70—

Class Acts

The publisher gratefully acknowledges the generous contribution to this book provided by the Frederick W. Hilles Publication Fund of Yale University.

Class Acts

SERVICE AND INEQUALITY
IN LUXURY HOTELS

Rachel Sherman

UNIVERSITY OF CALIFORNIA PRESS
Berkeley   Los Angeles   London

University of California Press, one of the most distinguished university presses in the United States, enriches lives around the world by advancing scholarship in the humanities, social sciences, and natural sciences. Its activities are supported by the UC Press Foundation and by philanthropic contributions from individuals and institutions. For more information, visit www.ucpress.edu.

Parts of chapter 4 are reprinted by permission of Sage Publications Ltd. from Rachel Sherman, "Producing the Superior Self: Strategic Comparison and Symbolic Boundaries among Luxury Hotel Workers," *Ethnography* 6 (2): 131–58, copyright © International Society of Adaptive Behavior, 2006. Excerpt from MAID IN MANHATTAN appears courtesy of Revolution Studios Distribution and Sony Pictures Entertainment. Excerpt from NINOTCHKA granted courtesy of Warner Bros. Entertainment Inc.

University of California Press
Berkeley and Los Angeles, California

University of California Press, Ltd.
London, England

Library of Congress Cataloging-in-Publication Data

Sherman, Rachel, 1970–.
    Class acts : service and inequality in luxury hotels / Rachel Sherman.
        p.   cm.
    Includes bibliographical references and index.
    ISBN-13: 978-0-520-24781-9 (cloth : alk. paper)
    ISBN-10: 0-520-24781-7 (cloth : alk. paper)
    ISBN-13: 978-0-520-24782-6 (pbk. : alk. paper)
    ISBN-10: 0-520-24782-5 (pbk. : alk. paper)
    1. Hospitality industry—Customer services—United States.
2. Hotels—United States—Management.   3. Luxuries—Social
aspects—United States.   4. Social classes—United States.   I. Title.

    TX911.3.C8S54   2006
    647.94068—dc22   2006003726

Manufactured in the United States of America

15   14   13   12   11   10   09   08   07
10   9   8   7   6   5   4   3   2   1

This book is printed on New Leaf EcoBook 50, a 100% recycled fiber of which 50% is de-inked post-consumer waste, processed chlorine-free. EcoBook 50 is acid-free and meets the minimum requirements of ANSI/ASTM D5634–01 (*Permanence of Paper*).

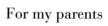

For my parents

Contents

Acknowledgments   ix

Introduction: Luxury Service and
the New Economy   1

1. "Better Than Your Mother": The Luxury Product   24

2. Managing Autonomy   63

3. Games, Control, and Skill   110

4. Recasting Hierarchy   154

5. Reciprocity, Relationship, and Revenge   184

6. Producing Entitlement   223

Conclusion: Class, Culture, and
the Service Theater   257

Appendix A: Methods   271

Appendix B: Hotel Organization   287

*Appendix C: Jobs, Wages, and Nonmanagerial
Workers in Each Hotel: 2000–2001*   291

Notes   295

References   325

Index   341

Acknowledgments

My greatest debt is to the workers, managers, hotel guests, and others who participated in this study. I am especially grateful to the workers at both hotels, who shared their workdays and their worldviews with me. Though they had no control over my presence, the vast majority welcomed me openly and warmly; several became friends. Although I suspect that this book is not what they expected, I hope they do not feel I have misrepresented them or abused their confidence. I am also indebted to upper-level managers in my sites, who permitted an inexperienced worker and researcher to participate in daily life in their hotels, and to their lower-level counterparts, who treated me on a par with other workers. And I thank my guest interviewees, who took the time to share stories and sometimes very personal feelings about their consumption of luxury service. Hotel managers outside my sites and other industry players were generous with their time and expertise.

I want to thank the staff at the HERE local at which I volunteered in

1995–97 for introducing me to the hotel industry and its workforce. Margaret Hunt, K. O. Odsather, and Mary Jo Martin intervened in indispensable ways at the beginning of the research. I am also indebted to the following sources of funding for the dissertation on which this book is based: the Clair Brown Graduate Study Fellowship from the Institute of Industrial Relations at the University of California, Berkeley; the Institute for Labor and Employment of the University of California; and the National Science Foundation's Dissertation Improvement Grant. I am also grateful for prior funding from the National Science Foundation and the University of California and for the assistance of the Frederick W. Hilles Publication Fund of Yale University, which supported the publication of this book.

I was lucky to work with an extremely supportive and helpful dissertation committee. Readers will see that I am indebted intellectually to Michael Burawoy; what they cannot see is the personal debt I owe him. Michael engaged enthusiastically with this project from beginning to end, reading and commenting on everything from my first tentative memos about the hotel industry to the conclusion of this book. His generosity with both his time and his ideas is a model for me as a teacher and adviser. Kim Voss and Raka Ray have been both insightful teachers and good friends. Kim helped me to stay grounded in my data and to link my findings to other research in the field. Raka shared my fascination with questions of entitlement, class, and subordinating interactive labor, and talking with her helped me develop my thinking about these issues.

In graduate school, I was fortunate to have the input of many wonderful fellow students, including Amy Hanser, Bill Hayes, Linus Huang, Anna Korteweg, Amy Schalet, Teresa Sharpe, Millie Thayer (who suggested the title), Michelle Williams, and Ann Wood. Christy Getz, Teresa Gowan, and Lissa Soep were sharp readers and remain invaluable friends. Leslie Bell deserves special thanks for her unfailing comradeship in this and many other endeavors. The dissertation also benefited from discussions with or comments by Arlene Kaplan Daniels, Laura Dresser, Gil Eyal, Steve Lopez, Ruth Milkman, Sean O'Riain, Myra Marx Ferree, Barrie Thorne, Roger Waldinger, Dick Walker, and Erik Olin Wright. The staff of the Berkeley sociology department, especially Elsa Tranter, gave indispensable practical and emotional support.

Many people generously provided helpful feedback as the project made the transition from dissertation to book. I particularly want to thank those who read the whole manuscript, in various incarnations, for their attention and insightful comments: Jeff Alexander, Dan Clawson, Jack Katz, Steve Lopez, Leslie McCall, Alondra Nelson, Diane Vaughan, Diane Wolf, and Julia Wrigley. I kept Rachel Heiman's annotated copy by my side during much of the revision. The manuscript was also improved by suggestions from Rick Fantasia, Christy Glass, Christine Wimbauer, Caitlin Zaloom, the participants in Yale's Center for Cultural Sociology workshop, and the members of the Work and Welfare group at Yale, run by Vicki Schultz. I thank Sam Nelson, Betty Yip, and Christy Glass for research help, and Noel Silverman for legal assistance. I am also grateful to the staff of the University of California Press. Naomi Schneider has been an engaged, insightful, and patient editor. Robin Whitaker greatly improved the book with careful and comprehensive copy editing, and Jacqueline Volin expertly shepherded the manuscript through production. All errors, of course, are mine alone.

My friends and family have been unfailingly encouraging during this lengthy process. Besides those already mentioned, Tanya Agathocleous, Jennifer Bair, Aaron Belkin, Emma Bonacich, Carolyn Chen, Averil Clarke, Dave Herbstman, Sarah Laslett, Zahavah Levine, Nancy Kane, Jackie Olvera, Meredith Rose, Stephanie Ruby, Diana Selig, and Paul Van De Carr were my daily support system, always curious to hear about the project and equally willing to provide distraction. Lynnéa Stephen was an enthusiastic and generous friend and a model of courage and perseverance. Karen Strassler deserves special mention here: a dear friend and intellectual fellow traveler for almost twenty years, she has commented on countless ideas and drafts, offering essential encouragement and insight in this as in so many aspects of my life. I also want to recognize Nancy Middlebrook, Margaret Hunt, and Judy Feins, who have always been generous with their own caring labor. With all my heart, I thank Laura Amelio for her unconditional love, joyful companionship, and unwavering faith in my capacity to finish this book.

Finally, I am deeply grateful to my mother, Dorothy Louise, and my father, Tom Sherman, not only for their consistent interest, encouragement, and love (and, in my mother's case, detailed copy editing), but also for shaping the values and personal history that inspired this project. I dedicate this book to them.

Introduction

When Mr. Jones, a guest at the five-star Luxury Garden hotel, began to prepare for an early business meeting, he realized he had forgotten to pack his dress shoes. Panicked, he called the concierge desk. Not to worry, said Max, the concierge. Max called a local department store, asked the security guard to help him contact the manager, and convinced the manager to open the store two hours early for the desperate guest. At the same hotel, room service workers know that when Mrs. Smith orders breakfast, they must slice her papaya along a straight line, forgoing the usual serrated edge. At the Royal Court, a small luxury hotel nearby, Mrs. Frank looks forward to the hazelnut butter on her French toast, which the chef whips up just for her. In a third upscale hotel, the gift shop does not carry the Silk Cut cigarettes Mr. White prefers. No problem, he is told; we can send someone to get them. Each time the guest returns thereafter, the cigarettes await him in his room. A legendary housekeeper in the same hotel has a habit of rifling through guests' wastebaskets; she is trying to identify their favorite candy bars and magazines in order to enter these into a computer database that helps workers keeps track of guests' preferences for the future.

I heard these stories from luxury hotel managers I interviewed in the late 1990s as part of my preliminary research on this book. I talked with mid- and upper-level managers in all different kinds of urban hotels— economy, midprice, convention, and so on—about the challenges of running the hotel, the service they offered, the types of guests they catered to, changes in the economic climate and the structure of the industry, and their views about unions. But managers in *luxury* hotels recounted especially captivating anecdotes. Like the examples above, these tales described hotel staff going to great lengths to observe guests' preferences, recognize each guest's individuality, and meet—even anticipate—the guests' wishes. These hotels promised, in the words of an ad for the Four Seasons, "service that cares for your every need."[1]

Managers and hospitality industry literature insisted that this caring service is more important than the physical characteristics of the hotel or its amenities. Asked what differentiated the Luxury Garden from its competition, for example, the hotel's sales director told me, "The service, because we all have beds and bathrooms." It was, managers said, the main reason guests paid daily rates as high as eight hundred dollars for rooms and three thousand dollars for suites. The staff played a crucial role in this enterprise. One manager commented, for instance, "The room helps, the views help, but it's really the people."

Managers characterized the guests who consume luxury service as "truly wealthy." As one manager put it, "They're not looking for discount coupons." Another told me that guest wealth "blows my mind." I wondered: if it blew the *managers'* minds, what did the *workers* think about it? Workers in these hotels earned ten to fifteen dollars per hour and in some cases tips and commissions; that could add up to a substantial wage, but it was nothing compared with guest wealth. And managers talked about the services their hotels offered as providing *care*. But *caring for* guests appeared also to mean *catering to* them. What was it like when your job was to ensure that the guest's every desire, no matter how insignificant, was fulfilled? Did workers feel subordinated by guests' seemingly unlimited entitlement to the workers' personalized labor and attention? And how did guests feel about luxury service, which seemed to involve a fair amount of potentially intrusive surveillance of personal preferences and habits, and about the workers who served them? Finally, I was curious about how managers tried to guide the production of this intangible, interactive service, especially given its dependence on the workers themselves.

Customized contacts with workers are a major part of what clients are paying for in many luxury sites, including high-end hotels, restaurants, spas, resorts, retail shops, and first-class airline cabins. However, the limited sociological literature on hotels and other service industry organizations has rarely focused on luxury.[2] And few sociologists since Thorstein Veblen, over a century ago, have investigated the luxury sector at all, let alone luxury service specifically.[3]

To understand luxury service, I decided I needed to participate in its production, which led me to conduct twelve months of ethnography in two luxury hotels. Based on the data I gathered and on interviews I conducted, this book looks at how managers, guests, and interactive workers negotiated unequal entitlement to resources, recognition, and labor as they produced and consumed luxury service. These issues matter for two reasons. First, they are important for our understanding of interactive work and its links to relationships and to selfhood. Second, they are significant for our conception of how work is connected to class. These questions are particularly important given the rise of both service work and economic inequality in the United States.

THE LUXURY MOMENT

The turn of the twenty-first century was an especially timely period in which to look at luxury production. In 1999, at the height of the high-tech boom, luxury spending in the United States was increasing at more than quadruple the rate of overall spending.[4] Demand was rising for luxury goods, including clothing, accessories, cars, exclusive housing, private jets, fancy wine, and premium cigars.[5] This active economic sector included many examples of extreme service as well as tangible products. New "boutique" medical practices, for example, offered services ranging from same-day appointments and house calls to heated towel racks and personally monogrammed robes in doctors' offices.[6] Services available to first-class airline passengers included chauffeured limousine pickups, customized meals, onboard massages, and "in-flight beauty therapists."[7] Some retail employees, such as those at the Dunhill store in Manhattan, were required to undergo butler training to improve their interactions with clients.[8] Wealthy people were increasingly hiring servants to care for their enormous houses, and training programs for these servants were expanding.[9]

After the bubble burst, around 2001, luxury consumption declined somewhat; but it rebounded quickly, thanks to high-end customers, who are often considered "recession proof." (After 9/11, for example, demand for chartered jets surged 40 percent, as wealthy people tried to avoid travel hassles.)[10] As of 2005, the sector has made its comeback. Spending on jewelry, private airplanes, and boats constituted 1.07 percent of consumer spending in the first quarter of 2004 versus .71 percent a decade earlier. Luxury stocks, such as those in Neiman Marcus and Nordstrom department stores, were up.[11] In the all-important Christmas retail season of 2004, luxury spending increased, while lower-end retailers saw a drop in revenues.[12] "Mass luxury" has been on the rise as well.[13]

Luxury is omnipresent in the media and popular culture. Reality television places "ordinary" people in Palm Beach mansions and European chateaux to be waited on as they vie for the million-dollar prize or the spouse of their dreams.[14] The media relentlessly detail luxury consumption among celebrities; a 2005 photo in *People* magazine, for example, shows tennis champ Serena Williams soaking in a five-thousand-dollar bath, consisting of a thousand bottles of Evian water, in the penthouse at the Hotel Victor in Miami.[15] The *New York Times* "Styles" section regularly features luxury services and products ranging from six-thousand-dollar haircuts, seventeen-thousand-dollar diamond-encrusted flip-flops, and sixteen-hundred-dollar pink sapphire tennis bracelets for toddlers, to at-home "tuck-in services" for adults (including a facial, a massage, crystal healing, and a bath) for only a thousand dollars.[16] The media also revel in stories of astronomical CEO compensation and spending; most famous, perhaps, is former Tyco CEO Dennis Kozlowski, who spent over two million dollars (half of which apparently belonged to his company) on his wife's birthday party in Sardinia, as well as six thousand dollars on a gold-threaded shower curtain. Wealthy party-givers pay millions for big-name acts to entertain at their birthday parties and their daughters' bat mitzvahs.[17] Best-selling novels of this period, such as *The Nanny Diaries* (the story of a young nanny's trials working for an overly entitled Upper East Side mother) and *The Devil Wears Prada* (the story of a young personal assistant's trials working for an overly entitled female magazine editor), satirize the entitlement of rich people and their mistreatment of assistants and servants.[18]

The rise of luxury consumption and production not only feeds a public preoccupation with the lifestyles of the rich and famous but also illuminates key features of what is often called the "new" U.S. economy. First, the new economy is a global one. Sites of luxury service are frequently what Manuel Castells calls "nodes" in the global "space of flows"—local places crisscrossed by movements of people and capital.[19] Luxury clients, purchasing services in London or Beijing, are often the mobile corporate executives who make the global economy run. Hotels and restaurants are located in the growing range of "producer services," which are used by high-end professionals but create nonprofessional and often low-paying jobs in the service sector.[20] At the same time, workers in hotels, restaurants, and retail are frequently immigrants from Europe, Asia, and Latin America. Luxury service companies are also often transnational, belonging to international chains and conglomerates that offer services worldwide.

Second, the new economy is a service economy. Like more than 85 percent of workers in the United States, luxury service workers (and usually consumers too) are employed in the service sector.[21] Many of these workers provide face-to-face, or "interactive," service, in which the product consists, to varying extents, of the interaction between workers and customers.[22] In contrast to "old economy" manufacturing jobs, in which the people who produced the products did not personally encounter the people who bought these products, the selfhoods of both worker and client come into play in these interactions. In luxury settings in particular, this interactive product is more than "service with a smile"; it is, rather, recognition of the customer's limitless entitlement to the worker's individualizing attention and effort.

Finally, the new economy is a deeply unequal one. It has created the conditions for the rise of luxury consumption by fostering higher incomes among the wealthy in what has been called the "new Gilded Age."[23] It is these astronomical incomes that allow consumers of luxury service to spend hundreds of dollars on lunch at five-star restaurants or on designer clothes at exclusive boutiques. High levels of income inequality are reflected in the relations between workers and clients in luxury sites, where workers can rarely, if ever, afford to purchase the services they produce.[24] Furthermore, in these sites, people who occupy increasingly distant positions in "social space" come together in "physical space."[25] The "top 1 percent," as one luxury manager often put it, stand face to face with the members of the middle and working classes.

Luxury service is not representative of the new economy in a numerical sense, because most people neither produce nor consume it. But studying luxury service can shed light on questions of interactive work and social class, because such service brings together structural inequality and subordinating interactive work in a particularly noticeable way. Structural inequality is the context for luxury service; interactive subordination of workers and the corresponding entitlement of clients are its content. Therefore, looking at luxury in light of what we already know about service work can shed light both on the specificity of luxury and on service work more generally.

SERVICES, SELVES, AND CLASS

From Industry to Interaction

For much of the twentieth century, sociologists of work were interested primarily in productivity, efficiency, and human relations, mainly in manufacturing workplaces. They took capitalist labor relations for granted and usually assumed a congruence of interests between workers and capitalists.[26] In 1974, Harry Braverman inaugurated critical labor process studies with *Labor and Monopoly Capital*, a scathing indictment of capitalist production methods and worker deskilling. Using a Marxist approach, Braverman looked at how the separation of mental and manual labor allows managers to control workers' labor power. Braverman's analysis spawned a generation of studies concerned with managerial control of workers within the labor process, in varying institutional and historical contexts.[27] Responding to what many believed to be an overly mechanistic and pessimistic view on Braverman's part, scholars in this tradition also began to look at worker subjectivity, agency, resistance, and gender.[28] The contemporary critical sociology of work remains indebted to the work of Braverman and his intellectual descendants.

For labor process theorists in the 1970s and 1980s, class was key. In this view, workers and owners by definition (in terms of their relation to the means of production) belong to different classes.[29] The challenge for capitalists and their managerial representatives is to control and appropriate workers' labor power in the service of securing profit (or other economic benefits). Thus, class relations are generated in the factory, through shop-floor domination. Consistent with this orientation, the vast majority of this literature has looked at manufacturing, Marx's paradigmatic site.

The study of service work, which Marx called "unproductive labor," was quite limited through most of the twentieth century, even as this sector grew and manufacturing declined.[30] But with Arlie Hochschild's groundbreaking 1983 study of flight attendants, *The Managed Heart*, service work—especially face-to-face service—began to garner attention. Subsequent researchers have looked at fast food workers, insurance agents, domestic servants, waitresses, temporary workers, nursing home workers, lawyers, paralegals, delivery drivers, bank tellers, supermarket checkers, business services workers, casino dealers, sales clerks, bill collectors, and hairdressers, among others.[31]

Much of this research focuses on two principal differences between interactive service work and traditional factory labor. First, the product of service work consists at least in part of intangible interactions between workers and customers. Rather than engines or electronics, the treatment of the client by the worker is a key part of what is being bought and sold. To describe this aspect of the product, Hochschild coined the term *emotional labor,* which refers to the paid worker's managing her own feelings in order to create a certain state of mind in the customer.[32]

The second, though related, difference is in the central role consumers play in service labor processes. In manufacturing, goods are sold in a market distant from the factory, which might be in Detroit or in Bangladesh, so customers who buy these products never see the workers who make them. Not so with service clients, who are not only physically present as the interactive product is created but also, in fact, participate in its production. A dyadic relationship between managers and workers becomes a tripartite one among workers, managers, and clients.[33] Interactive work also means that production and consumption occur simultaneously, linked in time just as they are brought together in space.

Self at Work

In regard to these characteristics—the importance of intangible worker-client interactions and the client's participation in the production of services—the literature on service work has tended to concentrate less on structure and class than on selfhood, interaction, and gender. First, scholars debate the effects that the performance of emotional labor has on workers who operate in what C. Wright Mills called "the personality market."[34] Hochschild drew on the Marxist notion of alienation to suggest that emotional laborers can be estranged from their emotions; subsequent work has looked at the pros and cons of emotional labor for workers in different settings.[35] At a theoretical level, some analysts have discussed the broader social and cultural effects of commodifying and routinizing emotional labor, especially the possible loss of authenticity in human interaction generally.[36] Despite research showing that emotional labor is not alienating for workers in all work situations, an implicit opposition between an "authentic," agentic self and an estranged, alienated, and performative one often marks this literature, with authentic selfhood, for the most part, seen as located *outside* work settings.[37] For example, researchers often talk of a self that needs to be "protected" at work or suggest that workers preserve their agentic selves through resistance.[38] Many scholars have also looked at how service work occupations and interactions are gendered.[39]

A second focus of this research has been on how the self is managed in interactive work. Because the worker's presentation of self and capacity to interact constitute part of the product, managers must control the worker herself in order to control production. This requires extending managerial influence to areas that have traditionally been private, which can incur worker resistance. Depending on the setting, managers can try to routinize work by developing standard procedures, scripting interactions, and controlling customers, as they do at McDonald's.[40] Or managers can attempt to transform workers' selves in a more fundamental way, through extensive training and techniques, to ensure what Hochschild calls "deep acting."[41] (This approach is more appropriate in luxury production, in which workers have more autonomy, as we will see.) Furthermore, these scholars point out, service workers have another kind of manager: the client. Customer feedback and monitoring create a "second boss," who supervises the worker even in the absence of managers.[42]

Service work researchers tend to cast both manager-worker and client-worker relations as antagonistic, involving subordination and struggles for control.[43] As in traditional labor process theory, the language of "control" and "resistance" remains dominant. Workers are seen as responding to managerial dictates and customer demands either with passive compliance or active resistance, which ranges from refusing to smile to cursing at customers.[44] Even when workers describe elements of their relations with customers as meaningful, scholars tend not to theorize the positive aspects of these contacts.[45] Robin Leidner has offered a less pessimistic view, suggesting the possibility of shifting alliances among workers, managers, and customers, but few scholars since Leidner have looked closely at positive moments of client-worker relations. Furthermore, these studies rarely incorporate, methodologically or theoretically, the client's perspective.[46]

In the Marxist manufacturing paradigm, how managers and capitalists benefit from extracting workers' labor power is clear: that extraction is the source of economic gain. Service work researchers have imported this sense of worker-manager antagonism into their view of the worker-client relationship, but they fail to theorize precisely how the client benefits from consuming workers' labor and why this benefit is antithetical to workers' interests. Partly this assumption has to do with the potential for individual customers to treat workers badly and with the belief that emotional labor has negative effects on workers, but these links are not often theoretically elaborated.[47]

In her ethnographic study of domestic servants and employers, Judith Rollins suggests that a moment of "psychological exploitation" stems from "the personal relationship between employer and employee." She sees this exploitation as giving employers "the self-enhancing satisfactions that emanate from having the presence of an inferior." Profit is not extracted, but the relation is exploitative because of its psychological benefit. Rollins also claims that domestic servants function to "validat[e] the employers' lifestyle, ideology, and social world, from their familial interrelations to the economically and racially stratified system in which they live."[48] In this way, Rollins usefully theorizes interactive subordination and links it to structural inequality; however, she tends to map the interactive moment very closely onto the structural one, denying the possibility of positive interactions between workers and clients. Indeed, Rollins focuses primarily on workers' deep resentment of and disdain for their client-employers, which she sees as stemming from this inequality. And although she implies that employers need the validation that workers provide, she does not investigate conflicts that employers might feel about their own entitlement to consume workers' labor.

One could argue, alternatively, that structural inequality benefits workers and that workers are happy to serve clients more affluent than they. Some researchers argue that wealthy clients or employers treat workers better than less-rich ones.[49] Another perspective suggests that workers identify with well-off clients and aspire to their lifestyle.[50] These scholars tend not to use a class analysis, coding interactions as ways to mitigate "social distance" rather than unequal class relations.

Overall, despite significant progress in understanding interactive service work, most researchers have adopted the critical tone of labor process analysis without rethinking its theoretical basis in Marxist analysis of manufacturing production. This tendency, which also leads to dichotomous formulations of control and resistance, authentic and inauthentic selfhood, work and not-work selves, and production and consumption, has been limiting in several ways. First, the exploration of selfhood in interaction has been circumscribed by a focus on managerial dictates rather than on workplace relations and by the assumption that the authentic selfhood of workers arises outside work. Second, and related, consumers of services have primarily been seen as a source of constraint on workers rather than as a source of enjoyment or alliance or as a subject of study in their own right as participants in production. Finally, the literature has generally not theorized the classed nature of interactions or the links between structural inequality and interactive work. My study attempts to break down some of these limitations, looking at both the multiple ways workers and guests negotiate asymmetrical relations and the consequences of these negotiations for the reproduction of unequal entitlements to material resources and attention.

LOOKING AT LUXURY

Luxury service, in particular the luxury hotel, is a good place to explore in more depth the connections among work, class, and self. First, the worker's self is deeply implicated in the highly personalized and attentive service she provides. And it is a self-subordinating service, as guests' every wish must be workers' command. Research has established that workers value dignity on the job above most other considerations,[51] but their dignity, in this case, seems constantly compromised by their subservience to guests. If any interactive workplace is likely to produce alienated and resentful workers, the luxury hotel is the one. On the other hand, the importance of service is a source of worker autonomy vis-à-vis managers, because the success of the guest's intangible experience rests largely on workers' shoulders. The discretion that interactive workers must exercise makes them hard to control, monitor, and standardize.[52]

Thus, workers might have more power and autonomous selfhood in these sites.

The upscale hotel is also a good place to look at customers and class. Like other luxury establishments, this site is structured by the unequal distribution of resources. Workers and guests nearly always occupy different class positions, by any definition.[53] Furthermore, asymmetries in power, authority, and entitlement also inhere in the relationships between workers and guests. Workers demonstrate deference and subordination; guests enact entitlement to human attention and labor.[54] As a result, both are constantly performing class differences, or "doing class."[55] Each actor must occupy her position appropriately in these classed interactions, thus also "doing self" in a classed context. Furthermore, in the luxury setting, both the structural inequality in which the interaction is embedded and the interactive inequality of which the luxury product consists are totally visible to both workers and hotel guests.

Thus, the following questions remain: How do workers reconcile their desire for dignity and power with the self-subordinating imperatives of their work? How do managers organize the production of this intangible, self-subordinating relation? How are workers' and guests' selves constituted or compromised? How do workers and guests make sense of their class differences and negotiate their unequal entitlements? Finally, what can the process of production-consumption of this interactive product, marked by inequality, tell us about classed identities and the legitimacy of class inequality more broadly? These are the questions that guided my research.

Sites and Methods

Via contacts obtained through the preliminary interviews, I gained access to directors of human resources in two luxury, nonunion hotels, the Royal Court and the Luxury Garden, located in a major American city.[56] I explained to these managers that I was interested in how their hotels defined and met a luxury service standard. Because managers themselves are very interested in this question, I persuaded them relatively easily to allow me to conduct ethnographic research in these sites.

This research took place in 2000–2001, when the labor market was extremely tight. High union density and activism marked the local hotel industry, meaning that even these nonunion hotels could not afford to antagonize workers for fear of union influence. This atmosphere made these sites especially favorable for looking at worker power vis-à-vis managers.

I first spent eight months (January–August 2000) working thirty-two hours per week at the Royal Court and then two months working on an on-call basis. The Royal Court is a 110-room, European-style downtown hotel with an award-winning restaurant and nightly room rates ranging from three hundred to five hundred dollars for a regular room to two thousand dollars for a suite. The Royal Court was independently managed, and its clientele was more or less evenly divided between business and leisure travelers.

I organized my research at the Royal Court to allow me to compare different kinds of work. I was formally hired, at a pay rate about half that of regular staff, and was treated like any other employee, except that I was allowed to do several different jobs. I started with interactive work: answering the telephone, reserving rooms, checking guests in and out at the front desk, doing concierge tasks such as making dinner and limousine reservations, parking guests' cars, carrying their bags back and forth, and running errands for them. In all I spent about twenty-five shifts, over six months, in each of the following jobs: concierge/front desk agent, bellman/valet parker, telephone operator, and reservationist.[57]

I then spent five weeks working the 3:00–11:00 P.M. shift in room service, both taking guests' phone orders and delivering their fried calamari and seasonal sorbets. During this period I also worked as a food runner in the restaurant on a few occasions. Finally, I spent a month shadowing housekeeping workers, mainly room cleaners (during the day) and turndown attendants (in the evenings).[58] Though my focus was on interactive workers, this comparison of interactive and noninteractive work allowed me to explore the specific characteristics of jobs that involved relations with guests, to look at racial and ethnic variation among workers, and to explore what interactive and noninteractive workers thought about each other.

When my stint at the Royal Court was over, I worked in a second luxury hotel, the Luxury Garden, for four months (November 2000–March 2001), in order to look at the effects of organizational features on the production and consumption of luxury service.[59] The Luxury Garden was larger than the Royal Court, with 160 rooms, and it was corporately managed. The hotel commanded the highest rates in the city—$500 to $750 a night for a room, as much as $3,000 for a suite—and catered mostly to business travelers.

For two months, I worked four shifts weekly as a concierge at the Luxury Garden, which primarily involved procuring restaurant reservations, car and driver services, flowers, massages, rental cars, and tickets to theater or sporting events, plus meeting other, more unpredictable guest requests. For another two months, I continued to spend two shifts each week at the concierge desk, but I also shadowed room cleaners, turndown attendants, bellmen, doormen, business center workers, telephone operators, and reservationists for two shifts each week, spending between one and five shifts in each area. Here I was an unpaid intern, though I was permitted to keep tips and cash commissions.

I socialized with workers from both sites, but especially those at the Royal Court, with whom I often went out for drinks after the evening shift. Both on and off the job in both hotels, I talked extensively with workers about their jobs, the work environment, and their personal lives. Though these were not formal interviews, they allowed me to get a sense of what workers thought about a broad range of issues, and I quote them frequently in the text.[60]

I participated in employee orientation and training sessions in both sites. I also analyzed comment cards and guest letters from both hotels, representing a four-month period in each case (approximately two hundred cards total). In addition, Luxury Garden management granted me access to detailed reports, comprising hundreds of pages, written by mystery shoppers whom they had hired to evaluate the hotel's service. During and after my ethnographic stints in these hotels, I conducted formal interviews with twelve upper-level managers, each lasting sixty to ninety minutes.

In addition to hundreds of ethnographic encounters with hotel guests,

I carried out formal, open-ended interviews with nineteen people (twelve women and seven men) who frequently stayed in luxury hotels. Many of these interviewees did not come from wealthy backgrounds, though all were currently quite well-off. These interviews were generated through snowball sampling unrelated to the hotels. (See appendix A for details about ethnographic access, ethical issues, the composition of the interview samples, and other reflections on the research.)

CONSENTING WORKERS, POWERFUL SELVES, NORMALIZED INEQUALITY

Both the sociological literature and popular books such as *The Nanny Diaries* led me to expect disgruntled workers and rude, demanding guests in the hotel. However, when I began work at the Royal Court, I was surprised to find that this was not the case. Rather than expressing resentment or alienation, workers were engaged in their work and wanted to do it well. They sometimes complained, avoided work, or adopted the falsely performative mode Hochschild calls "going into robot." But they did not appear to be trapped between passive, alienating acquiescence and active, empowering resistance. For the most part, in fact, they seemed to enjoy their jobs, often including their relationships with guests. This made sense, because guests treated workers quite well most of the time, thanking them, tipping them, and even bringing them gifts. On the other hand, workers rarely expressed either a desire to live as guests did or any belief in their own capacity to obtain such a lifestyle.

I was also surprised to find that unequal entitlement was both constantly invoked and completely unquestioned. Workers often told stories of outrageous demands guests had made or talked about the high prices they paid for rooms and fancy services. Yet these unequal entitlements had a taken-for-granted quality. Although workers frequently criticized or made fun of individual guests, they did not talk about class difference explicitly or critique the system that allowed guests so much more wealth than they. The gulf between workers' and guests' social positions and workers' obligation to provide self-subordinating service seemed commonplace, simple facts of life.

When I later worked at the Luxury Garden, I found the same held true there. Managerial styles and strategies were very different, because the Luxury Garden was more corporate and offered more consistently professionalized service than the independent, informal Royal Court. But workers at the Luxury Garden also became absorbed in their work, offering emotional and physical labor to guests willingly, for the most part. Likewise, inequality was always apparent but rarely discussed as such.

These findings led me to two concepts on which I draw throughout the book. The first is the notion of *consent*. Used most notably in Michael Burawoy's study of factory production, consent is active investment in work. In Burawoy's formulation, workers who have some autonomy become involved in and engaged with their jobs by means of small incentives and choices, which become meaningful in the context of particular shop-floor status hierarchies and cultures. In consenting to exert labor, workers unintentionally also legitimate the broader conditions of its appropriation. In the factory Burawoy studied, workers played the game of "making out," which allowed them to make choices about exerting effort. As they played the game, consenting to (and defending) its rules, they both ensured productivity and consented to the structural order in which the fruits of their labor (the surplus value they produced) accrued to the company.[61]

This concept, though rarely invoked in the contemporary work literature, is sometimes used (incorrectly, in my view) to connote passive, unresisting, or "coping" workers.[62] In fact, like resistance, consent highlights workers' agency. Unlike the concept of resistance, however, the concept of consent allows us to think of workers as using their agency to participate in work rather than to refuse to participate. Explaining consent entails taking seriously the reasons that workers like their jobs and the rewards they derive from them, without losing a critical perspective on unequal social relations of appropriation.[63] Like resistance, consent has the potential for oppositionality. Workers can withdraw their consent in several ways: by refusing to invest themselves in their work; by quitting; and by organizing some kind of collective action that challenges the organization of work or the distribution of rewards from work. As we will see, workers who withdrew consent in my sites (more common at the Royal Court than at the Luxury Garden) tended to do so individually, by exiting.

The second concept is the idea of *normalization*, which refers to the taken-for-granted nature of both interactive and structural inequality. Unequal entitlements and responsibilities were not obscured, because they were perfectly obvious and well-known to interactive workers. Nor were they explicitly legitimated, since workers rarely talked about them as such. Rather, they simply became a feature of the everyday landscape of the hotel. Conflicts over unequal entitlement were couched in individual rather than collective terms and in the language of complaint rather than critique.

In the bulk of what follows, I show how consent and normalization arose as functions of worker strategies for constituting themselves as not subordinate vis-à-vis managers, coworkers, and especially guests.[64] Rather than negotiate between authenticity and performativity or between agency and passivity, workers drew on a range of complex and sometimes contradictory strategies of self-articulation to cast themselves as powerful. First, they established themselves as autonomous, skilled, and in control of their work, especially by playing games. Second, they cast themselves as superior, both to their coworkers and to the guests they served, by using comparisons and judgments. Finally, they constituted themselves as equal to guests by establishing meaningful relationships with them on the basis of a standard of reciprocal treatment. These strategies were not necessarily intentional; as Bourdieu has repeatedly argued, strategic action is not always conscious.[65]

Organizational characteristics and conditions, often seen as oppressive to workers, actually became crucial resources in the creation of nonsubordinate selves. The features of luxury, including discretion, guest wealth, and luxury service standards, helped interactive workers recast themselves as powerful. Organizational elements such as corporate culture, the hotel's division of labor, and the distribution of authority, allowed workers to establish skill, professionalism, and prestige. Differences in the character of these elements between the two sites help to explain why workers at the Royal Court tended to withdraw consent more often than those at the Luxury Garden. At the Luxury Garden, it was easier for workers to forge powerful selfhoods, because managerial rhetoric emphasized professionalism, status, and organizational belonging, and managers more clearly defined workers' autonomy and prestige within the hotel. At the Royal Court, managers offered fewer such discourses, and they organized work in such a way that workers had more trouble seeing themselves as autonomous and privileged vis-à-vis their coworkers. Finally, guests also helped workers to constitute themselves as powerful. Guests provided the raw material for the games workers played; they served as objects of strategic comparison; and they acted as agents of equality through emotional and financial reciprocity. Far from being in constant tension with workers, then, guests played a central role in generating workers' consent.

Yet the work environment was not the only source of self-constitution; biographical and cultural resources were also important. At a personal level, the preexisting dispositions of individual workers were key to how they inserted themselves into the organization.[66] Some workers, for example, took on professional identities that led to investment in the hotel, while others cast themselves as independent of the workplace. At a broader level, workers drew on "cultural repertoires" in shaping themselves as powerful.[67] An especially central cultural narrative was the "norm of reciprocity" that both workers and guests articulated and practiced in their relations with each other.[68] This norm repeatedly emerged in a way that may be distinctly American, evoking as it does a sense of egalitarianism, of downplaying power differences in interactions.[69]

For the most part, workers' capacity to create powerful selves, sustained by guests and managers, engendered consent and muted the sharp edges of unequal entitlement. However, the path to normalization was not always smooth. Workers' right to power—even the limited power I am describing—was a site of constant negotiation and occasional open conflict. Workers struggled to maintain their power against coworkers who resisted their authority, incompetent or inconsistent managers, and guests who failed to respect their basic humanity. When workers' methods of establishing their own entitlements were thwarted, they avenged themselves by withholding labor or by enacting small punishments, usually imperceptible to managers and guests.

These actions constituted moments of resistance, but they were also mechanisms of consent. It was often precisely these instances of refusal or revenge that allowed workers to feel autonomous. And, in these transgressive episodes, workers were usually defending, rather than contesting, already-established rules about how they would be treated. These rules, and workers' symbolic enforcement of them, recast social relations as ties between individual workers and guests, managers, or other workers, rather than promoting collective identifications. Finally, these acts of resistance rarely had broader repercussions for production, the organization of work, working conditions, and so on. Thus, I argue, workers' actions can constitute both resistance to a specific imperative at a particular time and consent to a larger order in which guests are entitled to workers' labor.

Finally, I found that workers are not the only ones who constitute themselves in the production-consumption site. Guest selfhood is also enacted and created in a variety of ways in the hotel. Despite their enjoyment of luxury service and its pampering, most guests prefer to avoid thinking of themselves as excessively entitled or exploitative. To justify their consumption of workers' caring labor, they draw on a range of interpretations of themselves, from deserving or disadvantaged to especially moderate relative to others. And they cast workers as powerful, skilled, knowledgeable, and prestigious, mirroring workers' own constructions. Guests also go out of their way to constitute workers as equal, primarily through practices of emotional and financial reciprocity. On the other hand, luxury service itself continually reassures guests that they are entitled to consume the caring and self-subordinating labor of others. Workers thus school guests in both their rights and their obligations. In a sense, the hotel and its workers produce guest subjects who are comfortable with and equipped to occupy their advantaged class position.

My central argument, then, is that both workers' consent and the normalization of guest entitlement arise from workers' ability to construct powerful selves. This capacity is contingent on immediate, organizational factors *and* individual and cultural ones, though I focus primarily on organizational characteristics, which are illuminated by the comparison of the two hotels. The ways workers manage to create dignity and power in the face of subordination, paradoxically, lead them to accept rather than to challenge the inequalities that define their workplace, making it less likely that they will develop structural critiques of class inequality. Guest fears of not belonging and of exploiting others are put to rest by some of the same processes, which in fact constitute them as entitled subjects and thus further normalize unequal power relations.

From "Shop Floor" to "Service Theater"

If we are to move once and for all to studying the service sector in its own right, it is necessary to use an image that changes our perception of the space under consideration.[70] I have chosen the metaphor of the "service theater" instead of the manufacturing image of the "shop floor," for several reasons. First, resonances with the dramatic theater pervade the hotel. Both are spaces divided between front and backstage, which are themselves further subdivided.[71] Both are open to those members of the public who can pay to get in, and both depend on the reviews of professionals and publics to succeed.

A major similarity between the service theater and the dramatic theater is the importance of meaningful performance. Actors take on roles, which they may or may not be comfortable executing. Performance is guided by learning done outside the theater as well as by norms within it. In the service theater of the luxury hotel, we see both performances of subordination and performances of class. But *performance* need not connote "inauthenticity." As Hannerz paraphrases Goffman's view: "Even if the individual is aware of making a presentation, he may be doing so in all sincerity."[72]

The term *service theater* has other relevant connotations as well. The sense of "operating theater" calls to mind an arena of skill and of transformation. In the hotel, both social relations and personal identities are changed. The "theater of war" version connotes conflict. All three usages also describe, as I wish to, an arena of action set off from but linked to the outside world. Finally, like a theatrical spectacle or a surgical procedure, the hotel's service is produced and consumed at the same time. Therefore, throughout the text I also refer to the hotel as a site of production-consumption.

OVERVIEW

The focus in the first two chapters is on the luxury product, the organization of work, and the specifics of managerial regimes in both hotel sites. In chapter 1, I first offer a comprehensive description of luxury service in hotels, which comprises four elements: personalization; anticipation of, responsiveness to, and legitimation of guest needs; unlimited available physical labor; and deference and sincerity. Guests prefer to interpret luxury service as individualized, almost maternal care, but it rests on an imperative of self-subordination more analogous to domestic servitude than to mothering.

Many labor processes underlie the production of luxury service; these are codified within an especially stark organizational (and usually racialized) division between noninteractive workers, such as housekeepers, and interactive workers, such as concierges. Characteristics of both work and workers allow managers to use constraining measures to organize noninteractive work; these workers experience limited interactive subordination as a result of their limited contact with guests. Interactive workers, however, have significantly more autonomy and thus cannot be routinized or tightly controlled; at the same time, interactive workers face the imperative of self-subordination head on. For these workers, I argue, inequality is normalized, constantly discussed but rarely critiqued. The rest of the book focuses on how this normalization occurs among interactive workers, but with an eye toward the important role of their noninteractive counterparts.

One potential explanation for this normalization is that management transforms workers through corporate culture or sophisticated training sessions or both. In chapter 2, I look at this possibility, introducing the two hotels in more detail and comparing their managerial practices and rhetoric. The Luxury Garden's managerial regime was marked by "hierarchical professionalism." Managers drew on a sophisticated corporate culture in the context of a specialized division of labor to organize professionalized service. At the independently owned Royal Court, a focus on authenticity, minimal job differentiation, and inconsistent managerial authority led to a regime of "flexible informality." My ethnographic evidence reveals that, despite differences, overt managerial strategies of transforming identity were at best only partly successful in both hotels. Workers at the Luxury Garden responded to corporate culture as a mechanism of accountability as much as one of self-transformation; workers at the Royal Court, often more experienced than their managers, developed a fairly autonomous worker regime. In both sites, workers were largely self-regulated. The question of why this was so, however, remains.

In chapters 3, 4, and 5, I look at workers on the job, analyzing their efforts to recast subordination as power and describing the role of guests in that endeavor. In chapter 3 I take up another possible explanation of consent and normalization: workers' games.[73] Like manufacturing workers, hotel workers become absorbed in games, and this absorption fosters their consent to both managerial and customer appropriation of their labor. However, there are several differences between games in the service theater and those on the shop floor; the most important have to do with the guest's role in the labor process. I further show that games allow workers to think of themselves as autonomous, skilled, strategic, and powerful—in short, as not subordinate. The two hotel cases demonstrate that the character of each managerial regime affects workers' capacity to play games and to deploy certain strategies of self.

In chapters 4 and 5, I turn more directly to workers' views of and relationships with guests as they influence consent and normalization. The focus in chapter 4 is primarily on workers' discourses and practices related to social hierarchies. Workers invoke multiple symbolic rankings vis-à-vis their coworkers, the guests they serve, and their communities outside the hotel. Workers situate themselves favorably in relation to these other interlocutors, using strategies of comparison and judgment that draw on whatever advantages they can glean from their own work situations. Again, this process differed somewhat in the two hotels, according to the organizational and interpretive resources workers had at their disposal.

In chapter 5 I analyze the imperative of worker subordination as it plays out in worker-guest interactions and relationships. Building on the finding that guests treat workers quite well, I show that workers adhere to and enforce an implicit contract, according to which their labors entitle them to emotional and financial reciprocity from guests. When this reciprocity is forthcoming, the relationship can be recast as egalitarian rather than subordinating. When guests fail to meet workers' expectations, however, workers limit their own self-subordination in both symbolic and practical ways. Guests likewise articulate a sense of contract, describing their own rights and responsibilities vis-à-vis workers. In part, their reciprocal behavior stems from the generalized social norm of reciprocity, but it also arises from expectations constructed in the hotel. These relations are the cornerstone of normalizing guests' entitlement to workers' labor, because both workers and guests endeavor to see themselves as equal individuals.

In chapter 6, I look at guests' perspectives on their own consumption and discuss how their class privilege is legitimated within the hotel. As I have suggested, guests use a variety of practical and interpretive strategies, similar to those of workers, to assuage conflicts about their consumption of and entitlement to luxury service. These strategies are supported by particular features of the hotel setting. At the same time, guests are interpellated into a sense of class entitlement through their participation in luxury service; the service itself constitutes them as legitimate consumers. In the conclusion, I discuss the implications of these findings for our understanding of service work and class.

ONE 'Better Than Your Mother'

THE LUXURY PRODUCT

Then I pick up the telephone
and call Room Service.
Ooooooooo I absolutely love Room Service.
They always know it's me
and they say "Yes, Eloise?"

Kay Thompson, *Eloise* (1955)

One of my first interviewees was Martha, a white woman in her early fifties who frequently stayed in luxury hotels with her husband, the chair and CEO of a large recycling company. Asked to describe "incredible service," she mentioned a particular hotel, calling it "great" for the following reasons:

> Well, their linens, and the services, and they bring things, they're just so accommodating. They go out of their way to make you feel, y'know, like you matter. "If you weren't here, we would be very unhappy about

it." . . . They zero in on you, and they make you feel like you're not lost in this huge crowd. And I think that's really the nicest thing, because all of us, when we're traveling, we're not home. And to be taken care of and to have somebody who's gonna do things for you in a way that's, like, better than your mother! . . . It makes you feel good.

Martha starts by mentioning material items—the linens—but she quickly shifts to identifying the workers' treatment of guests as the main element of luxury service. She describes personalized, genuine attention, the exertion of extra effort, and the legitimation of needs. She is talking about a sense of being cared for and made to feel special in a way beyond what she might expect even from her mother.

Though they usually use different language, managers' comments echo Martha's intuitive emphasis on "positive human interactions" as the crucial feature of luxury.[1] For instance, Isadore Sharp, chair and CEO of the Four Seasons chain, stated that luxury "isn't just building a different kind of building and adding more amenities; it comes through the service element."[2] Although managers I interviewed mentioned the physical aspects of the hotels—sophisticated, distinctive design; unusual, high-quality amenities; and comfortable rooms—managers saw distinctive service as the key to separating luxury from nonluxury hotels and to distinguishing luxury properties from one another.

This chapter explores the defining elements of luxury service as they emerged implicitly and explicitly in interviews with guests and managers, in industry literature, and in ethnographic observation. These aspects include personalization; anticipation, legitimation, and resolution of guests' needs; unlimited available physical labor; and a deferential, sincere demeanor on the part of workers. Interactive luxury service entails more than broadly conceived "emotional labor," which Hochschild defines as "the management of feeling to create a publicly observable facial and bodily display" that is sold for a wage.[3] It is, in fact, akin to intersubjective "recognition," which Jessica Benjamin terms "that response from the other which makes meaningful the feelings, actions, and intentions of the self." Luxury service entails recognizing a person's "acts, her feelings, her intentions, her existence, her independence."[4]

Guests prefer to interpret luxury service as care, akin to that provided by the idealized mother Martha invokes. But this service is also similar to the labor of another kind of reproductive worker: the domestic servant, who provides both physical labor and deference while lacking authority. I explore the twin issues of care and subordination in the context of structural inequality. I also describe the organization of luxury service, showing how its production is divided up among workers with radically different jobs and personal characteristics, and I analyze what this division of labor means for worker consent and the normalization of inequality. I begin with a short history of the luxury hotel.

THE RISE OF LUXURY HOTELS

The word *hotel* came into use in the United States in the late eighteenth century to designate taverns and inns that served upper-class clients, a new distinction in hospitality practices.[5] The upscale Tremont Hotel, which opened in Boston in 1829, has long been considered the first "modern" hotel in the United States.[6] The Tremont and other hotels that followed it during the nineteenth century demonstrated impressive technical achievements in architecture, services, and amenities. In the early years, these included gas lighting, private rooms, and indoor plumbing; later, hotels introduced electricity and elevators to marveling guests. Luxury hotels were defined by their large size, tasteful aesthetics, cleanliness, high-quality food, and prime location, as well as the privacy and security they afforded and service marked by "faultless personal attention."[7] The "highest achievement of the first class hotel" was that "each guest may easily fancy himself a prince surrounded by a flock of courtiers."[8] These "public" institutions were seen to represent modernity, technological innovation, and progress.[9] Important social and political figures frequented or even lived in these hotels.[10]

By the 1930s, personalized service, replacing the earlier obsequious, racialized servitude, had surpassed technological innovation as the key selling point for and main managerial concern in grand hotels such as the Waldorf-Astoria.[11] But after midcentury, palace hotels declined in importance. In the 1950s, development of the "motor hotel," spurred by the growth of the national highway system and suburbanization, as well as the increasing importance of chain hotels and franchising, shifted the focus of the industry to midrange hotels in cities and on the road.[12] In the 1960s, convention hotels boomed; in the 1970s, limited-service and budget hotels emerged. Although luxury hotels did not disappear during this period, they were not especially prominent in the industry.

In the 1980s and 1990s, however, upscale hotels returned to visibility and growth. Rising international travel, for both business and pleasure, spurred demand. Intense competitive pressures in this period led to diversification of the whole industry through segmentation and branding, which further codified the luxury segment.[13] Favorable tax laws led to the building or acquisition of upscale "trophy hotels," even when they might not have been profitable. In the 1980s, a period of increasing income inequality, demand for "high-priced" lodging, including luxury, outpaced that for lower-priced hotel rooms.[14]

New ideas of luxury came to the fore, including innovations in design and available services. One general manager I interviewed attributed the "invention" of the "perfect luxury bathroom" to a particular hotelier in the 1980s, for example. Concierge services, twenty-four-hour room, laundry, and business services, flexible arrival and departure arrangements, fitness centers and spas, and a range of upgraded room amenities became widespread.[15] International luxury chains expanded in this period. The Ritz-Carlton company, for example, had closed all but one of its six properties by 1940. This Boston hotel and the rights to the Ritz-Carlton name were sold in 1982, and the company (owned by Marriott since 1998) now operates over sixty hotels globally. The Four Seasons chain likewise began with one nonluxury property in Toronto in 1960 and has expanded, especially since the 1980s, to over sixty-five hotels and resorts worldwide.

The national recession of the late 1980s and early 1990s and the savings and loan debacle brought crisis to the highly cyclical hotel industry. Like other segments, however, luxury rebounded by middecade when the industry reorganized itself to increase profitability and efficiency.[16] Developers began again to build luxury hotels.[17] Thanks to Internet startup millionaires and stock market high rollers, these hotels reaped record profits during the boom of the late 1990s, gaining more value than other industry segments.[18] In 1998, 5 percent of newly opened hotels were classified as upscale. Demand led to rate inflation; in 1999, hotel rooms with rates of five hundred dollars or more per night had increased threefold since 1994, and upscale hotel rates had risen by 31 percent since 1996.[19] Rates and occupancy declined in luxury hotels in the economic downturn after 2000, but luxury suffered less than other segments and has largely recovered.[20] For example, both occupancy and room rates in the Ritz-Carlton and the Four Seasons increased significantly during 2004, and luxurious concierge floors were increasingly popular.[21]

LUXURY SERVICE

Since the crisis of the late 1980s, *service* has become the watchword of the hotel industry as a whole, as a significant source of distinction and profits. Rejecting the old philosophy of "heads in beds," according to which the objective was simply to sell room nights to any client, hotels now devote significant attention to who is sleeping in the bed and how the hotel can maximize its profit from that particular customer over the long term. Yet service is defined differently in distinct industry segments. In luxury, it takes the form of extensive personalization; needs anticipation, legitimation, and resolution, including a willingness to break rules; unlimited physical labor; and deferential, sincere workers.

"They Zero in on You": Personalization

Consistent with the luxury hotel's emphasis on distinctiveness, service in these hotels is highly personalized.[22] First and foremost, managers and workers literally recognize the guest; consistent name use is one of the main tenets of service at any luxury hotel. The Luxury Garden's first service standard, for example, was "recognize guests personally through the use of their name, naturally and appropriately."[23] Management in both my sites encouraged workers to learn not only guests' names but also the names of their children or pets. (Another dimension of luxury service, of course, is to know when the guest prefers *not* to be recognized, at moments when he might want privacy or would be embarrassed at being acknowledged by staff.)[24]

Workers customize contact in other ways as well. To individualize their conversations with first-time guests, workers use information they already have or whatever they can glean. They might remember where the guest dined the previous night or that he is in the city for the first time. Or they might wish him a happy birthday or a happy anniversary. Luxury hotels also mark special occasions by providing complimentary champagne or other amenities.

For frequent guests, personalization goes even further. Workers greet returning guests on arrival with "welcome back." They remember details about guests' lives, families, and preferences. Upscale hotels devote significant energy to gathering and acting on information about the desires of repeat guests, including the type of room they want, particular services they require (such as ionizing the room to purify the air or not using chemicals when cleaning), special requests for blankets or pillows, favorite newspapers, and food preferences. These hotels also keep track of guest conditions such as alcoholism and diabetes in order to avoid offering inappropriate amenities.

Beyond customizing these basic elements of the guest's stay (some of which are also noted in nonluxury hotels),[25] the staff of upscale hotels observe preferences spanning a wide and unpredictable range. At the Mandarin Oriental hotel in Hong Kong, for example, a frequent guest's toy monkey always awaits her on the bed; in another Hong Kong hotel, workers iron one guest's shirt near his door "because he likes the feeling of warm cloth when dressing in the morning."[26] One repeat guest at the Royal Court required that a rented red Jaguar convertible be waiting when he checked in; another guest insisted on always being addressed as "Doctor." A guest at the Luxury Garden requested that laundry workers avoid putting starch in his clothes; another demanded that the head of his bed be elevated six inches off the ground; still another thought of a particular chair as "his" (he had reportedly carved his initials on it) and requested that it always be in his room when he was staying in the hotel.

Sometimes preferences are observed as a result of the guest's explicit request, as in the examples above. Yet luxury service also means fulfilling preferences when the guest has not explicitly articulated them. One manager at the Luxury Garden said that for him, luxury service was exemplified by a housekeeper's noticing that a guest had eaten a peanut butter cookie provided for him one evening but had left the chocolate chip one untouched; the next night she left him two peanut butter cookies. In fact, workers there were given forms to record any guest preferences they became aware of, to keep them on file for future stays. A Royal Court standard of the week exhorted workers hotelwide to "please tell the front desk anything you know to put in the guest history."

Many luxury hotels use additional strategies to recognize repeat customers. Some offer frequent guests gifts to mark significant stays (such as the fifth, tenth, twentieth, and so on). Often these emphasize the guest's individuality, such as personally monogrammed stationery at the Luxury Garden and monogrammed pillowcases at the Ritz-Carlton and the Peninsula Beverly Hills.[27] These hotels even make major structural modifications in order to meet the needs of repeat guests. For example, one Ritz-Carlton hotel installed a wood floor in a room for a frequent guest who was allergic to carpeting.[28] The Royal Court provided a shower curtain for Ms. Parker, a frequent visitor who did not like the open shower in the recently renovated bathrooms.

Research suggests that personalized attention is indeed an important element of creating customer loyalty. One industry study found four factors related to recognition, personal attention, and customized service to be among the top eight factors (of eighteen) that clients said engendered loyalty to a particular hotel; 87.5 percent of clients surveyed rated "the hotel uses information from your prior stays to customize services for you" as either 6 or 7 on a 7-point scale of important factors (with a mean rating of 6.4). The factors "the staff recognizes you by name" and "the staff recognizes you when you arrive" achieved a mean score of 5.6.[29] Other research has identified personal attention and recognition as two of the three factors determining the choice of a hotel brand.[30] Marketing research reveals that affluent frequent travelers in particular look for recognition by name and, in making reservations, "a direct line to the general manager, who inquires about a recent family triumph or tragedy, as any old friend would do."[31]

Most guests I interviewed likewise described personal attention as important to them. Many enjoyed being called by name; Christina, a young leisure traveler, appreciatively told me that at a Four Seasons hotel the staff had remembered not only her name and her husband's but also the names of her two dogs. Tom, a business traveler, had been "dumbfounded" when his preferences were observed at another Four Seasons hotel; upon arrival, he had received plain strawberries instead of chocolate-covered ones, because on an earlier visit he had mentioned that he was "a low-fat eater."

Guests appreciated being distinguished from others and having their personhood acknowledged, often describing this treatment in terms of "care" and feeling "at home." Betty, a training consultant, preferred luxury hotels because, she said, "they treat you like you're a person" and "they respect me as a person." Adam, a retired businessman, said of himself and his wife, "We feel [being called by name is] more a guest relationship and a human thing, that you're not simply a number or a unit. You're a person who is recognized and you can have a little conversation." Andrew, the president of a major manufacturing firm, echoed these ideas: "I think that that changes the whole equation for the entire hotel, when somebody who's at the door in the lobby—there's at least a sense of recognition. If he doesn't know your name he might say—like if you are coming back from dinner, he says, 'Did you have a nice evening this evening,' like he really cares, 'I care about you as a person.'"

By the same token, guests frequently complained if they did not get the personalized attention to which they felt they were entitled. On several occasions at both the Royal Court and the Luxury Garden, guests lamented, "No one here knows me anymore," or asked, "What happened to everyone that knew me?" A frequent guest at the Royal Court complained that during the recent renovation "they destroyed my room." One return guest at the Luxury Garden mentioned on a comment card that she felt "ignored" because the personalized stationery she and her husband received was always in his name.

A few guests I interviewed, all women, said they did not care if the staff used their names or appeared interested in their lives. They spoke of being "embarrassed" when they were treated this way, and they suspected that recognition was not authentic. These guests were more likely to consider recognition facilitated by technology as less meaningful, saying, for example, "I'm sure they have it in the computer or something." These guests cared more about the design and décor of the hotel and that the service be efficient rather than personalized. Some of them also mentioned a sense of surveillance or intrusion associated with recognition; one woman told me of a friend who was shocked when hotel staff knew something about her that she felt they could háve found out only by listening in on her private conversations. Nonetheless, most of these women also said they would notice if the staff failed to provide this kind of attention, indicating that recognition was still part of their expectation of luxury service.[32] (I discuss these guests further in chapter 6.)

"They Go Out of Their Way": Anticipation and Legitimation of Needs

In Robert Altman's 2001 film *Gosford Park,* Helen Mirren's character, the head housekeeper in an English country mansion in the 1930s, says to a young lady's maid: "What gift do you think a good servant has that separates him from the others? It's the gift of anticipation. I'm a good servant. I'm better than good; I'm the best. I'm the perfect servant. I know when they'll be hungry, and the food is ready. I know when they'll be tired, and the bed is turned down. I know it before they know it themselves."

Workers in the luxury hotel are likewise expected to anticipate guests' needs, a process in which the definition of "needs" expands to include what might otherwise be considered "desires." The Ritz-Carlton's credo, for example, includes the commitment to fulfill even the guest's "unexpressed wishes and needs." The general manager of the Peninsula Beverly Hills, Ali Kasikci, told a reporter, "Waiting for customers to tell you what they need is like driving your car by looking in the rearview mirror."[33] Workers must be on the lookout for needs the guest might not articulate or even be aware of. Concierges, for example, stood armed with umbrellas for guests who were on their way out and might not know that it was raining. Antonio, a guest services manager at the

Luxury Garden, advised me always to offer soup to guests who mentioned they were not feeling well, thereby actually creating a need rather than anticipating an existing need. Needs anticipation may also include withholding information or refraining from taking some kind of action; for example, I was cautioned not to tell a guest that he had been upgraded when the person he was traveling with had not been.

Needs anticipation also entails reading the guest's demeanor, picking up subtle cues to predict her needs and desires. Sydney, a guest services manager at the Luxury Garden, told me, "You have to know what they want that they aren't telling you, because if you don't they won't like what you get them." When a guest asks the concierge to recommend a restaurant, the concierge must (in addition to asking the guest about his tastes, of course) take into account factors such as where he is from, how old he is, and how sophisticated he appears, in order to increase the chances of making an appropriate choice. If the guest is older and appears unschooled in upscale dining, he may receive a reservation at a chain steakhouse; if a visitor from New York requests information on local entertainment, the concierge will not recommend the traveling version of the latest Broadway hit. In employee training sessions at the Luxury Garden, Alice, the human resources manager, encouraged workers to use visual clues to offer the guests something they might need. On one occasion she role-played a woman massaging her neck and seeming tired and another guest arriving with a crying baby, then asked what we would do to meet the needs they were not expressing verbally (the answers: offer the tired guest a place to sit down and give the mother a private space even if her room is not ready).

Guests appreciate needs anticipation. One visitor to the Luxury Garden wrote on a comment card: "Housekeeper apparently saw cold medicine next to the rollaway bed for our 10 year old daughter and thoughtfully left an extra box of tissues! Great attention to detail!!" Herbert, a businessman in food manufacturing, recounted approvingly that after hearing that his young son was going to a baseball game, workers at an upscale hotel left cookies, milk, and a baseball hat in the room for him. Shirley, a leisure traveler, was amazed when tea was delivered unexpectedly upon her arrival at one fancy hotel:

We'd checked into our room, and there was a knock on the door, and they brought chamomile tea and cookies. It was just those sorts of things, those unanticipated, delightful little things. You didn't even know you wanted chamomile tea, and it was the perfect thing. . . . I think it's a combination of anticipating your needs but doing it in a way that's sort of invisible, that doesn't draw attention to itself, that it sort of magically happens without you seeing how it happens, but it's as if they knew what you were thinking two seconds before you thought of it.

Although these practices are known in the industry as *needs* anticipation, these examples demonstrate that the process also creates *desires*, by providing things "you didn't even know you wanted," and then codes them as needs.

Workers also recognize clients by responding to the individual needs and problems they express. Managers in training sessions and in industry literature stress that the guest must be able to get whatever she wants, including having prescriptions picked up, salon shampoo delivered to the room, and a cell phone retrieved from the restaurant where she had lunch. But more extreme examples abound. At one Four Seasons property, for instance, the maitre d' lent his tuxedo to a guest who did not have one for a black tie event, and even had the trousers altered for him.[34] As I have mentioned, on two separate occasions, Max, the Luxury Garden concierge, convinced the manager of a local department store to open early for guests with urgent needs for clothing. Another concierge, Alec, literally lent the shoes off his feet to a guest whose own shoes had been misplaced by the housekeeping department. When a group of incoming guests at the Royal Court wanted to rent two new-model Mercedes SUVs, front desk workers found a rental agency that could provide them, though it entailed having the vehicles delivered from several hundred miles away. At the same hotel, I was asked to find a gauze bandage for a woman who had recently undergone knee surgery and then to assist her in dressing her leaky wound.

In both hotels, my coworkers and I were asked to perform many services for guests. A partial list, culled from my field notes, illustrates the broad range: "Find doctor; find live crab, feathers, balloons; find white truffles; take shoes to be fixed; take luggage to be fixed; find gown; reserve spa for six, rental van, all-day limo; obtain video of local performance; arrange babysitting; get cell phones, Japanese furniture, cigars; find sheet music; find blue roses; find jade jewelry; plan out-of-town day trip; find pediatrician; give directions to local farmer's market; find out about tea set used in hotel's restaurant; arrange for local golf; get kosher takeout menu; find Greek Orthodox church; arrange camera equipment rental; open package arriving for departed guest and send back to him; arrange for spa, watsu treatment, shiatsu; get symphony tickets; find yoga clothes, particular designer furniture; find computer equipment; find map store; arrange helicopter tour; find and make appointment with German-speaking dentist; get shoelaces; find tailor; make hotel reservations in New Orleans; get coat left at restaurant and send to guest; get birthday cake for tonight; find Catholic church; place T-shirts and welcome packages in incoming guests' rooms; get ginger root for tea; send champagne to incoming guests on behalf of a friend; find out about lobby furniture; find out about duvet cover in room; find artificial orchids; get baseball tickets; mail knife; put rose petals on bed; find lost child."

The list for one especially demanding Luxury Garden guest, Dr. Kramer, compiled over several visits, included "get electronics; get cotton jogging clothes; make hotel reservation; make copies; get stapler; get sushi; fix e-mail access; find battery for cell phone; get luggage fixed; get rental car exchanged; find access to Internet for his computer; fix luggage; get temps; get more temps; find Indian food; change room; fix cell phone; find CDs; get newspaper; give message to models waiting for him in lobby; find cell phone help; rent convertible; find directions to state park; make laptop work."

Recognition work also entails that the worker legitimate these needs by responding sympathetically. Workers are expected to show concern about any situation the guest finds difficult, from a missed flight to a cloudy day. This standard extends to moments when the guest is dissatisfied with the hotel service itself. Alice, the Luxury Garden human resources manager, emphasized five elements of responding to guest complaints, the second of which was "apologize first." She said that when she studied guest complaints, most guests claimed, "All I wanted was someone to listen and care," or said, "No one apologized." She said the appropriate emotional response was especially important in the luxury hotel because "we don't have clientele that count pennies," so monetary compensation when something went wrong was less meaningful to them. Sebastian, the general manager, told me in an interview that guests were most likely to complain that "their needs weren't met" and that "they weren't heard."

Guests value worker responsiveness to their needs and problems, seeing it as a key dimension of luxury service. For example, one guest at the Luxury Garden wrote in a letter to the general manager, "Antonio [the guest services manager] and his staff were extremely courteous and helpful when we needed to locate our lost luggage. I am sure that we seemed very high maintenance at one point when several calamities occurred at once. But Antonio and his people never complained nor seemed in any way reticent to attack each challenge as it arose." Asked in an interview what he meant by "caring service," Herbert invoked both recognition of needs and their legitimation, as well as personalization:

> When you're in the hotel and you order room service and—because I get up early, and I make a motion to the room service waiter that my wife and son are still asleep in the next room. The next morning the same waiter comes and delivers the breakfast and taps so quietly on the door I almost didn't know he was there because he noticed—that's sort of a very concrete example. He really did care that he didn't want to wake them and knew I wanted to have coffee in the morning, and that's really legitimate.

Guests also see it as a failure of service when workers do not acknowledge their problems. Christina described a stay at a hotel where "everything" had gone wrong; among other things, she and her husband were given a room much smaller than the suite they had reserved. She said, "If they had put flowers in the small room or a fruit basket or whatever, all would have been forgiven, but we were totally ignored."[35] Shirley described a bad experience in which the staff upgraded her but did not respond to her complaint that the room smelled musty: "They kind of pooh-poohed my concern and acted as if I wasn't being appreciative enough of the upgrade." Here staff failed to legitimate the guest's need, assuming that the bigger room would be more important to her than the odor.

Legitimation of guests' needs carries another dimension: a sense of unlimitedness. The imperative to "never say no to a guest" is a mantra in luxury hotels. Check-in and check-out times were rarely enforced at the Luxury Garden, for example; if a guest decided to stay another night, he was not refused, even if that meant overbooking the hotel. One manager told me that imposing these rules would violate "five-star service," especially given the rates guests were paying. The general manager at the Royal Court stressed several times in an all-employee meeting that "the guest needs to be able to get anything he wants." He said, "We can't let rules get in the way," berating the staff for turning a guest away from the restaurant because he had arrived five minutes late for breakfast. "For four hundred dollars," he said sarcastically, "we should be able to find a piece of bacon somewhere in this building."

Guests approved of this idea that rules could be bent or broken for them, and they often saw a willingness to transgress as a defining feature of luxury establishments in contrast to midrange hotels. One couple wrote a comment card to the Luxury Garden praising the hotel for providing breakfast at 10:30 P.M. On comment cards, several guests at both hotels lauded the chef for making vegetarian meals available. Tom, after citing an instance in which a Four Seasons had accommodated his request for a special meeting room, said of luxury hotels, "You just don't have problems. You just don't hear about rules and stuff—you know, they solve [problems]. They basically do everything humanly possible in these nicer hotels to meet whatever you want and make it a wonderful stay for you and your family." Betty, the consultant, described her experience:

> If I ask—like the Ritz-Carlton in Boston is one of my favorite hotels, and if I ask for something there they'll do whatever they need to do to fix it, to accommodate me. But if I would go to, say—I was staying in some [nonluxury] place in Washington about four months ago and all I needed was some pens for my room and I got an argument at the desk. . . . You know they're not going to go out of their way for anything

unless you have an argument with them, and that bothers me. . . . [In luxury hotels] you don't hear, "We don't do it that way," or "We can't do it that way," or "We don't have that here," that kind of thing.

Again, the guest is given the sense of unlimited entitlement in the fulfill-ment of her needs.

"Pampering": Displays of Labor

Another key element of luxury service, though it is not explicitly ac-knowledged as such either in the industry or among hotel guests, is the guest's entitlement to workers' physical labor—what some guests refer to as "pampering." Thorstein Veblen saw both abstention from labor and consumption of the labor of others as markers of the leisure class.[36] He would not have been surprised to find that guests in the luxury hotel are entitled both to avoid working themselves and to benefit from the unlim-ited labor of workers. But this available labor is not only physical; it also has an emotional dimension, indicating "care" to guests, just as a mother's preparation of dinner indicates love for her family.[37] I call these offerings "displays of labor"; they can involve visible human work or simply mark-ers of labor.

Many of the available services and explicit standards of the luxury hotel involve lavishing visible labor upon the guest. Both the Luxury Garden and the Royal Court, for example, offered packing and unpack-ing services on request. One of the service basics at the Luxury Garden insisted that all guests receive an amenity upon arrival, which "must be personally presented and not simply pre-set in the room." Standards at both the Luxury Garden and the Royal Court demanded that workers "escort guests" to their destinations within the hotel. (At hotels such as the Four Seasons, even animals are entitled to consume human labor; room service is offered to guests' dogs.) Available labor also inheres in the speedy service that characterizes the luxury hotel. The timely delivery of food or freshly pressed laundry indicates that plenty of people are ready and willing to meet the guest's needs.

Managers encourage workers to use "proper verbiage" regarding their efforts, such as "my pleasure" or "I'd be happy to," which minimizes guest perception that human labor is being exerted. They must respond enthusiastically when asked to run any kind of errand, from renting camera equipment to picking up chocolates for a guest's wife. They must be willing to wait on the telephone while the guest ponders the room service menu, for example, or confers with her husband about what type of restaurant strikes his fancy for the evening. Workers are exhorted to respond personally and immediately to any guest complaints; even if these are not the worker's responsibility, she should never tell the guest to call some other department. More than once in employee training at the Luxury Garden, Alice recounted a cautionary tale of sitting in another luxury hotel's lobby and listening in horror as a caller looking for a lost briefcase was bounced around from front desk to concierge to bell desk to housekeeping.

When management praises workers it is often for "going the extra mile." Managers at the Luxury Garden, for example, on separate occasions rewarded a doorman who called a taxi company after a guest left something in a cab, a front desk worker who taped a basketball game on her home VCR for a guest, and a business center worker who ran with a guest's package to the Federal Express office late one afternoon so it could be sent that day. Management at the Royal Court lauded a bellman for assisting a guest with her luggage when she moved to another hotel several blocks away.

A corresponding luxury service convention dictates that the guest himself should never exert any labor. At the Luxury Garden, for example, a manager who was training me said, "Never let guests fill out their own forms." Workers checking guests in at both hotels often requested a business card to save guests the labor of filling out the registration card by hand. One of the service standards at the Luxury Garden dictated that employees should pass on information about guest problems to their coworkers, so that "the guests will not have to repeat themselves." I was also told that "a guest should never touch a door." And, of course, guests should never carry their own bags, and the time they wait for any service must be minimized. The prohibition on guest labor is another way to acknowledge the guest's high status and limited time, thus recognizing his entitled personhood.

Tasks associated with certain jobs involve extreme amounts of visible labor. In my sites, bellmen not only escorted guests to their rooms but also carried their bags, set up luggage racks, and got ice for them if they wanted it. In the restaurants in both hotels, busers (often older immigrant men, known as "back servers") not only offered bread at each table every few minutes (rather than simply leave a basket) but also served it using the complicated method of manipulating two spoons or two forks with one hand rather than employ a simple pair of tongs. Concierges at the Luxury Garden were required to handwrite elegant cards giving guests pertinent information about their dinner reservations; at the Royal Court, all messages were delivered to the guests' rooms, so they did not have to call the operator. Inspired by the St. Regis in New York, some hotels offer the service of butlers, who will tidy guests' rooms during the day, run their errands, and draw them a bath, among other tasks.[38] Even some standard jobs, such as door attendant, function partly to indicate available human labor; automated technology is available, but the human touch is more luxurious. (Elevator operators and restroom attendants in other venues serve a similar function.)

Labor can also be demonstrated in the absence of workers. It is present in a variety of touches in the guest's room, in displays of labor that go beyond the typical folding of the toilet paper. At both the Royal Court and the Luxury Garden, for example, the guest's morning newspaper not only arrived in a fancy cloth bag that announced "Good Morning!" but was also hung carefully on the guest's door handle. The personalized stationery that awaited frequent guests in their rooms demonstrated labor, as well as serving the aforementioned purpose of customization. Andrew recalled that at a luxury resort, he and his wife had returned to their room to find a package adorned with an orchid awaiting them. Thinking it was a gift, they were surprised to find it was their laundry. Even objects in the room are indicators of labor, giving the sense that an invisible (caring) hand is constantly replacing bathrobes, slippers, ten or more different bathroom amenities, mountains of towels, fruit, fresh flowers, and so on.

Turndown service is an especially striking display of labor. Literally folding the corner of the bedding down, of course, serves no useful purpose; the gesture indicates, rather, that an invisible hand has been at work. Other elements of the elaborate turndown service in luxury hotels include switching on lights, turning on the radio, closing drapes, emptying trash baskets, cleaning the bathroom, replacing used towels, arranging the laundry bag and room service menu on the bed, and filling the ice bucket. At both hotels guests received, with their evening cookies, a card predicting the following day's weather; at the Royal Court, these were filled out by hand. These gestures primarily let the guest know that someone has been laboring on his or her behalf. As a butler at the St. Regis hotel told a reporter, "It's nice for the guest to see that the butler's been in."[39]

Although they did not refer to it explicitly as such, guests I interviewed saw labor, both visible and invisible, as a key element of luxury service. Asked what they thought constitutes luxury service, they often invoked indicators of labor, speed, and eagerness to serve. Herbert defined luxury hotels in part as places where someone will "pop up to help unload your car and offer to put it away for you." Bob, a young management consultant, said, "It's the little touches they do that impress me. . . . There's always a circle of people around you, and depending on how good the hotel is, it's either further away or closer to you and doing more or less for you." Linda, a leisure traveler, was impressed that little boys were available outside her room all night at an Asian resort hotel if she and her husband wanted anything.

Many guests, in interviews and on comment cards to the hotel, approved of workers' speed in tasks such as checking in, delivering room service or luggage to the room, or bringing their car from the garage. Mike, a businessman in his late thirties, mentioned speed of service as a difference between luxury and nonluxury hotels: "[Nonluxury hotels] are very bureaucratic in their handling. You know, you have to wait in line when you are checking in, even if you are a super-preferred kind of customer. The one that drives me completely nuts but is characteristic, particularly of the big convention [hotels], is that it takes twenty minutes to set up a wake-up call. . . . You know, room service takes an hour and a half to get there."

Workers' attitude about providing labor was considered important. Guests enjoyed getting the sense from them that "nothing is too much trouble," characterizing luxury service as "can-do." Virginia, who had stayed in a luxury hotel for three months because of damage to her home, described asking a worker for more dishes in her kitchenette: "If we were running low I would just ask her for—you know, 'We need more glasses' or something. In about three minutes we had an entire cabinet full of glasses. I wonder if we are demanding. But they never made you feel like you were asking them anything more than what they could willingly do for you. . . . They never batted an eye." Kim told me, "It's nice when you forget your toothbrush or something. Just to call up and say, can I get one, and they bring it to you. . . . Like when they ask you, can they take your bags, whether you want it or not. . . . 'I'll be happy to get that for you.' If you need some aspirin or you need some—just really anything, they'll just bring it to your room as opposed to you having to get it."

When workers withheld labor, guests often reacted unfavorably. Several people I interviewed and many hotel comment cards characterized as "bad experiences" episodes when they had to wait for staff or when dishes were not picked up around the hotel, and negative comment cards were full of criticism about failures of labor. One irate Luxury Garden guest wrote a letter complaining that the hotel's staff had disappointed him by, among other things, not providing the American cheese he preferred with his eggs and not offering to go out and buy him cigarettes when the hotel's gift shop did not carry his brand. (This was a failure of personalization and legitimation as well as one of labor, because his individual needs were not acknowledged.) I violated the code of unlimited labor when a couple staying at the Royal Court asked me to wrap flowers they had ordered for their room so they could take them home; I responded, "I'll deal with it," prompting the man to comment to his wife (right in front of me), "'Deal with it'—that makes it sound like a problem."

Clients could also be extremely sensitive to transgressions of their own entitlement *not* to perform labor. For example, in 1999, the Luxury Garden placed cards in the bathrooms suggesting that clients who did not want their towels changed every day for environmental reasons hang them up, whereas if they did want them changed to leave them on the floor. The hotel received "a flood" of negative comment cards in protest, according to the general manager. He described the attitude that they communicated: "I pay top dollar, I shouldn't have to worry about this." Andrew associated his own exertion of labor with a lack of intimacy: "When you're standing in line, I mean, it's a little colder, a little more matter of fact."

Guests also interpreted labor exerted on their behalf as "personal" service. In telling me about a luxury resort in Asia, Andrew said:

> The beach boys, they just almost hover around you. They put the towel around the pad on the beach [chair]. Of course, the first thing they ask you is if they can bring you a drink and you get that. They come around periodically with towels that have been soaked in some sort of smelling water, rose water, and put in the freezer, because it's so hot. And you kind of cool off with that. Again, it's a special personal service more than anything else. It isn't the size of the room, it is not the amenities. I mean, I don't think I've mentioned the word TV or VCR or that type of thing. It's the feeling of getting personal service.

Even objects communicate to the guests a sense of personalization, though they are also demonstrations of labor. Kim, a young business traveler, said of the bowl of fruit in the room, "It's as if they're saying, 'Oh, we knew you were coming.'" To Mike, room amenities associated with frequent stays communicated, "We're glad you're back." A guest of the Luxury Garden wrote on a comment card, "I am very impressed. . . . Very nice *personal* touches with the fruit and the bathroom facilities" (emphasis added).

While guests often appreciated the small touches in the hotel, they never described these as involving work. For example, Shirley liked a hotel where "apples *would appear* at one o'clock in the afternoon" (emphasis added). Instead, guests (like managers) often referred to these efforts as "attention to detail." Asked what he liked about luxury service, Herbert responded: "Attentiveness to detail. They pay attention to small things. If you went into the dining room to get a newspaper at breakfast, they would all be lined up in a nice little straight row. There would be no crumpled ones, you know. The flowers are going to be real flowers, and there aren't going to be a bunch of petals lying on the table next to it."

Everything this guest mentions involves labor, but he does not acknowledge that. Instead, he perceives these practices as indicators of *aesthetic* attentiveness.

Labor involving interaction, as we have seen, is supposed to appear voluntary on the part of the worker; noninteractive labor is supposed to remain invisible. When a guest at the Royal Court requested that red rose petals be strewn about his room as a surprise for his girlfriend, for example, he probably did not imagine that Ginger and Inga would spend an hour or so methodically yanking the heads off the long-stemmed flowers. When "invisible" labor was made apparent, guests often became uncomfortable. As one guest I interviewed, Sally, said, "I expect not to be bothered . . . if they want to turn down the beds, just make sure I'm not there." Here she indicates not only that labor must remain invisible but also that she prefers to imagine that the workers turned down the beds because they desired to rather than because it was their job. If the occupants were in the room when the turndown attendant knocked on the door, they almost always requested that she come back later or refused the service altogether. On the couple of occasions I witnessed in which the guests allowed the housekeeper (and me) into the room, they stood around awkwardly waiting for her to finish the service. (These were also the only occasions when I saw turndown attendants receive tips.) As I wrote in my notes after one of my first turndown shifts, "Most people were pretty nice but a tiny bit irritated at being interrupted. It's weird because it's a fine line—we are trying to do something nice for them, but it only works if it's done in kind of a mysterious way. If not, then we are just bothering them."

"They Really Care": Deference and Sincerity

Luxury service is not only about what workers do; it is also about how they do it. As the examples I have given indicate, workers in my research sites were required to demonstrate a range of emotions in their demeanor. First, they had to display deference to guests. They had to call guests "Mr. X," for example, while guests used workers' first names. Workers were also required to smile at guests, regulate their own appearance, and allow guests to initiate and terminate interactions, thereby occupying a "subordinate service role."[40] The deference imperative also inheres in the more elaborate strategies of legitimation and unlimitedness I have mentioned. Managers told workers, "There is no right or wrong, only the guest's perspective." Second, as I have shown, workers were required to display enthusiasm, appearing eager to exert labor on guests' behalf. As Arlie Hochschild wrote of flight attendants, "Seeming to love the job becomes part of the job."[41]

Most important, however, was that workers appear sincere in their concern for guests. The Royal Court's service handbook directed workers to "show genuine care and concern for guests' needs." One Luxury Garden service standard instructed workers to "engage guests with eye contact and a warm, sincere smile." Alice, the training manager at the Luxury Garden, told workers that guests need to perceive "that you care, that you care I [the guest] am here, and you're going to do your best to make sure I'm happy. . . . [Guests] need to know they can trust you to do what they need." Managers also encouraged workers to see guests as dependent, casting them as tired after traveling or as disoriented in a new city and therefore deserving of sympathy.

Guests also identified genuine care as a central part of luxury service.[42] Betty said, "I guess the biggest thing is, people want your stay to be comfortable, and they don't just say that. They really do." She immediately gave the example of doormen allowing her to leave her car at the curb instead of parking in the garage, as would have been required in a less upscale hotel; for her, genuine care was related to the sense of breaking rules and accommodating needs. As he approached the front desk, an older guest at the Royal Court said to Jasmine and me, "What perfect smiles! That's a real smile, right?"

Some guests contrasted sincerity to routinized interaction, which they viewed with distaste. As Adam put it, "I think good service begins at the front desk. . . . With a welcome that seems sincere . . . where people look at you, look you in the eye, instead of looking down at the computer and handing you a card without even looking at you. That ticks me off." Herbert commented, "In a first-class hotel, the staff that works there generally looks you in the eye when they walk by you in the hall. And when someone comes up and asks you, 'Is there anything I can get for you?' or 'Are you enjoying your stay?' they look you right in the eye, and they're really asking that question as opposed to saying that 'I have to walk into the lobby at an eighteen-minute interval and see if anybody wants anything.'" Martha, whose computer had been stolen at a midrange hotel, compared the distant reaction of the workers there with the more genuine response she imagined she would have had at a luxury property:

> It was really sort of an upsetting event. And I thought the difference, in retrospect, between if my computer had been stolen in the lobby of the Four Seasons as opposed to the [Hotel X], the people at the Four Seasons would have been, like, slashing their wrists! [Laughs.] You know? And the people at the [Hotel X] were like, "Well, our insurance is five hundred dollars, and that's it." So, it's a difference.

By the same token, guests did not like workers to be overly formal or aloof. As Shirley put it when describing a hotel she had not enjoyed, "There was a formality there where I didn't feel welcomed in any kind of intimate way. . . . It was a coolness." Violations of the sense of authenticity, as well as a sense of rote behavior, rupture the guest's sense that her individual self is being recognized.

MOTHER OR SERVANT? CARE AND SUBORDINATION

Horst Schulze, the former president of Ritz-Carlton, described the findings of a study his company had conducted on guest desires: "The first results that came back said that the guests wanted to feel at home, but I didn't believe that. So we did a further study and found out that what they really wanted was to feel like they did when they were in their mother's house." Gilbert explains, "This meant that they wanted an environment where nothing went wrong: light bulbs didn't blow out and food wasn't burnt."[43] Schulze might more accurately have spoken of a *fantasy* mother's house, of course, as few real mothers can provide an environment where nothing goes wrong. Like an idealized mother, the luxury hotel provides a sense of nurture, noting all individual preferences and quirks, anticipating and fulfilling needs, and showering the guest with genuine care and unlimited labor. As we have seen, this is largely what guests value in their hotel experience.

By the same token, luxury service also involves some of the elements of paid "care work" as it is defined in the literature on socially necessary work, such as child, health, and elder care.[44] As a home health care aide defined good care, for example, "It's not always the clean bed, it's not always some food or medication, but it's a smile or I'll get that for you or I'll do that for you."[45] In fact, many of the intangible components of care that compose luxury service are precisely those that are eliminated in the rationalization of other kinds of care, especially elder and health care.[46] In the hotel, however, these components are a primary source of profit—they differentiate a hundred-dollar room from a four-hundred-dollar room— and management thus emphasizes them through standards and rewards. Using standards, managers make explicit the components of care that are mystified in family settings or characterized as an intuitive "mother's wit" in nursing homes.[47] They also encourage workers to develop ongoing relationships, often seen to characterize care, with frequent guests.[48]

But there is, of course, a crucial difference between hotel workers and these other kinds of workers. Mothers have power over children, and even workers in traditional caring occupations exert some authority over their physically or emotionally dependent charges, who are usually children or elderly or infirm adults. But hotel workers lack this power, at least explicitly. Indeed, their relation to guests is in many ways more analogous to that between domestic servants and their employers than to the relation between mothers and children or paid caregivers and other kinds of dependents. Two kinds of racialized, gendered domestic servant tropes are relevant here: the female servant of color who typically does housework and sometimes child care, and the butler (or valet), usually a white man performing personal and household services.

The image of the butler connotes professional, skilled, unobtrusive service, while the female domestic brings to mind overtly subordinated labor; both of these dimensions are visible in luxury service. Furthermore, the deference, willingness to serve, and needs anticipation that are implicit in the work of both types of servants are codified and emphasized in the hotel.[49] Also like household servants, workers in hotels are required to create client entitlement by subordinating themselves. By drawing on images of maternal care, guests interpret workers as exerting power over them (and, as we shall see in later chapters, they are sometimes afraid of workers). But, of course, guests are entitled to more personal attention, more legitimation of self, and more labor than those who serve them. Guests are entitled to recast all desires as needs, to consume the unlimited labor of others while not performing labor themselves, and to be recognized in their individuality while not reciprocally recognizing that of workers. And, like domestic servitude, luxury service depends on unequal allocation of resources, for its consumers can afford it while its producers cannot.

However, the hotel is not like the private home, in which the caring mother, the obedient and deferential female servant, and the professionalized male butler labor. In the hotel, no single person (mother or servant) produces the service. The client is not the employer, which is usually the case among domestic servants.[50] Rather, this intangible feeling of having someone to care for and wait on the consumer is bureaucratized, emerging from a formal organization comprising layers of workers and managers doing a range of different jobs. The self-subordination required of workers is formally codified by managers, and in some cases their tasks are more limited than those of household workers.[51] In the remainder of the chapter, I look at the complex division of labor in the hotel that underlies the provision of luxury service, including job characteristics, worker demographics, and the possibilities for managers to control workers and routinize work.[52] I then analyze workers' experience of self-subordination, which differs according to their placement in the hotel, setting up the rest of the book's focus on interactive workers.

PRODUCING SERVICE: AUTONOMY, CONSTRAINT, AND INEQUALITY

The service theater of the hotel comprises a wide range of workers and jobs, a variation that is mirrored in the hotel's complex topography. Front desk agents and concierges stand all day behind a desk in the lobby, checking guests in and out and attending to their dinner reservations and unpredictable requests. Door attendants govern a narrow outdoor space between the hotel's front doors and the curb, loading and unloading guests' luggage and keeping an eye out for meter readers. Valet parkers run or drive from the door to the garage and back, rarely entering the hotel. Bellpersons roam around the building, guiding brass carts piled high with guests' bags through hallways and into elevators. Telephone operators and reservationists outfitted with headsets sit in windowless offices, staring at computers as they connect callers or discuss room availability. Housekeepers alternate between the small housekeeping offices, where their assignments and supplies are kept, and the floors where the rooms they clean are located, as they labor to finish their assigned quota. Restaurant servers shuttle between the hushed, intimate dining room and the loud, chaotic kitchen, while sweaty cooks and kitchen staff are confined behind the cooking line or next to the steamy dishwasher.

How do managers organize all these labor processes? They first split them into two categories: interactive and noninteractive positions. In the industry, the public areas of the hotel are known as the "front of the house" and are home to concierges, front desk agents, bellpersons, door attendants, valets, and restaurant servers. The private areas of the hotel are known as the "back of the house." Here we find workers who rarely have contact with guests, such as room cleaners, turndown attendants, and laundry workers. In a gray area between the front and back of the house, we find what I call "semivisible" workers, who have limited face-to-face or exclusively telephonic contact with guests, including reservationists, telephone operators, room service workers, and housemen or runners.[53] This division of labor is defined in terms of worker visibility to guests.

Less obviously, these jobs also vary according to the tangibility of the product. Workers in the front of the house provide most of the elements of interactive service, which consists mainly of intangible emotional labor (personalization, needs anticipation and compliance, and deference) as well as visible physical labor. Workers in the back of the house, in contrast, primarily produce the noninteractive elements of recognition, mainly invisible physical labor. Their products—clean rooms, turned-down beds, hot food, and so on—are tangible (though usually not portable, as most material goods are, because they cannot be taken off the premises).

Wages and working conditions vary between these two groups, as we will see in more detail in subsequent chapters (also see appendix C for wages in my sites). Back of house workers are paid less than front of house workers as a rule (one or two dollars less per hour in my sites). Many interactive workers regularly received tips (and sometimes commissions), which was less common for back of house workers (except for room service servers). All of these differences have consequences for workers' experience of work. As we have seen, back of house workers are more highly regulated and tightly supervised, while front of house workers have more autonomy and control over their work. At the same time, invisible workers are not required to interact often with guests, while interactive workers must offer more self-subordination.[54] Table 1 summarizes the key characteristics of these areas.

This division of labor maps onto demographic distinctions.[55] (See appendix C.) Front of house workers are usually white (though bellpersons and door attendants, who perform more physical labor, are often men of color). Workers in the back of the house are generally people of color, often immigrants from a wide range of countries. These distinctions held at the Royal Court, though the norm for front of house workers did not hold at the Luxury Garden; there, those workers were more diverse, many of them Asian and Asian American. Back of house jobs are usually stratified by gender (turndown attendants and room cleaners are always women), as are certain front of house positions (bellpersons, valets, and door attendants are almost always men). However, both men and women perform front desk and concierge work.[56]

The Back of the House: Invisible Workers

Workers in the back of the house provide few of the interactive elements of service, for their primary role is to furnish invisible physical labor. Room cleaners and turndown attendants display labor by doing the myriad tasks involved in both morning and evening maid service. As I have suggested, the maintenance of the room's aesthetic, particular to luxury service, indicates labor. Luxurious appointments create extra work for housekeepers not found in nonluxury hotels; they change the covers of

TABLE 1 Comparison of Front and Back of House Work Characteristics

	Front of House Work (Visible)[a]	Back of House Work (Invisible)[b]	Front and Back of House Work (Semivisible)[c]
Client contact (visibility)	High	Low	High (telephonic) or low (face-to-face)
Tangibility of product	Low	High	Low (reservations and telephone) High (runners and room service)
Customization	High	Low	Some
Emotional labor	High	Low	Some
Physical labor	Low (high at front door)	High	Low in reservations and telephone High for runners and room service workers
Discretion	High	Low	Some
Routinization	Low	High	High
Monitoring	Low	High	Some
Worker demographics[d]	More often white Almost always men at front door	More often people of color Almost always women in housekeeping	Both white and people of color Women and men in reservations and telephone; mostly men as runners and in room service
Remuneration	Higher wage, tips, commissions (concierge)	Lower wage, few tips	Higher wage, some commissions (reservations)

[a]Concierge, front desk worker, door attendant, bellperson, valet.

[b]Room cleaner, turndown attendant, laundry worker.

[c]Reservationist, telephone operator, runner, room service server and order taker.

[d]These characteristics vary according to the hotel's location.

down duvets every day, replace ten towels, tie sashes of bathrobes, and so on.[57] These workers also implemented guest preferences by leaving special amenities or objects in the rooms, but they did this on the order of managers.

Hence, as I have said, the product these workers provide is tangible. As a result, their work is easily routinized. Room cleaners and turndown attendants are given a certain number of rooms to clean or turn down each day, which for room cleaners rarely varies. Management gives workers extremely detailed specifications on what the room should look like, including how many hangers belong in the closet, how to tie the sashes of bathrobes, and where to place amenities and towels in the bathroom or items on the desk and bedside table. Room cleaners often train one another and over time develop their own preferences as to when to do different tasks and which implements to use. Once they find the fastest individual system, however, most do not vary it much from day to day or room to room. They do make some small choices, such as whether to replace a bedsheet when they notice a tiny hole or a stain. And guest behavior, which determines the time housekeepers can enter the room as well as the effort necessary to clean it, does introduce variation into their work. But in general these workers exercise very little discretion.

As a consequence of this tangibility and quantifiable "output," room cleaners are also easily monitored. Although room cleaners generally work alone, supervisors examine the rooms they have cleaned, holding glasses up to the light to look for spots or running a finger along the windowsills checking for dust. Supervisors are inconsistent about this task, because the amount of time they have to inspect rooms varies daily. However, room cleaners do not know when their rooms will be checked, and clear standards make measurement of performance very simple.

Furthermore, tangibility makes back of house workers vulnerable to guest complaints. Guests frequently call the housekeeping office or the front desk to complain about problems in the room or services they have failed to receive. Housekeepers (and even supervisors) in my sites lived in fear of guest dissatisfaction and remembered seemingly small incidents for years afterward. Socorro, a room cleaner with whom I worked at the Royal Court, was especially anxious about guest complaints. She worried about acquiring a "bad reputation" when there was a mark on the wall in one room, though she had reported it to the supervisor. She put extra soap in one room, even though there was some in the shower, because she said it was the kind of thing guests might complain about. Workers sometimes feared misunderstanding guests because of the language barrier.[58] It is notable that these housekeeping workers, who had least contact with guests, were most afraid of their complaints.

In addition to their highly regulated work, these workers were especially dependent on their employment at the hotel, because they had few labor market options. Housekeeping workers spoke little English, usually lacked higher education, and frequently told me they had "no choice" when I asked them if they enjoyed their jobs. They primarily liked working at the hotel, not for the content of the work, but because they had good benefits and consistent days off, which was crucial to organizing their child care. Some of them had also suffered much worse in their home countries or as recent immigrants.[59] For all of these reasons, these workers were fairly easily controlled by managers.

Semivisible Workers

Some work is neither exactly visible nor invisible. Room reservationists, telephone operators, room service workers, and housekeeping runners have frequent guest contact, but it is either fleeting (for runners and room service delivery people) or telephonic (for telephone operators, room reservationists, and room service order takers). In my sites, these workers were housed in different departments and not generally thought of as all belonging to the same category. Room reservationists and telephone operators have more in common with front of house workers in terms of their race (they are primarily white) and the intangibility of their work.[60] Runners and room service workers in both hotels were more akin to housekeepers, in that their work involved a tangible product and they were almost all immigrants of color. However, the labor processes of all these workers share some common elements and differ from either "pure" front of house or back of house work. Hence I call them semivisible workers.

These jobs are most similar to those Leidner discusses in her study of fast food.[61] Although the McDonald's employees she focuses on worked in the "front of the house" at the counter, their jobs were similarly routine and involved only brief contact with clients. Also, both semivisible hotel workers and fast food workers are constrained by the technology that supports them: computers in the case of reservationists, telephone operators, and room service order takers and computerized cash registers in the case of counter workers at McDonald's.

Thanks to the brevity and routine nature of their contact with guests, semivisible hotel workers must observe the interactive elements of luxury service more than housekeepers but less than front of house workers. They must, of course, appear deferential and sincere; Royal Court managers counseled telephone operators to answer the phone "with a smile," for example. Workers customize interactions by using the guest's name and title of address as they appear on the computer screen. Reservationists and telephone operators are sometimes expected to anticipate guests' needs on the basis of information they glean in conversation. Runners and room service workers provide speedy physical labor as well as some interactive customization, such as using the guest's name. They must take cues from guests about how much interaction they want, lingering in the room to chat if the guest desires it or responding to unpredictable guest requests.

Semivisible jobs can also be routinized (though not as thoroughly as housekeeping work, as a result of customers' unpredictability). Room service servers at the Royal Court, for instance, had a prescribed way of setting up the tray or table. They had been trained very specifically on details of the presentation (and they vigorously defended putting the knife to the right of the plate if I unwittingly moved it to the left, for example). They did have some discretion over charging guests for extras or giving them special treats. Telephonic encounters are also fairly routine. The telephone operator's contact with the caller is short and varies little; rarely does she exchange more than a sentence or two with the person calling. The questions the reservation agent asks the caller never vary, and she types the answers into prescribed spaces on her screen. After many shifts in reservations, I wrote in my notes, "It is starting to feel kind of like a factory."

Semivisible workers in my sites used scripts to some extent, some of which were imposed by managers. Royal Court management posted exactly what the telephone operator was supposed to say to callers, which differed according to whether they were inside or outside the hotel. In reservations, I was trained to say "fully committed" instead of "sold out" or "booked." Instead of saying "no" to callers, I was supposed to say "I can put you on the waitlist" or "I can check other dates for you." Yet interactions were rarely fully scripted and usually involved some spontaneous conversation; management certainly made no attempt to eliminate improvisation, as it made the interaction seem more genuine. Workers were expected to respond to cues from guests in customizing their interactions. Routinization, however, sometimes serves to insulate hotel workers, because it controls the client, just as it does for McDonald's employees in Leidner's argument. Scripts protect reservationists from insistent callers, for example, allowing workers simply to repeat "May I check another date for you?"

Supervision of semivisible jobs varies but in general is minimal. Reservationists, telephone operators, and room service order takers are subject to the de facto supervision of coworkers and managers who can hear their interactions with callers, and of course the callers themselves can complain about these workers' behavior. These checks may prevent them from being overtly rude, but they do not give these workers particular incentives to go out of their way to offer extra care or labor to guests; these extra elements of service are by definition unexpected, so guests are likely to be impressed when they are forthcoming but not notice when they are not. Runners and room service servers interacted with guests completely out of sight of managers, though housekeeping supervisors occasionally complained that runners did not respond to pages, and guests might grumble that room service delivery was not fast enough. The tangibility of the product in these cases ensures that guests know when they have (or have not) received it, so it is easier for them to complain.

The Front of the House

Front of house work contrasts strikingly with both invisible and semivisible work. The workers in front of house positions provide the highest level of intangible, recognizing service. Workers at the desk and at the front door greet guests by name, anticipate their needs, chat with them, and provide deference and legitimation. Front desk workers and concierges especially remember guest preferences and offer emotional labor. Front door workers not only make conversation and personalize interactions but also carry bags, open doors, and retrieve cars, exerting physical labor on the guest's behalf. Managers in the front of the house also provide a fair amount of luxury service.[62]

Leidner argues that complex jobs in which customers resist routines and in which customization is a key element of the product are harder to routinize.[63] These factors, plus unpredictable guest demands and behaviors, make front of house work in the hotel especially difficult to routinize. Hotel workers must often respond to highly specific and unpredictable situations. Furthermore, to anticipate and fulfill guests' needs, workers must discern clients' immediate desires on the basis of their self-presentation as well as their explicit requests. Because guests value authentic interactions with workers, these must not appear scripted or routine. Thus the challenge for managers in the front of the house is to elicit nonroutine behavior from workers on a routine basis.[64]

Recognition of guests may be what I call "engineered," meaning that it is supported by technology that allows workers to call guests by name and acknowledge their VIP or repeat visitor status and their preferences even when workers do not know them personally. In my sites, these mechanisms included the phone display, computer databases, credit cards, and luggage tags. Nonetheless, most interactive work must be personalized in the moment, not scripted in advance. Mechanisms that help to engineer this recognition must be employed at the worker's discretion, in terms of both using the guest's name and collecting information useful for future standardization. Thus, the customization imperative means workers enjoy a high level of discretion in their work.

Front of house workers in my sites were subject to less surveillance, especially in terms of the content of their interactions with guests. Video cameras in public areas of the hotel (the loading dock, elevator, and so on) recorded workers' movements, although this was not their only purpose. Also, workers often had to initial their job tasks and use their names to log onto computers; thus, mistakes they made could return in the future to haunt them. These mechanisms of surveillance, however, did not facilitate supervisors' evaluation of the extra effort and genuine interaction workers were expected to offer. And supervisors did not have time to oversee the worker's interaction with guests. They witnessed these interactions only if they happened to be present at the time, which was rare.

Of course, clients also monitor interactive workers, as other researchers have pointed out.[65] They make their views known through conversations with managers, comment cards, and letters to upper management. Both my sites also employed "mystery shoppers," who knew the standards of the hotel and reported on workers' behavior, but these visits were rare. As we will see, comment cards in my sites were overwhelmingly positive. The potential surveillance inherent in any customer interaction certainly prevented workers from being rude to guests, but it did not force them to make the special efforts that luxury service is supposed to entail, because these efforts by definition go beyond the guest's expectations. Interactive workers, unlike the more vulnerable housekeepers, rarely articulated fear of guest wrath.

Interactive workers also had more choices on the labor market than their back of house counterparts. They spoke good (if not always native) English, were usually white, and often had some higher education. They were also harder to replace, especially when workers were scarce. Thus, both their personal characteristics and the differences in their work meant these workers could not be subjected to routinization and close monitoring, as back of house workers were. Eliciting the consent of interactive workers to care about and serve guests was further complicated by the self-subordination required in this work and the higher visibility of stratification for these workers.

OBSCURING AND NORMALIZING INEQUALITY

As I have suggested, inequality takes two forms in the hotel: the structural asymmetry between workers and guests and the interactive self-subordination of workers to guests. Interactive workers in my sites were more aware of the structural asymmetry than their invisible counterparts and much more responsible for the self-subordination.

Back of house workers, most of whom were immigrants from developing countries, were more disadvantaged structurally in relation to guests than their front of house counterparts, who earned more money, enjoyed greater job opportunities, and usually did not face racial discrimination. But these back of house workers had less direct contact with either structural or interactive inequality in the course of their work. They knew that the guests were wealthy, of course, but they were not constantly confronted with evidence of that wealth. In both hotels, housekeepers I worked with were unaware of the room rates or believed them to be lower than they actually were. It is unlikely that these workers were cognizant of the expense of the belongings they found in the rooms, if they even had time to notice them, which in my experience they did not.[66] They rarely commented on guests' wealth. Also, because they had little contact with guests, these workers did not have to enact the self-subordination characteristic of luxury interactions. For back of house workers, then, inequality was obscured.

Some semivisible workers, such as telephone operators and runners, were likewise rarely confronted with either structural or interactive inequality. Others, however, did know about guest spending. Room service workers knew how much the meals cost, and they occasionally commented on the exorbitant prices of the food or wine that guests ordered. Reservationists were well aware of the hotel's high room rates. But because they performed little interactive recognition work, most semivisible workers were insulated from the subordination characteristic of visible work. The scope of guest requests was usually quite narrow. Furthermore, routines protected these workers from having to manifest extreme deference, giving them some power in the interaction. They rarely had to legitimate outrageous behavior or demands. Reservationists also tended to interact with travel agents or guests' assistants at least as often as with the guests themselves and thus could withhold deferential treatment.

In the front of the house, in contrast, interaction required workers to face disparities in wealth between themselves and the guests more directly. Front desk workers, who handled guests' accounts, knew how much the guests often spent on their rooms, their food, and other services in the hotel. Concierges procured extremely expensive products and services outside the hotel; guests in my sites spent hundreds of dollars on tickets to the theater, symphony, or sporting events, as well as on meals, flowers, massages, and travel. Concierges knew where guests ate, shopped, and pursued expensive recreational pastimes such as golfing. They sent cars to pick up guests from their private planes or directed them to restaurants where they could buy three-hundred-dollar bottles of Cristal. Doormen and bellmen also saw the guests' expensive cars and luggage and were familiar with the high price of the car-and-driver services guests often used. Thus, guest wealth was by no means obscured to front of house workers and some semivisible ones.

Front of house workers also enacted interactive self-subordination to a much greater degree than other workers, deferring to guests, anticipating and responding to their every need, customizing interactions, and transgressing limits for them. Workers in these jobs must subordinate their own selves to those of the guests and restrain impulses to say what they really think.

But despite this increased knowledge and experience of unequal entitlements, inequality was normalized for most of these workers. In their conversations about guests and their desires, demands, and behaviors, workers constantly invoked guests' wealth. They bandied about numbers in the hundreds and thousands of dollars without batting an eye. However, they rarely critiqued or voiced discomfort with either the material inequalities between themselves and guests or the subordinating imperatives of their jobs (although workers sometimes judged *individual* guests for behaviors related to their wealth, as we will see in chapter 4). Indeed, in coding my field notes I became frustrated with the lack of explicit mentions of the guests' wealth in a critical vein.

Interactive workers discussed disparity and subordination only because I mentioned it in answering their questions about my research. Joel, a Royal Court doorman in his early forties, asked about my project, and I mentioned that I was interested in the disparity between workers and guests. He seemed confused, so I asked, "Do you ever think about that black Jag parked at the curb and wonder why you don't have one?" He responded, "That has never crossed my mind." He told me, "Sometimes people can be rich and think they're entitled to anything they want, and I know that's not true." But otherwise, he said, he did not think about it.

Contrast that experience to a conversation I had in the Royal Court locker room with Millie, a young woman who had just been hired as a hostess in the restaurant. I asked how she liked it. She responded that, in comparison to her last restaurant job, "here, you have to kiss a lot of ass." I was surprised, because I had never heard anyone voice this imperative so openly.

It was not coincidental that Millie was struck by this during her first few days of working in the hotel. I came to see that many workers went through a process in which guests' wealth and the imperatives of luxury service came to seem normal; it was apparent without being problematic. The restaurant manager at the Luxury Garden told me, "It's interesting to watch how the staff evolve over time. At first they worry about nickel-and-diming the guests, until they realize that the guest doesn't even look." I asked Sarah, a reservationist who had held her job for thirteen years, if she thought about how much the clients were spending. She said, "I used to think about how these people are spending my monthly rent to stay for one night." But, she said, "they can afford it, so it doesn't matter."

Other longtime workers also invoked this kind of relativism, saying, "It's not a lot of money to them." Annie, a part-time college student in her early twenties, told me one evening over drinks that she did not think about the high rates guests paid. She said, "It's all relative. To them it's not that much; to me it would be a lot." In this way they constituted guests as members of another universe, where money has different meanings. This was one kind of discourse I heard in the hotel about wealth acquired over time. I, too, went through a similar process. I had been fascinated by managers' stories of wealthy guests and outrageous demands, but soon after actually beginning work, I ceased to notice them.

Elena, a young, well-liked assistant manager who had studied hospitality management in college and had worked at the Luxury Garden for about a year, was the only person in either hotel who articulated the critical stance that I had expected to be more common. One day in the locker room she told me she was thinking seriously of leaving the industry. She said she was tired of her work and that it seemed meaningless. She commented that guests "put so much energy into getting an upgrade," oblivious to an earthquake in India or homeless people in the United States. She described them as "clueless" and told me she didn't want her job to be to "make sure that assholes enjoy their stay." At one time, she said, she had been committed to providing good service, but "now I don't care." She made fun of the idea of "wowing" guests. A couple of weeks later, Elena told me again that she thought it was "silly to care about rich people getting everything they want." In these comments, she linked the consumption of luxury service to larger social concerns and to individual entitlement associated with class inequality. The process of normalization had stopped working for her. As she began to question the inequality inherent in her work, Elena's investment in her job diminished. She became more and more unhappy and eventually left the hotel and the hospitality industry. Thus, the breakdown of normalization and the withdrawal of consent were closely intertwined. The question I will address in much of the rest of this book is why this breakdown and withdrawal happened so rarely.

This question is especially salient for interactive workers. It is not hard to see why back of house workers rarely contested their working conditions or left their jobs, given their unfavorable labor market position and limited skills. And for them, structural inequality was obscured, and self-subordination to guests was virtually nonexistent. Better-educated front of house workers, on the other hand, had more options, especially in the tight labor market that existed at the time of this research. Why did they choose to stay in jobs that exposed them incessantly to class inequality and required them to subordinate themselves to—and to appear to care for—hotel guests? How did this inequality come to seem normal?

The answers to these questions lie partly in the characteristics of the interactive work I have laid out here. After all, front of house work is autonomous, varied, often challenging, and fairly well paid, at least relative to back of house work. But a more complete answer lurks in Joel's comment above, that rich people are *not* "entitled to anything they want." As we will see, despite the hotel's call to provide unlimited labor, workers symbolically constituted guest entitlement as limited. They also constructed themselves as entitled in a variety of ways—to skill, to status, and to equal treatment. These constructions, as we will see, helped workers to reframe their own subordination while at the same time normalizing it. They also facilitated workers' active investment in their work. And they often depended on the use of back of house workers as a foil. Throughout my discussion of these processes, I will highlight workers, like Elena, who withdrew consent when their strategies for managing their own subordination proved inadequate.

The characteristics of the hotels themselves and their managerial regimes helped to shape workers' visions of themselves and others. Chapter 2 offers a more detailed discussion of both.

TWO

Managing Autonomy

Luxury service, as we have seen, depends largely on the commitment of the workers who provide it. Managers thus face a difficult task. They must convince their employees, especially those in the front of the house, to go out of their way for guests, satisfying and surprising guests in largely intangible ways. The managers I interviewed and worked with were all too aware of this dilemma. Their chief complaint was that it was too hard to find workers, especially workers who would provide high-level service. The food and beverage director at the Luxury Garden described his greatest challenge as "without a doubt the [worker] management aspect." The general manager at the Royal Court told me his biggest problem was finding qualified labor; he said he didn't understand why it was "so bloody difficult" to get clients' phone messages and packages straight, because "it's not brain surgery."

A tight local labor market exacerbated this problem. Most of my research took place in 2000, at the height of the national and local economic boom, which meant that many hotel workers had left to seek employment in other industries. Internal problems, including unpopular managers at the Luxury Garden and renovation at the Royal Court, had also prompted an exodus in each hotel. Alice, the head of human resources at the Luxury Garden, told me there had been a 34 percent turnover in 2000, which was high for the hotel. (She claimed it had been under 20 percent since 1993.) Alice named employee retention as one of her biggest challenges. Nicole, the Royal Court's human resources director, told me turnover had reached 43 percent in 1999 and was at 23 percent as of April 2000. The front desk staff, including line employees and managers, had been decimated. (When I started, almost all the front desk workers and front office managers had been at the hotel for less than two years.)[1]

Managers were similarly constrained by the requirements of interactive work. As we have seen, luxury service cannot be routinized because of workers' discretion in the face of unpredictability. Coercive approaches would not work among interactive workers either, especially given the tight labor market. So what strategies did managers use to convince scarce autonomous workers to provide luxury service? In this chapter, I introduce the two hotels and compare their managerial regimes. Although managers faced many similar constraints and had similar options for regulating workers, the two hotels produced luxury service very differently. The hierarchically organized and highly regulated Luxury Garden offered professionalized service; the Royal Court provided more informal, friendly service in the context of flexible organization and lateral authority. These managerial regimes could not, in and of themselves, ensure worker cooperation and consent; rather, they provided different kinds of resources for workers in the constructions of selfhood that I explore throughout the book.

THE HOTELS

In many ways, the Luxury Garden and the Royal Court were alike. They strove to provide a comparable level of service, competed for many of the same clients, and faced similar recruitment and training difficulties. They were both fairly small (160 and 110 rooms, respectively), with worker-to-room ratios of over 1:1 (standard in luxury hotels). They had a similar organizational structure. (See appendix B for details.) Because the city's hotel industry was highly unionized, both hotels, which were nonunion, more or less adhered to the terms of the master contract that governed unionized hotels in terms of wages and disciplinary procedures (though Royal Court workers earned slightly less than unionized workers). Workers were paid hourly and scheduled on three daily eight-hour shifts. Benefits at both hotels included health care, lower room rates for workers and their friends and family, free food in an employee cafeteria, and free uniforms and uniform laundry. However, the hotels differed in their ownership and management structures, types of accommodations and service, characteristics of guests, types of workers, and their managerial regimes. Guest responses to the service were similarly positive but varied in character; reflecting contrasts in service styles, guests saw the Luxury Garden as "professional" and the Royal Court as "friendly." Table 2 summarizes the differences between the hotels.

The Luxury Garden

The Luxury Garden was located in the city's business district, in an imposing skyscraper that also housed offices. A gold-coated doorman, positioned near carefully cultivated flowering plants, greeted guests. Inside, neatly uniformed white, Asian, and Latino workers, mostly older than thirty, stood behind the desk looking into the lobby, decorated in black granite with red and gold touches. The hotel's 160 rooms boasted a glorious view of the city; they were decorated with dark woods and Asian accents, such as bamboo and Chinese ceramics. Large bathrooms featured capacious tubs and sinks, as well as a separate shower, two kinds of bathrobes, and soft slippers. Like most luxury hotels, the Luxury Garden boasted twenty-four-hour room service, an award-winning restaurant, same-day laundry service, twice-daily maid service, packing and unpacking service on request, valet parking, and a complimentary chauffeur-driven house car in the mornings and evenings. A fruit or flower amenity awaited each new guest in the room. A business center, a fitness center, and a gift shop were located within the hotel.

TABLE 2 Characteristics of the Luxury Garden and the Royal Court

	Luxury Garden	Royal Court
Corporate structure	Multinational conglomerate	Independently owned and managed
Service	Formal, professional Meets standards	Friendly, informal Doesn't meet all standards
Clients	Business (global) Mostly men Mostly white	Leisure and business (local) Women and men Mostly white
Worker demographics, front of house	White (U.S.-born), Asian, Asian American, Latino Older (30s–40s) (Immigrant men at front door)	White (U.S.-born and European) Younger (20s) (Immigrant men at front door)
Worker demographics, back of house	Primarily Chinese	Chinese, Filipino, Central American
Remuneration/benefits	Higher	Lower
Managerial regime	Hierarchical professionalism	Flexible informality
Client responses	Positive ("professional")	Positive ("friendly")

The Luxury Garden's room rates ranged from $500 to $750 for single and double occupancy rooms, and from $1,400 to $3,000 for suites. Mobil, the industry's most important ranking organization, had awarded the hotel five stars, its highest rating. Other publications, agencies, and reader polls in travel magazines had also given it extremely high ratings. The hotel employed 200 workers, of whom about 165 were nonsupervisory. It was owned by a private Asian company. Management was part of the Luxury Garden Hospitality Company (LGHC), which managed luxury properties worldwide and was expanding, especially into the United States. The LGHC was itself a subsidiary of an enormous multinational conglomerate.

Luxury Garden workers earned slightly more than workers covered by the union contract in other hotels. Front desk workers made $15 per hour, as did concierges, though concierges garnered significant additional income from tips and commissions (approximately $2,000 per month, including an average of $150 per week in tips). They also received perks such as free restaurant meals, theater tickets, and gifts from vendors such as massage therapists. Bellmen and doormen respectively earned $9 and $10 per hour, plus about $100 and $150 per day in tips. Housekeeping workers made $13–14 hourly. Telephone operators and reservationists at the Luxury Garden earned $14 per hour. (See appendix C for details.)

Service at the Luxury Garden was highly professionalized and relatively formal. Doormen, bellmen, and front office workers consistently greeted guests with "welcome to the Luxury Garden" or, when appropriate, "welcome back." They used the guest's name frequently. Using engineered recognition, workers consistently noted and respected guest preferences and frequently anticipated their needs. They were cordial but not overly friendly or familiar, as a rule, though some had developed relationships with frequent guests. Workers generally used what managers called "proper verbiage" rather than informal talk, which preserved distance.

The professional service the hotel offered was well-suited to its business-oriented guests, who brought fat wallets and high expectations. The Luxury Garden's clientele was overwhelmingly composed of business travelers (70–90 percent, according to different managers), usually senior executives from a variety of companies, especially in the financial services industry. Approximately three-quarters of the guests were men, and at least 80 percent hailed from the United States. The rest came mainly from Asia and Europe, especially London. Although most guests were white, the hotel housed more African American and Asian or Asian American guests than the Royal Court did during my research (which may have been related to the preponderance of business travelers). Most of the business travelers paid lower corporate rates. At least 21 percent of guests were frequent, meaning they returned at least twice in a twelve-month period, and many more were repeats. The hotel hosted few groups and no conventions.

The Royal Court

Though located on a busy downtown street, the Royal Court was unobtrusive; you could walk by it a hundred times and never know it was there. Visitors entered through glass doors under a white awning; the décor of the spacious but intimate-feeling lobby was understated but elegant, featuring marble floors, high ceilings, European-style furniture, including some antiques, and a large flower arrangement. Featured colors included peach, cream, and gold. Employees uniformed in basic black—mostly young white women—stood at the ready behind the desk. Classical music played softly in the background. The hotel's 110 rooms were being renovated; new rooms were decorated in earth tones with bright accents, large mirrors, and natural woods; sizable bathrooms featured open glass showers and soapstone sinks and counters. The available services were similar to those at the Luxury Garden, though the hotel lacked business and fitness centers and a gift shop and offered slightly fewer amenities. The laundry was on-site, however, making service faster.

The Royal Court's room rates ranged from $300 to $500 for single or double occupancy rooms and from $550 to $2,000 for suites. The hotel was ranked with four Mobil stars. (Because it lacked some services, it was ineligible for a fifth, but the general manager told me the hotel merited "4.75 stars.") A major travel publication rated it among the top ten city hotels in the United States, and travel magazine reader polls gave it consistently high rankings. The hotel employed about 160 workers, of whom about 130 were nonsupervisory, for a worker-to-room ratio of slightly over 1:1. Since its initial opening in the 1980s as a nonunion luxury property, the hotel had had two different owners and been run by several management companies. At the time of my research, it was owned by a private Asian firm and independently managed.

Wages and tips were slightly lower than those at the Luxury Garden. The most notable difference was among the front desk workers, who also did the concierge work; they were paid thirteen dollars per hour, in contrast to fifteen, their tip/commission income was lower (probably reaching only fifty to one hundred dollars per week), and the perks associated with concierge work were fewer, because their front desk work depleted the time they could spend doing concierge tasks. Other workers in general were paid slightly less than their Luxury Garden counterparts. (See appendix C.)

Management strove for "authentic service," encouraging workers to be friendly and relatively informal in their treatment of guests. The hotel's founder called this unpretentious service "luxury with a cheerful face." The doormen often joked around with guests. Front desk workers spoke to guests in a casual but warm way, often eschewing formal terms of speech ("my pleasure") for those that sounded more relaxed but authentic ("sure"). When they did not know the answer to a guest's questions, which was often, they would acknowledge their ignorance and call the guest back with the information. The hotel observed guest preferences in terms of rooms and food, and some frequent travelers had their own special requirements. However, workers did not often record the kinds of information required to surprise guests with needs anticipation, instead taking note of only complaints or problems.[2]

The friendly service was well-matched with the Royal Court's clientele, which was composed of at least half leisure travelers and about half women.[3] Most of these travelers were not affiliated with convention or tour groups. The sales manager told me that 85–90 percent of the guests were from the United States; many of the leisure travelers lived in the area and would come to spend a weekend in the city. Most of the rest hailed from Japan, Canada, and Great Britain. At least 25 percent had stayed in the hotel before. The overwhelming majority of the guests were white; a few were Asian or Asian American, but I very rarely saw African American or Latino guests.

MANAGERIAL REPERTOIRES

Managers in both hotels drew on a similar repertoire of explicit strategies for regulating worker behavior, primarily having to do with hiring, training and standards, and the regulation of workers' self-presentation. First, managers I interviewed frequently argued that hiring the right *type* of worker was key to providing luxury service.[4] They consistently talked about finding the right person rather than creating him, saying specific skills could be learned if the worker's personality was appropriate for the job. Sebastian, the general manager of the Luxury Garden, said in an interview, "People don't get into the business for the money; they have to want to serve, and you can't teach this." The Royal Court's general manager, Mr. Weiss,[5] told me that he wanted workers with "a positive outlook toward the human race"; he felt the job required "80 percent personality, 20 percent skills." The tight labor market, however, constrained this strategy of selection. In September 2000, I asked Nicole at the Royal Court what she looked for in a prospective employee. She responded, "At this point it's speak English, be available, smile, be personable." She characterized the hotel as "desperate" for workers.

Second, managers in both hotels used a variety of means to regulate workers' selfhood and their interactions with guests. They standardized appearance by requiring that workers adhere to particular (and gendered) norms; as in many service enterprises, these included specifications about fingernail length, jewelry, makeup, hairstyles, beards, and so on. Managers also attempted to develop standards of behavior, which were sometimes quite specific, to guide employee interactions. Training workers in regard to these standards was, at least theoretically, a major managerial concern. Finally, both hotels used mechanisms of surveillance and especially customer feedback to monitor workers, as I have mentioned in the previous chapter.[6] At the Luxury Garden, not just regulation but also transformation of self was a major theme.[7]

Looming over managers in both hotels was the example of the Ritz-Carlton, the most prominent company in the industry to use the empowerment and corporate culture strategies common among enterprises trying to produce high-quality service interactions.[8] Awarded the Malcolm Baldrige National Quality Award in 1992 for its Total Quality Management (TQM) program, the Ritz-Carlton was the first hotel company and one of only a few service-industry businesses to receive this major honor, and its program has become very well-known.[9]

The Ritz-Carlton program includes efforts to ensure quality, create standards, and promote employee identification with the company. Each employee is given a card to carry at all times with the company's "Gold Standards": the "credo," the "motto," the "three steps of service," the "employee promise," and the twenty "service basics."[10] These are primarily statements of company philosophy and standards of conduct, not routines.[11] Uncommon in the industry, Ritz-Carlton hotels employ a "quality manager," who produces daily "quality improvement reports," which list the "defects" of the previous day, both "external" (guest-related) and "internal" (employee-related). Employees identify these problems and their solutions by filling out "quality action forms." The program also features extensive on the job training, as well as philosophies of careful employee "selection," team development, and "empowerment" (including allowing workers to spend up to two thousand dollars without managerial authorization to solve any guest problem). The hotel purports to value its employees as highly as its clients (describing workers as "internal customers"). As we will see, this program provided both an inspiration and a foil for management at the Royal Court and the Luxury Garden.

The two hotels' use of management rhetorics and strategies, especially corporate culture, training, and self-transformation, differed in important ways. But explicit strategies are not the only ingredients of a managerial regime. In examining these regimes it is important to look at how they play out in daily life in the worksite, rather than focus primarily on the elements of corporate culture as managers define them. Corporate characteristics and managerial decisions about hiring workers and organizing work, as well as local cultures of authority—what managers do and how they actually treat workers, as opposed to what they might say in interviews—are also important facets of the environment. I thus focus on three elements: the hotels' organization of work, especially the division of labor and worker demographics; managers' attempts to regulate workers' selfhood and behavior and to gain their loyalty; and the way authority relations played out in daily life.

At the Luxury Garden, a specialized division of labor, highly developed corporate culture, a clear managerial hierarchy, and consistent monitoring of worker performance led to a regime of worker accountability and professionalized service, which I call "hierarchical professionalism." The Royal Court, in contrast, was characterized by "flexible informality." Primarily as a result of the hotel's size and lack of corporate ties, this regime was marked by a flexible division of labor, including blurred boundaries between managers and workers; limited corporate culture and training with a corresponding emphasis on worker "authenticity"; and inconsistent managerial authority and surveillance. Instead of top-down, hierarchical

TABLE 3   Comparison of Managerial Regimes

	Hierarchical Professionalism	Flexible Informality
Organization of work	Specialized division of labor	Flexible division of labor
	Internal labor markets	External labor markets (limited)
	Higher wages	Lower wages
Organizational identity	Professional	Authentic
	Corporate culture, standards	Limited corporate culture
	Limited worker sociability	High worker community
Authority relations	Hierarchical (managers)	Lateral (coworkers)
	· Managers regulate workers	· Workers regulate one another
	· Workers accept managerial authority	· Workers challenge managers

organization, the Royal Court was characterized by a flexible, laterally organized process, largely regulated by workers themselves, and friendly authenticity was the hallmark of the hotel's service.[12] These differences are important for consent and the normalization of unequal entitlements, because they shape the ways workers can think about themselves; they are resources for nonsubordinate constructions of self. In later chapters I show how variation in these resources affected workers' strategies.

Table 3 summarizes the two regimes along the dimensions I will discuss in the rest of the chapter.

HIERARCHICAL PROFESSIONALISM AT THE LUXURY GARDEN

Who Does What: Diverse Workers, Internal Labor Markets, and Specialization

The first element of the regime of hierarchical professionalism consists of the organization of work and the choice of workers. Although this dimension is not an explicit aspect of managerial rhetoric or culture, it constitutes the foundation of the regime as a whole. Interactive workers at the Luxury Garden were slightly more diverse ethnically than is usual in the industry. Workers at the front desk and concierges during my research there were Asian, Asian American, and Latino, as well as white, though I was told that usually more white people worked at the front desk. The semivisible reservationists and telephone operators were also ethnically diverse. And middle managers in the front office were white, Latino, and Asian American. In other respects, worker demographics were as we would expect from my discussion in chapter 1.

Front desk workers and concierges were all older than twenty-five, and several of them were over thirty-five (including all but one of the concierges). Most of these workers were married and many had children, which as we will see was a contrast to the Royal Court. Many of them, including all the concierges, at least one bellman, and several front desk workers, were college-educated. Most had previous experience in hotels.[13]

The hotel created active internal labor markets (possibly especially so, given the tight external labor market). Three of the front desk workers had started in other departments (housekeeping, telephone operator, and sales); these workers were Chinese, Latina, and Asian American, suggesting that the practice of internal promotion contributed to greater diversity at the front desk. Becky, a white concierge, had been promoted from the front desk. In the four months I was there, at least six workers and managers were reassigned to higher posts within the hotel.

The corporate nature of the enterprise also conferred advantages on workers in terms of career ladders. The existence of other properties worldwide provided potential mobility (and possible places for workers to stay on vacation at reduced rates—a perk of the job). Both Jaya, a front desk worker from the Philippines, and Fred, a bellman from China, had worked for the Luxury Garden hotels in their native countries before immigrating to the United States. The possibility of promotion not only created a clear incentive for workers but also established hierarchies among particular jobs and between managers and workers.[14]

The internal labor market was supported by a specialized division of labor (see appendix B). This specialization was demonstrated, first, in the arrangement of particular units or departments in the hotel. The front office (mainly the front desk) was separate from guest services (the concierge staff, the business center, and the front door), which meant primarily that the guest services workers had their own assistant managers (though both were supervised by the rooms division manager). Reservationists were part of sales,[15] and telephone operators were under the supervision of the controller's office (mostly because their offices were adjoining). Security, laundry, the gift shop, and valet parking were subcontracted to outside companies.

The division of labor was also codified in a strict delineation of job tasks. Concierge workers and front desk agents did none of the same work; concierges focused on entertainment and guests' needs outside the hotel, while front desk agents checked guests in and out and executed other administrative tasks. Front desk workers were not trained at the telephone operator station. Business center workers, organizationally separate from the front office, sent out faxes and packages for guests, logged their incoming faxes, and did their Xeroxing. Workers were only minimally cross-trained. High specialization also characterized the back of the house for both semivisible and invisible workers.[16] As we will see, this separation of tasks contrasts with the organization of the Royal Court.

The spatial organization and aesthetics of work matched this division of labor at the Luxury Garden. Concierges worked next to the front desk agents, but telephone operators were located in the basement, and reservationists were upstairs in the executive offices. Room service had its own office on a floor above the restaurant kitchen. The laundry center and uniforms were in the basement, near workers' locker rooms, and the housekeeping office was upstairs. Workers wore different uniforms depending on their position: the doormen's gold coat differed from the bellmen's outfit, and the concierges' sober uniform contrasted with the gold and black apparel of the front desk agents. Reservationists wore suits, and telephone operators wore their own special uniform as well.

The front office managerial hierarchy was highly differentiated. François, the rooms division manager, supervised Patricia, a front office manager, who in turn oversaw several assistant managers and one supervisor. François never worked at the desk, and Patricia rarely did. Managers' responsibilities were clearly distinguished from those of line employees, although assistant managers spent some time relieving workers for breaks and shared some of their work, especially on the evening shift. The exception to this rule was at the concierge desk, where the two assistant managers sometimes took on regular concierge tasks, though they spent most of their time in manager meetings or working on special projects.

"Who We Are": Building Identity and Accountability

The second element of hierarchical professionalism at the Luxury Garden was a sophisticated program of standards and training, including the cultivation of a common identity and "culture." In this effort, management used many common techniques, including encouragement of deep acting and self-transformation, explicit standards and training, and practices of reward. More than transform workers' selves, however, these techniques served to clarify what workers were expected to do and to let them know that they would be held accountable.

CORPORATE CULTURE   Probably emulating the Ritz-Carlton, Luxury Garden management at the corporate level had developed an elaborate "culture," including a corporate philosophy, service and operational standards, and a training program. The most salient facet of this culture was a continued effort to establish a communal identity. When I interviewed Sebastian, the general manager, he frequently brought up culture as a feature of identity, calling himself "the carrier of our culture." He referred to a new standards program as "one of the tools that make us who we are." Managers referred to employees (and employees were supposed to refer to one another) as colleagues. Postings throughout the hotel about other properties in the chain, company news, and budget numbers attempted to create a feeling of belonging and participation in a common enterprise.

The company had a "mission statement" and "guiding principles," which Alice told us in the orientation had been "hammered out" by the general managers of all the properties. In addition to the corporate mission statement, the hotel's local management had come up with its own credo: "Above All Else: Dignity, Excellence, Enchantment." On several occasions I heard Alice tell the story of how managers at this property had spent months designing and implementing a new program for the hotel; this historical narrative seemed to be an integral part of the culture itself, as it often is in training sessions.[17] As at the Ritz-Carlton, workers were given a card to carry with them that included the credo, the four practices for each term, and the hotel's motto, "Enchanted moments come from living our credo."

The initial employee orientation reflected this concern with establishing a common identity and a sense of belonging in a luxury environment.[18] Alice handed out special pins to be worn on each employee's uniform when she talked about "who we are" as a way to introduce the mission statement and guiding principles. Company-made videos emphasized the mission statement, workers' commitment to service, and the luxurious elements of the Luxury Garden experience. She also emphasized the high status of guests, frequently describing the hotel's clientele as "the top 1 percent."

Procedures for recognizing workers and creating community in the hotel were well-developed at the Luxury Garden and linked to these elements of "culture." The primary recognition program rewarded workers for "enchanted moments" they provided to guests (nominally it also applied to workers enchanting one another, but I never saw an instance of this). When a worker went out of his way to assist a guest, he received twenty-five dollars; his photograph and a description of what he had done were posted in the workers' area in the basement. Seven or eight of these appeared during my four months at the hotel.[19] Managers posted guest letters of praise in their departments. François, the resident manager, told me in an interview that he tried to recognize workers by name "just like we do to guests" and to compliment them verbally or in writing (using special "five star cards") for good work. The human resources department conducted an employee satisfaction survey each year and publicized the results around the hotel.

Managers created community in other ways as well. The human

resources department organized community events such as a pumpkin carving at Halloween, a children's party, and a fancy holiday party in the ballroom of another local hotel. The Luxury Garden also produced a (more or less) quarterly newsletter, which announced the employees of the quarter and the year (who received cash awards) and mentioned employee and company news. Workers were encouraged to participate in committees, whose tasks included coming up with new ideas for bettering service ("to improve the 'wow' situation," as Alice said in the orientation), addressing environmental issues within the hotel, and improving the food in the employee cafeteria.

However, the sense of community also carried a dimension of accountability or coercion.[20] The language of many of the communications from upper management to workers often manifested two facets: one of community building and free choice, and the other of surveillance and compulsion. Typical of this attitude were the flyers posted around the back hallways of the hotel advertising a general assembly meeting; their tone promoted a fun, voluntary social activity ("Come enjoy refreshments!"), but at the bottom they stated baldly, "Attendance is mandatory."

Alice told me in an interview that the corporate culture, which she characterized as "pretty darn strong," served to clarify expectations and weed out those who did not "fit in." If employees did not observe these norms, she said, they would "stick out" and "feel out of place." This meant that workers knew they could not shirk work and that if they brought friends in as employees, they knew the friends had to be good. Thus, Luxury Garden corporate culture was in part a culture of accountability; this culture also included elaborate standards and company surveillance.

CORPORATE STANDARDS AND TRAINING   The credo "Dignity, Excellence, Enchantment" codified broad standards of behavior; written in the first person, these standards also implied a certain kind of selfhood, telling the worker what kind of person to be. They included, for example: "I respect my guests' and colleagues' individuality." "I show empathy." "I listen actively." "I keep my promises." These are norms of personhood as well as behavior, conscripting the self in the service of the hotel's product and the guest's experience.

Training sessions at the Luxury Garden, especially the orientation, encouraged workers to use strategies of deep acting to induce real feeling for guests.[21] Much like trainers at the airlines Hochschild studied, managers told workers to "act like the hotel is your house" and to "pretend the [complaining] guest is a relative, so there's still a sense of caring." This approach promotes deferential behavior "by invoking a familiar situation in which such behavior does not imply subservience."[22] Alice also told workers to "think about the hotel as if it were *your* business" when trying to solve a problem.

Managers also suggested that making the guest feel better would benefit the worker herself. One video Alice showed in the orientation included a scene in which a worker relates to another worker a story (supposedly true) about a guest who arrived upset and treated the worker rudely. Although she was already having a bad day, the worker went out of her way for the guest, because she realized that he had been traveling for a long time and was tired. Afterward she felt good about having made the extra effort. At the end of the scene, her coworker comments, "So I guess by making *his* day, you made *your* day as well." This video and other stories communicated that workers have to make allowances for people, because one never knows what has happened to them, and that the worker has the power to make someone feel better, which will benefit her psychologically too.

Training also focused on specific ways to handle guest needs and complaints, which gave workers resources as well as standards to which they would be held accountable. In the orientation, we played the "customer service pyramid game," for example, in which workers answered questions in nine categories of customer service ("Who ya gonna call?" "Service with a smile," "Anticipation," and so on). Alice showed a video that emphasized the importance of meeting the guest's needs in different interactive jobs. We also had training on guest complaints, which included statistics about repeat clients, psychological interpretations of guests' underlying desires in situations when they complained, extensive role playing of unhappy guests, and five steps to handling guest complaints ("Don't interrupt," "Apologize first," "Identify the problem," "Take immediate action," and "Follow up"). This part of the training also included an animated video entitled *A Complaint Is a Gift*.[23]

The hotel also used more specific service standards developed at the company's head office, known as Celebrated Quality Standards (CQS). Binders containing dozens of standards were kept in each department. These included very specific ways of doing tasks in each department in the hotel, such as how many minutes it should take for the guest to check in (five) or when the worker should acknowledge the approaching guest (when he is fifteen feet away). These were not routines in the strictest sense, at least for interactive workers, because the workers had discretion about when to use them. But they were a sophisticated attempt to codify as many of the hotel's practices as possible. This program was accompanied by the Celebrated Standards Training, or CST. Alice told new workers that the CQS and the CST had been developed in order to maintain the high level of service "on so many continents."

TRAINING ON THE JOB   Despite these elaborate standards, corporate culture was often more a matter of image than of practice. Training on the job was less elaborate than I had expected, given the emphasis on standards during the orientation. My own training from managers was somewhat spotty. When I first started, Antonio gave me a packet that included many of the relevant standards, but no one ever reviewed them with me. Training was inconsistent for other workers as well. Several workers told me they had simply been thrown into their jobs. Carolyn, Elena, and Patsy told me they had never been trained on the hotel's standards; Javier, a bellman who had been at the hotel for over a year, did not know that the red dot on the guest's key envelope indicated that the guest was a repeat. Max, who had helped to develop the guidelines, said, "No one ever uses them."

However, it was also clear that many workers had been trained very well, which may have depended on what department they were in and how long they had been with the hotel (those workers who had been through the original CQS "rollout" a few years before were more familiar with the standards). Luxury Garden workers seemed to get far fewer write-ups than those at the Royal Court, where discipline was used in place of training. Also, some attention was paid to ongoing training. During my time at the Luxury Garden, in addition to a two-day "etiquette training," concierges, bellmen, and front desk agents attended a "guest services training," the first in what François said might become a series. Managers also attended a training after which they had to solicit feedback from workers on topics such as recognition, career goals, and optimal working conditions.

IMPLEMENTING NEW STANDARDS   Corporate culture's multiple functions—promoting community and loyalty, demonstrating the impressiveness of the company, and establishing legitimate managerial authority and worker accountability—were illuminated in the "rollout" of a corporate-led initiative to modify the company's standards. The program, called Celebrated Quality Experience (CQE), was kicked off in a hotelwide meeting led by Sebastian, the general manager, about halfway through my time at the hotel. Workers gathered in a large meeting room decorated with yellow and red helium balloons and posters proclaiming the CQE. Before the meeting, workers were given numbered tickets. After calling workers to order, Sebastian said, "Those of you who know me know I like to give money away." He drew a number and gave an envelope with fifty dollars in it to the housekeeping worker who waved the corresponding ticket as a human resources manager snapped their picture.

Sebastian used a slick PowerPoint presentation to introduce the new program. He said that the CQS was becoming the CQE, a shift from over 1,000 "standards" to 175 "experiences." He explained that the very specific Celebrated Quality Standards had proven unwieldy, because the company's various properties had constantly requested certain kinds of exemptions, needed because of the particular circumstances of each hotel. The U.S. properties, for example, could not implement standards that required excessive amounts of labor, which was much more expensive here than in Asia. The new standards would allow flexibility while retaining consistency among all the Luxury Garden properties worldwide. Sebastian said they also permitted a greater focus on interactions with guests, were more concise, and allowed each Luxury Garden property to "express its uniqueness." Although workers were encouraged to retain specific standards appropriate to their work areas, the shift was toward the use of general core standards rather than specific routines. This shift also demonstrates the flexibility needed to provide the "experience" characteristic of luxury service.

Sebastian detailed the process by which corporate management had arrived at these standards via the creation of a task force; like Alice's portrayal of the development of the hotel's credo, this approach centered on creating a common history and identity. He introduced the "eight mantras" of the new approach. He talked about the time line for implementing the new standards and how they would be measured by the mystery shopper company the Luxury Garden used. Finally, he talked about how management would "keep it alive" through continued training and visuals posted around the hotel. He concluded the presentation by saying that the CQE "will become a heart of our culture; it's what we do, what we're about," and that we should "incorporate it into our daily lives." The meeting ended with Sebastian asking simple questions recapping what he had said; workers who raised their hands and answered correctly received twenty dollars. On our way out we were each given a newly reprinted credo card that included the eight mantras.

This introduction was followed by "train the trainer" sessions, in which Alice helped workers designated as departmental trainers to understand the program and the implementation process. I attended two of these sessions (lasting one and four hours), which featured professional-looking binders filled with training materials about facilitation, learning styles, lesson plans, and evaluation. Of the more than twenty employees who participated in these two sessions, at least fifteen were managers, both high- and midlevel, demonstrating that, in fact, managers would be primarily responsible for the training (in contrast to the rhetoric about worker trainers). Most workers who had been chosen were clearly of the more professionalized and committed variety. During the training, Alice laid out a time line for the updating of manuals and training of coworkers; she also directed role plays and other activities that offered trainers possible ways of communicating the concepts of the new program to workers.

Some of what she encouraged was obviously unrealistic. Trainers who were not managers or concierges would not be able to send e-mails to the executive committee or to one another, because they did not have e-mail access. Some of the standards were also extremely difficult to implement. One standard exhorted the worker always to accompany the guest to his destination. But practicalities made that impossible; for example, workers could not take guests to the restroom, which was located far away from the desk. Alice's response to this situation was to acknowledge the problem and suggest vaguely that workers figure out creative ways to meet standards in their own departments.

In interviews, Luxury Garden managers appeared to believe that workers were socialized into a particular identity via the corporate culture and training, and certainly they tried to promulgate this sense of commitment among workers. Some workers did seem identified with the hotel and proud to work there. However, worker attitudes toward the corporate culture and standards programs were not necessarily enthusiastic. I rarely heard nonmanagerial workers refer to one another as colleagues, as they were supposed to do. On my first day there, Dirk, a white doorman in his thirties, made a disparaging joke about the hotel but then checked himself, saying that he should "seem more committed" in front of a new worker. After the CQE rollout meeting, Lupe, a front desk agent, shrugged and opined, "Es algo más que tenemos que hacer" (It's something more we have to do). Other workers made fun of the "rah rah" nature of the meeting or commented simply that it had been short. Polly, a Chinese housekeeper with limited English skills, had been asked to participate as a trainer because, as Alice had pointed out publicly during the session, she usually trained new workers in her department. When I asked her if she had understood the presentation, she said, "Some of it," and added, "They just said 'go to the training,' so I go."

Rather than only induce commitment to the hotel and its standards, these elaborate practices also served to make the worker feel as if he or she had some kind of accountability. There was a sense that workers might be held responsible and that managers were paying attention.

Standards were generally clear, which made violations more noticeable. As we will see, these characteristics contrast with the more laissez-faire regime at the Royal Court.

Who's in Charge: Hierarchy and Consistency

The third facet of hierarchical professionalism at the Luxury Garden was a consistent, vertical distribution of authority in daily life. Managers supervised workers reliably, respected their investment in their work, and supported them when they had problems. But mechanisms of surveillance and accountability reinforced their authority.

In general, worker-manager relations were cordial but professional. The advanced division of labor I have described established clear boundaries between workers and managers. Line employees did not function as supervisors, and areas of managerial responsibility were clearly demarcated. The active internal labor market for managers was an incentive for them to take responsibility. Although they were friendly with workers, when managers were called on by guests or workers to exercise authority they always did so, without appearing ambivalent about it. When they had to correct or train workers, they spoke in a friendly and educational tone. They also gave workers the support they needed to perform their tasks appropriately (such as reimbursing concierges for expenses related to familiarizing themselves with new restaurants and providing adequate computer systems). Managers rarely, if ever, socialized with workers outside work.

In general, workers accepted managerial authority without comment. Conflicts between workers and managers usually revolved around scheduling rather than coercive communication or lack of availability (though concierges did criticize concierge managers).[24] Rarely did workers talk about new managers changing procedures significantly for no apparent reason. Although some workers complained about a lack of recognition, managers offered more praise than their counterparts at the Royal Court.

The other face of a benevolent authority was worker monitoring, which was fairly sophisticated. Surveillance cameras were placed in several locations throughout the hotel. Though it was rare, managers occasionally disciplined workers for violations caught on camera; one bellman was written up for knocking over a lamp with the bell cart and not stopping to pick it up, for example. Workers were required to punch out for breaks, which was another form of technological surveillance. Managers told workers at the door to keep a log of the car tickets they handed out. Sebastian and François often spent an hour or so in the evening standing near the front desk; ostensibly they were there to greet guests, but they also kept an eye on the workers. Workers were aware that managers might be watching them. Lou, a young bellman, was nervous about showing me his personal Web site on the concierge computer, because he thought Patricia might come by and get angry. When Sebastian and François came within earshot, Alec refused to finish a juicy story he was telling, saying they disapproved of gossip.

Workers also knew that mystery shoppers might be in the hotel. The Luxury Garden employed at least two different mystery shopper companies to rate performance several times a year. These guest spies wrote extensive reports comprising hundreds of pages, evaluating every possible detail of their experience in the hotel, naming workers, and enumerating their mistakes. Managers posted the results of these inquiries—minus identifying characteristics of the workers—in the back of the front office. Managers also posted comment cards and letters from guests, including both positive and negative feedback.

Worker Relations

Hierarchical professionalism led to the establishment of relations among workers that were friendly but neither especially intimate nor marked by mutual authority. Workers in the same area paid attention to one another's work and interacted often, but they did not constitute an independent regime of mutual regulation like the one I describe below at the Royal Court. The division of labor at the Luxury Garden made mutual training and surveillance difficult, both because workers were separated spatially from one another and because the jobs were differentiated such that fewer people surrounding the worker were qualified to criticize him (for example, only concierges would know about a mistake another concierge had made). Managerial authority made mutual regulation among workers unnecessary.

Personal relations among workers were cordial but not especially close, and they were usually organized by department. At the end of my first week, I noted, "People haven't been that friendly to me except Alec and Max. They seem not to have much of a sense of humor, and there's something kind of insular about them." Miyako, a part-time front desk agent, confided to me that she felt her colleagues were "cliquey." Over time I became more comfortable with the workers in my immediate area, who did have fairly warm relations. However, they interacted only minimally with workers from other parts of the hotel. They said hello in the cafeteria but often did not know one another's names. Most workers ate lunch with other workers from their department, especially those of the same ethnicity. Upper-level managers also usually shared a table. Because most workers were older and had partners and children, they rarely socialized with one another off the clock except at hotel-sponsored events.

I discerned no overt animosity among ethnic groups or between white workers and workers of color, though there was more affinity among workers who shared a language. White workers mingled companionably with their coworkers of color at the desk and the front door, but they complained about the limited English skills of some back of house workers, who for the same reason were somewhat marginalized in public gatherings such as training sessions. I was also struck by a tendency among some Asian and Asian American workers in the front of the house to make and laugh at jokes about Asians (especially mimicking stereotypical accents) that seemed fairly racist and to welcome white workers' participation in these jokes. Chinese and non-Chinese workers alike laughed about the "Chinese mafia table" in the cafeteria. In these ways race and ethnicity were marked, but did not seem to be a source of open conflict.

Overall, then, managerial decisions about hiring and promotion, job specialization, a well-developed corporate culture, and reliable managers helped to constitute hierarchical relations between workers and managers and fairly distant relations among workers. These elements, especially the highly elaborated standards and rhetoric of accountability, also contributed to a professional demeanor among workers and a consistent adherence to the standards of luxury service. The Royal Court, in contrast, developed a regime of lateral authority and friendly authenticity.

FLEXIBLE INFORMALITY AT THE ROYAL COURT

Zeke, a white Royal Court doorman in his thirties, told me one evening that he was thinking of trying to get a job at the Luxury Garden through a friend who worked there. He characterized the Luxury Garden as a "real hotel" that had "policies." He explained that the hotel rewarded workers when they did not call in sick for a year, which the Royal Court did not. He also described the Luxury Garden as "more organized" and "more corporate." Zeke's critique highlights some of the negative features of the Royal Court's regime of flexible informality: minimal rewards for workers and a high level of managerial disorganization and inconsistency, largely born of the hotel's independent status. But the regime—marked also by limited labor markets and a flexible division of labor, a focus on authenticity rather than self-transformation through "culture," and lateral rather than hierarchical authority—gave benefits to workers in terms of control and autonomy.

Who Does What: Young Workers, European Labor, and Flexibility

The typical racial/ethnic division of labor between front and back of house workers was stark at the Royal Court. Front office workers, many of whom were European, were white; the only nonwhite worker at the desk was Inga, a young Swede of Asian descent. Three of the four doormen were white, and one was Ethiopian. Bellmen and valets were men of color, almost all immigrants. Semivisible workers in the front office and front of house managers were also white. The back of house workers were immigrants of color, as were the housekeeping managers and supervisors.

A striking and important feature of the front office workers at the

Royal Court was their youth. Annie, Jackie, Betsy, and Ginger, white front desk/concierge workers, were all under twenty-three; Jackie had recently finished college, but the others, as well as Jasmine (who was twenty-eight and already had one BA), were putting themselves through school. All the European workers were under thirty, and most were in school in Europe, working in the United States on temporary visas, or had recently finished studying. Even Petra, the front office manager, was only twenty-eight. All of these workers were also unmarried and childless. As we will see, the youth of these workers was a significant factor in the development of the hotel's flexible and friendly regime.

Possibilities for promotion were limited because of the size and independent status of the hotel, which the general manager pointed out when I interviewed him. Though front office workers could become assistant managers, other possibilities for moving up were few. The chance to ascend by changing properties was nonexistent, because the Royal Court lacked sister hotels elsewhere. Also, because front office work was not hierarchically organized, the internal ladders that might exist at other hotels (and did at the Luxury Garden) were limited. In hotels with a more extreme division of labor, the hierarchy might ascend from telephone operator to reservationist to front desk to concierge. But the policy of cross-training prevented this possibility, except at the front door.[25]

Instead of promoting from within, the hotel had developed a strategy of circumventing the tight labor market in the city by bringing European hospitality students over on visas that allowed them to work for eighteen months. Petra, Juliane, Ralf, and Peter had all entered the hotel this way prior to my arrival. While I was there, at least seven other workers arrived from Germany, Sweden, Holland, and Denmark through similar means. This practice had clearly been going on in the hotel for several years, although it seemed to have become more important during 1999 and 2000. The increase may have been related to the general manager's European nationality, or it may have been amplified in response to the labor market. Managers perhaps felt that it was better to take these workers, who had some training and could not change jobs for the eighteen-month duration of their visas, than to risk hiring U.S. citizens, who could potentially work for longer at the hotel but were not guaranteed to stay at all. Thus, career ladders existed in the industry as a whole, not in the Royal Court itself, which contributed to a sense of lateralism rather than hierarchy in the hotel.

Lateralism was also reflected in the Royal Court's minimal specialization, largely because of its size. The front office department included front desk agents/concierges, front door workers, reservationists, and telephone operators, and the department featured significant cross-training among workers. New hires were usually trained first at the telephone operator station, then in reservations. Later (how much later varied widely), they moved up to the front desk, where they performed both front desk and concierge tasks. However, these workers were also usually scheduled with some frequency at the telephone operator job even after this training (no full-time worker served exclusively as telephone operator).

Beyond cross-training, each job also entailed a broad range of tasks. Unusual in the industry, the Royal Court did not separate concierges and front desk agents, so the same workers did the routine jobs of checking guests in and out as well as the varied duties of the concierge. The telephone operator performed multiple tasks not related to answering the phone, including writing the "weather cards" forecasting the next day's weather for guests, logging incoming and outgoing packages, updating guest histories, taking reservations in off hours, and sending and receiving guest faxes. Bellmen ran the errands that concierges might undertake in another hotel. A minimal division of labor also characterized the back of the house.[26]

The physical layout of work spaces and workers' attire reflected these overlapping tasks. The small front office area housed the telephone operator, the reservationists, and the front desk agents. Front desk workers stood behind the desk, facing the hotel's lobby; the telephone operator sat to their left in a corner mostly obscured from guests' view; and the reservationists sat behind a wall in the same area, where they could hear what went on at the desk but not see it. In contrast to the Luxury Garden, Royal Court workers' uniforms varied little; all the workers behind the desk (front desk agents/concierges, reservationists, and the telephone operator) wore the same basic black (except that men wore pants and women skirts), and the doormen's and bellmen's uniforms were very similar.

This flexible work organization extended to managerial duties, blurring the boundaries between managers and workers (see appendix B). The hotel had no rooms division manager, and a single front office manager, Petra, supervised several assistant managers.[27] Assistant managers labored alongside front desk workers; Petra told me they spent 60 percent of their time at the desk, which was congruent with my experience. Unlike mid- and upper-level managers at the Luxury Garden, Petra herself spent about 30 percent of her time working at the desk or filling in for workers on breaks. (She was often scheduled as the "manager on duty" because of the shortage of assistant managers.)

Line employees also often took on managerial responsibilities. Ralf, Peter, and Jasmine were occasionally scheduled as assistant managers for certain shifts, again because of the shortage of managers (Ralf and Peter were too inexperienced to become full-time assistant managers, and Jasmine had refused the position). Their responsibilities included preparing and checking rooms for incoming guests, helping new workers, and covering breaks. During my stint there, Petra created the "supervisor" category for these workers. These blurry boundaries between workers and managers were essential to the hotel's flexible character.

"You Can Be Yourself": Authenticity Replaces Culture

The second element of flexible informality was the Royal Court's focus on "authenticity" and the absence of the elaborate programs of corporate culture, standards, training, and reward that existed at the Luxury Garden and the Ritz-Carlton. These elements, which I had understood to be a significant element of the production of luxury service, were almost completely lacking at the Royal Court. Management made only minimal attempts to tie workers' identities to the company or to codify luxury standards.

LIMITED CORPORATE CULTURE   Primarily because of its independent status, the hotel lacked a meaningful corporate culture; that which did exist was in name only, for workers were often unfamiliar with its elements. Assistant manager Brad told me that upper-level managers had "tried to establish a culture, but it's been hard because of the renovation and the crisis of turnover." He told me that managers had developed a credo but admitted that "not much has happened with it." The credo (presumably modeled on that of the Ritz-Carlton) was "Try-Create-Surpass." However, the credo was never mentioned in the orientation for workers. The hotel's mission statement was "Where superlative service goes beyond high expectations." One day this mission statement came up in a conversation between Brad and Jasmine, who had worked at the hotel for four years; she said sardonically, "What is it? We meet guests' expectations—and beyond?" She laughed, and Brad said, "You've been here four years and you don't know the mission statement?" This exchange exemplified most workers' attitude toward attempts at establishing corporate culture or identity.

Managers sometimes emphasized that workers had been "selected" to join a privileged community. In the orientation, Mr. Weiss said, "We've been looking for you for six to eight weeks," and "We hired you because of your attitude." However, he also talked about recent high turnover and the tight labor market, implying that the hotel was desperate. Nicole, the human resources director, likewise made no effort to hide management vulnerability in this regard. In a hotelwide meeting,[28] for example, she asked workers to try to bring in new employees, highlighting the hundred-dollar referral fee for anyone who recommended a worker who stayed at least thirty days.

Some recognition programs for workers existed. Upper management named an employee of the quarter and of the year. Workers were invited to dine in the restaurant and spend a night in the hotel after they had completed three months on the job. In the front office, when a guest praised a worker in a comment card or letter, the worker received a star next to her name on the "star board." Letters and comment cards complimenting workers by name were also displayed. At the end of an arbitrary period (usually about three months) the worker with the most stars received a small gift, such as a twenty-five-dollar gift certificate to Tower Records. Again, however, workers were not rewarded for exerting effort in particular instances, as in the "enchanted moments" program at the Luxury Garden. Nicole admitted publicly in the orientation (and in private conversations with me) that recognition was limited in the hotel; she seemed to feel this situation was acceptable, telling workers, "That's life."

Managers made some efforts to create community among the hotel's employees. Nicole called the small size of the hotel an advantage, saying it was "like a family." She and her assistant, Amy, tried to make the workplace seem familial and caring. They planned activities such as a ski trip, a bowling night, and an Easter egg decorating contest, and they arranged annual events such as the off-site employee holiday party (though the restaurant was less upscale than the one where the Luxury Garden's party was held). The cafeteria featured special treats on holidays and a monthly birthday cake (for all workers born in that month), and workers received birthday cards both from their coworkers in the department and from the hotel's executive committee. However, the rhetoric of common identity inculcated at the Luxury Garden was absent, as were instruments and benefits such as a newsletter, committees, an employee assistance program, and so on.

SHIFTING STANDARDS   General standards, such as those we have seen at the Ritz-Carlton and at the Luxury Garden, were not consistently reinforced at the Royal Court. In the worker orientation, both Nicole and Mr. Weiss emphasized service, stressing name recognition in particular. Nicole showed the same video I had seen at the Luxury Garden about the importance of good service in a variety of interactive jobs, and she talked about telephone etiquette, "proper verbiage," and anticipating needs. We participated in an exercise that emphasized the need for attention to detail. However, service "basics," standards which were the subject of hours of training at both the Ritz-Carlton and the Luxury Garden, were written in a handbook, which Nicole said workers should look at in their spare time; the rest of the orientation focused on attendance, discipline, grooming standards, benefits, safety, a tour of the hotel, and so on.

This approach was spurred at least in part by a focus on authenticity as a key element of service. Managers explicitly prized sincerity among workers and suggested that the lack of formal culture contributed to maintaining that sincerity. They often contrasted their vision to the standardized service of the Ritz-Carlton. In a 1998 interview, Mr. Weiss told me that "the Ritz philosophy is highly scripted." He said he preferred to "nurture people [workers] as individuals" and encourage them to "use personal terminology," rather than to say "My pleasure to connect you," as telephone operators did at the Ritz. He wanted workers to use guests' names but not to repeat particular phrases, such as the Ritz doorman's "Welcome to the Ritz-Carlton." He called this strategy more risky but more authentic.

Nicole, who had worked at the Ritz, also frequently invoked that hotel's philosophy as too constrained; in the orientation, for example, she called the Ritz service "kind of canned" and alluded to it as "robotic," as did other managers. She told workers in the orientation, "Fun is my motto." In some ways this rhetoric simply made a virtue of necessity, for circumstances made it difficult to instill a culture, but the philosophy of authenticity was clear.

Some standards in day-to-day operations did exist, though they were not consistently implemented. Front office managers were supposed to post a weekly service standard in the hallway behind the front office; these standards included exhortations to "always thank our guests for staying with us and make sure to invite them back," to "please tell the front desk anything you know to put in the guest history," and to "answer the phone in three rings and use the guest's name as much as possible." However, these standards were rarely changed (workers referred to them jokingly as the "standard of the month") and were not part of any ongoing training. At infrequent intervals a manager might suddenly appear and demand, "What's the standard of the week?" But there was no penalty, beyond momentary embarrassment, for not knowing it; indeed, managers often seemed not to know it themselves.

Likewise, few consistent standards for particular jobs existed in writing, in contrast to the Celebrated Quality Standards at the Luxury Garden. Managers provided no written training materials to new workers (rather, they were given a binder full of *blank* pages with job headings, which they were supposed to fill in themselves). In contrast to the Luxury Garden, specific operational and communications standards also changed constantly, largely because managers tended to create new procedures quickly in response to problems or complaints, without taking the time to design a coherent set of standards. Approximately once a week, a new memo appeared on the front office bulletin board on such topics as what to include in guest histories, special procedures for guests staying longer than three nights, and how to deal with garage tickets on guests' cars. But changes were rarely followed up by face-to-face training, explanation, or encouragement, which contributed to the cycle of inadequate implementation.[29] In the context of limited corporate culture, minimal incentives combined with lack of accountability made workers unlikely to alter their habits.

MINIMAL TRAINING   Congruent with shifting standards, workers received very little training in the Royal Court. Employee orientation was only five hours, in contrast to the two-day orientation sessions that existed at other luxury hotels (including the Luxury Garden). This orientation led me to believe that workers would receive more training in their specific departments. As it turned out, however, little ongoing professional training existed for any workers in the hotel.[30] Nicole repeatedly stressed in an interview that managers lacked the time to train workers. What minimal training did exist seemed so irrelevant to managers that Petra would frequently complain about having to "send someone to training," rather than carefully select participants, as managers did at the Luxury Garden. Extra workers were not scheduled to pick up the slack for those who were out at training, so training became a departmental liability.

On the job training was even less comprehensive than at the Luxury Garden. Managers rarely took charge of new employees, leaving them immediately in the hands of other workers, without allocating any extra time or space to focus on training. In practice, new workers just had to watch how the trainer did her job, while the trainer had little opportunity to explain how the work was done. As a consequence, new workers understood only those procedures that had happened to occur during the shifts on which they were trained, and they often had not had a chance to do the related work themselves. Managers often scheduled workers to work alone in a job for which they were not fully trained. In fact, workers were sometimes scheduled to be *trainers* for jobs on which they were not fully trained. One restaurant server referred to this "sink or swim" approach to training as "the Royal Court way."

Unlike the concierges at the Luxury Garden, who arrived on the job with previous training, most of the front desk/concierge workers at the Royal Court knew little about the job. Petra repeatedly told these young and inexperienced workers to walk around the city and look at the restaurants and shops they would be recommending, and she lamented to me that workers did not often do this. But she did not encourage them to try to *experience* these services, nor did the hotel pay for concierges to try new restaurants, as the Luxury Garden did. Stan administered a "concierge test" to the whole front office staff, including those who had never done concierge work; the test served to show workers what they did not know, but he never returned it or gave out the answers. Nor did it provide the basis for further instruction. The computer systems were much less advanced and contained less information than those at the Luxury Garden; workers were rarely trained on how to enter new information, which perpetuated the inadequate system.

Disciplinary "write-ups" sometimes took the place of training. Workers were not written up consistently, however; some frequently received write-ups from managers when they made mistakes, while others rarely or never did. Furthermore, the write-ups had no real meaning, because they were not attached to disciplinary proceedings (as in unionized hotels, where workers receive a verbal warning and then a written one, different from a write-up, on their way to being suspended or fired). Immediately before my arrival, Brad introduced the "oops I forgot" forms, which were intended as less severe write-ups for workers who had done something wrong; often the worker had never been told the correct procedure. But these forms were discontinued less than five months later. Workers rarely received official evaluations; often, neither the three-month nor the annual evaluations were done when they were supposed to be. (I did not receive my ninety-day evaluation until I was leaving the front office after six months, when I requested it.)

Given this state of affairs, it should not be surprising that Royal Court managers made few attempts to transform workers' sense of self though encouraging deep acting or other mechanisms. The standards and training that might have encouraged a certain self-presentation and self-conception were largely absent. Nor did managers emphasize the prestige and status associated with working at a luxury hotel. Again, the emphasis on authenticity was both a reason for and a justification of these choices.

Who's in Charge: Flexible Authority

A third dimension of flexible informality was the inconsistency of managerial authority, especially in the front of the house, and the concomitant expansion of mutual regulation among workers.

INCONSISTENT MANAGERS   Managerial inconsistency was partly related to managerial turnover at the Royal Court. About eighteen months before I was hired there, Keith, the assistant general manager, had left after nine years at the hotel, as had Jessica, who had been the front office manager for over five years. A subsequent rooms division manager, named Bruce, had left after a year, and Mr. Weiss had promoted Petra to front office manager despite her youth and lack of experience. The assistant managers she supervised had all been at the hotel for less than a year (indeed, several were hired while I was there). As a consequence, managers were often newer and less well-trained than the workers themselves, interfering with their own establishment of authority. The labor shortage probably also led to the hiring of new managers who were younger and less qualified than those who might otherwise have been hired. Hans, for example, had never worked at a luxury property before.

Mainly white men in their twenties, assistant managers had little management experience and few incentives within the hotel to maintain a professional demeanor. They were poorly trained in their specific jobs and received no training, as far as I know, on general principles of management. As we have seen, their opportunities for advancement were limited. Furthermore, the minimal division of labor between workers and managers obscured differences between them. The authority of line workers who occasionally acted as "manager on duty" or "supervisor" was especially murky.

Assistant managers demonstrated ambivalence about their authority. They did not manifest the professionalism and commitment to the company that often differentiates managers and workers. In front of workers they complained about upper management, gossiped about other midlevel managers, and griped about their own work. Managers used positive feedback only sporadically in daily operations, as I have suggested. Assistant managers rarely took on the authority to compliment workers, and Petra was too busy to do so, except intermittently.

It was often hard to get managers' attention, because they were running around dealing with momentary crises. Workers also frequently complained about assistant managers who would "hide in the back office," doing paperwork at the computer; they did not come to the desk and help when it was busy, even when untrained workers were on duty there. The food and beverage managers were similarly unhelpful; Hao, a room service worker, told me, "The only thing Patrick [the restaurant manager] ever does is come into the kitchen and say, 'How's the floor?'"

Determined to maintain their laissez-faire attitude, managers made fun of workers who seemed to care too much about doing a good job, rather than support them. When Jasmine, somewhat stressed, asked Stan to help her with something, he said, "Simmer down, easy there, killer." When I asked how to make a limousine reservation (I had recently started working at the front desk, and no one had trained me on this very basic task), Brad told me, in a tone of sarcastic condescension, "First, pick up the telephone, then push the buttons. . . ." Rarely did managers commend workers for pointing out problems or asking for help.

As a rule, assistant managers appeared more comfortable *aligning* themselves with workers (to whom they were demographically similar) than supervising them, seeming to consider themselves primarily workers' friends and thereby establishing a kind of lateralism. Managers often joked and bantered with workers on the job. Sometimes they used their authority to workers' benefit, accommodating special scheduling requests and letting workers take extra smoke breaks when it was slow. In contrast to the Luxury Garden, managers frequently sat with workers in the cafeteria (ethnicity, more than rank, was the organizing principle) or kidded around with them in the halls. Outside work, managers socialized with workers and with other managers quite frequently, going for drinks after work at least a couple of times a week.

Managers did, of course, have to exert authority sometimes. Unsure of themselves and poorly trained, they did this sporadically and symbolically rather than supportively. Often authority was couched in what I call a "coercive joking" form, in which managers made quasi-humorous, usually sarcastic remarks that actually served to establish their authority over workers while retaining the semblance of friendliness. On the aforementioned concierge test, for example, Stan wrote, "The winner gets to wash my car." Managers seemed to think that this joking was a way of bonding with the workers and hanging around with them rather than an exercise of their own power. I never saw this tactic at the Luxury Garden.

New managers also changed minor aspects of operations in order to demonstrate their authority. This practice was common in the industry; a female former general manager I interviewed called it "pissing on trees" and associated it especially with male managers. When Stan came on at the Royal Court, he changed all the blue stars on the employee-recognition star board to green smiley faces (although he eventually changed them back to stars). Stavros, the overnight manager, reprogrammed the fax machine to print out a confirmation of every fax that was sent; this move infuriated the environmentally conscious reservationists, who sent most of the faxes and therefore saw how much paper was wasted. Restaurant workers also complained that new managers made changes, such as removing items from the menu, without telling them.

Another dimension of the informality of authority was the inefficiency of mechanisms of surveillance. Workers were not required to clock out for breaks. I never heard of a worker being disciplined for activities caught on the surveillance cameras, though front office workers were aware of the monitor of four video feeds above the telephone operator's station. Workers also were aware of cameras near the elevators and right at the employee entrance. They knew that the computer tracked the worker who had been using it. Sarah cautioned me to be careful about making unnecessary changes to reservations, since any alterations would be traceable to me. However, such mechanisms of surveillance require someone to look at them, and as a rule managers were so busy attending to immediate needs that workers knew it was unlikely they would notice any but the most extreme mistakes. In fact, managers rarely cared, so workers seldom bothered to cover up when they were goofing off or otherwise breaking the rules in minor ways. Lucille, a part-time telephone operator, openly made and received personal calls throughout her shift.

Guests played some role in worker surveillance, although the vast majority of the comment cards I reviewed were positive toward workers, and almost none singled out a particular worker for complaint. Managers did not post negative comments from guests, in any case. The hotel claimed to hire professional mystery shoppers to come in and evaluate the service. However, in contrast to the Luxury Garden, where the shoppers came quarterly and management made the results available throughout the hotel, I never saw any results of these evaluations. I do not know if this is because management did not share them with workers or because no shoppers came into the hotel during my eight months there. But for the most part, workers were not made aware of negative guest feedback, and it was rarely tied to managerial discipline.

Workers griped that they did not receive enough positive recognition from managers, especially for sticking it out during the renovation. In a department meeting, Juliane said she wanted financial compensation for her loyalty; Peter said, "All I want is a kind word." They also grumbled about managerial absence and incompetence, which made their jobs more difficult.[31] Annie and Jasmine told me, "You have to tell Stan what to do," and Sarah frequently complained that he did not know what was going on. Restaurant workers made fun of assistant managers Patrick and Bobby; one worker described Bobby, who had shown up an hour late for his shift one busy morning, as "useless on the floor." Longer-term workers assessed the current management regime as less committed and using lower standards than previous regimes. Clint told me that the assistant managers in the past "really knew what they were doing, but now they don't."

Their frustration with managers' unavailability sometimes led workers to become less invested in their work and in the hotel. Giovanna, a front desk agent, told another worker in my presence that it was "hard to care" about doing a good job when others did not care and coworkers were not well trained; she said it made her "stressed out." Usually a vigorous participant in department meetings, one week she was nearly silent, commenting afterward, "It's not going to change, so why bother?" Joel the doorman told me when he returned from a different department meeting that it was "fine . . . you just have to get through it."

However, workers also valued the autonomy and authenticity they enjoyed on the job, thanks to managerial unavailability (or incompetence or both). Like managers, they contrasted the hotel's service to that of the Ritz-Carlton. Zeke appreciated that "you can be yourself." Joel prized the "friendly" service the hotel offered and appreciated that he could put his "own stamp" on the job. Annie characterized service at the Royal Court as more genuine and personal than at the Ritz, and she and Jackie both felt that managers had emphasized hiring "naturally" outgoing and compassionate people. I never heard workers complain about managers trying to instill a sense of identification with the hotel, as they sometimes did at the Luxury Garden.

Workers also enjoyed the independence that came from managerial absence. Zeke told me he liked Petra because "she doesn't come out here and tell us to do shit we're not going to do," such as lock the luggage closet (which made it more time-consuming to get guests' bags out). Workers at the desk liked being able to make personal calls or take extra breaks. Annie once commented, "I love working at a place where my [computer] password can be *bitch*." The workers who were less critical of managers also tended to socialize with them more, seeing them as peers rather than authority figures.

Inconsistent managerial authority and freedom from surveillance-related discipline also allowed workers to avoid work. Workers were never told exactly how much the guest had to consume from the minibar before being charged, so some workers simply threw away the minibar charges under five dollars rather than post them to the guest's account. Some workers tossed out the in-room movie charges as well. They could also avoid work such as entering information from guests' registration cards into their computerized guest histories. And they could let mistakes slide, because they knew no one would be checking up on them. Thus, the managerial regime did not always channel worker discretion productively, allowing it to leak out in these avoidances.

Managerial absence also meant work was often simply fun, because there was time and space to chat and make jokes. I frequently ended up doubled over with laughter when working with Sarah (who had attended clown college) or Jasmine; we sang show tunes, told knock-knock jokes, and dueled with umbrellas. Workers sometimes laughed so hard they had to leave the desk. Joel and Carlos at the door had invented a special dance they would perform in the lobby for the front desk workers when no guests were around. Annie and Clint had hatched a half-serious plan to call up candy companies, saying they were looking for new room amenities in order to get free samples. Workers speaking with guests on the telephone often used their own performance as entertainment for their coworkers, rolling their eyes or speaking in a strange voice.[32]

LATERAL REGULATION AND SOCIABILITY   It may seem surprising that a high level of service was ever maintained at the Royal Court. I was confused by this when I began to comprehend managerial neglect of workers. But I came to see that, in fact, the workers themselves basically ran the hotel, taking on quasi-managerial functions. They trained and monitored one another, exchanged positive feedback, and helped one another out. And they often valued the freedom they had as a result of managerial neglect. The regime of flexible informality, therefore, led to mutual regulation among workers.[33]

Established workers often continued to train their newer coworkers even after the official training was over. Sometimes this training was unsolicited, as more experienced workers kindly corrected newer ones; also, when workers had questions, they tended to seek out other workers rather than managers, who were usually unavailable anyway. Hugh, a white front desk worker in his forties, corrected Annie on more than one occasion, for example admonishing her, "Don't say 'you guys' to guests." Hugh and Giovanna actually composed the concierge test Stan administered. After listening to me fail to use the guest's name during a wake-up call, Ginger said gently and almost conspiratorially, "I always call them by name, so they think it's all personalized." My coworkers at the door, especially Joel and Clint, clearly took pride in explaining to me the ins and outs of the jobs there. Though it occasionally led to conflict, as we will see, this peer training was generally accepted by all and, in fact, was often useful to workers frustrated by managerial inattention.

Workers often lent a helping hand to their colleagues when they could. For example, Jasmine told me one day that she was doing extra tasks on the morning shift so that Annie would not be too overwhelmed in the evening, when it was going to be busy. The doormen tried to maximize tip opportunities for the bellmen. In contrast to the Luxury Garden, mutual assistance was also prevalent in the back of the house, where room cleaners assisted their friends (usually members of the same ethnic group) when they had no vacant rooms of their own to clean.

Mutual training was predicated on mutual surveillance, which in some cases replaced managerial supervision. First, the close proximity of workers to one another, especially in the front office, allowed one's coworkers to hear everything one said. This setup led workers both to compliment and to correct their colleagues. Because the telephone operator was responsible for printing and sending messages from front desk workers to guests, for example, he or she often read them and pointed out spelling or other errors. The limited division of labor in the front office facilitated this mutual surveillance, because most workers knew how to do each job and could critique other workers' performance.

Congruent with their role as trainers and monitors, workers often provided more positive feedback than managers. Carlos, a bellman, commended me to Jasmine, saying that I did "a good job" at the front desk, because I was "thorough" when he overheard me talking with guests. Ginger was very excited one day because Giovanna told her she was doing a better job than anyone else at the desk. Though the formal division of labor did not support a hierarchy, workers established a flexible one through mutual training.

Managers explicitly fostered this culture of mutual worker training, surveillance, and recognition. On one occasion, Giovanna told Petra she had noticed a mistake Annie had made (taking a guest's Discover card when the hotel did not accept Discover), and Petra told Giovanna to talk to Annie about it herself, thus situating Giovanna as Annie's superior. About four months into my research, Stan instituted the "stars of reception" program, in which workers were supposed to recognize one another. His memo, written in a typically jovial tone, read:

> Folks, as we provide the best possible service to our guests, it is nice to be recognized not only by the guests but also by your fellow employees. Sure, we all get the "great work Bongo," and "nice job Truman" every now and then, but what if we were constantly reminded that we do make a difference.
>
> Well guess what? Now we can. We are starting an employee recognition program called Stars of Reception, and this is how it works. You are working alongside your colleague and something he or she does for the guests makes you stop and say wow, that was really nice, or really creative, or really whatever. In addition to telling them that was a great idea you have the option of writing this on a Stars of Reception form and posting it wherever you want in the back office! . . .
>
> In the future, we will determine if we should award those with more Stars of Reception forms than others. Have fun! The Royal Court Front Office Team Rocks!

This memo suggested that it was workers' responsibility to give positive feedback to other workers; managers were not differentiated, which reinforced the sense of flatness in the managerial hierarchy and absolved managers of responsibility for motivating workers. The program supported a pattern of mutual surveillance by workers. However, it gave workers no incentive to participate, either by lauding their colleagues or by improving service themselves in order to be recognized. After a brief spate of mutually appreciative remarks from workers to their colleagues, the program fell into disuse.

Workers talked disparagingly about constraints on their authenticity and discretion under previous management (as well as under current management, which we will see in more detail in chapter 3). Workers saw Bruce, the previous rooms division manager, as a proponent of extreme standardization. He had given workers a set of standardized guidelines similar to those used at the Ritz-Carlton, wrote people up for minor infractions, and required them to respond with "excellent" when he asked how they were. As a consequence, he had not been well-liked; Zeke the doorman, for example, referred to him as a "Nazi." Jasmine talked to me about the old ways when we were taking a break. She said somewhat disdainfully that there had been "higher standards" and more "professionalism." Previously, workers were also more likely to be reprimanded: "You had the fear in you." Now, she told me, she could do things she never would have done then, such as chat with the people in reservations for fifteen minutes: "Before, you could just stick your head back there from the front desk for a second maybe to say one thing." A former executive committee manager told me in an interview that, in the past, "they'd hang you by your thumbs if you made a mistake."

Yet, workers with experience of previous management formed the cornerstone of the worker regime. Sarah, Haile, Zeke, and Jorge had all been at the hotel at least nine years, Juliane six, and Jasmine four, and these workers knew more than most managers. The training they had received in the past supported their current behavior. When he trained me at the bell station, Clint, one of the few workers who had liked Bruce, the "Nazi" manager, gave me a copy of Bruce's written standards. Workers' characterizations of the past regime indicated that standards had been inculcated, even if workers did not like the managers in charge. Sarah said that Jessica, the former front office manager, was "a bitch, but she ran a tight ship."

Relations among front office workers were generally friendly, although the usual gossiping and backbiting occurred. Clint told me that he stayed in the job for its "social aspect." Often workers brought in food for everyone, as when Ginger brought candy on Valentine's Day. Jasmine liked to make chocolate chip cookies; Joel picked up doughnuts for another worker's last day on the job. And just as managers often socialized with workers, workers also socialized with one another. The younger front desk workers often went out after work together, and they were frequently joined by Frankie and Haile, who worked at the door, as well as by the young managers. Ginger, Annie, and Inga were inseparable at different points; Inga became Annie's roommate and, later, Petra's.

Exceptions to this camaraderie occurred when new workers violated their colleagues' superior authority. Experienced workers expected deference and respect from new staff and became irritated when they did not get it. Betsy, a new telephone operator, irked her colleagues by failing to attend to the rules, making a lot of personal phone calls and taking her breaks without ensuring there was someone to replace her. Jasmine, Annie, and Sarah were all annoyed with her and commented repeatedly that she had made personal calls "on her first day"; when she called in sick in her first week, Annie thought she was lying. These workers did not care about personal calls and sick days for the sake of the hotel, but they resented that new workers behaved as if entitled before understanding the local relations (this was what was often exasperating about managers as well). These reactions illustrate limits established within the worker regime. Conflicts over tipping and work also occurred, as I discuss in detail in chapter 3.

As a whole, worker relations in the hotel were friendlier and more integrated than at the Luxury Garden. Workers from all departments joked around in the small cafeteria and called one another by name. Front and back of house workers did not necessarily become close friends, because a language barrier existed for many; as at the Luxury Garden, white interactive workers sometimes complained about the limited English abilities of immigrant housekeepers.[34] Likewise, most workers ate with others of their ethnic group (including supervisors and managers) when they could. However, there was a general sense of familiarity and collegiality among workers from different departments.

This worker regime kept the hotel running on a daily basis; workers who had previous training in the hotel or in European hospitality schools compensated for managerial inattention. However, the system was unstable. The fragile balance between worker discretion and self-regulation on the one hand and managerial authority on the other was fraught with problems. The provision of authentic service, which depends on experienced workers, was complicated by turnover and lack of training (which sometimes allowed "authentic" to shade into "inappropriate"). Managerial absence and inconsistent managerial intervention caused workers to withdraw consent, as I discuss further in the next chapter.

The year I was at the Royal Court was an especially chaotic period at the hotel because of the turnover and the renovation. By the end of my stint, it appeared that more systematic procedures and training were being implemented. Several months later, I was told that the front office had hired a consulting company to help develop training manuals and that the whole front office staff was being retrained. Also, some measure of stability seemed to have been attained in terms of worker turnover, because several front office workers had been there for over a year.

Nonetheless, when I chatted with workers at a party two years after I exited the field, most of them told me that "nothing has changed," despite the slack labor market and the end of the renovation. All the assistant managers I had worked with had left. A newly appointed manager was at risk of being deported to Europe because his visa had not been extended (and he had lied about it). Ginger, now twenty-three, was the most senior assistant manager, though she had held the position less than six months. She cracked up as she told me how the previous night she and Annie had gotten into a war, squirting canned cheese at each other.

GUEST RESPONSES AND THE CREATION OF EXPECTATIONS

Guest comments about each hotel's service echoed the distinction between professionalism and informality. In comment cards and letters, clients at the Luxury Garden used words such as *courteous, pleasant, well-trained,* and *professional* to describe the staff. Their opinions described the professionalized service the hotel strove to provide. At the Royal Court, in contrast, guests often used language evoking authenticity. The words *friendly* and *helpful* appeared repeatedly on comment cards. Guests frequently made observations in person, such as "The staff here are so friendly," as one woman told me when I was escorting her to her room on her second stay in the hotel. One comment card writer praised the "great mix of friendliness and service—not obsequious but helpful and alert." Another lauded the "great genuine personalities and interest in the guests' needs; warm and friendly."

Guest behavior toward workers also varied along these lines. Although they were polite, guests at the Luxury Garden tended to have a fairly businesslike approach to workers. At the Royal Court, guests joked and chatted with workers much more often. They made confidantes of front desk and other workers, telling them about a variety of personal issues from a botched haircut to a new job or a pregnancy. Guests at the Luxury Garden made fewer such disclosures and shared these with only a limited set of workers (concierges and sometimes doormen).

As I have suggested, the Luxury Garden's emphasis on professionalism led to greater adherence to luxury standards of service. The Luxury Garden personalized service more, especially in terms of preferences and engineered customization. Guests' needs were anticipated more fully, and workers used "proper verbiage" more often, exhibiting a more professional demeanor overall. However, somewhat paradoxically, guests at the two hotels were similarly positive in their comments.

In addition to high rankings the Luxury Garden received in magazines, the opinions of its guests, expressed in comment cards and letters and in person, were largely favorable. Of 73 cards submitted in a four-month period in late 2000, 63 included some written comments; of these, 28 were only positive, 15 were exclusively negative, and 20 were both positive and negative. Complaints almost always had to do with problems in the room, not with the service. Almost all of the 20 unsolicited letters I looked at from that period were overwhelmingly complimentary about the service.

Guests' responses to the service at the Royal Court were also extremely positive. Of the 121 comment cards I reviewed that included written comments (three months' worth), 60 were exclusively positive, only 26 were negative, and 35 were mixed. The comments that guests made to workers in person were almost always favorable. As at the Luxury Garden, almost all the complaints I recorded in field notes or saw on comment cards had to do with the rooms, largely referring to their size or to problems arising from the renovation.

In part the difference between expectations of business and leisure guests probably explains the positive evaluations in both hotels. People traveling for pleasure are perhaps more likely to value service that is "friendly" and feels authentic and to enjoy talking with workers as part of their vacation experience. Oscar, a doorman at the Luxury Garden who had worked as a bellman at the Royal Court for years, told me that the guests at the Royal Court had more time to "hang around and chat" with the doorman. Business travelers tend to be especially concerned with professionalism and dependability. This division may also explain the greater number of comment cards returned at the Royal Court; in my experience, guests there also more often told workers in person how much they had enjoyed their stay. The difference in price between the two hotels may also be a factor, of course, because those paying five hundred dollars for a room may have expectations different from those paying three hundred dollars. (On the other hand, the business travelers at the Luxury Garden were less likely to be paying out of their own pockets.)

I suspect that worker and guest demographics played an important role as well; the young, white, female front desk workers at the Royal Court may have seemed less intimidating to white clients than their older concierge counterparts at the Luxury Garden and more familiar than the workers of color at the front desk there. Female travelers, who made up a higher proportion of guests at the Royal Court, are perhaps more likely to "bond" with workers, especially young women like those who worked at the Royal Court. However, this explanation is not sufficient, for a much greater proportion of male guests at the Royal Court than at the Luxury Garden were also prone to joke and chat with workers.

A final reason for these different but equally positive guest responses has to do with guest expectations being constructed *within* the hotel, as I suggested in chapter 1. When guests believe they are staying in a luxury hotel, the hotel tends to seem luxurious unless something goes drastically wrong. Because the point of luxury service is to surprise the guest, he will not expect particular kinds of attention and, in fact, may be satisfied with the distinctive touches in the room or whatever minimal customization he does receive. However, some guests enter the hotel with certain expectations, perhaps formed in other luxury hotels; when they are not met, the guests complain. Some guests did gripe that the Royal

Court did not have a "real" concierge, for example, demonstrating a pre-existing expectation of luxury service.

THE LIMITS OF MANAGERIAL INFLUENCE

Research on managerial strategies often focuses on managerial rhetoric, practices, and intentions without looking ethnographically at how these play out among workers.[35] Ethnography shows that the overt strategies of selection, surveillance by customers, corporate culture, and self-transformation invoked in the literature are often less influential than managers indicate. In preliminary interviews, managers in my sites made elaborate claims about culture, standards, and philosophy; only after sustained participation did I see how related rhetoric and practices affected workers. I have thus argued that a useful conception of managerial regimes includes not just management rhetoric but also less obvious features, such as the division of labor, worker demographics, internal labor markets, and practical cultures of managerial authority and worker relations. These features in turn depend largely on corporate characteristics.

At the Luxury Garden, attempts to encourage personal transformation and identification with the company were only partly successful, because workers rarely seemed invested in corporate identity. As critics would predict, managerial attempts to foster a sense of empowerment and community also served to highlight worker accountability—to show workers what was expected of them and to let them know managers were paying attention.[36] Manager responsiveness to and recognition of workers, higher wages, and internal job ladders provided positive incentives; surveillance and monitoring practices were the coercive side of the regime. But are the twin practices of reward and accountability, or veiled coercion, all that are necessary to elicit consent, even among autonomous workers in a tight labor market? Even more striking, the small and independently managed Royal Court offered a corporate culture that was nominal at best, few consistent standards, and incoherent managerial authority. Yet guests and other sources rated its "authentic" service highly. That the hotel produced luxury service at all indicates that the regime itself is not the key factor. In the absence of accountability, why do workers bother to self-regulate?

I suggest in the next three chapters that the answer has to do with the ways workers become invested in their jobs and constitute themselves as powerful. In my analysis, managerial attempts to regulate worker behavior do matter, but not so much for their direct effects on workers as for the ways in which managers' discourses and practices serve as resources for constructions of nonsubordinate selfhood. The features of hotel regimes described in this chapter helped interactive workers to see themselves as professional, superior, skilled, and independent. Managerial regimes also contribute to defining and circumscribing practical cultures of entitlement and consent among interactive workers. As we will see, these organizational contexts contributed to differences among workers' behavior in each hotel and to their more frequent withdrawal of consent at the Royal Court.

Although worker practices of self-constitution overlap, I have tried to disaggregate them for clarity. Chapter 3 shows how workers construct an *autonomous* self through playing games on the job, which allows them to emphasize skill, control, and professionalized or independent selfhood. Chapter 4 focuses on the constitution of a *superior* self, in which workers reimagine hierarchy through comparisons with both coworkers and guests. Chapter 5 describes the forging of an *equal* self, which emerges from workers' reciprocal relationships with guests.

THREE Games, Control, and Skill

NINOTCHKA: *(To railway porter)* What do you want?

PORTER: May I have your bags, Madame?

NINOTCHKA: Why?

KOPALSKI: He's a porter, he wants to carry them.

NINOTCHKA: Why? Why should he carry other people's bags?

PORTER: Well, that's my business, Madame.

NINOTCHKA: That's no business, that's social injustice.

PORTER: That depends on the tip.

Ninotchka (1939)

If you were a fly on the wall of a luxury hotel, you would not ordinarily observe workers standing around talking about managerial standards of service or about delighting guests or about being themselves on the job. You would see them *working:* the reservationist and telephone operator intently scanning computer screens as they rattle off rates; the concierge writing a message to a guest confirming her reservation at the city's fanciest new restaurant; the door attendant whistling for taxis; the bellperson straining to move heavy bags into rooms. What you might not notice at first, though, is that workers are doing more than their jobs as they perform these tasks. They are also playing games. These games do not involve cards, chips, or dice, but they do entail strategy—about how to finish tasks quickly, control the pace of work, and maximize tips. In playing these games, workers make their jobs meaningful, become invested in them, and construct images of themselves as skilled and autonomous.

Games workers play, especially in factories, have long been a subject of sociological study. In the industrial relations literature of the mid-twentieth century, workers' games were seen to constitute *opposition to management*, a way of wasting time and a source of inefficiency. Michael Burawoy turns this notion on its head, arguing that these games are, in fact, the basis of *consent to produce*.[1] Workers in the factory he studied played the game of "making out" by negotiating effort around piece rates, attempting to beat the machine and the production quota. Through making choices about how much effort to exert, they became invested in the game and consented to its rules.[2] At the same time, workers also consented to the rules of production and distribution arrangements. Thus, the game served to obscure unequal relations of authority on the shop floor and the appropriation of surplus and to constitute workers as individuals rather than as members of a class. According to Burawoy, making out was the center of "shop-floor culture" in the factory, because it determined noneconomic incentives such as prestige (through status hierarchies) and influenced lateral relations among workers.

Studies of service work have mostly neglected to follow up on Burawoy's analysis by looking at how games differ between services and manufacturing.[3] In this chapter, I compare both the games of hotel workers with those of factory workers and the games of hotel workers in different jobs with one another. I follow Burawoy's definition of games as entailing "a set of rules, a set of possible outcomes, and a set of outcome preferences," which is to say that outcomes have to be variable and matter to workers; workers also have to feel that they can influence outcomes.[4] Games take place in a collective context, and they are linked to workers' status relative to that of other workers. Workers require some autonomy in order to play games, so highly controlled and routinized workers doing repetitive jobs are unlikely to participate in the kind of games I am describing. (Housekeepers, for example, employ different strategies in their work, but they do not play games with variable outcomes.)[5]

Consistent with the variety of types of work they do, interactive workers in the service theater play multiple games rather than a single game organized around piecework quotas.[6] I focus on two types of games among workers producing largely intangible products. First, workers in visible and semivisible jobs attempt to master the "raw material" of guest requests and the demands of luxury service in games of skill and control. Second, tipped workers play money games, similar to "making out" among factory workers, in which they strategize and negotiate effort around gratuities.

As in the factory, hotel games depend to a certain extent on workers' autonomy, on their relations with other workers, and on parameters set by management. However, the key difference from manufacturing is that the guest becomes one of the "agents of production" that Burawoy identifies as crucial to the game. Guests' actions and desires, from what kind of room they prefer to their propensity to tip well, generate the unpredictability central to these games, which in the factory comes from the behavior of the machines. Furthermore, guests often determine the outcome of games. That is, in the hotel, guests provide the material rewards of tip-related games, whereas in the factory, rewards are established by the "time-study man," who sets piece rates.

Beyond their form, the functions of hotel games are in some ways similar to those in manufacturing. Like making out in factories, hotel games help to pass the time, reduce fatigue, and establish skill.[7] They allow workers to make choices about when they exert effort, casting it as voluntary. And they individualize rewards and relations. The rewards associated with game playing—social, material, and psychological—underlie workers' consent to exert effort, their active investment in work. The importance of lateral relations with coworkers in games deflects attention from the hierarchical relations with managers (and in this case, with guests). For the most part, as in the factory, workers' and managers' incentives are coordinated,[8] but in some cases the possibility of their divergence exists.

Again, however, the presence of the guest means that hotel games serve another function as well: to normalize unequal entitlements between workers and guests. Burawoy argues that as workers defend the rules of the games, they unwittingly consent to "some broader set of outcomes . . . such as the generation of profit, the reproduction of capitalist relations of production, and so forth."[9] In this case, the broader outcomes also include guest entitlement to workers' labor. Hotel workers consent not only to managers' and owners' appropriation of labor power for economic gain but also to guests' appropriation of workers' interactive self-subordination for guests' psychological and physical fulfillment.

This process occurs in two key ways. First, games alter the meanings of unequal entitlements, which are rearticulated to benefit workers materially and psychically. Second, games provide resources for the construction of an autonomous and nonsubordinate selfhood. Workers use games to recast the subordination associated with their jobs by thinking of themselves as strategic, controlling, powerful, and manipulative. Some workers use this constellation of meanings to constitute a professional identity, while others employ it to construct themselves as independent of the hotel. When the worker's strategy of self dovetails with the managerial regime—professionalism at the Luxury Garden, independence at the Royal Court—workers consent. When managers interfere with games and with strategies of self, workers withdraw consent both by withholding labor and by exiting.

GAMES OF SPEED, SERVICE, AND CONTROL

In the front of the house at the Royal Court and the Luxury Garden, guests largely determined the pace of work, by driving up to the hotel curb to check in, requesting restaurant reservations, or calling to ask about the price of rooms. Because of the unpredictability of these demands for workers' labor (unlike the more predictable checking in and out that affected housekeepers), managers could not set any kind of production quota for workers in the front of the house, as they did in the back. Thus, expectations of worker output, often intangible anyway, were variable, and they depended on guest behavior.

Workers managed this unpredictability by playing certain games that took guest demands as their raw material. These included processing guests quickly, selling rooms at high rates, allocating rooms, and meeting luxury standards; their object was for the worker to maintain control over his own time, meet standards, and conserve his own labor by avoiding guest complaints. Workers used strategies of prediction and typology to control the "opponent"—the guest.[10] They constituted themselves as skilled and in control, not subordinate to either the volume or the content of customer demands. These games tended to maximize managerially defined outcomes and involved few material incentives for workers.

Controlling Unpredictability

Clint was a rugged, part-time white worker in his fifties, who worked variously as a reservationist, telephone operator, and relief doorman at the Royal Court. He had been a fire marshal and approached his job with a seriousness of purpose worthy of firefighting. When training me at the telephone operator station, he insisted that speed was of the essence. He told me to answer the phone on two rings every time and get rid of callers as quickly as possible. He kept repeating, "Get 'em off, get 'em off." Echoing this sentiment, Sarah, a longtime reservationist at the Royal Court, told me, "A successful call is a fast call." Like Sarah and Clint, many semivisible workers and some front of house workers played games emphasizing speed as a way of negotiating unpredictability.

Workers used routines to control the speed and content of the conver-. sation. Reservationists rattled off the questions necessary to fill in the blank spaces on their screens, not stopping to chat unless it would be overtly rude not to. Clint gave me ways to finish more quickly, suggesting particular words to use in starting a sentence so as not to get involved in a long conversation with a caller.

It was also important not to embark on lengthy interactions with guests from which it would be difficult to extricate oneself if the phones lit up or a line formed. One evening, for instance, Clint trained me at the bell station and advised me on how to wait for guests who were checking in; I had to be available to help them with their bags but not unavailable to others who might need me before they did. He told me to take the luggage cart with the bags up to the desk only when I could see that the worker was about to hand the key to the guest. He said, "If you commit yourself to the guest, you're dead," because it became impossible to abandon him for something else more important. These practices helped workers to maintain control over their time, giving a sense that they were not simply subject to the onslaught of guest demands.

Focusing on speed not only subordinated the guest to the worker's routine but also introduced an element of challenge and risk. Sarah used typologies and prediction to make calls go faster, typing the answers to her questions before the caller answered them, guessing whether the guest would be a smoker or trying to anticipate which credit card he would use. The skill of the game lay both in being able to predict correctly and in having the dexterity to correct mistakes without interrupting the flow of the conversation. After a few weeks in reservations, I found myself doing this, to pass the time and to create a challenge for myself.

Similarly, semivisible room service workers took pride in processing food orders quickly, setting up trays and tables in a flash and coordinating multiple deliveries. Although I did not experience many busy shifts in room service, it was clear that workers had strategies for dealing with an onslaught of calls. Even their jokes made a similar point: on my first evening in room service, when I was upstairs with Hao delivering a meal, the order taker covered the grease board with orders just to see the terrified look on my face when I returned and thought we were going to be insanely busy. The practical joke indicated that, although I might not recognize this because we were slow, one needed certain skills to perform the job well in the face of unpredictable guest requests.

Maximizing Sales

Workers also made a game out of volatile guest demands for rooms. Selling out the hotel was a game for full-time room reservationists and other workers who took reservations (including managers and front office workers). Early in the morning, Sarah and Juliane would ask Petra how many rooms they needed to sell to sell out and how far over capacity Petra wanted to go. The general rule was to overbook 10 percent of arrivals, on the theory that 10 percent of incoming guests would cancel, or "no-show," but the rules for same-day reservations were different. The reservationists felt victorious if they had managed to sell out by the end

of the shift and disappointed if they had not. Invested in the outcome of
the game, they would arrive the next morning and ask if the hotel had
sold out or if anyone had been "walked" (relocated) to another hotel as a
result of overbooking.[11]

Workers used a variety of strategies in this game. If they feared cancellations, they wait-listed people so they would have a backup. They
often oversold the cheapest category of rooms in order to sell out the
hotel, knowing that they could upgrade people later. They used typologies to predict cancellations; for example, when Sarah and I were looking
at dates that were sold out partly because of a banking convention, she
told me, "Bankers and doctors always cancel." One day in reservations at
the Luxury Garden, the workers were abuzz about the fact that five
guests had been walked the night before, a nearly unprecedented situation in the hotel. Edith, the manager, was kicking herself because she had
failed to factor into her calculations that many of the incoming guests the
previous day were part of groups, which did not usually no-show (and
hence were not subject to the 10 percent rule).

Maximizing rates, as well as the number of rooms, constituted another
game. Workers tried to sell rooms at high official, or "rack," rates (rather
than cheaper corporate rates) or sell them in the more expensive categories.[12] It was much more satisfying to sell an $800 suite than to sell a
basic room at a corporate rate for $225, which hardly felt like an achieve-
ment. Sally, a former reservationist at the Luxury Garden, told me that
yield management (maximizing revenue through rate manipulation) was
"like gambling" and that she liked to do it when she was bored. Front
desk workers also used "upselling" when guests checked in and seemed
to need more space; they received a small commission for convincing the
guest to take (and pay for) a larger room. The outcomes of all of these
games were consistent with managerial objectives of selling the most
rooms at the highest rates possible.

Room Blocking

At the front desk at the Royal Court, room assignment, or "blocking,"
constituted another game, and workers even referred to it as such.[13]
Reservationists assigned certain rooms in advance, because quantities

were limited (smoking rooms, disabled access, suites, connecting rooms, and so on). Front desk workers also blocked rooms on the day of arrival, deciding which guest would be assigned to which room, including who would get upgraded and who could be walked to another hotel if ours was overbooked. The worker allocated rooms on the basis of various factors, such as how many nights the person was staying, whether he was traveling alone, if he had stayed at the hotel before, and his room rate. Workers could upgrade guests but never downgrade them. The game was won when all guests were placed in appropriate rooms; the game was lost if guests had to be walked. This game dovetailed with managerial interests in that winning the game preserved revenue for the present (by not walking people unnecessarily) and for the future (by not alienating the more important and high-paying guests). It was also an ever-changing puzzle, because the characteristics of incoming guests were never the same from one day to the next.

Workers used a variety of strategies in blocking rooms. But the main goal was to preclude guest complaints by assigning the least desirable rooms to people who fit a certain pattern: ideally, a first-time guest, paying a low rate and staying for only one night. Workers tried to avoid upgrading people more than one level and made use of their right to assign any room to guests who were paying the lower "house choice" rate. When things became complicated, they would ask guests who arrived early to wait for their rooms rather than rearrange the blocking to accommodate them. Workers also used typologies in this game; for example, Juliane told me, "Business travelers don't usually mind being assigned a room with two beds."

Unpredictability arose not from immediate guest demands but rather from not knowing how the rooms reserved on any given day (a function of incoming guests' desires) would fit with the rooms available (determined by guests who were already in-house). My notes from one shift at the Royal Court demonstrate the multiple challenges Jasmine faced when assigning rooms for that evening:

> Jasmine was looking at the daily report, which suggested that Mr. Weiss [the general manager] wanted her to upgrade an incoming guest. She said, "Fuck [the guest], we're minus-1 on the Platinum King today, and I don't care if he's a V-V-VIP per Mr. Weiss." But the Platinum King

problem was resolved anyway, because the in-house guests who had wanted to move into the Platinum King (who had priority) decided not to. Jasmine also suggested the Super Double for the Pallisers, who had a Silver King and some other rooms, just because we were minus on the Silver King. Jasmine also put a couple who are here for their anniversary in a Gold King instead of upgrading to a Platinum King as Petra had requested. Jasmine said, "We'll give them champagne, that's enough."

As this example shows, the game involved juggling various conditions and demands. It not only presented a puzzle to work out but also gave the worker a sense that she was minimizing the likelihood of having to deal with an unhappy guest.

Luxury Service Imperatives

The interactive workers in my sites also made games of luxury service imperatives. Rarely involving direct material incentives, luxury-imperative games served primarily to help workers develop a sense of themselves as skilled and to code the unlimited labor they were required to provide as voluntary. Winning these games involved meeting the luxury standard in an uncertain context. Thus, rather than resent guests' and managers' demands, workers used these demands to constitute themselves as skilled. The "opponent" in the game was the worker's self, his capacity to meet demands, but the raw materials were the guest's desires and behavior. For the most part, these games were in line with managerial goals of recognizing guests and fulfilling their desires.[14]

Name use and recalling details about guests was one luxury-imperative game. Jorge, a bellman at the Royal Court, prided himself on remembering the names of frequent guests. He was very annoyed with himself one day for having to check the luggage tags of a frequent guest to remember his name; on another occasion I noticed him mouthing a guest's name as she approached the door to check in, making sure he remembered it correctly. Joel, a Royal Court doorman, usually came in about half an hour early for his 7:00 A.M. shift, in order to make a list of guest names, room numbers, and car ticket numbers, which he used to address guests by name (and to keep track of how many cars were in the garage at any given time). Front desk workers and concierges, especially at the Luxury Garden, also made a game of calling the guest by name; it felt strategic, for example, to find a way to glean the name surreptitiously from the computer while conversing with the guest across the desk. Dirk told me that, in order to remember guests' names, "I pretend I own the hotel and I'm getting those four-hundred-dollar rack rates."

Needs anticipation was another such game, which depended in part on typologies. As we have seen, concierges had to match the services they offered with guests' personal characteristics in order to please them. Reservationists and front desk workers might assign rooms with larger bathrooms to older people. This kind of prediction not only met luxury standards but also prevented complaints; workers thought about ways to make sure guests would be satisfied and thus less likely to make trouble.

The ability to read guest demeanor also arose from the imperative of needs anticipation, and workers saw it as a skill. Charlie, a server at the Royal Court restaurant, told me that guest expectations varied; some people, he said, wanted him to participate, "join in the fun," while others wanted him to be unobtrusive. Coding himself as skilled, he told me he could "gauge from the beginning" how the table wanted him to be. Saul, another server, independently claimed this type of reading as a skill; as I noted after our conversation, "He thinks he's good at figuring out what people want and then giving it, whether it's staying out of their way or being more interventionist."

Responding to specific guest requests and demands was another game. Rather than resist guests' high expectations and their demands, workers coded these as challenges. Jorge, the Royal Court bellman, told me I "couldn't have handled" one older male guest, because he was difficult, his bags were unwieldy, and he had special demands, such as placing the luggage racks a specific distance from the wall. For concierges, it was a personal challenge, and thus a game, to obtain a particular designer gown for a guest, find a store that sold special high-end furniture or antique maps, or send five air-to-sea vehicles to Saudi Arabia (as the concierges at a five-star Manhattan hotel had to do one day when I was given a tour).

In my first meeting with them, Luxury Garden concierge managers Sydney and Antonio spent a lot of time emphasizing the demanding nature of the job, presenting the game as especially difficult. They described guests as highly demanding and "unforgiving," because they were paying so much. Reservations, tickets, and cars were the easiest part of the job, they said, claiming not even to notice these mundane tasks. They focused on more challenging demands, such as planning weekends out of town; Antonio mentioned that the previous week he had had to locate and purchase a ninety-five-thousand-dollar Hummer for a guest. They clearly coded dealing with these demands as a skill acquired only through experience.

Securing restaurant reservations was indeed a common daily task for concierges and, in fact, was one of these workers' main games. Here workers negotiated two kinds of unpredictability: what the guest wanted and what was available. One challenge of the game was to figure out what guests would like, as we have seen. Another was to minimize effort while maximizing payoff in terms of the caliber of the restaurant. A third challenge was to maintain relationships with restaurant reservationists; when guests asked us to cancel reservations at prestigious restaurants, we often kept them in case another guest wanted to dine there, but we had to cancel with enough notice that the reservationist did not become irritated with us. Workers became quite invested in this game; for example, one day Jasmine referred to herself as being "on a mission" to get a table for two guests at a prestigious restaurant that took only same-day reservations, and she spent at least an hour calling the always-busy number.

This reservation game also involved manipulating guests, controlling them while subtly placing limits on workers' own labor. For example, when I arrived one day at the Luxury Garden, Max cautioned me, "If Mr. Wong asks, tell him that [a local restaurant] is the trendiest and best one, because that's what he wants to hear." Max and Alec had not been able to make reservations elsewhere, and it was easier simply to make the guest think he was getting what he had requested. Similarly, Giovanna at the Royal Court told a guest who had requested "trendy" restaurants that for her first night in town the hotel's restaurant was the best place to eat.

Giovanna confided conspiratorially, "Everything else around here is pretty touristy, and you don't want that," thus avoiding the work of getting the woman a reservation elsewhere while also confirming the guest's sense of herself as *not* a tourist. In these practices, workers used the guest's trust in them to assert their power and minimize their labor.

Concierges also interpreted their cultural capital as a skill. They manifested this expertise as a routine part of their work in discussions of restaurants, theater, museums, and high-end shopping. They valued their cultural authority over guests and felt gratified when guests took their advice. Their membership in local and international concierge associations reinforced the concierges' sense of themselves as knowledgeable, as specialists in a kind of craft.[15]

Another aspect of luxury service that workers saw as a game involving skill was saying no to guests—the ultimate luxury taboo, but necessary sometimes nonetheless. One day Pearl, a young front desk worker who had been at the hotel for only a few months, received a positive mention in a letter from guests to hotel management. She jumped up and down gleefully, saying she had finally "learned to play the game," which meant "knowing how to say no." She told me that at the bank where she had worked previously "everything was black and white" and she could just "say no," but at the hotel "everything has a gray side." She said, "You have to pretend to check even if you know the answer is no, and you have to say 'unfortunately' and tell the guest something that makes him think he's getting something good."

Training from others helped workers to interpret saying no as expertise. Carolyn, an assistant manager, told Pearl after a run-in with a guest who had been refused the upgrade he wanted, "You have to say it very nicely and with a smile." She also admonished, "Don't say, 'I can only upgrade you to whatever'; make it sound good." After a caller at the Royal Court became irritated with me because I could not give her the corporate rate she had requested, I said to Sarah, "She hated me." Sarah responded, "It's because you told her no. You'll get better at it." She told me that was why she always offered to check another date, to give callers the message that the conversation was over and there was nothing else she could do.

Reframing Subordination and Money

Games helped to normalize disparity by changing the meaning of money. First, the behavior of wealthy guests allowed workers to exert less effort, control their own time, and avoid complaints. Many workers and managers told me that wealthy guests created less work because they were not preoccupied with how much everything cost. Telling me that reservation seekers generally did not ask about children's activities, as they would at a larger and less exclusive hotel, Sarah pointed out that the wealth of the guests "makes our job easier." Conversely, less wealthy clients often demanded long interactions that consumed the worker's time without a corresponding payoff. For example, Sydney moaned one day that she had to fetch a guest's clothing from the nearby dry cleaner because he was "too cheap" to pay for it to be cleaned in the hotel. Less wealthy people also sometimes demanded more emotional labor. As one Luxury Garden manager put it, "Their expectations are disproportionate to the rate they are paying," increasing the likelihood of complaints.[16]

Second, the resources of rich guests allowed workers to win reservation games that depended on garnering higher room rates. Thus, guests who were financially more similar to workers themselves became less desirable. Linus, a Luxury Garden reservationist, told me that he became annoyed with the penny-pinching guests, feeling that they were wasting his time, even though he mentioned that he couldn't afford to stay in the hotel either. Taking reservations at the Royal Court, I found myself irritated with a woman who refused to comprehend that six people would not fit into a two-bedroom suite. Afterward, I noted: "I realize now why Sarah has this attitude of 'get rid of them,' because it's annoying to have to deal with them and also because there are people waiting, or there could be at any time. Also of course the more quickly you get rid of them the more free time you have. On the other hand you might have thought I would be sympathetic to this woman because she obviously didn't have all the money in the world and was trying to figure out how to economize." As a consequence, workers grew accustomed over time to dealing with large amounts of money and began to see these amounts in terms of how they related to the hotel rather than how they related to the workers'

personal lives. Annie told me on one occasion that a promotional rate of
$250 "seems cheap now for a room." Max at the Luxury Garden said of
one guest's rate, "Six hundred, that's nothing." This recasting of the
meaning of money also distanced guests from workers, who often said,
"It isn't a lot of money to them."

Finally, the very self-subordination that workers are supposed to provide as part of luxury service became a source of competence, as these
examples have shown. In contrast to McDonald's, where routines con-
strain workers, or airlines, where behavioral specifications are a form of
emotional "deskilling,"[17] luxury hotel workers can code themselves as
skilled not in spite of but *because of* the interactive requirements of their
work.

MONEY GAMES

Workers who received tips and commissions in these sites also played
games around these material incentives, developing myriad strategies
and using predictive typologies to negotiate their effort. Of the games
hotel workers play, the tipping game is closest to "making out" on the
factory floor, for several reasons. It involves a financial incentive that is
somewhat predictable but not so predictable as to become boring, and
the worker is able to negotiate her effort in a way that seems related to
the outcome. It helps to pass the time and establish a sense of worker control. Workers become increasingly involved in their work as they become
invested in the outcome of the game. The tipping game also constitutes
workers as individuals because of the individualized nature of the
reward. Finally, as in the factory, managers implicitly condone this game,
most of the time; but, like making out, its logic could eventually contra-
dict managerial goals—in this case, the provision of unlimited labor to
hotel guests.

However, the tipping game differs from those played in the factory,
both in the character of "output," which is intangible and difficult to
quantify in the hotel industry, and in the importance of the guest, who
generates unpredictability. No time-study man determines pay rates;

rather the guest, in the context of social norms (which he may or may not know), decides whether and how much to tip. Thus, the guest provides the monetary incentive and serves as the worker's primary interlocutor, the "machine" against which the game is played.

Nearly a half-century ago, Fred Davis described the strategies and typologies that cab drivers used to minimize the unpredictability associated with their fleeting relationships to their "fares." He argued that cab drivers used the tipping game not because it actually increased their income but because it passed the time and made the work more interesting:

> In the last analysis, neither the driver's typology of fares nor his stratagems further to any marked degree his control of the tip. Paradoxically, were these routinely successful in achieving predictability and control, they would at the same time divest the act of tipping of its most distinguishing characteristics—of its uncertainty, variability, and of the element of revelation in its consummation. It is these—essentially the problematic in human intercourse—which distinguish the tip from the fixed service charge. And although another form of remuneration might in the end provide the cabdriver with a better wage and a more secure livelihood, the abrogation of tipping would also lessen the intellectual play which uncertainty stimulates and without which cabdriving would be for many nothing more than unrelieved drudgery.[18]

As this quotation suggests, the tipping game is organized around income maximization, but that is not its central function. The game engages the worker's mind and structures his investment in the work. In the hotel, as in manufacturing games, income maximization is important because it coordinates the interests of managers (and guests, in this case) with those of workers; the tip provides an independent incentive for workers to behave toward guests according to the standards of luxury service. This is why, for the most part, managers allow and even encourage workers to play tipping games.[19] But these games also confirm workers' skill, pass the time, and organize relations with coworkers and guests. As in the factory, when workers cannot obtain these other satisfactions from playing the game, they cease to participate, as I will show. Workers are not simply rational income-maximizing actors; rather, they use the tipping game to constitute themselves as autonomous. In some cases, workers' desire to establish autonomy and earn tips came into conflict with managers' need to provide consistent service.

Money games also help workers to invert the subordination associated with their interactive work. Rather than feel their inferior status confirmed by tipping practices, these workers used the tip to recast subordination. This inversion occurs primarily not through overt moments of resistance but through a construction both of self as strategic and autonomous and of the exertion of effort as voluntary. Furthermore, the tipping game normalizes unequal entitlement to wealth and labor, first, by making guests' money beneficial to workers and, second, by engendering consent to the rules of the game, which structure guests' entitlement to consume workers' labor (not just managers and owners' right to appropriate the fruits of this labor).

Rules of the Tipping Game

As we have seen, concierges and front door workers were the primary recipients of tips at the Luxury Garden and the Royal Court. Guests usually tipped concierges for making dinner reservations or other arrangements (five to ten dollars for a reservation or two, twenty to fifty dollars for more extensive arrangements and occasionally a generous hundred). They tipped doormen and valets a dollar or two for getting a taxi or bringing a car around, and doormen and bellmen usually garnered five or ten dollars for unloading or loading luggage or bringing it up to or down from a room. I will elaborate on the rules of the game for guests in later chapters; here, the rules that matter most are those that workers used to regulate the allocation of tips, which were often elaborate and varied by work area.

For concierges and front desk workers in both hotels, rules about tips and commissions were established by management. Concierges at the Luxury Garden pooled the commissions they obtained from massages, car and driver services, rental cars, and so on, although they kept individual cash tips.[20] At the Royal Court, concierges kept their cash tips and their own commissions. At the front door at both hotels, workers had established and continued to regulate the complicated rules governing tip allocation. Experienced workers explained the rules to new hires, thus inserting them into the game (though not all were equally forthcoming about how to win it).

At the Royal Court, the bellman and the doorman observed a strict spatial division of labor, in that the doorman executed all tasks between the door and the curb (mostly loading and unloading luggage) and the bellman did everything inside the hotel (bringing bags up or down). They split tips for guests who were checking out if only one of the two received a tip. When guests were checking in, however, this rule did not apply (which meant that the day shift doorman, with more check-outs, made more in tips than the evening shift, with more check-ins). The doorman kept tips intended for the valet if the car the valet had brought around was a "check-out car" (the guest was leaving), but the valet received the tip if it was an "in-and-out car" (the guest would be coming back later). At the end of the shift, consistent with his quasi-managerial status, the doorman might share tips with the bellman or the valet. These relations were complicated by the new division of labor that attended the renovation, because bellmen and valets were put into the same category and paid the same hourly rate; yet managers failed to define when each would work inside, as a bellman (which was more lucrative in terms of tips).[21]

At the Luxury Garden, in contrast, bellmen instead of doormen often loaded guests' luggage into their cars, though if the bellman had already been tipped he might pass the bags on to the doorman in hopes that the guest would tip him as well. The two bellmen on duty alternated in escorting the guests to their rooms, thereby evening out the chances of being tipped, unless one worker was doing especially badly. Workers shared gratuities that came from well-known big tippers, in order to minimize competition to serve those guests. Because the valets were employed by the garage rather than the hotel, they usually kept their own tips. (Dirk, a doorman, told me that if the guest tipped the valet and not him, the valet should give up the tip, "and I'll make that clear to them if I have to." But Oscar, another doorman, told me that he always shared his tips with the garage workers.) At both hotels, managers filling in for workers were never supposed to accept tips. Just following the rules was a kind of game, because it was challenging to remember who owed what to whom, and workers doubtless also tried to circumvent these rules on occasion.

Strategies of the Game

As Davis might have predicted, some workers believed that it was not possible to elicit tips from guests strategically. Annie told me, "People will tip or they won't based on who they are, not on what you do for them." Max felt that tipping was totally unpredictable. He said he could "move heaven and earth" for guests and they might not tip him, or he could do something he felt was very minor and receive a big tip. (He gave the example of a guest to whom he had lent his cell phone for the afternoon; he said he had thought nothing of it, but when she left she gave him an envelope containing five hundred dollars.) Joel at the Royal Court told me one day not to stand there looking as if I were waiting for a tip after I brought a car around. He said, "You shouldn't take it personally if you don't get tipped." His approach, he said, was to give the guest his spiel, do whatever he was supposed to, and then step away; if the guest wanted to tip him, "great, but if not that's fine too." In this way workers presented themselves as not invested in the money, and this philosophy helped them maintain distance from the tip's significance as a judgment of their service.

Despite their opinion that the tip could not be controlled, workers mobilized a variety of strategies to elicit tips.[22] First, they offered guests effort and recognition. Javier, a bellman, was explicitly tactical about his relationships with guests. One guest had mentioned to Javier that he wanted to stay an extra night, but the hotel was sold out. Javier had gone to the desk and set up the extra night for him, and the guest ended up tipping him fifty dollars. On another occasion, Javier had asked about a returning guest's family and specifically his favorite son. The guest responded, "Oh, you remember my son?" and tipped him well. Dirk, the Luxury Garden doorman, anticipated the need of guests who were going jogging by offering them towels and water; he invoked the tip as the reason, telling me that the guest probably wouldn't have cash for a tip when she returned but might "remember" him later. Thus, the personal attention characteristic of luxury service provides raw material for winning the tipping game.

Workers also subtly highlighted their labor in order to increase the tip. Concierges tried to ensure that their communications with the guest identified the concierge who had done the task; handwritten reservation cards, messages on the guest's voice mail, and notes left in the computer for incoming guests, all of which included the worker's name, discreetly reminded guests that work had been done by particular workers. Workers followed up with guests about their experience, asking how they had enjoyed the meal or manicure the concierge had arranged for them, for example. Because this follow-up seemed to increase the chances of being tipped, providing individual attention was a strategy for winning the game as well as an imperative of the job. By drawing attention to their effort, however, workers delicately transgressed the luxury norm that labor be unlimited and seemingly effortless.

Performativity could be a tip strategy and at the same time a source of skill. Joel, for example, was widely noted for his style of joking with guests. He walked the fine line between friendliness and excessive familiarity. One day he said something vaguely rude to a customer, in jest, and I asked if he had ever gotten in trouble for talking to a guest like that. He told me that he had with managers but very rarely with customers. He said he could tell when they were becoming offended and could "usually turn it around." He also mentioned that a coworker at another luxury hotel used to use Joel's lines, but he could not quite pull it off, so guests would get angry with him. Joel's hamminess was probably partly a strategy to make himself memorable and thus increase his chances of receiving a tip, and clearly he also thought of this capacity as a skill.

Workers also encouraged guests to consume in particular ways when it was to the workers' own monetary advantage. For example, when a guest asked Jasmine if it was more romantic to have flowers waiting in the room for his girlfriend or bring them himself, she told him to have them in the room, because if he ordered them in advance she would get a commission from the florist. She told me afterward that if she really thought it made a difference she would be honest, but in this case it didn't matter, "so I might as well get the commission." Edward, a server at the Royal Court restaurant, would ask guests, "Bottled water or just tap?" which subtly encouraged them to order the expensive water, increasing the check total and thus, presumably, his tip.[23]

Workers shared these strategies with new colleagues, establishing a collective repertoire. Alec at the Luxury Garden told me specifically to make sure to let guests know my name so that they would remember who had helped them. After I obtained an exclusive restaurant reservation fairly easily, Alec told me to "make the guest think you worked hard" nonetheless. Joel counseled me not to load bags into the guest's car until the guest was present and could "see what's happening," meaning that she would be reminded that I was working.

Predictability, Effort, and Investment in the Game

Much as in the factory, where discussion of who was making out was widespread on the shop floor, tipped hotel workers frequently asked each other how they were doing, though specific amounts were not always mentioned.[24] Daniel, a bellman at the Luxury Garden, was irritated by how often his coworkers at the door, with whom he did not get along especially well, asked him how much he was making. Concierges at both hotels often mentioned when they had been tipped an unusually large or small sum; at the Luxury Garden, they frequently complained that they were not making much, perhaps commenting euphemistically, "The guests haven't been very generous lately." (Concierges usually evaluated their tip earnings weekly, because they varied widely from day to day, while bellmen and doormen talked in terms of each shift.) This practice not only established the game as collective but also located practices of comparison among workers rather than between workers and guests.

Just as Burawoy and Roy were sucked into the logic of making out on the factory floor, I felt myself being inserted into the tipping game, learning the strategies, and, most important, beginning to care about it. Having never expected to make any money doing this research, I was flabbergasted when I received my first tip (which happened to be a gen-

erous twenty dollars for bringing a couple's luggage up to their room).
But I soon became accustomed to receiving cash from strangers, and I felt
myself becoming more invested in receiving tips. As I noted on two separate occasions after initial shifts at the door:

> I felt like I was getting too stressed and greedy about the tips. . . . the
> whole setup made me want more money, when it had never really
> occurred to me I'd ever make anything.

> I realized that the stakes are somehow raised because I think I am going
> to get tipped. It used to be that if they gave me money I was elated and
> felt like they were giving it to me for no reason. But now I am irked
> when they don't tip me.

Daniel agreed with me that the job fostered greed, saying that he had to
force himself to take his whole break instead of running upstairs early
from the cafeteria at the prospect of more money.

However, hotel workers sometimes set limits on effort even when it
meant potentially losing income. They used their discretion and freedom
from surveillance to avoid working when the game seemed unwinnable,
giving up the potential tip just as manufacturing workers gave up the
possibility of increased income when they could not make out on a given
machine.[25] Like Davis's cab drivers, who developed categories for their
fares such as "the sport," "the blowhard," and "the lady shopper," hotel
workers frequently used typologies to classify guests in order to increase
predictability related to tipping.[26] Alejandro in room service told me that
if the guest is concerned about the price of the food, "they never tip."
Zeke the doorman mentioned that businessmen traveling alone usually
carried their own bags (eliminating the chance of a tip for him and for the
bellman), "especially on Monday nights." Workers not only prepared
themselves not to receive a tip; they also negotiated effort according to
these typologies, going out of their way for likely tippers and holding
back for those who they thought might not tip, including repeat guests.

Workers also constantly weighed the potential tip against the difficulty
of the exertion it would involve and negotiated their effort accordingly.
One particular high-end restaurant, for example, was booked for months
in advance, and the phone number was always busy; concierges had to

dial many times before they reached a reservationist, who nearly always refused the request. Consequently, workers at both hotels, without even picking up the phone, routinely told guests that the restaurant had no availability. Even Antonio, the guest services manager at the Luxury Garden, told me more than once not to bother trying to get through. When guests asked concierges to try to change their airline tickets, which usually required spending long periods on hold, workers might simply tell the guest nothing else was available. Sometimes workers subtly indicated to guests that one of their options was better than another; for example, in order to avoid having to move the guest's bags, Paulo, a bellman, told Dr. Kramer about the disadvantages of a room he was thinking about changing into.[27] In all of these instances, the potential of the tip was uncertain enough that the worker deemed the effort not worth making.

Unlike Davis's cab drivers, who experienced "fleeting encounters," hotel workers also used previous experience with guests to make these calculations, for frequency tends to increase predictability of client behavior.[28] One guest at the Luxury Garden was so legendary for giving enormous tips that workers took only a short break or skipped it altogether when he was expected. Doormen at both hotels identified their own favorite guests on the basis of tips; as Dirk said to me one day, "Sometimes our VIPs out here are different from [indoor workers'] VIPs." When Mr. Melmot, a frequent guest, asked Max to make restaurant reservations for him in a nearby town, Max graciously suggested that it was better to ask workers at the hotel there to do it, because they would have better local connections. Later he told me that if Mr. and Mrs. Melmot were good tippers, he would work harder for them, but "they only tip ten dollars every ten visits."

At the Royal Court one afternoon, Joel subtly refused to load Mr. Woodhouse's luggage, which surprised me, because this frequent guest was beloved at the front desk. I came out with the guest and the luggage cart and found Joel standing far away from the car, which I had never seen before. I said, "Joel?" and he said, "You go ahead." I inexpertly put the bags into the trunk, and Mr. Woodhouse tipped me two dollars. I asked Joel later why he hadn't want to do it, and he responded, "Because that guy is so cheap." He preferred to let me do all the work and get all the tip, because he knew it would be small. The message was that Joel refused to scrounge for a dollar. Conserving his own effort and retaining his sense of dignity in this case was more important to him than the money. (Workers also claimed to turn down gratuities from guests who were rude to them or tips that seemed so small as to be insulting.) The recognition imperative of luxury service—remembering the guest—thus also coincides with the worker's interest in predicting who may tip well and who may stiff him. Taken to an extreme, this refusal to exert could affect service negatively by limiting the labor available to guests.

Workers became annoyed when their discretion was minimized by guest demands that could not be avoided, especially when a typology led them to predict they would not receive a tip. In these situations the game was shut down, and workers were simply forced to exert effort without using strategy or exerting control. Alec was faced with this dilemma one night at the Luxury Garden when some German guests asked him to try to change their plane tickets and hotel reservations in Houston. This meant waiting on hold forever, first at the Hilton and then with United. He told me, irritated, "I know I'm going to do this for them, and I'm not going to get one thin dime." I had to finish this task after Alec's shift ended, and he was right—they did not tip either of us.

Likewise, when unpredictability was eliminated the game could no longer be played. For example, guests sometimes tipped workers before asking them to do anything. Workers often reacted negatively to this practice, which is somewhat surprising, given that the tip is then guaranteed. Annie told me that she felt bad if guests tipped her before she did anything for them, "like it's an obligation." I was happy when a guest tipped me a hundred dollars before I had done anything significant for him. "But," I noted, "it is a little like he is temporarily buying himself a slave when he tips first." Though the tip guarantees the material payoff, it removes the "intellectual play" that Davis mentions and the sense of voluntary exertion of labor, bringing back the element of subordination and obligation.[29]

Limited unpredictability also influenced room service workers' practices concerning tipping. They were quick to execute guest orders but sluggish and grumpy when it came to untipped tasks for which they did not feel responsible, such as answering the restaurant phone. However, I never noticed tip-related games among these workers; while they sometimes mentioned that particular guests were generous tippers, they never talked about strategies for eliciting bigger tips. This was because the tip was much more predictable in room service, in two ways. First, like most tips on food, it was calculated by a percentage of the check; second, and of course more important, it was added automatically to the guest's bill. With its limited unpredictability and minimal space for negotiating effort, room service provides an example of work oriented toward income maximization but without a corresponding development of games.

Illicit Income Games

Front door workers played games beyond tips and legitimate commissions to maximize income and create a sense of themselves as strategic decision makers. These games involved illicit practices, which other researchers have found common in the hotel industry.[30] At the door in both of my sites, the doorman controlled the white curb outside the hotel where incoming guests pulled up, and this control led to various modes of income generation.[31] One practice, common at both hotels, was for day-shift doormen to hold the cars of people not associated with the hotel—usually wealthy local women, at the Royal Court, or businessmen, at the Luxury Garden—while they shopped, lunched, or attended meetings in the area around the hotel. At the Royal Court, they usually tipped the doorman about twenty dollars when they returned; at the Luxury Garden one businessman consistently tipped ten dollars, and others probably tipped more. Zeke told me there were about fifty of these "regulars" at the Royal Court.[32]

Holding cars for locals required strategic thinking. The doorman juggled many variables: Would the guest want his car before the doorman's shift ended? Before the meter readers came at the hours when the curb must be clear? Would the doorman need the space for other, more important cars and be forced to send these "cash cars" to the garage, thereby annoying their owners? Would something happen to the car while it was at the curb, causing the car's owner to complain, or would the owner recognize the prestige and special treatment accorded him by leaving the car out and tip the doorman handsomely?

Zeke told me he started thinking about his strategy at noon, wondering which cars would leave before he did at 3:00. He said sometimes he had to take care of "regulars" even if they would return after he had left and he would miss being tipped that day. He said he would leave them to "hit" (tip) Haile because "Haile is my buddy." He said, "That's when it gets hard," referring to the decision between engineering a tip for Haile and receiving one himself. Dirk at the Luxury Garden made similar calculations, telling me he had to weigh the potential tip for keeping the car at the curb against the possibility it would be damaged somehow.

Of all the games, money games posed the greatest potential threat to the central managerial goals of providing service to paying guests. Workers had a clear incentive to withhold service from bad tippers, compromising the quality and consistency of service. In the car-parking games, the doormen might prioritize the local regulars over the hotel guests, because the owners of the cars had a financial relationship with the doormen but not necessarily with the hotel. (As we will see below, this contradiction led to open conflict at the Royal Court.) On the other hand, the tips of hotel guests provided independent incentives for workers to provide luxury service to them; even if managers were ineffective, workers' relationships with guests still engendered consent. We will see in chapter 5 that the emotional qualities of these relationships were often as important as the financial dimension.

Normalizing Wealth

Playing money games not only helped workers avoid "unrelieved drudgery," as Davis put it, but also deflected the experience of interactive subordination by recasting asymmetrical relations as favorable to workers. Rather than highlight stratification or subordination, the large tip or high rate indicated that the worker had won the game. Rich, "sophisticated" travelers were thus a boon to workers in terms of money games. Wealthier people possessed the resources to pay higher rates, tip more generously, and consume expensive services for which workers received commissions. These guests' demand for workers' labor tended to generate tips. They were also more likely to know the rules of tipping and, as we shall see later, of emotional reciprocity.

Much as six hundred dollars came to seem like "nothing" to room reservationists, tipped workers also grew accustomed to dealing with large amounts of money. As I have said, while twenty dollars initially seemed like a fortune to me, and receiving cash from strangers was a thrill, I soon became accustomed and felt entitled to it. Only when I received my first hundred-dollar bill, several months later, did I experience that excitement again.

Furthermore, tips and commissions provided a kind of distraction; guest expenditures were important to workers for their effect on workers' incomes, not for what they signified about the guests' consumption or their structural position. As I noted one evening after a front desk shift at the Royal Court, when I had arranged for a van to pick up a group of guests at the airport: "When I made the van reservation for Mr. Bertram, he said that he didn't know when the flight got in, and I assumed he just didn't have the information. Then he said it was a private jet, so he wasn't going to know for a few days. It only flashed through my mind for a second how rich he must be, and then I forgot about it and concentrated on my commission." Given that an interest in wealth and inequality was motivating my research, it is especially surprising that I would hardly notice the blatant disparity between us, indicated by this guest's owning his own plane. Even in writing my field notes, I had recorded the commission before I made the entry above; and if I had not been writing down what happened on each shift (which, of course, my coworkers were not), I would likely have forgotten the incident.

Thus, money games served to recast relations between workers and guests, shifting them away from structural inequalities. As I show in the next section, this recasting was also linked to workers' relations with their colleagues.

LATERAL RELATIONS

Burawoy argues that in the context of making out in the piecework machine shop, conflict between managers and workers is reconstituted as lateral conflict among workers.[33] Machine operators depend on auxiliary workers to make out; when management interferes with the supply of such workers, lateral conflict arises. Conflict among workers also occurs in the hotel when workers interfere with one another's games and tips. But this conflict obscures potential hierarchical antagonism with guests as well as managers; becoming embroiled in these conflicts distracts workers from the massive gulf between themselves and those handing out the tips. Furthermore, lateral relations are organized not only around conflict in terms of games but also around comparison in terms of competence. Workers use judgments of others to constitute their jobs as challenging and themselves as experts.

Lateral Conflict

Workers in my sites, especially those who labored in the same areas, collaborated in order to win games. They told each other about strategies to minimize work or maximize tips. They sometimes tried to increase tips for their colleagues even when there was no material benefit in it for them. However, mutual interference in games created ongoing tensions and conflicts among workers, especially when incentives conflicted. Again, guest demands and interactive imperatives were often the basis for these conflicts.

The pace of guest demands sometimes created irritability among workers, especially given the necessity for speed in responding to guests' requests. Workers clashed over access to the computer terminals, the phones, or the attention of managers when they needed questions answered. Conflict also arose when one worker's decision or error led guests to complain to another worker, which usually created more subordinating interactive labor for the worker receiving the complaint. For example, a worker might fail to confirm or notify a guest about services he had requested, such as reservations or theater tickets, so whoever happened to be at the desk when the guest asked about it often had to pacify the guest's irritation. This problem also occurred in the wake of decisions made during the day about overbooking, because the evening workers would have to face the angry guest who was getting walked.

Because front desk workers were more visible, guests often complained to them about problems that were the responsibility of back of house workers, again creating interactive work and leading to conflict. On one occasion, for example, Jasmine had to mollify an angry guest because room service had failed to attach a card to some birthday gifts the guest had sent to his father's room. Consequently, the father had believed that the gifts came from the hotel and that his family had forgotten his birthday. The son was "really pissed" when he found out. Jasmine thought it was "stupid" of room service not to leave a card or wait until the guest was in the room, saying this should have been obvious because the son had requested that someone sing "Happy Birthday." The angry guest was at the desk while we were talking about it in the back; Jasmine told me, "I don't want to go out there." Although the workers at fault in these situations are not interfering with the material incentives of the coworker who must deal with the problem, they are preventing that worker both from controlling her relations with guests and from avoiding the performance of deferential emotional labor. (Workers in the back of the house complained about front of house workers occasionally too, though less often; but these gripes were mostly about information failures, which interfered with speed rather than generated negative treatment from guests.)

Workers also sniped at one another when one left work for another to do if no tip was involved. Reservationists, for example, were irritated when sales workers changed reservations multiple times, thus creating more work for the reservationists. Extra work conflicted with the workers' goal of accomplishing their tasks speedily and interfered with the limits they had set on how much labor to exert.

However, workers also competed for work when it did involve tips, which gave them an incentive to lunge for the phone or to accost passing guests, asking if they needed assistance. This competition was more obvious at the Royal Court, because commissions were not shared and because so many workers were eligible for them (because of the merged concierge and front desk positions). Luxury Garden concierges told me that tension had existed there before they starting sharing commissions, and conflict over work still surfaced at times.

Workers also complained when others interfered with their potential tips and hence with the game. Trina, a restaurant server, disliked Millie, a hostess, because she failed to "count covers"—that is, keep track of the number of diners seated in each station so that every server waited on the same number of people, equalizing the tip opportunity. Joel was annoyed with a taxi driver who closed the cab door for the guest instead of allowing him to do it, because he saw that moment as the guest's chance to tip him.

Workers at the front door were especially prone to conflicts over tips, thanks to complicated tip-sharing rules and limited managerial involvement. Haile told me that tension had arisen between Frankie and Ethan, a new bellman, because Ethan was taking all the work, "jumping on people's bags." Ethan asked Frankie what he was doing with some luggage, and Frankie responded, "Do I have to tell you always what I'm doing?" Ethan replied, "I need to make money too." The conflict became serious and ultimately required Petra's intervention.

I had a similar clash with Carlos one day when I was working outside, mostly as a valet, and he inside as the bellman, which meant he received more tips. While he was on break, I brought some guests' bags downstairs; later when they needed the bags loaded into the car, Carlos was nowhere to be found, so I carried them out. Carlos appeared, saw me loading the bags, and asked sarcastically, "Are you going to do *all* my work?" Finding this unbelievable, I said, "Shut up, Carlos, that's outrageous," and continued working. He then asked for half of the ten-dollar tip I received, because he had stored the bags in the luggage closet. I reluctantly gave him two dollars (which he later returned because he said the guest "got me on the way out"). Irritated, I also suggested that I work inside for half of our overlapping shift, challenging his right to the more lucrative job. Eventually we discussed the problem and made up, but the incident demonstrates to an embarrassing degree how invested I had become in receiving tips as well as how little I trusted Carlos to observe the rules of sharing them.[34]

Burawoy argues in regard to manufacturing that lateral conflicts among workers that revolve around games are compounded by managerial decisions about the rules of the game.[35] This was true in terms of tipping games at both my sites, especially the Royal Court. As we have seen, decisions about who would receive commissions could cause tensions and competition for work. Likewise, as the example of my clash with Carlos demonstrates, the failure of managers at the Royal Court to define the bellman and valet positions or institute some kind of rule about tip sharing led to conflict among workers. With other bellmen/ valets (including me, after our conflict), Carlos instituted a tip-sharing system. But, he said of Jorge, who was more senior and therefore worked inside, "You can't hit Jorge up to share with you; he'll bite your head off." In the absence of managerial decisions about seniority, Jorge had to enforce his own hierarchical prerogatives interactively, causing friction with Carlos.

Tension also arose when managers skimped on scheduling in order to save on labor costs. Front desk workers and concierges griped about having to answer the phone for the workers in the understaffed restaurants and pick up faxes for business center workers. The problem of parking guest cars was endemic at the Royal Court. Joel often called the desk to ask if someone could help him park cars, and when no one was available he frequently became irritated with his coworkers rather than with the managers who made staffing decisions.[36] Jasmine complained about Joel's tendency to call the front desk for help, saying, "The guest is going to yell at me anyway, not him." She joked, "I'm going to call the door when it's busy in here and tell him I need some help at the desk."

In order to avoid managerial reprimands, workers in one area sometimes took actions that interfered with other workers' games. For example, Zeke complained that front desk workers asked bellmen to bring guests' bags to their rooms when the guests were not there (what was known as a "dead move").[37] He said, "If a bellman brings up bags to an empty room, he makes no money." Later, I asked Jackie at the front desk if she usually sent up the bags to the empty room, and she said, "Yes, just to get them out of the way." I mentioned that the bellmen did not receive a tip for the "dead move," and she said, "Well, I can't always look out for the bellmen." Jackie was responding to managerial dictates to get the bags moved quickly, and she knew that if she waited she might get busy and forget about it, which could bring a reprimand. Thus, managerial decisions affected these relations by creating the context for conflict or cooperation.

Lateral Comparison

Lateral relations also presented workers with opportunities for certain kinds of self-conceptions. As the examples I have used above indicate, workers in the same department shared a culture of skill, in which they trained one another in particular strategies and practices of their jobs.[38] In so doing, they also taught one another to think of these practices as skills, thereby constituting competence. However, a process of relentless, though subtle, comparison with other workers underlay these self-conceptions. Their talk was filled with explicit and implicit evaluations of other workers and other jobs, and their strategies of superior expertise sometimes created conflict. The sense of skilled autonomy depended in part on their comparisons with others. Like conflicts, these comparisons also served to reframe hierarchical antagonisms as lateral ones.

Workers stressed that their particular job or shift was especially challenging. Giovanna told me, for example, "People think the day shift is harder," but she argued that, in fact, the night shift was more difficult, because it involved more paperwork as well as checking guests in and out and doing concierge duties. Workers also explicitly used their colleagues as a foil in order to cast themselves as competent. Noting with irritation that Clint had done a sloppy job putting a fax into an envelope, Hugh told me, "That's his trademark." Oscar, a doorman at the Luxury Garden, was annoyed with Daniel one day because he couldn't "handle the door" alone, so Oscar had to cut his break short to help. Ginger at the Royal Court complained of Stephanie, "She can't even answer the phone right, because she won't put people on hold to get other calls."

Sometimes workers criticized one another for not observing particular standards, again casting themselves as skilled by maintaining these luxury imperatives. Dirk became extremely annoyed when other front door workers did not bother to write the guest's name on the car ticket (this practice enabled whoever gave the car back to the guest to call him by name). Giovanna groused when she called room service or the restaurant and the worker answered the phone with "Hello?" instead of "Room service [or restaurant], X speaking," though the worker could tell from the telephone display that it was another worker calling.

These critiques of competence also applied to workers in the back of the house. As we have seen, guest-related mistakes made by invisible workers created more work for interactive workers. But invisible workers were also a convenient foil for front of house workers, especially because interactive workers had little knowledge of housekeeping work, making it easy for them to code these workers as incompetent. Joel said, "Ninety-eight percent of the workers in housekeeping, when you look up the word 'useless' in the dictionary, their picture is there." Annie went out of her way to confirm with a guest that he had requested a wake-up call, because she did not trust the housekeeping supervisor who had notified her about it. As I have mentioned, front of house workers also frequently criticized housekeeping and room service workers, behind their backs, for their limited English. This kind of criticism was implicitly racialized, given that the front office workers were mostly white and the housekeeping workers were all people of color, although explicitly racialized language was not used.

Workers even extended these lateral comparisons into workplaces outside the hotel, evaluating the abilities of restaurant reservationists, travel agents, assistants, secretaries, and even workers at the garage where the guests' cars were parked. Sarah frequently complained, for example, that travel agents "don't know what they're doing," calling them "idiots" or "unprofessional." Antagonisms with these workers, as with their own colleagues, helped hotel workers constitute themselves as more competent.

PROFESSIONALS AND INDEPENDENTS

Games, conflicts, and comparisons fostered a sense of self as autonomous, but this autonomy played out in different ways among hotel workers. Most, especially at the Luxury Garden, used autonomy to underpin what some would call "role embracement."[39] These workers saw themselves as professionals.[40] They took every opportunity to stress the skills involved in their work, and they compared themselves favorably with other workers in terms of competence, as the examples above have shown. Workers who prided themselves on their skill and professionalism responded negatively to violations of their sense of competence, often responding defensively when coworkers pointed out mistakes they had made. Giovanna was not amused when Annie showed her that she had misspelled "Peninsula" in a message to a guest that confirmed his reservation at the "Penisola Hotel." Charlotte at the Luxury Garden bristled when a front desk worker pointed out that she had failed to record a sedan pickup in the concierge log. These workers also objected to managers who seemed not to respect their ability and knowledge of luxury standards.

Some workers' self-concepts, however, emphasized a *lack* of investment in their at-work identities, manifesting "role distance." Workers using this strategy were usually less concerned with defining their work as skilled, difficult, or prestigious. Most of these workers were young and did not foresee a career for themselves in the industry. They were less committed to the hotel as an institution, and they often saw themselves as more authentic at work, again implying freedom from being told how to act.

These workers tended to use comparisons with other workers to mark themselves as independent of the hotel. For example, Zeke repeatedly contrasted himself to Joel, who was much more invested in his doorman identity. One day when I was working with Zeke outside, Joel came out of the hotel to go home, still wearing his uniform. Zeke said, with a hint of sarcasm, "Got an interview?" Joel said no, explaining that he wore the uniform to work because it was easier. He told us it was his own pants and his shirt (he told me on another occasion that he had them dry cleaned outside the hotel rather than have housekeeping do it free of charge, because he had "to know that it's going to be ready"). After he left, Zeke commented, "Live the job, love the job." With this contrast, Zeke distanced himself from hotel work as career or profession. When Annie heard that Giovanna was criticizing workers in other departments for not identifying themselves when answering the phone, she responded, "Who cares how they answer the phone? Just say, 'Who is this?'" Oscar and Dirk were Luxury Garden doormen with differing styles; more relaxed than Dirk, Oscar was gratified when a female guest with whom he had a good rapport referred to Dirk as a "wooden Indian."

Workers were not always consistent in their views of themselves, expressing ambivalence about their commitment to their work and the hotel. As we have seen, for instance, Max had a lot of professional pride. But he contrasted himself to other local concierges, whom he saw as having their "whole selves" invested in their work. Both he and Alec mentioned to me that something they liked about their job was that they could leave it behind after eight hours.

Many workers drew on repertoires of both professionalism and independence, but the hotel context made a difference in which strategy predominated. At the Luxury Garden, managerial consistency and other regime characteristics created a stable context for games and supported a professional orientation among workers. In contrast, the Royal Court's unstable regime threatened the conditions of games and encouraged a more independent orientation among workers. This state of affairs at the latter hotel led to a paradox: the workers who saw themselves as professional and skilled withdrew consent, while workers who saw themselves as independent of the hotel remained engaged.

Playing by the Rules at the Luxury Garden

While management at the Luxury Garden was more formal and hierarchical than at the Royal Court, managers also respected workers' autonomy more consistently. In particular, they stayed out of workers' tipping schemes. Managers were aware, for example, that doormen kept nonguests' cars at the curb; but, aside from requiring that all claim tickets be logged in to prevent illicit practices,[41] they did not interfere with the doorman's authority in that zone, his right both to money and to independent control of the door. Oscar said that Sydney, who as a guest services manager supervised the door workers, had told him that "she didn't even want to know what was going on at the door." Dirk told me management knew that "the doorman has to have autonomy." He said that his "regulars" might not be staying in the hotel at that particular moment, but they would eventually, and "management knows it's good to keep them happy." Whether or not this service imperative was their rationale, managers apparently believed that letting the doormen govern the door brought more benefits than negative consequences.

Managers also facilitated game playing by sticking to rules and not skimping on the number of workers per shift. Managerial consistency relieved all but minimal conflict among workers over the allocation of tasks, though some tension still arose over mistakes and other problems related to guests. (I suspect, however, that more antagonism occurred than I was aware of, especially at the door, because I worked there for only a short time.) Workers did not have to enforce rules of games interpersonally because of managerial inattention or inconsistency. The clear division of labor lessened workers' conflicts over responsibilities and tips, though there was some grousing about workers who did not do their jobs well.

I heard about one instance, months before my arrival, when upperlevel managers tried to break the rules of the game by channeling concierge commissions to the hotel itself. This shift would have significantly affected the concierges' income and changed their ability to play the game. Sydney—herself a low-level manager—represented the concierges in the matter: eight months pregnant, she walked into Sebastian's office and told him and François that the concierges "wouldn't stand for it." The managers quickly backed down. Alec told me later that it was because of her action that the commissions had been saved. He told me the story several times and clearly felt grateful to her for defending the concierges. In a sense this was a moment of resistance, because Sydney's defiance challenged managers' authority to change the rules. Her action, however, also defended the broader rules of the game (concierges were entitled to commissions as long as they provided luxury service) and thus constituted consent to those rules.

At the same time that the Luxury Garden regime preserved workers' autonomy as it was needed in certain games, that regime also regulated workers' discretion by providing greater symbolic resources, both implicit and explicit, for constructing a professional identity. First, the organization of work helped to reinforce a sense of skill, particularly for concierges, who did not have to do any of the more routine and seemingly easier front desk tasks. Second, being older, better trained on luxury standards, and more accountable supported a general sense of professionalism among workers. Third, managers explicitly encouraged workers to see themselves as skilled and professional, stressing the challenges of providing a luxury product (an "experience") and the "responsibility" that accompanied the hotel's "reputation for excellence." Emphasis on selection of workers supported this notion: "We hired you because you're the best," as Alice said in the orientation. Explicit standards and training on the finer points of guest relations also reinforced the notion of skill.

As a consequence of this regime, most workers at the Luxury Garden consistently used a strategy of professionalism. A few occasionally complained that their jobs were boring or made irreverent comments about the hotel. The front door workers on the night shift liked to goof off (and used at least one illicit income-generating mechanism that I know of, linked to the car service). But for the most part the managerial rhetoric of professionalism, skill, and responsibility dovetailed with workers' self-presentation.

Conflict and Contestation at the Royal Court

As we saw in chapter 2, managerial neglect of workers sometimes reinforced their consent, by allowing workers to "be themselves," giving them time to have fun on the job, and reinforcing their sense of autonomy and control. One might assume, then, that the Royal Court's focus on authenticity and managers' de facto respect for workers' autonomy would have led managers to respect workers' games. However, managerial inconsistency led to both contestation over games and variation in worker self-conceptions.

Though they usually seemed uncomfortable about exerting authority, managers occasionally attempted to establish control by changing the rules, which led to conflict and the withdrawal of consent. This sometimes occurred on an individual level. At the desk, Petra violated Jackie's sense of autonomy by telling her she should not have upgraded a guest into a much more expensive suite than the room he was paying for; afterward, Jackie told me that workers became less invested in their work "because they just have to do what she says." A couple of months after I left the hotel, I heard that Jorge was quitting after working there for seventeen years. Haile said this was because Petra, the front office manager, had begun to schedule him on the 10:00–6:00 midshift rather than his usual morning shift, which was more lucrative. By limiting Jorge's capacity to "make out," in a way that violated not only his income but also his sense of seniority and entitlement on the job, this decision led him to withdraw consent by leaving.

The rules of the game as they applied more broadly were also unstable, leading to an ongoing struggle between front door workers and management. As we have seen, doormen at the Royal Court accepted large tips from people not associated with the hotel for holding their cars while they shopped or did business in the area. Management was not explicitly aware of this practice ("and you better not tell them," Joel warned me when I asked if they knew). However, about three months into my fieldwork, one of the drivers from the car service company the hotel used sent an anonymous letter to management, complaining that the doormen refused to let the drivers park at the white curb while they were awaiting guests, because the doormen were using the space for nonguest cars. This letter prompted Petra to talk to the doormen individually about what was going on. Most of them told me they had said there were not enough valets to take the cars to the garage, and she had told them not to worry about it. Nonetheless, assistant managers, who had largely stayed away from the door in the past, began coming outside more often and asking the doormen what each car was doing there, micromanaging the allocation of curb space. Petra also posted a new memo: "All cars are to be taken immediately to the garage."

These new practices curtailing their autonomy irritated the doormen, partly because their income was threatened, but also largely because they did not want to feel they were being supervised and deskilled. As Zeke put it, "The managers are getting more managerial lately." He complained, "Now I don't just have to look out for meter maids; I have to watch out for managers as well. . . . After ten years in this job I don't like anyone looking over my shoulder." Joel grumbled about Petra's elimination of discretion, saying her memos were "too black and white" leaving "no gray area." He was disgruntled about the loss of money but also commented, "They don't want me to think." Haile likewise referred to Petra's memo as "too clear" and told me management was treating him "like a piece of furniture" to be moved around. He said, "They don't want me to use my brain." These workers' responses to managerial intervention illuminate how playing the game was intertwined with constructing an autonomous self.

Like Dirk at the Luxury Garden, workers used the language of service to justify these car parking practices as a way of suggesting there was no difference between their interests and those of the hotel. They usually said that it was important to take the cars of local shoppers, because they occasionally dined at the hotel or put up their out-of-town visitors there. But managers did not accept this rationale, as they did at the Luxury Garden. Haile was furious that Petra had accused the doormen of lowering the standard of service, saying, "Shoppers patronize the hotel too." He also declared that Keith, the previous long-term manager, "never cared what was going on at the door."

The lack of clear rules led to more conflict among workers as well. The doormen's car parking business required the cooperation of the valets, but the doormen failed to compensate the valets to their satisfaction. Knowing that the doormen were in a vulnerable position vis-à-vis management already, thanks to the limo driver's accusations, Arnold and Carlos took revenge by complaining to Petra that the valets were not tipped enough, partly because they were not allowed to hand car keys to the guests, and by telling managers about the doormen's practice of holding cars for nonguests. The conflict continued for weeks, with various workers not speaking to one another, and still had not been resolved when I left the hotel. The doormen's failure to maintain good relations with the valets led the valets to challenge the rules of the game as the doormen had decided them, and in so doing the valets jeopardized the game itself.

These changes threatened worker consent. All three doormen began to talk about looking for other jobs. Zeke said to me of managerial surveillance, "This job has been bad enough with the renovation [because of reduced tip income], but now it's really bad." Not long afterward, after ten years at the hotel, he took a job outside the hospitality industry. Joel explicitly threatened to withhold consent, telling me that if the situation did not improve, he was going to think of himself as "hourly"; he would stop arriving early to make his guest-identification sheet, and he would "call managers out [to help] more." He was always an "hourly" worker, of course, but here the term signals his refusal to make the extra effort that constitutes active consent. A few weeks later Joel told me he never came in early anymore or hung around in the cafeteria after his shift, saying, "I just come to work in my uniform and go home after." He had settled for just showing up.

These examples demonstrate the difficulty of constituting autonomy under an unpredictable managerial regime. But other features of the regime also made it harder for workers to use a strategy of professionalism. First, the minimal division of labor eliminated the possibility of distinction in terms of skill. It is more challenging to conceive of oneself as a concierge, for example, when one is also doing the routine tasks of the front desk and answering the telephone. (When I began work at the Luxury Garden, I mentioned to Alec that the Royal Court concierge and front desk tasks were combined; he responded, "That kind of cheapens it.") Second, the hotel's choice to hire young workers increased the likelihood of their being students or otherwise not committed to the industry for the long term. Third, the lack of training made it difficult for workers to see their jobs as skilled, for training implies that skills exist.

Workers thus commonly saw themselves as independent of the hotel. Some male workers at the Royal Court described their true calling as located outside their paid work, implicitly defining themselves as what Jennifer Pierce calls "occupational transients."[42] Zeke had taken the doorman job when he was fresh out of college; he had kept it for ten years because it allowed him the free time necessary to work on his band. He commented one evening, "After spending all day trying to book dates for our tour, it's nice to be at work." Saul, a restaurant server in his forties, had been trained as an architect. He was gratified when some guests asked if he had another career, saying, "We're sure you haven't been in food service all your life." Although they did not always identify an alternative profession, most of the young, female concierge/front desk workers (several of whom were in school) were reluctant to take on the status of true professionals that their counterparts at the Luxury Garden treasured, rarely developing relationships with restaurant reservationists and other service providers.

Not all the workers took this independent stance, however. Some were invested in thinking of themselves as professionals. Several of these had been at the Royal Court for a long time and trained under previous management. Others had come to the hotel with experience in the industry. And some were the European hospitality students in training for a profession they would exercise in Europe. Thus, most of the professionally invested workers had imported their sense of professionalism from outside the current regime.

Somewhat counterintuitively, the flexible regime of the Royal Court in some ways supported the self-conception of workers who cast themselves as professionals. Managerial incompetence made workers feel more skilled, and some workers reinforced their sense of superior knowledge in their constant criticism of managers. By the same token, the mutual surveillance and training of the worker regime allowed workers to constitute themselves as knowledgeable and skilled vis-à-vis other workers (as long as they were the ones doing the surveilling and training).

However, the flexible regime did not always engender consent among this group of workers, largely because of the lack of institutional support for these self-interpretations. This was especially true of the workers who did not expect to return to hotel jobs in Europe. Giovanna and Hugh exemplified how managerial absence and the organization of work impeded the development of this sense of self and led them to withdraw consent. They considered themselves professional concierges, and they wanted the concierge responsibilities to be separate from the front desk. Hugh felt that workers should have to spend ninety days in the hotel before they could be called concierges. He was frustrated that he could not join the local concierge association because he was not a full-time concierge, given his other duties. Both of them also resented having to do

the telephone operator job; Giovanna was so resistant that she was scheduled there only once in my six months in the front office.

In contrast to the attempts of others to avoid work, Giovanna actually
created work for herself as a way of feeling that her job was challenging.
She hated giving up tasks to her coworkers and consistently refused help
that I and others offered her. Yet she also had to talk about how busy she
was in order to sustain that self-conception, which made her difficult to
work with. Giovanna also fostered her own sense of superiority by frequently telling other workers how to do things or complaining about
their mistakes. Beyond the friendly mutual training common among
most Royal Court workers, she became so bossy and quasi-managerial
that she created antagonism with other workers, showing how the
regime of mutual worker regulation could go awry.

Yet even Giovanna's extreme attempts to create a sense of professionalism in this unfavorable environment did not sustain her. Both she and
Hugh resigned while I was there, withdrawing consent not through contestation but through exit. Hugh was offered a job at a larger hotel with a
permanent schedule and no telephone operator or front desk work, and
Giovanna left without another job simply because her frustration had
become so great (she was later hired as a concierge at another prestigious
local hotel). These workers did not fit into the culture of informality,
authenticity, and lateral authority that suited their younger colleagues.

To summarize, the Luxury Garden regime was marked by both preser-
vation and regulation of autonomy in games and strategies of self. This
led to correspondence, for the most part, between management's representations of workers and workers' strategies and practices of professional selfhood, and also to workers' consent. At the Royal Court,
however, managerial inconsistency led managers to violate workers'
autonomy in games in a way that negatively affected their strategies of
self. Thus, workers such as Zeke and Jorge withdrew consent by leaving;
Joel reduced his investment in the work and the labor he was willing to
offer. Furthermore, fewer institutional resources supported workers' self-
conceptions as professional. Workers who saw themselves as independent from the hotel were more likely to remain, while more professionalized workers, such as Giovanna and Hugh, withdrew consent by exiting.

GAMES AND SELVES

The games hotel workers play are broadly similar to those found in the factory; they depend on autonomy and unpredictability, the organization of job tasks, and relations among workers in the context of managerial rule setting. Beyond the goal of income maximization, money takes on meanings linked to workers' identities and competencies.[43] It is through these games and self-interpretations that workers insert themselves into and invest in their work and make it meaningful and rewarding. Finally, while these games involve momentary resistance to managerial and guest authority, they also organize consent to social relations in production.

In the hotel, however, workers play multiple games, organized around unpredictability, incentives, and variety offered by guests. Not all of these games are organized around income maximization,[44] and those that are clearly serve psychological and social functions as well. (It seems unlikely that eliminating tips and raising tipped workers' wages to the same levels would engender consent in the same way that permitting tips does.) The sense of skill, control, and autonomy fostered by game playing underpins different self-conceptions among workers, which play out in discourse and lateral comparison as well as in practice and conflict. Finally, unequal entitlements are normalized in games, because money takes on new meanings. Workers grow accustomed to guest wealth, which becomes beneficial to them in games. Lateral conflict replaces potential hierarchical tensions as workers scrap with each other for crumbs rather than question either managerial authority or the distribution of wealth.

These interactive games illuminate the specificity of luxury service in several ways: workers are both constrained by luxury standards and able to make games and challenges of them; the presence of repeat guests allows workers to use typologies; and many of their games rely on the discretion associated with luxury service work. However, it is likely that service workers in other industries play games that are similar and likewise dependent on client behavior, although the specifics may differ. Games of speed and control among semivisible workers, for example, are comparable to practices other researchers have described (though not always referred to as games) in routinized or constrained interactive jobs, such as fast food and grocery work.[45] And front of house games organized around gratuities are surely akin to those in other tipped work.[46]

Beyond the comparison of service and manufacturing games, the link between games and workers' concepts of selfhood sheds light on the controversial question of where worker subjectivity is produced. Many scholars have pointed out the tendency for service workers doing deferential or subordinating interactive work to code themselves as skilled by emphasizing the aspects of their jobs that require expertise.[47] But these scholars have tended to see workers' self-interpretations as independent, not connecting them to opportunities arising from the content and organization of work. The same is true for discussions of resistance, which usually posit an authentic self that struggles against the confines of the workplace. Burawoy, in contrast, claims that consent is shaped at the point of production, that identities and attitudes that workers bring in from outside the shop floor are irrelevant to the game of making out.[48]

My findings confirm a softer version of Burawoy's claim: that worker practices are significantly shaped by the contexts in which they occur and are not determined solely by attitudes imported from outside. One of these contexts is the luxury sector, as I have shown. Another context is the organization. The division of labor, the organization of work, managerial intervention, and corporate rhetoric and culture provide resources on which workers draw to constitute themselves. A third context is the job itself, which offers possibilities for strategies, games, and rewards, all of which shape the worker's sense of self.

Contra Burawoy, on the other hand, preexisting selfhood also matters. Different workers are not simply inserted into games to emerge as undifferentiated and automatically consenting. Were this the case, Giovanna and Hugh would simply have become "independents" instead of "professionals," and they would still be working at the Royal Court. Workers clearly brought to the job their self-conceptions, probably related at least in part to both age and previous work experience, and these self-conceptions could be fostered or inhibited by the workplace. I am not suggesting that workers have preinstalled attitudes or beliefs that legitimate inequality in advance. Rather, individual characteristics interact with organizational resources to foster the development of certain strategies of self on the job. Key to consent is the congruence of available strategies of self with the sense of self the worker brings to the workplace. Moreover, the rewards these games bring—a sense of autonomy, competence, professionalism, and independence, as well as money—are themselves culturally constructed as desirable.

We have seen that sometimes games are not enough to engender consent. In the next chapters, I turn to other practices that underlie workers' construction of a powerful and consenting self. In chapter 4, I show that workers constitute other elements of selfhood, especially prestige and character, by locating themselves at the top of symbolic hierarchies involving coworkers and especially guests.

FOUR

Recasting Hierarchy

> To serve people takes dignity and intelligence, but remember
> they are only people with money, and although we serve them
> we are not their servants.
>
> Lionel Bloch, head hotel butler in the film *Maid in Manhattan*

At the Royal Court and the Luxury Garden, guest desires and behaviors not only provided the foundation for workers' games but also constituted a main topic of their conversations. Listening closely to their talk, I was struck by contradictions: workers told disbelieving stories of guest extravagance, occasionally commenting that "people have too much money," but they also laughed at guests who seemed cheap. Concierges poked fun at guests who wanted "the fanciest restaurant" but then bragged about the free meals they themselves had consumed at the city's top eateries. Workers proudly repeated that some guests were VIPs and CEOs but referred to others condescendingly as "trailer trash." Front desk workers kindly attended to guests who seemed lost in the luxury environment and then made fun of what they were wearing as they walked away.

At first these incongruities confused me. But I came to see that workers' paradoxical comments about guests actually served a consistent purpose: that of reframing and limiting workers' own subordination and unequal entitlement. We have seen how workers used games to recast asymmetry as autonomy. In more explicit comparative talk about their colleagues and clients, workers presented themselves as superior rather than subordinate. They invoked multiple, symbolic hierarchies of worth and advantage— status, privilege, intelligence, competence, morality, and cultural capital— and mobilized these hierarchies selectively to establish themselves as superior to others. Asserting capacities and advantages that others lacked allowed workers to resituate themselves as powerful.[1] Ironically, this move led them to constitute guests' entitlement as legitimate.

This chapter is, in a sense, an ethnography of symbolic boundaries, which pays special attention to how these boundaries are strategic, contradictory, and organizationally embedded. First, I show that workers constituted themselves as superior to their peers. In addition to the comparisons related to competence described in the last chapter, workers emphasized the perks associated with their jobs (vis-à-vis their coworkers') and the status of the hotel and its guests (vis-à-vis other people in their communities or workers in other hotels). Second, I discuss how workers coded themselves as above guests, by using both condescension toward and negative judgment of them. They also combined strategies of status and judgment by symbolically limiting guests' entitlement to stay in the hotel. Workers created this repertoire collectively, subtly introducing new workers to appropriate ways to think about themselves and discourses to use in representing themselves and others. Yet at the same time, these comparisons individualized guests and workers by highlighting personal traits and behaviors.

Workers' comparisons drew on culturally determined standards of evaluation and prestige, involving aesthetics, morality, and knowledge.[2] Yet the comparative repertoire also depended on a variety of features of the luxury hotel, including guest wealth and status, the imperatives of luxury service, and workers' intimate access to guests. Organizational context also played a role; each hotel provided different resources for workers' self-constitution.

PERKS AND STATUS: SUPERIORITY TO PEERS

Privileges of the Job

We saw in chapter 3 that workers used comparisons to cast themselves as skilled vis-à-vis their colleagues. They also invoked these comparisons to emphasize advantages associated with their jobs, especially prestige, authority, and material privileges. Workers linked competence and challenge with status, using the difficulty of their work to signify a higher position relative to those of their colleagues.

Workers cast their own jobs as the most important; for example, Sydney told me in my first meeting with her, "The concierge is really the one providing the luxury service. At the desk they are just checking people in and out." (Realizing how this sounded, she immediately corrected herself, saying, "They are important too, of course.") Workers also tried to dissociate themselves from low-prestige jobs. Workers at the Royal Court, for example, saw the telephone operator job as lowly. Men in particular seemed especially anxious to distance themselves from this "women's work"; they repeatedly stressed how unchallenging it was, calling it "too easy" or comparing it to secretarial work.

Workers also constituted status by emphasizing their authority over particular areas of the hotel and over lower-status workers. At the Royal Court, workers enjoyed exerting authority over their newer colleagues through training them, as we have seen. Front office workers there disliked Betsy, a new telephone operator, because she acted as if she knew how to do her job before she really understood it, failing to defer to more senior workers. These workers also often competed for concierge tasks in their effort to define themselves as concierges rather than front desk workers.

Doormen and concierges, who were well-placed on internal hierarchies, often emphasized both authority and income. The doormen at both hotels felt it was their responsibility to "run the door," as Joel said, deciding how to allocate the labor of bellmen and valet parkers. They also saw themselves as governing the curb; Dirk at the Luxury Garden told me, for example, "I let the sedans park here." As well as enjoying power over others, doormen were paid significantly more.

They tended to see this favored status as something they had earned by rising though the ranks. Commenting on the valets' complaints about not getting a cut of the doormen's tips for holding cars, Zeke, the doorman at the Royal Court, said, "Yeah, that's why you work your way up to being a doorman." Zeke disliked Joel partly because he had been hired as a doorman rather than working his way up from other positions or shifts, as Zeke and Haile had. Zeke grumbled that Joel "never had to work graveyard or anything." As we have seen, Ethan, a new bellman, overstepped his bounds by assuming entitlement to particular tips early in his tenure at the hotel, which caused conflict with Frankie.

For their part, concierges played up their cultural capital and corresponding authority by publicly discussing travel, fancy restaurants, and the arts. Hugh at the Royal Court liked to show off his knowledge of different food styles; Luxury Garden concierges often discussed foreign travel. One day Charlotte and Max were talking about Venice. She commented, "I think it's a more beautiful city than Paris." Max replied, "That depends if you can smell the canals." These conversations took place within earshot of front desk agents, who were unlikely to be familiar with anything concierges were discussing. Indeed, other workers—including managers—saw concierges as repositories of information having to do with culture and consumption and often asked them, for example, what restaurants they should try for special occasions.

Like doormen, concierges also emphasized the material advantages associated with the job, especially comparing their pay and fringe benefits with those of their colleagues. Concierges received a variety of perks, from free theater tickets to designer chocolates, and they took pleasure in and talked about these extras. Concierges at the Luxury Garden and Giovanna, Hugh, and Jackie at the Royal Court frequently mentioned restaurant or theater openings they had attended or lavish meals they had eaten free of charge in local restaurants. All the workers at the Luxury Garden desk knew that concierges received elaborate gifts from vendors, especially at Christmas (the year I was there, one massage therapist gave us all old-fashioned popcorn poppers). (At the same time, however, concierges wanted to avoid the impression that they were desperate for minor perks. Referring to an invitation to a restaurant's opening event designed specifically for concierges, Max told me, "I don't do openings or stand-up cocktails"; Charlotte asserted on another occasion, "I don't do cocktails.")

Concierges reinforced this sense of their own privilege more subtly as well. Concierges at the Luxury Garden were paid the same hourly rate as the front desk workers (fifteen dollars), with whom they labored side by side, but concierges received significant income from tips and commissions. Acutely aware of this discrepancy, Sydney told me on several occasions not to mention the "c-word" (commissions) or to talk too explicitly about money. Other concierges also tiptoed elaborately around the subject. This conspicuous avoidance of the topic felt to me like a subtle way for concierges to remind themselves of their privileged position vis-à-vis that of these other workers. On at least one occasion the concierges also bought gifts for the front desk staff, rearticulating their advantage through this ostensibly compensatory gesture.

Just as they disliked having their competence questioned, these higher-status workers, especially concierges, responded negatively to violations of their sense of authority and privilege. At the Luxury Garden, concierge and front desk positions were organizationally separate, but concierges still occasionally had to police these boundaries interactively. One day Damien talked about how well he had been treated at a local restaurant because he was from the Luxury Garden; he often made comments like this, attempting to emphasize privilege. Indicating that he was overstepping his bounds, Charlotte shut him down by responding, "And you're not even a concierge!" (which infuriated him). Alec told me one day to "keep an eye on" Damien, who would sometimes answer our phone when we were busy. I thought he was trying to help us, but Alec saw him as infringing on our territory. This boundary maintenance surely had to do in part with maximizing possibilities for tips, but it also served to foster the concierges' sense of organizational privilege.

Concierges were also irked when workers in other services, such as restaurant reservationists or travel agents, violated their sense of superiority, especially by talking down to them or telling them what to do. Irritated, Sydney said of a rude reservationist at an upscale restaurant, "She needs to remember she's working there, not dining there." Max complained about Dr. Kramer returning to the hotel, saying, "The worst part is that his little assistants are bossing us around." These comments imply that some people—the guests themselves—*are* entitled to exert authority over these workers. But by focusing on those below them, concierges emphasized their superior prerogatives.

Not surprisingly, workers' attempts to highlight their own perks and authority created conflict. Damien, Oscar, and Joey disliked Charlotte because she ordered them around. Daniel, a bellman at the Luxury Garden, told me the concierges "all think they're better than me." He saw them as obsessed with their tips and "compliments" from the guests, not caring about the workers who were "lower" than they. Daniel said that Alec ordered him around, on one occasion bellowing, "Daniel, come here right now!" Still irked, Daniel told me, "I am not a slave!"

Establishing authority and privilege relative to other workers overlaps with the emphasis on competence we saw earlier, because it depends on lateral comparisons and also leads to lateral conflict. But these comparisons also establish workers' superiority to their coworkers, arising from their greater authority, responsibility, and status. Focusing on their relative advantage is one strategy for minimizing the disadvantages high-status workers face in relation to hotel guests.

Status by Association

The high caliber of the Royal Court and the Luxury Garden and the high status of their guests also allowed workers to constitute themselves as superior to others by "borrowing prestige," as C. Wright Mills called it.[3] Interactive workers without high status or authority within the hotel, such as front desk workers, used this approach often. Their real or imagined interlocutors were not their immediate coworkers in this case but rather workers in other hotels and peers in their communities.

Workers at both of my sites were invested in the status of the hotel.[4] Clint at the Royal Court told me, "You get status from working here that you don't get from working at the Hyatt." Alec told me he liked the "glamour" of his job. While most workers did not make this kind of explicit claim, they took opportunities to emphasize their hotel's prestige, using indicators of luxury service as markers. Damien, a front desk worker at the Luxury Garden, told me proudly, "We never relocate our guests," meaning that the hotel never overbooked and therefore never walked anyone to another hotel. (He even used the more formal term *relocate* rather than *walk,* despite the informality of our conversation.) Sarah, in reservations at the Royal Court, was preoccupied with the possibility that the hotel would lose a star from its Mobil rating because the front desk was understaffed, saying, "Stars will be falling from the sky." On various occasions I heard front desk workers speak proudly of how much the rooms cost, using the high rates to signal exclusivity.

Jorge, the longtime bellman (who later resigned when his shift was changed), revealed how salient the hotel's high rating and high level of service were to him in his responses to my questions when he was training me. When I asked if there were coffeemakers in the rooms, he scoffed and said, "This is a five-star hotel" (which, as we know, it was not). I commented that it seemed like a hassle to go downstairs to get free coffee in the bar, and he answered, "There's always room service." When I responded that room service was pricey, Jorge said, "Well, it's a luxury hotel; it's expensive." He appeared to feel that if the guests had enough money to pay for the room, they would not mind paying for room service; in fact, he signaled that it was unconscionable to ask them to do anything for themselves or even to provide them the opportunity to do so. I also mentioned the limited-menu room service, asking what time the limitation started. Jorge misunderstood the question and replied, somewhat defensively, "It's not limited; it's twenty-four hours!" I said, "Yes, but it's a limited menu," and he responded, "Oh, yes, but of course it is," suggesting there was nothing wrong with that. In this exchange, Jorge coded guests' entitlement to consume workers' labor and not to exert labor themselves as a positive feature of the hotel, using an implicit comparison to less fancy hotels with lower standards.

Workers in various positions also explicitly differentiated their own work from that of workers in similar jobs at other, less prestigious hotels, casting themselves as more professional and providing superior service. One evening I was chatting with Oscar, a Luxury Garden doorman, about another hotel that had just opened. He said disparagingly, "Every time I walk by there, the doormen have their hands in their pockets." One day at the Royal Court I tossed Joel the keys to a car I had just parked, and he said, "Let's hand 'em. That's what they do at the Holiday Inn, throw keys. We're a little better than that; it's tacky." Concierges commented that they were happy not to work at a local convention hotel, where the limited means and high volume of the guests prompted concierges simply to send guests to the same restaurant and tourist attractions all the time, rather than confront the varied demands of a high-end clientele.

Luxury service standards thus allowed workers to intertwine prestige and competence. As the Luxury Garden's food and beverage director told me in an interview, "We can all pour coffee, but it's great to make them say 'wow.'" Workers who criticized colleagues for not observing luxury standards were also implicitly faulting them for failing to uphold the hotel's status. Alec told me, "You have to act very professional when you are dealing with other hotels, because they think of the Luxury Garden as the best." Hao, a Royal Court room service waiter, disparaged the restaurant's new chef for refusing to customize orders for guests; the former chef, Hao said, would whip up whatever the diner requested.

Guests could violate this sense of superiority by failing to recognize the status of the hotel, which irritated workers. If they asked about frequent points programs, associated with midrange chain hotels, workers frequently commented afterward, "Who do they think we are?" or "Tell them to try down the street at the Hilton." Ginger spoke to a caller who wanted a two-bedroom suite for $250 and said afterward, "What kind of idiot was that? Maybe at the Embassy Suites."

Yet exclusivity was marked not just by the hotel's stature but also by the wealth and status of the guests, which workers often emphasized. When I first began working at the Royal Court, Frankie the bellman told me proudly that the clients of the hotel were "always VIPs—presidents or CEOs or vice presidents of companies." Hugh, the Royal Court concierge, commented, "I love this hotel, the small size and the caliber of the guests, very refined." Alec explicitly constructed the status of the Luxury Garden guests as key to his capacity to do his job, saying, "I'm such a snob that I can't do this for people at a lower social level than me."

As we have seen, guests' wealth became an advantage for workers in that it allowed them to win games; here we see how it also helped them constitute status. Workers also felt that high-status guests were more entitled than others to consume their labor.

Workers distanced themselves from identification with the working class. They never referred to one another or themselves as workers, usually using the terms *staff* or *employees*. When my family was staying in the hotel, my father and I picked up cookies as a parting gift for my coworkers (this was common practice for workers' family members, who stayed at reduced rates). As we walked into the hotel, I said to Joel, "Look, we got cookies for the workers." He responded sarcastically, "Yeah, the *proletariat*," speaking, as I wrote in my notes, "in this way that was like the proletariat had nothing to do with him." I was unaware of any discussion of union organizing in either hotel, with the exception of a rumor that Royal Court restaurant workers were thinking about trying to unionize, which I heard only once.

One might assume that workers admired guests' wealth because they identified with guests or aspired to be rich themselves.[5] In my twelve months in both hotels, however, I spoke with only two workers who explicitly dreamed of consuming at the same level as guests.[6] Few workers seemed to believe or even wonder whether they could reach these heights of consumption, and often they criticized guests for their extravagance. Rather, the wealth of the guests fostered status by association as guest privilege symbolically rubbed off on workers.

CONDESCENSION AND CRITICISM: SUPERIORITY TO GUESTS

In my two sites, workers' capacity to see themselves as superior to others in their social and professional worlds depended on guests' higher social position and made a virtue of inequality. At the same time, however, workers found ways to look down on guests, turning their social advantages into indicators of psychological, social, and moral flaws. Workers cast themselves as powerful in relation to guests in two ways: sympathetically, constituting guests as disadvantaged, and critically, mobilizing a range of (sometimes contradictory) judgments to cast them as deficient.

As other authors have noted, workers' capacity to see themselves as superior often depends on their proximity to intimate aspects of clients' lives, what Judith Rollins calls "consciousness of the Other."[7] Interactive workers in both hotels had access to personal information because of the small size and high standards of the hotels, and this access encouraged them to notice and remember intimate details about the guest. Private information about guests was not only available in the guest history database but also circulated informally among workers. The frequency of guest stays also contributed to the accumulation of knowledge on which workers drew in judging guests.

Guests as Needy: Empathy and Condescension

Because workers knew about guest vulnerabilities, from a fear of heights or earthquakes to serious health problems, they could constitute themselves as powerful by feeling sorry for guests or protecting their personal information. They often demonstrated empathy for a difficult situation. For example, Sarah, the Royal Court reservationist, sympathetically counseled a female caller who was planning a stay at the hotel in order to avoid a psychotic neighbor. Restaurant workers felt compassion for a woman dining alone on her wedding anniversary because her husband had died two years previously. After saying hello to a restaurant guest, Haile told me that she had "stayed here when she had facial surgery, but we shouldn't talk about that." These were not hollow performances of empathy demanded by the standards of service, for workers expressed these feelings even in the absence of guests.[8]

Workers sometimes saw guests as deserving of empathy because they were somehow disadvantaged or dependent on workers. For example, they felt sorry for business travelers who had to work long hours. Charlotte, at the Luxury Garden, told me of these guests that "time is more important than money to them," casting them as disadvantaged because they lacked something that Charlotte, with her eight-hour shift, did have. Sydney, the guest services manager, told me, "The guest is depending on you to have a good time, or is depending on you for their business to go well." Workers also sympathized with guests when something went wrong for them. At the Royal Court, workers felt for guests who had been disturbed by the renovation, often commenting, "I'd be pissed too," when the water ran cold or loud drilling echoed in the building.

Workers often articulated their power over guests in a way that emphasized nurturing and care. Saul, a server at the Royal Court, told Annie and me over drinks one night after work that he enjoyed "making guests feel better." He told us about a couple who had dined in the restaurant the previous week. When they arrived, they were upset because they had missed a plane, but Saul "got them excited about the food, and they had a good time." Jackie described herself as "by nature a person who wants to make people happy." She found "something very nurturing about giving people a place to sleep," and she took pleasure in making them comfortable.[9]

Workers also established themselves as powerful through condescension to guests. Max told me that a "part of [his] heart" loved to give people a good time and give them service, "especially when it's a special occasion for them or they aren't used to this kind of traveling." Here he invoked an authentic self that gained pleasure from helping people who acted less entitled than other guests. Charlotte, who was new at the Luxury Garden, said she had enjoyed assisting guests more at her old job, at a larger and less high-end hotel, because they weren't "seasoned travelers." She thought that over time she might not be as inclined to serve the more demanding and entitled guests at the Luxury Garden.

I experienced a similar sense of condescension when a Luxury Garden guest asked several questions that revealed him as less experienced and possibly less wealthy than most. He asked how he and his wife could take flowers they had ordered for their room with them on a train; where they could find a McDonald's so they could get breakfast; and if we knew of a good Chinese restaurant that was "authentic" but where English was spoken. I wrote in my field notes, "He was clearly intimidated by the possibility of not being able to communicate. I kind of liked him because he was unsophisticated (also maybe didn't have much money since they were going to take two dozen roses with them). He gave me five dollars, and I didn't mind that as I had with [another guest]. Maybe this is what Charlotte was talking about in terms of helping people at her old job." These less worldly guests cast workers as experts, especially when they so clearly deferred to workers' authority.[10]

In general, many guests asked questions of workers involving directions, restaurants, entertainment, what they should wear to dinner, and so on. Guests frequently lacked confidence about whom to tip or how much or how other procedures worked within the hotel. They often told workers something along the lines of "We'll leave ourselves in your hands." Just as workers prized their authority over their coworkers, they valued this power over guests, manifesting both pride in their superior knowledge and satisfaction in being able to control guests in a certain way. One day at the Royal Court, for example, I was discussing some guests from the previous night with Giovanna; she said proudly, "They came in with a whole page [of possible restaurants] from the newspaper, but they ended up going where I wanted them to go."

Workers objected when guests violated their sense of self as knowledgeable and authoritative. Jasmine was irritated with a guest who requested driving directions and then disdained her advice; she asked, "Why did he ask if he already knows?" Charlotte was annoyed with two men who requested a dinner reservation at "someplace trendy" and then rejected both of the reservations she made for them. They had stopped by one of the restaurants early and told her that "nothing was happening." She said to me, "They went at like 5:00; of course nothing was happening." She was offended by the implication that she didn't know what she was doing, as well as annoyed that they failed to appreciate an 8:00 reservation at a desirable restaurant. By disputing the workers' authority, guests revealed the asymmetry of the relation and the worker's fundamentally subordinate status.

When they could not feel superior in terms of knowledge or experience, workers sometimes used guests' wealth as a way of feeling sorry for them, commenting that rich people were not necessarily content.[11] Workers sometimes said they felt sorry for guests because they "have to pay us to be friends with them." Sometimes they even used mistreatment by guests as an opportunity for condescension. For instance, Peter at the Royal Court speculated almost sympathetically that Mrs. Ingram, a highly demanding frequent guest, was rude to us because "she has no friends and has to abuse someone."

The requisites of luxury supported workers' self-conceptions as powerful. Jennifer Pierce and Arlie Hochschild have shown that paralegals and flight attendants empower themselves in relation to attorneys and passengers by likening them to children.[12] In the case of hotel service, however, knowledge about the guests allows workers to constitute this kind of caring condescension on the basis of real characteristics rather than infantilizing analogies. Furthermore, the capacity to focus on the guest's vulnerability is facilitated not only by the knowledge but also by the time workers have; if the volume of interactions were greater and more routine, as they were in the speeded-up airline industry that Hochschild studied and as they are in nonluxury hotels, this strategy would be less feasible.

Guest Transgressions: Entertainment and Judgment

In a contradictory but simultaneous move, workers also constituted themselves as superior through criticism rather than empathy. Here superiority was based not on guest vulnerabilities such as illness or lack of time, experience, or knowledge, but rather on individual idiosyncrasies or character flaws. Workers used their intimate access to make fun of guests and judge them on a wide and sometimes contradictory range of criteria. They told countless lurid tales of sexual, illegal, or disgusting acts of various kinds. One evening a frequent Royal Court guest urinated in his wastebasket, presumably because he was drunk; by the next day all the workers in the hotel knew about it. They also gleefully discussed another frequent guest who had invited a prostitute to his room, called the desk at 4:00 A.M. "all coked up," according to Brad, and the next day overflowed his bathtub. At the Luxury Garden, workers knew that one repeat guest stashed pornographic magazines in the hotel and that another had received an erotic fax. As these examples demonstrate, workers shared intimate information and created a kind of culture of entertainment based on it.

Sometimes workers reframed demands for labor or complaints as a source of amusement, often evaluating guests on the basis of their intelligence. One guest at the Royal Court called the desk because he could not get his computer connected to the Internet; Jasmine could not help him over the phone, and so Brad reluctantly went up to his room. When he returned, he told Jasmine, "You have to say, [in patronizing voice] 'Are you sure you checked all your connections, Mr. D'Angelo?'" The lesson was never to assume that the guest had any basic competence. One Luxury Garden guest complained about absolutely every aspect of his visit. Because his window would not stay open, he propped it ajar with his telephone, which of course fell over twenty stories to the ground; the staff all made fun of him. Just as they constructed their colleagues as incompetent on the job, workers saw these guests as incompetent in the basic operations of life and thus in need of workers' assistance. As one Luxury Garden assistant manager put it, "The more money guests have, the less common sense they have."

Although they sometimes felt positively inclined toward unsophisticated guests, as I have said, concierges also evaluated them on the basis of their taste, thereby establishing themselves as superior in terms of cultural capital. Workers frequently made fun of guests for requesting items that the staff thought of as tacky or inappropriate, such as "the fanciest restaurant" and, on one occasion, blue roses.[13] Max often referred to guests as "Philistines." When Charlotte saw that I'd made a reservation for a guest at a restaurant she considered overrated, she said, "Eew, did the guest request that?" as if she were trying to decide whether it was me or the guest who was in the dark (if it had been me, she would have worried that the guest would not like the restaurant). At the Royal Court restaurant, workers made fun of guests who were unfamiliar with the *amuse-bouche*, the tiny pre-appetizer delivered compliments of the house to each diner. (But at the same time, they distanced themselves from this cultural marker by calling it the "Amish bush.")

Workers judged guests, especially women, on the basis of their appearance, which in some cases was also an issue of cultural capital. Stan, a Royal Court assistant manager, said of a woman wearing a tight leopard-skin pantsuit, "Why don't they put a leash on her?" When a woman in a particularly atrocious outfit walked by, Max commented,

"Wait until you see what they wear for the holidays." At the Luxury Garden, Antonio referred to one woman as a "blond Barbie"; Carolyn typed into the computer for me to see that another guest looked "like she's wearing a lab coat." Workers also made fun of guests who had had face-lifts or other obvious plastic surgery; Royal Court workers in particular frequently speculated about which guests had "fake breasts."

Workers also evaluated guests on a moral scale, criticizing them for selfishness and lauding them for altruism.[14] Mrs. Bennett was both demanding of my time and indecisive about what restaurants she wanted to go to, saying that she was concerned about her son's enjoyment; when I expressed frustration to Sydney, she said, "She doesn't really care about the son; she only cares about herself." Max, who had referred to the Melmots as "black holes of darkness," later said, "The thing that redeems him in my eyes is that I've heard him on the phone with his son, and he sounds like a good dad."

This moral evaluation sometimes had to do with guests' use of money. Workers judged guests negatively for being tightfisted even when the workers would not have benefited materially from the guests' spending. One guest called the concierge desk at the Luxury Garden to ask if he could transport his twelve-year-old son to a small city about an hour away on a train or bus; several workers expressed shock that the guest would even consider not sending the boy with a car and driver. Front desk workers also derided a male guest who was in the hotel with his mother and sisters (celebrating the mother's birthday) because he allowed his mother to pay for the family's stay.

Yet workers also judged guests' extravagant spending habits negatively, coding them as excessive. Charlotte raised her eyebrows when describing a couple who had spent ten thousand dollars to travel up the coast in a helicopter and then fly on short notice to England. Max acerbically described one frequent guest: "She wears a diamond the size of a quarter, and her maid sleeps in the room with her in case she needs anything in the night." He told me she had spent three thousand dollars to go to Canada for the day.

Another moral failing related to money was to act too entitled. One day a young German woman asked us to find a German-speaking dentist, which we did; but she took forty-five minutes to get ready to go, by which time the dentist had left for the day. Alec said, explaining his lack of concern for her toothache, "She looks a little spoiled." Giovanna at the Royal Court had to tell a French couple that the suite they had been upgraded to on a previous visit was not available, and they grumbled about it. She commented afterward, "People are so spoiled." (As she made this moral critique, however, she let me know that she had understood everything they had been saying between themselves in French, demonstrating her own cultural capital.)

Workers sometimes gleaned satisfaction from seeing guests confronted with poverty. Annie told a story about guests who had gone to a local restaurant in a somewhat dicey neighborhood; they were sitting at a window table, and "there was a big white Cadillac outside, and some guy came along and got on top of it and took a big ol' shit." She giggled as she recounted how horrified the guests had been upon their return to the hotel. Celine, a restaurant manager, said she laughed when people requested a window table, because the window looked out on an alley; she said, "All they see is trash and homeless people."

Thus, money was reframed as only one of a variety of individual characteristics, subordinate to moral and other aspects of the guest. Furthermore, it was not even an especially desirable attribute; Joel told me, for example, that he had learned over time that "having money doesn't mean you are happy or a good person or have any integrity." As Lamont has written, "By subordinating social status to what they perceive to be the 'real' value of a person, workers create the possibility of locating themselves at the top of the hierarchy."[15]

In these moral judgments and entertainments lurks the possibility of a structural critique of disparity, similar to what Paul Willis has called "partial penetration."[16] Workers sometimes cast individual guests' extravagance and entitlement as unnecessary and even morally wrong. For example, after complaining guests left the desk, Giovanna commented, "I don't have much compassion for them—there are people dying in the world." These judgments emerged especially when guests made demands that interfered with workers' own strategies of self, making it hard for workers to downplay their own subordination. More often, however, the moralization of wealth tied it to individual personality rather than to an asymmetrical social system.

Concierges, who possessed significant cultural capital but limited economic capital, were especially ambivalent about high-end consumption. Sometimes they aligned themselves with guests by letting it be known that they consumed at the same level. On our way back from an errand to buy wine for a guest, for example, Max suggested we stop by a cashmere store, where he pointed out to me the items he already owned. More explicitly, Hugh, one of the more professionalized concierges at the Royal Court, commented to a frequent guest arriving exhausted after a flight from Indonesia, "Whenever I go to Asia, I have to take a sleeping pill." In chatting with a guest about property she had recently purchased, Antonio mentioned that he had been thinking about buying land in a similar area.

Concierges also emphasized their privileged access to the same services guests paid through the nose for, as we have seen, but at the same time questioned their value. Hugh mentioned repeatedly one evening that he had been invited to a fancy restaurant opening. But he was not planning to attend, he said, explaining, "On my night off I'd rather stay home and eat a peanut butter and jelly sandwich." I asked Giovanna if she had ever paid four hundred dollars for a hotel room; she replied, "No, and I never will." However, a few weeks later, she was very excited about an upcoming trip to another city, saying, "I get to stay in a fancy hotel for a hundred dollars" because of her industry connections. It was thus largely their own *special access* to the same services guests consumed that gave concierges a sense of advantage over their coworkers and over guests. In a sense concierges were caught in a kind of contradictory class location; their strategy was to invoke their cultural capital while distancing themselves from economic capital.

A few workers said that their expectations about their own consumption and their sense of taste had changed since they had begun working in the hotel. Alec at the Luxury Garden mentioned one evening that he was going out for margaritas after work; he said he drank only "top shelf" tequila now, explaining, "You get accustomed to better things in this job." Naomi, the assistant to the general manager, agreed with him. I have mentioned that other workers often asked concierges for advice about local restaurants; this process was one of self-education in cultural capital that was facilitated if not caused by their experience in the hotel. Often managers made the same point; the Luxury Garden general manager, Sebastian, told me in an interview that he and his wife had begun to live a more elegant lifestyle since he had arrived at the hotel, which was also true of a food and beverage director at the Luxury Garden.

"WHAT MORE DOES HE WANT?"
LIMITING ENTITLEMENT

Combining elements of status and judgment strategies, workers also acted as the self-appointed guardians of boundaries around guest entitlement to stay in the hotel and to consume luxury service. Articulating symbolic limits allowed workers to negotiate their own effort, to reinforce their sense of the high status and exclusivity of the hotel, and to cast themselves as powerful gatekeepers. They coded having money as a necessary but insufficient criterion for access. In making distinctions among guests, workers symbolically reduced the number of people who were entitled to their subordinate labor. Yet by casting some guests as unworthy, they implicitly acknowledged that others *were* legitimately entitled.

Workers consistently complained on finding that a person requesting services was not a guest. On my first day at the Luxury Garden, an older couple came by the desk and asked if we knew of a prix fixe lunch. After searching in the computer and making a few calls, Max finally found a place they could go, and they left. Then Lou, a bellman, came over and said they were not guests—they had come in to use the bathroom. Max said, "If I'd known that, we would have had a very different conversation." Jack, a doorman at the Luxury Garden, told me his biggest headache involved workers from the nearby office building who expected him to get them taxis.

Workers also disliked guests who were staying at low rates, seeing them as not entitled to consume either the hotel's service or the workers' labor. One day a woman checked into the Luxury Garden at a special XYZ club rate. Damien commented that she couldn't be an XYZ member, because it included only very wealthy people, and he knew she was the sales manager at another hotel. He was upset about it and wanted to ask her for the XYZ card to expose her, even though it was clear the Luxury Garden sales manager had given her the better rate as a favor. I said, "What difference does it make? It's so slow, we need to sell the rooms." Damien responded, "We shouldn't sell them so dirt cheap." Reservationists at both hotels similarly tried to make sure only people entitled to corporate rates received them, and they poked fun at callers who "fished" for lower prices by pretending to be from a company with a low corporate rate. Though guests who paid low rates might have had more in common economically with workers, they violated the hotel's exclusivity and, by extension, the workers' sense of prestige by association. In serving these guests, workers felt they were subordinating themselves to the wrong people.

Workers often considered the complaints of guests who were paying less to be less important and resented having to exert effort for them. One older man at the Royal Court said he loved the hotel but complained that the phone in his room only rang twice before voice mail picked up. While we were looking into the problem, Giovanna said to me, annoyed, "He's not even paying for it." When I forgot to confirm a guest's sedan pickup at the airport until immediately before the scheduled pickup time, Alec checked her reservation, noted the low rate she was paying, and said, "It's all right; she's a nobody."

Workers also drew limits around entitlement to VIP status, which they coded as something to be earned. A Luxury Garden sales worker muttered to herself about an incoming guest, "He *thinks* he's a VIP, but he's not." When a man complained that no one recognized him even though he was a frequent guest, Becky, a concierge, derided him to her coworkers, saying, "He's been here five times. I hate to tell you, but you're not a frequent guest. Talk to me about Mr. X, Y, or Z" (whom she thought of as real frequent guests). One evening when we were oversold at the Royal Court, Petra told us to be sure to save rooms for four men who were coming in together, because one of them had been walked to another hotel the previous week and so was entitled to better treatment this time. Giovanna scoffed at the idea that they were to be treated as VIPs "just because we walked one of them."

By the same token, workers became annoyed when guests demanded a better room, seeing them as unappreciative of upgrades or low rates they had already received. They would moan, "What more does he want?" As I noted after one shift at the Luxury Garden:

> People kept trying to get upgrades, saying that if we were slow why couldn't we give it to them. This annoys the workers. One guy in particular was really pissing off Pearl and Carolyn, because they had already upgraded him five categories and he wanted more. Carolyn said to Pearl to just "tell him it's not available," but Pearl wasn't able to satisfy him so Carolyn had to talk to him. . . . It's not only that they want the upgrade but the fact that they don't appreciate the upgrade they already got— Pearl was pointing at the screen and saying "Five!" about the number of categories he'd already been upgraded.

One might assume that it would not matter to workers which room the guest stays in or how much he pays. But when they demand more from workers, guests do not see that they have already received more than they "deserve." Their misplaced sense of entitlement again denotes failure to recognize both the hotel's status and the condescending benevolence of the worker herself.

Mr. Weiss, the Royal Court's general manager, referred to guests who were constantly trying to get something for nothing as "sportsmen of price," adding that he withheld labor from these guests when they complained unreasonably. As I paraphrased in my interview notes, "The sportsman will whine, and you have to decide what's valid, sometimes give nothing but an apology. . . . Mr. Weiss makes the money-grubbing guest work, whereas with a guest he likes he might give more than the guest asks." By making this distinction he also suggested that some people are not entitled to luxury service (and asserted his own sense of control over the guest).

Workers also judged entitlement to access on the basis of a range of guest behaviors and characteristics beyond the conditions under which they were staying in the hotel. Workers criticized guests' appearance, for example, not only because the workers did not personally like what the guests wore, but also because informal or ugly outfits violated a sense of how they *should* look in the hotel. Hugh, the fastidious and professional Royal Court concierge, dismissively shunted a group of informally dressed potential guests off to me, working as a bellperson, when they wanted to see a room. I thought he was unusually cold to them. I later realized why when he commented placidly as they left, "It's rare to see a person in our hotel dressed in sweats." On another occasion a male guest sported tattoos all over his arms; while he was conversing with another worker, Annie and Ginger stood in the back and laughed about them.

Critiques of guests' cultural capital also enforced this kind of mental boundary. Max predicted that one couple would complain about the price of a trendy restaurant I sent them to, because they had also asked about a much less prestigious locale. Implying that they were not entitled to such consumption, he said that by setting up the reservation, I was putting "pearls before swine." Damien, the front desk worker at the Luxury Garden who prided himself on his own sophistication, frequently referred to guests as "trailer trash." He labeled one guest as "not refined enough"—the *enough* suggesting that the true Luxury Garden guest must possess some minimum level of refinement. A server at the Royal Court restaurant came into the kitchen one evening to prepare hot hand towels for a guest who had requested them; he was muttering to himself, "I know you're white trailer trash, so get off your high horse." Although he was required to perform this highbrow service, his response shows that he felt the guest was not entitled to request it. This stance contrasts with the sympathetic condescension that workers sometimes felt for unsophisticated guests. The difference might be simply the worker's mood, though sometimes harsh criticism emerged when guests were not sufficiently deferential to workers (which I discuss further in the next chapter). Their lack of cultural capital here becomes the basis for symbolic exclusion rather than empathy.

The most striking example of transgression of these boundaries occurred at the Royal Court when a group of musicians and journalists from a well-known rap magazine stayed there. This group was unusual for the hotel, because they were all African American and they dressed very differently from and were more boisterous than most guests. As I wrote in my notes, "there were a lot of raised eyebrows all the time" among workers throughout their stay. Giovanna made fun of one of them for calling the desk and asking, "What kind of fish do you have today?" as if that were ridiculous, even though it happened because the room service telephones had mistakenly been forwarded to the front desk. These guests were a hot topic of conversation among the workers, who criticized them for playing loud music in their rooms until 4:00 A.M. and for calling the front desk demanding alcohol in the middle of the night. This criticism arose partly because workers had to pacify other irate guests. But these clients also clearly violated a racialized behavioral norm.

Again, workers also judged guests for not having or spending enough money, making such judgments not only as entertainment but also in order to create boundaries. Jorge's comment about the coffee mentioned earlier ("Well, it's a luxury hotel; it's expensive") showed that he expected guests to be able to pay for coffee delivered by room service. Jasmine made the same point explicitly when I said I thought there should be coffeemakers in the rooms; she responded that it wasn't necessary, because "these people have enough money to order room service if they don't want to come downstairs" to get free coffee in the bar. Melinda, who worked in the business center at the Luxury Garden, told me to watch out for guests who wanted to do the copying themselves instead of paying us to do it. She thought this practice was outrageous, declaring, "This isn't St. Anthony's; we are not a charity." Sometimes, as we have seen, this was an issue of winning games, because guests who consumed minimal worker labor did not usually tip. But it was also a more general issue of the type of guest whom workers felt it was legitimate to serve, articulated even by those who had nothing to gain materially.

In these ways workers limited the range of people who were "really" entitled to their service, in contrast to the unlimited expenditure of labor expected of them in the luxury environment. They categorized guests into those who were legitimately "above" them (and from whom they could glean status by association) and those who were not (toward whom they could manifest condescension and negative judgment). These limits were mostly symbolic, because workers could refuse to offer service in only the subtlest ways. But, like the other strategies I have described, these distinctions and judgments made hierarchy beneficial to workers in terms of how they thought about themselves.

MANAGERIAL REGIMES AND HIERARCHY

Workers in both sites used all of these strategies of superiority, which might therefore seem to arise independently of the managerial regimes of the two hotels. This might be the case for two reasons. First, moral and aesthetic judgments were embedded in broad cultural repertoires common to workers in both hotels (although workers possessed different amounts of cultural capital to use in making judgments). And second, guests varied little between the two hotels in terms of their behavior, providing relatively constant objects of both empathy and judgment. Indeed, I suspect that a closer look at other kinds of service work would reveal a similar use of comparison, in which workers draw on cultural repertoires, working conditions, and relations with clients to situate themselves as powerful and entitled.

Again, however, these particular strategies are embedded in their contexts and affected by them.[17] A comparison of the two hotels shows that managerial regimes, the division of labor, and internal labor markets contributed to workers' opportunities for using comparative strategies of self.

Supporting Superiority at the Luxury Garden

The characteristics of the Luxury Garden dovetailed with workers' strategies of superiority, as they did with regard to the games and professional selfhood I have discussed. The rigid and visible division of labor made superiority to other workers easy to establish. The concierges were privileged vis-à-vis the front desk workers, who were themselves higher up than the telephone operators, and so on. The high rating of the hotel constituted a resource on which interactive workers with more routine work—especially at the front desk—could draw to gain a sense of status by association. And internal labor markets allowed these workers to move up from less prestigious jobs within the hotel, which reinforced the internal occupational hierarchy.

The more developed corporate culture at the Luxury Garden also fostered strategies of status and empathy. Managerial rhetoric explicitly highlighted the status of the hotel and its guests, allowing workers to glean a sense of prestige by association. Training sessions were peppered with references to the elevated status of guests ("the top 1 percent"), as well as to the high ranking and multiple awards of Luxury Garden properties around the world. The videos that Alice showed in the orientation emphasized the high quality of the Luxury Garden product.[18] She told workers about a time when a man at a conference saw her name tag and asked, "The Luxury Garden, what's that?" because he had never heard of it; a woman passing by turned and said, "Just the best hotel in the world." Here, Alice used the hotel's lack of name recognition in the United States as an indicator of exclusivity rather than obscurity.

Indeed, managerial rhetoric encouraged workers to undertake self-transformation in relation to class behaviors. Workers were subtly encouraged to adopt the class mannerisms of guests (or perhaps ideal-typical upper-class manners), such as not chewing gum and wearing only "tasteful" amounts of makeup and jewelry. Managers and written materials also emphasized the use of proper vocabulary, avoiding words such as *hi* and *okay* and replacing them with *good evening* and *my pleasure* or *certainly*. The hotel required workers to attend a two-day etiquette training, in which they learned to eat with the tines of their forks pointing down and not to touch guests. The cultivation of a particular appearance, vocabulary, and behavior not only constrained workers but also gave them a resource for self-constitution, indicating that they could adopt a particular class identity by virtue of their association with the hotel.[19]

Trainers at the Luxury Garden also coded guests as dependent on workers and thus deserving of empathy. While managerial rhetoric sometimes helped workers to see guests as "above" them, it also brought the guest "down" to the worker's level, encouraging her to see the guest as "just human," with basic needs similar to her own. Alice invoked Abraham Maslow's "hierarchy of needs" in more than one training session I attended, thus framing the guests' desires as objective, fundamental needs.[20] In the same vein, she emphasized in the orientation that clients might be lost in an unfamiliar city or tired after an arduous journey. Even after acknowledging that guests were very wealthy—"probably not me or you or our friends"—she said, "The things money can't buy for them are great service and quiet." Here, she situated the worker as having something the guests needed, something simple that with their hectic lives they could not often obtain. And she presented that something as decommodified, as if money were not buying it in this instance but rather workers were giving it of their own accord.

Hence, workers at the Luxury Garden could easily draw on strategies of privilege, status, and condescension and were less likely than workers at the Royal Court to articulate these explicitly. It went without saying—because managers had already said it—that the Luxury Garden was the best and that its workers therefore commanded status. For example, concierges could reinforce their privilege vis-à-vis front desk workers, as we have seen, by avoiding mention of their commissions instead of repeatedly invoking them. Luxury Garden workers often took pride in their responsibility for guest secrets (they still talked about them, but less openly than workers at the Royal Court). And workers there did not constantly compare themselves aloud with their colleagues. The style of these workers was also more delicate than that of Royal Court workers. Though workers often judged guests, especially on the basis of cultural capital, these judgments were wittier and more veiled. They referred to guests as "Philistines," "psychos," and "beasts" (as in, "the beasts are starting to awake," as Sydney said to me one Sunday morning when the concierge phone began to ring).

Luxury Garden workers especially emphasized exclusiveness and cultural capital in their views of guests. They tended to articulate limits to entitlement more frequently than their Royal Court counterparts. They saw VIP status or upgrades as attainable only to a chosen few. And their condescension toward guests was based more on guests' lack of experience, which reinforced workers' own greater knowledge, than on guests' personal difficulties.

"Authentic" Empathy at the Royal Court

At the Royal Court, as we have seen, workers (often younger than their Luxury Garden counterparts) had fewer resources with which to constitute themselves as professional as a result of the organization of work, inconsistent managerial intervention, and a lack of training and corporate culture. The same was true of these comparative strategies of self. The flexible and fairly flat division of labor made comparisons with other workers in terms of status and material advantages more difficult. The division of labor also limited the perks of the concierge job. For example, front desk/concierge workers at the Royal Court received fewer invitations to restaurants and events than their counterparts at the Luxury Garden, partly because the concierge list named twelve people in contrast to the usual four or five.[21] And because a smaller percentage of their work was concierge-related, they received fewer tips than their Luxury Garden counterparts.

Managerial discourses about the status of the hotel and its guests and about workers' advantages over guests were also limited. In the orientation, Nicole, the human resources director, repeatedly characterized the hotel as a luxury property. The sales director described the accolades of the hotel, telling workers, "You should be very proud to be working at the Royal Court." She handed out copies of the sales packet that described awards the hotel had won, which workers could "show off" to their friends. But this was the extent of playing up the hotel's prestige. Managers did not emphasize themes of empathy and responsibility either in the orientation or in daily communications with workers (which, as we saw in chapter 2, had an informal tone).

Thus, again, two varieties of worker strategy—professionalism and independence—predominated. The same workers I identified in the last chapter as using professionalism strategies—the front door workers and Giovanna and Hugh at the concierge desk, as well as most of the young European workers—used the same approaches that their Luxury Garden counterparts invoked: job privilege, status by association, and judgment of guests on the basis of cultural capital and entitlement to access. For doormen, institutionalized structural privilege made this easier. The internal labor market at the door and the doormen's clear authority in this department facilitated a sense of prestige relative to other workers. Concierge workers, however, had to distinguish themselves without the help of an official division of labor, hence their repeated and explicit denigration of the telephone operator job and competition for concierge tasks. Whereas Luxury Garden concierges went out of their way not to mention their privileges vis-à-vis front desk workers, for example, Giovanna seemed always to be talking about her free consumption at fancy restaurants.

The less-professionalized workers at the Royal Court, in contrast, avoided judgments of guests on the basis of cultural capital (as their own was limited) and entitlement to access, although they did try to emphasize the hotel's status vis-à-vis nonluxury properties. Concomitant with the hotel's emphasis on authenticity, their strategies of condescension more often invoked empathy for a difficult situation than the pleasure of providing a good time for inexperienced travelers. They tended to use cruder forms of entertainment and judgment than workers at the Luxury Garden did, focusing primarily on guests' ridiculous behaviors and their appearance rather than their entitlement. It was common for the less-professionalized workers to laugh outrageously at guests behind their backs. These workers used cruder language in relation to guests (words such as *asshole, bitch,* and *big fat ho*). These workers overtly circulated more personal information about guests as well.

Lucille, a middle-aged Chinese woman, exemplified the way managerial behavior and structure influenced workers' self-conceptions, especially the link between the hotel's status and worker professionalism and pride. After years as a housekeeper at the Luxury Garden, she had been promoted to full-time work at the front desk there; she also worked part-time as a telephone operator at the Royal Court. She was very invested in the success of the Luxury Garden, but she continually disparaged the Royal Court. I worked with her first at the Royal Court, where one day she told me that the Luxury Garden had finally been awarded its fifth

Mobil star. She was gleeful about this and excited about the "big party" management was planning to celebrate. A few weeks later, she told me proudly that one of the concierges at the Luxury Garden had won a local award and pointed out that no one at the Royal Court had won one. In these ways, Lucille used the Royal Court as a foil in order to construct the Luxury Garden's superior prestige. Furthermore, her behavior and attitude were notably more professional at the Luxury Garden than at the Royal Court.

THE COMPARATIVE SELF

Goffman wrote, "Perhaps we should . . . [define] the individual, for sociological purposes, as a stance-taking entity, a something that takes up a position somewhere between identification with an organization and opposition to it, and is ready at the slightest pressure to regain its balance by shifting its involvement in either direction. It is thus *against something* that the self can emerge."[22] The discourses I have analyzed in this chapter illustrate the comparative constitution of self that Goffman invokes and its contradictory dimension. Mobilizing a range of discourses of self and other, workers attempted to neutralize their subordinate position by establishing a superior ranking on alternative hierarchies. First, workers focused on the elements of their jobs that gave them advantages in relation to others (perks and the caliber of the hotel). Second, their perspectives on guests reduced the possession of money to just one of many possible good qualities, such as being competent, attractive, knowledgeable, or morally upright. Indeed, often workers' judgments suggested that many of these latter qualities are especially difficult for rich people to achieve, making wealth a kind of liability. Third, workers' policing of guest entitlement reinforced both the workers' own status and the idea that money alone does not guarantee the right to their subordinating labor. Theorists of symbolic boundaries tend to look at how privileged groups' exclusion of less powerful ones reproduces social inequalities. In this case, symbolic exclusion of the rich by the workers legitimated and normalized stratification.

Michèle Lamont has usefully shown that workers find ways to locate themselves favorably on symbolic hierarchies, but she neglects the way these strategic locations shift. An ethnographic look at practice, rather than interviews, indicates that workers do not carry around consistent "mental maps," as Lamont suggests people do.[23] We have seen that workers' symbolic locations were flexible in two ways, both linked to the strategic deployment of particular discourses and interpretations. First, these interpretations were contradictory, often appealing to seemingly incongruous values and judgments.[24] Workers articulated shifting opinions of guests rather than a single standard of *the* desirable guest, for workers' criteria changed according to which hierarchy benefited them. They judged guests on both stinginess and profligacy, on lack of experience and the behavior of excessive entitlement. They looked up to guests symbolically, gaining self-worth from guests' status, but they also looked down on guests, either condescendingly or critically. The same characteristics that sometimes made guests sympathetic, such as a lack of familiarity with the luxury environment, could also be used as entertainment. Second, workers could not simply automatically apply a predetermined boundary to determine who was in and who was out; rather, they had to *work* to locate themselves above others. They had to take into consideration (albeit implicitly) the circumstances and behaviors around them in order to mobilize appropriate judgments. Like the luxury service product itself, these boundaries were thus formed within organizations and interactions.

In these discourses, workers invoked contrasting understandings of inequality and money. They valued material and status advantages over those who were below them on these hierarchies (other workers and peers) but cast these advantages as minimal in terms of those who were above them (guests). In so doing, workers used this collectively constituted repertoire of judgments to recode wealth as an individual characteristic, on a par with traits such as intelligence and morality, instead of a structural condition. Thus, income disparity and unequal entitlement were normalized through their recasting as individual.

These "alternative measuring sticks," as Lamont calls them, include the seeds of a more critical approach to social structure.[25] And some of the practices and critiques I have described did constitute momentary resistance to the imperative of self-subordination. However, for the most part workers simply limited entitlement without challenging it. As workers placed boundaries on access to the hotel and to their labor, they indicated implicitly that some people did have the right to consume that labor. Keeping some people out allowed others in and complicated the emergence of a structural or comprehensive critique. Thus, the resistance workers enacted tended to be toward *less* wealthy guests, whom the workers did not see as entitled to consume their labor. Furthermore, these limits were primarily symbolic; though imaginary boundaries allowed workers to construct a not-subordinate self, workers still had to provide access and labor to all guests.

These discourses, like the games we saw in chapter 3, blurred distinctions between "inside" and "outside" work as sites for the creation of selfhood in the service workplace. On the one hand, workers' capacity to make strategic interpretations, like their ability to play games, was constructed within the production-consumption process.[26] The hierarchy that made lateral comparisons possible, the prestige of the hotel and its guests, and managerial rhetoric and practice all influenced workers' strategies. Workers in the two hotels, as we have seen, had different opportunities for self-constitution; those in nonluxury environments might draw on other possibilities entirely.

At the same time, however, workers' strategies of self illuminated the fluidity of boundaries between the "point of production" and the rest of the world. The interlocutors with whom workers engaged literally and metaphorically, especially in their strategies of status and prestige, such as their own friends and peers and workers in other hotels or in lateral services, often resided physically outside the hotel. The judgments workers made of guests, positive and negative, also depended on broader cultural criteria that are not shaped solely within work. Finally, these judgments also depended on guest behavior, which is imported into the workplace. Chapter 5 examines this behavior and the relations between workers and guests as they mutually construct a version of legitimate entitlement that depends on reciprocity.

FIVE Reciprocity, Relationship, and Revenge

When I first started working at the Royal Court, at the telephone operator station, I was shocked by how friendly callers were. They were gracious, sympathetic, and funny: for example, one guest commented jokingly when I answered the phone, "You were on last night, Rachel! Do they make you work every night?" They even seemed to use *my* name more often than I, not having quite figured out the telephone display, used theirs. Over time, I saw guests express gratitude to workers, tip them, and even go out of their way to bring them gifts or do favors for them. My experience of this reciprocal treatment reached its height at the Luxury Garden, when an incoming guest for whom I had planned dinner reservations for several nights, as well as entertainment on New Year's Eve, had to cancel his trip because of a death in his family. He sent me a bouquet of orchids worth seventy-five dollars, included an apologetic note, and called the next day to make sure I had received the flowers.

Also in my first few weeks at the Royal Court, I noticed that many workers spoke positively about guests and often enjoyed longstanding relationships with frequent visitors. One day during my reservations training, Juliane and Sarah chatted animatedly about Mrs. Flite, who turned out to be an elderly lady known for her collection of outrageous hats, and told me how much they looked forward to seeing her. One afternoon a few weeks later, Peter was looking at the list of that day's arrivals and said, "Oh, the O'Learys are coming in today, good!" He told me proudly, "They've stayed here over a hundred times." Workers at the Luxury Garden were eager to see Mr. Henry and talked about how nice he was; when he arrived, he gave Dirk the doorman a baseball cap from his business.

These practices and relationships confused me. Weren't service workers supposed to be resentful of clients, and weren't customers supposed to be rude? And in the luxury setting, wouldn't wealthy and entitled guests be especially abusive to workers? Guests had told me in interviews that they always treated workers respectfully, but I was skeptical of these claims. And I had heard the denigrating comments, described in the last chapter, that workers made about guests.

As it turned out, however, the great majority of guests in both hotels treated workers respectfully and often generously. Indeed, they went out of their way to establish parity with workers rather than subordination. Workers valued these relationships and reciprocal treatment, seeing it not as denigrating but as humanizing. In fact, reciprocity was the key mechanism regulating worker-guest interactions. Both workers and guests coded reciprocity as an obligation, which established an implicit contract between them.

On the basis of these reciprocal relations, workers constituted themselves as not subordinate in a new way—not as above guests, as we saw in the last chapter, but as equal to them in terms of sharing a common humanity and entitlement to equal treatment. Unlike the autonomous and comparative dimensions of self we saw in previous chapters, which take guests as objects to be manipulated or judged, the equal self is constituted intersubjectively, in relationship. Investment in these relationships fostered workers' consent and helped to normalize inequality by casting these relations as individual. Enacting symbolic and practical revenge on guests who did not behave as workers thought they should, thereby violating the contract, was a form of resistance. But it was also a way to police a set of rules governing guests' behavior. These relations remained both structurally and interactively asymmetrical—guests still held more authority and greater entitlement to labor and recognition—but reciprocity helped to recast this asymmetry as parity.

Guest practices of respectful treatment and reciprocity arose partly from a "moral norm of reciprocity"[1] that governs social interactions in a wide range of spheres. Guests also had individual motivations; they wanted to avoid feeling exploitative, and they wanted their relations with workers to feel genuine. Interpreting workers' attentions as voluntary rather than commodified required guests themselves to perform interactive work. Yet features specific to the luxury product and environment also facilitate positive guest behavior, which is one of the reasons my findings differ from those of other researchers in this regard. Characteristics of the luxury hotel setting, the service, and the guests themselves make reciprocal behavior especially likely. Thus, the very asymmetry of the relation enables personal interactions and genuine relationships to develop.

RECIPROCAL RECOGNITION

As might be expected, worker-guest relationships ranged from fleeting encounters in which one-time guests asked little of workers to relationships developed over years with frequent guests.[2] However, at all levels of relationship, guests tended to exhibit reciprocal behavior toward workers, by recognizing both their basic personhood and their effort. In this sense they constituted workers as entitled to a certain kind of treatment. Though some guests were demanding or even abusive, these were a small minority; most either adhered to or went beyond basic norms of politeness and courtesy.[3]

"What's Your Name?" Recognizing Personhood

Guests recognized workers' personhood in several ways. First, they were generally pleasant and respectful in their dealings with workers, often using a solicitous tone when addressing them. As I wrote in my field notes about the telephone operator job: "Some people just have a warmer tone of voice when they call, like they think you are a real person on the other end of the phone." Guests, especially men, often joked with workers at the desk or front door and sometimes flirted with female workers, especially at the Royal Court. Workers did not seem to construe this kind of friendliness as offensive or denigrating but rather as a genuine attempt at connection. As Arlie Hochschild has pointed out, workers value a sincere response from clients, because it helps them to be sincere in their interactions.[4]

Guests also valued workers' professional knowledge, as we saw in chapter 4, and often respected their time. Rather than simply order workers around, guests might ask, "Do you have a minute?" before requesting services. Occasionally guests acknowledged apologetically that they were creating work or other inconveniences for workers. One couple at the Royal Court excused their demands by making a self-deprecating joke, saying, "We're hard to get along with—we have all these special requests—that's what happens when you get old."

Guests also personalized interactions with workers. They reciprocally used workers' names, particularly over the phone after workers identified themselves ("Hello, Rachel, I was wondering if you could . . ."). I also noticed this tendency during my reservations training; I wore a headset to listen to Sarah's conversations with callers, who frequently used her name in the conversation. Guests who saw workers repeatedly during their stay often remembered them and would ask in a tone of joking concern, "Do you do everything?" or "Don't they ever let you go home?" Sometimes guests inquired more deeply into the worker's life, perhaps asking where the worker was from or how long she had been working at the hotel.

Some guests recognized workers' personhood in a way that cast them explicitly as equal individuals. Frequent guests sometimes asked workers to call them by their first name, for example, or they simply identified themselves by their first name when calling the desk. When I was in reservations at the Royal Court, one man explicitly attempted parity by asking my name and then saying, "I'm George, just so we're on a level playing field." A well-known film actress endeared herself to Alec when she unpretentiously offered him the name and phone number of her local chiropractor.

Similarities between guests and workers, such as being from the same city, often led guests to establish these "boundary-open" relations.[5] I saw pregnant female guests bond with Gina at the Luxury Garden and Juliane at the Royal Court, who were also pregnant. On several occasions guests made comments to me such as "Oh, my daughter's name is Rachel" and "My best friend's name is Rachel." Some guests spoke Italian to Giovanna, the Royal Court's Italian concierge. Mr. Ryan, a Luxury Garden guest, bonded with Max when he found out that their partners had a similar medical condition. Mr. Ryan asked for Max's e-mail address, and the two couples began to socialize outside the hotel. Casting the worker as similar to the guest and attempting to connect with him carries an implication of equality that goes beyond simple politeness. This example also demonstrates the personal confidences guests sometimes shared with workers.

Guests' comments in interviews echoed my ethnographic experience of this kind of treatment. Most travelers I interviewed said they treated workers politely and respectfully, sometimes invoking common humanity or friendship in their characterizations. I asked one couple, Adam and Rose, if they had a philosophy about how workers should be treated. Adam responded, "That they're peers as people." Rose added, "Absolutely. We always say good morning, good evening, thank you." Tom told me, "I treat them really nicely . . . you know, like they're your friends. I shoot the breeze with the doorman, you know, front desk people. I say hi to everybody." Eric, a middle-aged businessman, said, "I try to treat them like an equal. . . . Just be friendly, cordial." Although these guests might not have acted as friendly as they claimed to, these statements indicate that at least they valued treating workers as equal. (And, as we will see later, this kind of treatment mitigated guests' own discomfort with disparity.)

"Thank You Very Much": Recognizing Effort

Guests also recognized workers' effort by reciprocating in both emotional and material ways when workers performed services for them. At the most basic level, guests almost always thanked workers. They also often said they had enjoyed the activities workers had planned for them, such as dining, theater, and walks around the city, and often recounted details of their experiences. They often expressed gratitude to the worker in writing. For example, one guest whose dinner reservations I had arranged wrote me a note that read, "Thank you very much for being so attentive."

Guests who sent letters to management or filled out comment cards often included positive feedback about the staff as a whole or about specific workers, such as "Dirk is an asset to your establishment" and "Kenneth from room service was very accommodating, as was Alec the concierge." In fact, notes and comment cards that mentioned specific workers almost always praised them, in contrast to the emphasis in the literature on negative guest feedback as a mechanism of worker control.[6] Managers posted complimentary letters in public areas of the hotel and, at the Luxury Garden, gave copies to workers who had been mentioned by name. Managers also noted praise from guests on the star board at the Royal Court and through the worker recognition program at the Luxury Garden.

Tipping was the most common material form of recognition of effort for workers in tipped jobs. The amount of the tip usually varied with the amount of labor the guest believed the worker had exerted; concierges might receive five dollars for setting up a couple of dinner reservations, and twenty or fifty dollars for making more complicated arrangements. Doormen and bellmen typically received a dollar or two for hailing a taxi but five or ten dollars for helping guests with their luggage, depending on the number of bags.

Guests rarely tipped without also expressing some emotional recognition, usually delivering the money with a friendly thank you or an appreciative note. For example, Mrs. Vanderbilt brought her elderly mother and several other women into town to shop, spend the day at a spa, and sightsee. Max and I had made these arrangements in advance, which involved several phone conversations. Mrs. Vanderbilt was effusive when she saw Max and me, exclaiming, "Max! It's so nice to meet you! And Rachel!" She dropped off envelopes for us when she went out to dinner; mine contained fifty dollars, and Max's probably held more, because he had done more for her. In this way guests characterized the tip as *part of a relationship* rather than a naked payment for services, although this approach entailed more labor for them.

This financial recognition was decommodified in two other ways. First, it was coded in the language of care; both workers and guests euphemistically referred to tipping as "taking care of." Workers asked one another, for example, "Did the guest take care of you?" A guest might ask a worker, "Did my husband take care of you?" Second, when guests tipped workers they rarely handed them cash openly, preferring to enclose it in an envelope or to fold up the bills.[7] By the same token, it was bad form to look at a tip when the guest was present. Workers usually accepted the tip and quickly tucked it into a pocket, thanking the guest; only later could they look and see how much it was. This implicit agreement to deny the exchange of money (and hence the commodification of the interaction) helped to cast the relationship as a voluntary one on both sides and the tip as a gift rather than a payment. (An unintended consequence of this obscuring of commodification was that workers sometimes had no idea who had given them large tips that they found in their pockets at the end of the shift, which made it difficult to strategize around particular guests.)

Combining material and emotional dimensions in another way, guests gave workers gifts or did unsolicited favors for them. Gifts tended to be items workers would use and enjoy (in contrast to the old clothes, furniture, and other unwanted objects given by employers to their domestic servants).[8] Guests returning from day trips brought coffee, wine, or bread to concierges who had made plans for them. Having spoken with workers at the Luxury Garden front door about a new Mexican restaurant, a guest brought them a menu after dining there. A guest at the Royal Court who knew the desk had run out of current shuttle schedules brought some back to Annie. A Filipino pop star staying at the Luxury Garden gave copies of his CD along with personalized notes to Oscar the doorman and to Pearl and Jaya, Filipina front desk agents.

Frequent guests often developed longer-term relationships with work-ers, and their tips, gifts, and notes focused on recognition of personhood beyond specific instances of service or effort. Haile, the doorman at the Royal Court, had highly developed relationships with many guests. When he was about to go home to Ethiopia for a month, several guests gave him cards and money, saying, "Have a good trip" and "Be sure to come back." He proudly showed me a card a guest had given him that said, "Bring something to your family," referring to a hundred-dollar bill tucked inside. He talked about how good this made him feel, repeating several times, "People care about me." Referring to these relationships, he said of the hotel, "There's something special about this place." Haile clearly experienced reciprocal recognition from guests as care. Further-more, this exchange took place right around the time management was irritating the doormen by trying to regulate their car parking strategies. It illustrates the role guests play in fostering worker consent even in the presence of conflict with management.

Sometimes frequent guests expressed thanks toward the staff as a whole. Mr. Franklin, a regular guest at the Royal Court, brought the workers chocolate treats made by his fiancée. During the holidays, a cou-ple who stayed often at the Luxury Garden brought in a big wrapped box of candy for the workers and a card that read, "To the greatest staff at the greatest hotel" and "Happy New Year." Workers were very enthusiastic about both these guests and the gift.

Max, the concierge at the Luxury Garden, had a particular knack for developing relationships with guests, and they exercised reciprocity with him to an extreme degree. Guests asked him out to lunch, brought him photos, sent him cards, and gave him gifts of wine and symphony tickets. An older male guest and his wife had invited him to their villa in France. Max told me, "It's a very intimate kind of relationship."

Max was an older white man (like most of his clients), and he was highly educated, holding a master's degree. His demographic similarity to guests, I believe, made him an especially likely candidate for a "real" relationship, though he also participated actively in forging these ties. The drawback of these relationships, he explained to me, was that some-times these guests began to think of themselves so much as "friends" that they ceased to tip him. This tendency is surprisingly similar to the propensity of employers of nannies to code their employees' work as a "labor of love" and express feelings of betrayal when these employees seem to care about their wages.[9]

Guests I interviewed also described practicing reciprocity toward workers, especially in places where they stayed frequently. Herbert, a fifty-year-old business traveler, spoke of developing relationships with hotel staff: "I've been to a resort in the Caribbean, a very nice place down there, a number of times. And I ended up taking a pair of combat boots to the dive master because he couldn't buy them anywhere. He's in the reserves, the [national] military. So you develop those kind of things." Mike, a management consultant in his thirties, talked about developing relationships with particular workers in hotels where he stayed often: "You just tend to talk about more personal kinds of things [than in hotels where you are not a frequent visitor]. There's a broader scope of conversation. The bellman [at one hotel he frequents] likes to bow hunt. So once you find that out, it's deer hunting season, you can talk to him about deer hunting." These frequent guests not only reward workers but also customize their relations with them, doing free of charge what workers are paid to do for them. They participate in the production of the luxury relationship.

"THAT'S WHAT THEY SHOULD DO": WORKER EXPECTATIONS

These practices of reciprocal recognition were not exclusively positive, of course, and they were predicated on asymmetry and commodification. Guests decided what the tone of their interactions with workers would be, and workers had to respond politely no matter how the guest treated them. Guests retained ultimate authority, and they did not hesitate to use it when they felt they were forced to. Their confidences to workers were predicated on never being in the same social circle with them, so these could be seen as evidence of subordination rather than equality.[10] Finally, of course, the recognition that guests provided to workers was much more limited than that which they consumed, for there were clear boundaries to the labor they were willing to exert. Workers maintained their subordinate status.

Furthermore, these practices could create work for workers. A gift or tip required workers to perform gratitude that they may not have felt. Guests sometimes wasted workers' time by telling long personal stories that required the worker to appear interested even if she was not. Sometimes guests who apologized for their demands created more emotional labor. I wrote in my field notes: "Some people are actually aware that they are taking up a lot of the workers' time, but then you have to tell them 'That's what we're here for' or something like that." Indeed, the worker's job sometimes included sustaining the guest's image of himself as the kind of person who is nice to hotel workers.

Nonetheless, workers usually coded respectful and reciprocal treatment by guests as desirable.[11] They frequently evaluated guests on the basis of "niceness," valuing "nice" guests highly. Early in my stint at the Luxury Garden, Max told me how the actions of nice guests mitigated the behavior of rude ones, saying, "There are lots of bad people, but for each one of them there are a lot more people who are nice." Workers also enjoyed making connections and developing relationships with guests. Stephanie, a Dutch worker, told me she liked the Royal Court better than her last job at a bigger European hotel, partly because "you can get to know the guests."

These evaluations emerged especially with frequent guests popular among workers, whom I came to think of as "positive legends." Luis, a Luxury Garden bellman, told me that the Stillwaters were "nice." When I asked if they tipped well, he said no, they never gave him more than five dollars, but "she's just really nice." On one occasion at the Luxury Garden, I noted that Oscar "was happy Ms. Morris was back, because she drinks at the bar and then comes out to smoke and chat with him—he thinks she's really nice." (Oscar also called this guest by her first name.) Workers looked forward to the visits of these positive legends. They often exchanged personal information with these guests, rather than simply listen to them talk about themselves.

Workers also appreciated guests' material expressions of gratitude for their efforts. In contrast to the idea that gift giving and tipping are demeaning,[12] I never saw workers respond negatively to receiving gifts or talk about them as denigrating in any way (except when tips were too small). As we have seen, tipping provided the basis of many worker games. Recognition of effort was also an acknowledgment of the worker's professional skill; when guests enjoyed whatever the worker had done for them, the worker could feel powerful in the condescending way discussed earlier. Finally, the tip, constructed as "due" the worker, established the worker and the guest as equal.

In fact, these practices of emotional and financial reciprocity became the standard by which workers judged all interactions with guests as well as the guests themselves. Both parties adhered to an implicit contract, in which guests owed workers for exerting labor on their behalf. When guests recognized workers' personhood, authority, knowledge, and labor in ways that seemed to workers to be commensurate with their effort, which the majority of guests did, their interactions became fairly routine.[13] Workers commented only infrequently on these guests and often did not remember them later. This was business as usual. It was when guests either failed to meet or exceeded the terms of the contract that they stood out and became memorable.

Workers rarely articulated the elements of this contract explicitly, usually revealing them in comments about guest behavior. When I received my first concierge tip at the Royal Court (twenty dollars for arranging a hair styling and manicure, which awaited me in an envelope with a thank-you note), a coworker told me, "That's what they should do." When a guest tipped me after I had spent several hours procuring camera equipment for him, Alec said, "I hope he gave you something good; you deserve it." Here workers articulate a sense of themselves as entitled to a particular treatment, relying on an implicit discourse of rights,[14] and they inculcate that sense of rights in their new coworkers.

Workers' responses to guest behavior that violated the reciprocity contract also illuminated it. For example, workers very much disliked guests' failure to recognize their basic personhood. They particularly detested being treated as invisible. Dirk at the Luxury Garden told me that business guests were more likely than leisure travelers to be talking on a cell phone or otherwise distracted when they walked through the door he held open; he said, "I hate that." He also made fun of guests for being afraid they were going to have to tip someone and talked about those who had the "Heisman look" (referring to the Heisman trophy in football, which depicts a player strong-arming his opponent away as he moves single-mindedly toward the goal). As Dirk talked, he acted out a guest running toward his car, head down and arm outstretched, without a sideways glance at the doorman. Giovanna at the Royal Court despised the young "dot commers" who came up to the desk while talking on cell phones, didn't listen to her, and then asked, "What did you say?" She said, "I want to punch them." She explicitly articulated the emotional quid pro quo when she complained in a front office meeting about guests who "want an upgrade without even saying hello to you."

Sometimes guests failed to recognize the worker's professional personhood in particular, by refusing to respect her authority or her knowledge, as we saw in chapter 4. Guests could violate workers' sense of equal personhood not only by treating workers as invisible but also by behaving imperiously or expecting them to perform tasks they felt were beneath them. For example, Max and Alec were annoyed that Mr. Melmot, after attending a karate class that Max had located for him, would hand them his sweaty outfit to be laundered. However, this happened very rarely in my experience. Indeed, on several occasions in both hotels, male guests who had been rude to workers later apologized for those actions, or wives apologized for their husbands' behavior. As we will see, worker practices also served to neutralize the bad behavior of more demanding and entitled guests.

Guests might also fail to acknowledge workers' effort. Most obviously, they sometimes neglected to tip. On two separate occasions, after guests for whom we had gone to great lengths failed to leave us any money, Jasmine commented sarcastically under her breath as they departed, "Thanks for that big tip for everything we did for you." I felt ripped off after I had spent many hours over a period of several weeks discussing and arranging Mrs. MacKenzie's New Year's Eve plans, and she did not leave me a tip or a note. Sometimes guests did not recognize effort because they did not realize how much work they were creating for workers. As we have seen, workers tried to highlight their labor in subtle ways to make sure guests understood. Guests might also actively waste the worker's time, as often happened when they changed their minds about what they wanted or failed to be clear about it.

Workers indicated their expectations by telling stories about people who either had failed to observe the rules or had exceeded expectations, often comparing these guests with one another. For example, I noted that Annie from the Royal Court talked about a guest "who came in tonight and gave her a ten-dollar tip because she'd gotten him a reservation somewhere—he was a Royal Court restaurant guest but not staying in the hotel. She contrasted this with guests who'd wanted a dinner reservation for nine people last night at the last minute and . . . they didn't even thank her." Giovanna described a similar experience: "Giovanna got a fifty-dollar tip from a guy for whom she'd only made dinner and limousine reservations. She was comparing him to some other people who had three rooms and had asked her to get theater tickets and a bunch of other things and 'didn't even say thank you.'" Basic gratitude is revealed here as the minimum that guests "should" provide; on the other hand, tips that seemed out of proportion to the effort exerted surpassed the requirements of the contract. We see that the standard of what workers expect from guests is flexible, varying according to the amount of their labor that guests consume.[15]

The emotional and material dimensions of reciprocity were equally important, contradicting a simple materialist view of workers' motivation. As well as highly valuing guest "niceness," workers appreciated specific instances of praise or thanks.[16] As Sydney commented to me, "Sometimes it's better to get a letter than money." Although workers did exert special effort for guests who were known as generous tippers, as we have seen, they also went out of their way for guests who were nice to them. They also expected that the tip be delivered in a respectful or friendly manner. A conversation I had with Max early on at the Luxury Garden illuminated both emotional and financial dimensions of the contract, which Max associated with different types of travelers. He told me he liked leisure guests, because, having more free time, "they can form relationships." But he also said he liked business guests, because "they don't take up a lot of your time and they're generous."

Strikingly, some workers were ambivalent about their own response to caring treatment; sometimes they seemed to feel that they *should* prefer material gratification to emotional gratitude. One day Jasmine received a handwritten card from some guests, which said they had had loved celebrating their twenty-fifth anniversary in the hotel and that Jasmine had been especially helpful. She was excited about it, yet commented, "But I'd rather have money." I asked, "Would you?" and she said, "No, actually." She mentioned the card several times during the rest of her shift. Oscar, the Luxury Garden doorman, had a similarly ambivalent stance. He told me he thought "being nice is just as important as tipping well," but only after joking, "If they don't tip I don't care about them." This ambivalence may reflect workers' conflicts between seeing guests instrumentally and seeing them intersubjectively.

Despite this occasional ambivalence, a culture of expectation existed among workers in terms of guest behavior. Guests and other workers showed new workers how guests "should" behave, as the examples I have given above demonstrate. Reciprocity and compensation, like voluntary and obligatory behavior, were intertwined. Commodification was minimized in some ways and emphasized in others. When guests met workers' expectations, which varied according to the worker's effort, their interactions took on a routine or business-as-usual tone. However, when guests failed to observe the contract or exceeded its requirements, workers took notice and changed their behavior.

REWARD AND REVENGE

Guests could surpass the requirements of the implicit contract. When they did so, workers rewarded them by exerting extra effort on their behalf. I often noticed myself going out of my way for guests after they thanked or tipped me. Sarah, the reservationist at the Royal Court, occasionally arranged special amenities for guests who had been especially nice to her on the telephone, such as an after-dinner drink for adult guests or a teddy bear for their child. Max used his discretion to order complimentary champagne or snacks sent up from room service to particular guests. In these practices, workers code their labor as something they control, casting it as voluntary even when they offer more of it.[17]

Workers rewarded positive legends with extra labor or special perks. Max explicitly connected his level of effort to the treatment he received; referring to particular frequent guests he liked, he told me, "I'd do cartwheels" for them "because they're pleasant." One evening Haile gave prime curbside parking to a restaurant guest rather than send his car to the garage, saying he wanted to reward "people who take the time to know me." On another occasion, Haile referred to some frequent guests as "my VIPs," stating, "They know my name; I should know theirs." Here he invoked his treatment of guests both as voluntary and as a matter of common courtesy rather than as a requirement of his job.

In contrast, when guests violated the contract, workers reacted very differently. On rare occasions they would get upset when guests were rude to them, perhaps shedding a tear or two or having to step away from the desk to regroup. But for the most part, workers responded by enacting a variety of types of revenge, reestablishing their power vis-à-vis guests.[18] Again, workers did not often explicitly describe these behaviors as retribution (though Max, who tended to talk more explicitly than most about his own motivations, told me he occasionally enacted some kind of retaliation against overly entitled guests "to maintain the cosmic balance").

First, workers used what Goffman calls "negative deference" or "standard forms of ritual contempt."[19] They rolled their eyes behind guests' backs or gave them the finger under the desk. Workers typed derogatory epithets into the computer, such as *psycho, evil,* and *nudge,* often while the guest was standing right there. Workers at both hotels modified the names of unpleasant guests to make fun of them, transforming Mr. Buttercup into "Butt-cup" or Dr. Kramer into "Dr. Crazy." Sometimes workers imagined revenge when they had no chance to act it out. Elena fantasized about calling the guests names to their face, telling me, "I wish I could say 'freak' to guests, like 'Have a nice day, freak.'"

In this same vein, workers invoked the harsh criticisms discussed in chapter 4, especially toward guests who violated the contract. Guests who transgressed in some way were more likely to be judged negatively or made fun of behind their backs. For example, all the workers hated Ms. Ingram, a frequent Royal Court guest. One day she walked up to the desk and told us she was expecting people for lunch and she would be receiving them in the lobby, which had no relevance to us. As she walked away, Jackie said under her breath, "And you have a big water stain on your jacket." I asked, "Should we tell her?" Jackie said no, explaining that, first, "she doesn't want to hear that from us" and, second, "I think it's kind of funny." Jackie then referred to her as "Mrs. Facelift," criticizing her plastic surgery and telling me how she could recognize it because of Ms. Ingram's hairline. Later, when Ms. Ingram walked by, I told Jasmine about the stain; she responded, "I love that."

But revenge took more consequential forms as well. Using their discretion about negotiating effort, workers acted in ways that reversed their invisibility without being obvious enough to attract the notice of guests or managers. First, they sometimes withheld emotional labor. For example, Sarah at the Royal Court mentioned repeatedly when she was training me that she was not especially friendly to people who were not nice to her. Charlotte told me a guest had asked her for a reservation at a "trendy" restaurant, which Charlotte arranged; the woman then asked her, "If it's so trendy, how could I get in?" Angry, Charlotte had refused to engage, just asked if the reservation was "acceptable." She told me, "I didn't care, because she talked to me in that tone of voice."

On another occasion, Lupe, a front desk agent at the Luxury Garden, was annoyed by a woman who talked on her cell phone while checking in, which made it impossible for Lupe to ask her questions. Lupe responded by entering the information she had into the computer and then laying the key, in its glossy paper jacket, on the counter. When the woman turned off her phone and looked around for it, Lupe said pleasantly, "It's over there," rather than pick it up and hand it to her. The guest took the key and left; Lupe commented, "She was so rude, I'm not going to be all like, [in a deferential tone] 'Here's your key, ma'am.'" Here Lupe withheld her emotional labor and deference as a way of punishing the woman for not paying attention to her but without being overtly disrespectful.

Another way workers withheld emotional labor was to become more performative, as other authors have noted.[20] Hans, an assistant manager

at the Royal Court, told me his strategy was to "kill them with kindness."
After my family had stayed in the hotel, I thanked Jackie for being so nice
to them; she responded, "I'm always like that—except when I'm being
fake nice." When people were rude, she told me, she would say, "I'm
working on it," in an insincere way, meaning "I'm smiling, but I'm also
being a bitch." Damien, a front desk worker at the Luxury Garden, combined performativity with wasting the guest's time. He called Dr. Kramer
to ask him something, and Dr. Kramer asked him to call back in a minute.
Annoyed, he called back ten minutes later instead of one, put Dr. Kramer
on hold when he didn't need to, then picked up the phone and was fawn-
ingly nice.

Workers might also withhold physical effort or time from guests who
had broken the contract. For example, Dirk told me when he would
approach a car at the curb and the driver was on the phone or for some
other reason not responding, his policy was to back off. He explained,
"Then they have to get *my* attention." On one occasion, he pointed to a
gray Jaguar and told me, "The man who owns that car likes to whistle to
me like I'm a dog to get my attention." I asked, "What do you do?" He
said, "If there is absolutely anything else I need to do, I do that first."
Sarah spoke to an arrogant caller who invoked his frequent stays in the
hotel as a reason she should give him a room when the hotel was already
full. She said afterward, "I don't care if he's stayed here four hundred
times; if we're sold out we're sold out, and that attitude doesn't work
with me. . . . If you're nice I'll try to get you in."

Workers also used the discretion characteristic of luxury service to
enact punishment. They made decisions that affected the guest's stay
negatively, but in such a way that the guest would not realize it, in a practice I think of as "reverse customization." Possible strategies included
giving the guest a good or bad room or rate. One day, for example, Sarah
hung up after talking with a rude caller and announced, "No discount for
you!" In reservations training, Juliane told me that her room assignments "depend on how I feel about the person." I asked Walker, the
Royal Court sommelier, if he told people when the expensive wine they
were considering did not go with their food. He responded, "It depends
if the person's an asshole."

One evening Annie talked about how she treated guests who were being "unreasonable" (the very notion of reasonableness, of course, suggests a contract). She told the story of how she had downgraded a guest the previous week; he had unknowingly been upgraded before he arrived, but he came in at 2:00, an hour before check-in, insisted that he have a room immediately, tossed the pen down, and "basically threw the registration card" at her. He was paying $300 for a Silver King and had been upgraded to a Gold King, but she put him back in a Silver King that was available. Then he hated the room and ended up paying $365 for a Gold King.

Doormen used their discretion about where to park cars as a mechanism of revenge. Joel at the Royal Court told me he had once threatened to have a guest towed when he parked in the white zone; when people were not nice, he said, "I won't accommodate them." Zeke used a similar strategy. One night he was annoyed by people who had said, "We're just going to be ten minutes," and then stayed an hour. He said that after much more than ten minutes had elapsed, he "put their car way at the end of the street," where it would take longer to retrieve. Dirk told me that when nonguests asked him for a cab, they had to treat him "with respect," which included tipping him. He would refuse to whistle for cabs for people in the nearby office building if they had repeatedly "stolen" an available cab from "his" cab stand. He told me that sometimes nonguests lied about being guests in order to use the valet parking, "because they're too lazy to park themselves." He knew when a nonguest was lying, because the person entered and then immediately walked out of the hotel; he would tell the garage workers that the person was not returning until midnight, so they would "bury" the car.

Workers sometimes avenged themselves by charging the guest for services, literally making them pay for their transgressions. I asked Frankie, a bellman at the Royal Court, if guests paid to leave their cars at the curb; he responded, "If the person is snobby, you charge what the garage would have." When guests gave Max postcards to mail, he told me, he charged them for the stamps depending on "whether I like them or not."

Consistent with the findings of other authors,[21] workers also refused tips as a form of revenge when guests were unpleasant or the tip was too small, or at least they claimed they declined such tips (I never actually saw anyone do so). Daniel, a bellman at the Luxury Garden, was offended when a famous musician's minions tipped him a handful of pennies and dimes. He said that ordinarily he would refuse a coin tip and say, "No, that's all right, but let me know if I can do anything else for you." But in this case he could not do that because "they were leaving and it was rushed." He told me he had later thrown the coins into the trash. One day, a guest asked me to change his ten-dollar bill for two fives, then tipped me with one of the fives. When I told Charlotte about it, she declared, "I'd have said, 'Don't worry about it,'" making a gesture of refusal. In both of these imagined rebuffs, the worker's explicit response suggests that the guest is *not* responsible for compensating the worker, that the worker is magnanimous with her labor; yet at the same time, the worker's attitude lets the guest know he is transgressing the contract, in which he *is* responsible for compensation.

These practices fostered a sense that the guest was in the wrong, helping to neutralize the interactive power of guests who violated the contract by acting overly entitled or demanding. For example, one evening a guest at the Luxury Garden became infuriated with me as a result of a mix-up with a restaurant reservation. I apologized, saying, "I'm sorry it was not to your satisfaction," and he responded, "It was more than not to my satisfaction; it was incompetence, and I'm going to write to your general manager about it. And I want someone besides Rachel to help me with my bag!" I wrote in my field notes, "This was really the first time anyone had yelled at me, and I felt kind of bad but *not that much — he was such an asshole.*" I felt a little worried about what would happen if he did complain (which he did not), but my coworkers all supported me; Will, the manager, said, "If he writes a letter I'll tell them [upper management] what really happened." The incident triggered anxiety about management, but I was not emotionally affected by the guest's tirade (and I was never treated that way again in either hotel).

When frequent guests transgress the contract, workers can avenge themselves during the guests' future visits. Sometimes this future revenge is more theoretical than practical. For example, Zeke at the Royal Court told me one night about a local shopper who became upset because his car, parked at the curb, had been spattered with mud. Zeke said, "Now I know the guy, I'll park his car in the garage." Here, he was willing to give up the extra income he could pocket by keeping the guest's car at the curb in order to punish him and avoid the hassle of dealing with him. By taking this stance, workers equalize themselves mentally with the guest, even though it is entirely possible that he will never return.

Some guests did repeatedly receive vengeful treatment from workers simply because of their reputation from the past. As we saw earlier, workers used the predictability associated with frequency to negotiate effort (Joel subtly refused to load Mr. Woodhouse's luggage because he knew Mr. Woodhouse was a lousy tipper, and Max did not go out of his way to obtain a difficult reservation for the Melmots). Dr. Kramer, known as "Dr. Crazy," was a universally hated guest at the Luxury Garden; Max described him as "one of the most evil guests we have ever had." The first time he arrived when I was working there, Antonio assigned Charlotte to take care of his demands, which were sure to be numerous. She told me with an air of satisfaction, "We are going to charge him for *everything*." Vengeful treatment was preordained even before the guest had done anything on this visit.

Workers also desired that guests be consistent in their behavior, because lack of predictability interfered with strategies of both self-protection and games. Repeat visitors whose behavior varied between friendliness and rudeness toward workers were generally coded as problem guests. Ms. Parker, who stayed frequently at the Royal Court, was an especially good example. Hugh referred to her as "a Jekyll/Hyde," because she could shift from being extremely friendly to irritable and imperious in a moment. Though she was often very pleasant to workers, on one occasion she almost made Stephanie cry when Stephanie failed to transfer her calls correctly. When I first called her "Ms. Parker," she indicated that she wanted me to use her first name by snapping at me brusquely: "Penelope!"

For the most part, workers' emotional and material foot-dragging was quite subtle, in contrast to more blatant examples of revenge documented by other researchers.[22] I rarely saw workers defy guests in any obvious way. Dirk characterized himself as "passive aggressive," which was, he said, "the only way I can be," since he could not say anything to the guest directly. In some instances, the subtlety of hotel workers' revenge may be linked to their fear of losing a tip.[23] Also, despite the tight labor market, workers in the luxury setting would likely be disciplined for open insubordination. (On one occasion, Alec was visibly rude to a guest who was clearly not listening to him, and Antonio reprimanded him afterward.)[24] Instead, workers found ways to make their agency perceptible while remaining invisible, using their discretion to reestablish themselves as powerful by limiting effort and meting out small punishments.[25]

Other authors have shown that interactive workers negotiate their own effort or punish rude or transgressive clients in other ways, often calling these practices "resistance."[26] The preceding examples were indeed instances of resistance to the guest's attempt to ignore or devalue the worker, and they often had a perceptible, if minor, effect. However, workers did not withdraw consent in more consistent or overt ways, nor did they explicitly challenge the general entitlement of guests to their labor through individual or collective action. Moreover, references to structural inequality rarely emerged in their practices of revenge. Workers judged entitled guests on an individual level for being "spoiled," but they did not critique the system that allocates wealth unequally.

Rather than constitute resistance, revenge practices compose the enforcement side of the implicit contract, which establishes both norms of behavior and responses to transgressions of those norms. Like the other strategies I have described, these revenge strategies help workers to see themselves as powerful, minimizing the subordination imperative in their work as well as neutralizing particular rude or entitled guests who violate the workers' sense of personhood. This sense of power fosters active participation and investment in the work, or consent. The contract also normalizes subordination by limiting it symbolically and recasting guests and workers as equal on an individual level. Just as objecting to violations of the rules of the game in the factory legitimates these rules,[27] protesting transgressions of the worker-guest contract—whether or not these protests are perceived by guests—likewise legitimates the rules of interaction. And these rules are not just prescribed by managers but also set by workers, in the context of the social norm of reciprocity.

WORKPLACE CULTURES

Drawing on broad cultural norms of reciprocity and egalitarianism, reward and revenge practices form part of a workplace culture of expectation. As the examples I have used indicate, workers in my two sites were inserted into this culture when they arrived at the service theater. From other workers and from guest behavior itself, new employees learned both what to expect of guests and how to respond when these expectations were violated. They also learned about negative and positive legends, so they could prepare themselves. One evening, for example, Stan, Jasmine, and I told Inga, who was new, about Ms. Parker, the Jekyll/Hyde guest mentioned above; I wrote in my notes afterward that we were "indoctrinating Inga into the legend of Ms. Parker." Through inculcation, workers learned not to take guest behavior personally. For example, after a guest grumbled that the restaurant I had sent him to did not offer exactly the cuisine he wanted, Paulo the bellman approached me and said, "That guy always finds something to complain about; don't worry about it."

Workers also recoded mistreatment as a kind of hazing. Though I only rarely saw or heard of guests making workers cry, Pearl at the Luxury Garden told me that the first time she broke down, her fellow workers congratulated her. This practice supports the idea of integration into a particular local culture, in which a negative emotional experience is transformed into a rite of passage.

Because the culture of reciprocity and revenge relied on guest behavior, which varied little between the Royal Court and the Luxury Garden, it was fairly similar at the two hotels. However, there were some differences, which mirrored the flexible informality of the Royal Court and the professionalism of the Luxury Garden. At the Royal Court, relations were fairly casual. In general, as I have noted, guests joked around with workers more than was the case at the Luxury Garden. The preponderance of leisure travelers at the Royal Court explains this tendency, because people traveling for pleasure are more likely to value their relations with workers as part of their vacation experience. The lower prices and more informal demeanor of Royal Court workers (in part resulting from their lack of training and their age) perhaps made this group of workers seem less intimidating to guests; the "intimate" feel of the hotel encouraged confidences and joking.

These friendly relations were also more overtly gendered, especially at the front desk: male guests flirted more with female workers, and more women guests confided in female workers about their problems. Both the greater number of female guests and the predominance of young, white, female workers probably contributed to this tendency. Negative legends were also highly gendered; more women seemed to be perceived as problem guests, likely to be inconsistent or demanding.[28] In terms of revenge, I saw workers talk back to guests more often at the Royal Court than at the Luxury Garden (though it happened rarely in either hotel).

At the Luxury Garden, relations were more professional. Older, better-trained workers interacted primarily with men traveling for business, who were short on time. They tended to exercise reciprocity through tipping and minimal politeness rather than through extended friendly conversation (though there were many exceptions). These relations seemed to me quite androgynous; although there were many more male than female guests, I very rarely saw male guests flirt with female workers. Any propensity toward joking or flirtation may have been checked by the intimidating and professionalized environment. On the other hand, workers' relations with frequent guests were more developed at the Luxury Garden, probably because there were more repeat guests and lower turnover among workers. Frequent visitors more often asked workers to call them by their first name, and they were more generous with tips than repeat guests at the Royal Court.

RESPONSIBILITIES AND RIGHTS:
GUEST EXPECTATIONS

Guests in my sites were paying for luxury service and might well have felt entitled on that basis alone. Somewhat surprisingly, however, guests independently articulated the notion of contract. They described feeling both responsibilities *toward* workers and particular expectations *of* them.

And they distinguished between their relations with individual workers and those with the hotel as an institution or with management.

Guest Obligations

Mike, a management consultant, explicitly articulated the sense of contract, linking it to customized service, and characterized it as something he had to learn:

> There are internal cultural norms of how you manage yourself in those places, and early on you don't know what those norms are. . . . The hotels tend, for example, to be more personalized, right? So the quid pro quo to that is you actually have to, in a way, *merit that kind of treatment*. So it's being friendly and casual with the check-in clerks and knowing how much to tip people. . . . I mean understanding what those norms are of both interaction and transaction, if you will, is useful. (Emphasis added.)

Bob, another young consultant, said, "There's definitely a professional courtesy law, which is an amount you would show them, and an amount they would show you." Betty, a business traveler, made a similar point when she said, "None of us are so independent that we're not dependent on other people. And if we want that experience, we need to be respectful and appreciative of the people that provide it."

Guests also believed it was their contractual obligation to tip workers for services rendered. Most guests in my sites did tip workers, and almost all the guests I interviewed said they tipped hotel staff as a matter of course. One evening at the Royal Court, I delivered a message to a guest's room, and he began searching for his wallet to tip me; I said sincerely that it was not necessary (because the task was so minor), but he insisted, saying, "No, I'd feel guilty." In some instances, the tip was clearly offered as a quid pro quo, though it was never explicitly articulated as payment. For example, guests who called to make time-consuming requests before they arrived often promised, "I'll take good care of you."

It might seem likely that guests tipped workers or were friendly to them primarily because guests wanted better service. However, my evidence indicates that instrumental motives were combined with a sense of contractual obligation, owing both to hotel norms and to a generalized norm of reciprocity. Guests could not separate the obligations of any social interaction from those inhering in a service they were paying for. Kim, a young business traveler, invoked a general norm of behavior when she told me how she treated workers: "Just like you treat anybody. I mean, you just be nice." Virginia, a middle-aged traveler, characterized herself as obliged to acknowledge the workers' efforts despite the fact that she was paying for those efforts. She mentioned the norm of reciprocity, inculcated by her father, as a reason additional to the direct principle of exchange, what Gouldner calls a "second-order defense of stability":[29]

> That was a ground rule from my father. . . . I mean that was something he told all of us, that it doesn't make any difference what level somebody works at, what their job is. You treat them with respect. You call them by their name, you thank them when they do something nice for you, because there but for the grace of God, you know, that could be you doing the same thing. . . . Sure, you expect it because you're paying for it, but there's no reason not to thank the person for doing it.

Guests also explicitly denied instrumental motives, invoking the norm of reciprocity. I asked Herbert if he received special treatment if he was nice to the workers, and he replied:

> No, I've never had that happen. Never look for it to happen either. But every word connects to somebody and makes their day a little better; *they're doing the same to you*. . . . It takes two seconds more to say "Gosh, I hope it doesn't rain this afternoon," you know, talk back to somebody. But they think that somebody walking down the hall with a five-hundred-dollar briefcase and a suit on that they'll never be able to afford, you know, maybe it's a human being instead of just being a guest of the hotel. . . . It's sort of hypocritical to expect wonderful service and a caring environment and not to offer it yourself. (Emphasis added.)

This guest thought of emotional reciprocity not only as a generalized social obligation but also explicitly as mitigating inequality through creating an individual connection.

Guests often tried to code workers' treatment of them as voluntary and decommodified. Betty, a business traveler, appealed to an idea of voluntary labor in her discussion of reciprocity, saying the worker "is doing it because it's their job, but also because they want to, and you're obligated to be respectful of them and to thank them." Casting the worker's efforts as voluntary brings in the obligation of emotional reciprocity; presumably, this responsibility would not be present if it were simply a financial transaction, as the guest's entitlement would be based solely on his payment.

Nonetheless, an assumption of unequal entitlement lurked in guests' comments. Andrew, a businessman, said of his relations with workers: "I truly enjoy that relationship. When we were at [an Asian luxury hotel], the whole family got a big kick out of getting to know some of the people there, and they got a kick out of getting to know us. The elevator boy—a small thing, but we got to know him by his first name. Of course, we were always Mr. and Mrs. Armstrong to him."

Virginia told me she greeted hotel workers every day, as she did with the people that worked in her own apartment building. I asked if she called them by name, and she responded: "Yes—well, if they wear their [name] tags. I mean, I can't remember my own children's names unless I write it down. . . . I remember one of the guys helping us with our bags one time didn't have his tag. And I said, you know, 'This is really horrible, because I can't even say, "Hello, Joe," because you don't have your tag on. You can't expect me to remember it [your name].'" Here she casts the worker as responsible for enabling her to treat him well. She glosses over the inequality by suggesting it is not because he is a worker that she cannot remember his name ("I can't remember my own children's names"). The worker, of course, does not have the right to forget Virginia's name, though she is wearing no tag.

Guest Expectations

Guests described their own expectations of workers as well as obligations to them. These varied somewhat; for example, business travelers tended to expect reliable and professional service, while leisure guests often wanted to develop more of a relationship with the staff. But in general, guests assumed that their requests and needs would be met, service would be personalized, and labor would be available.

Guests also expected workers to exhibit a particular demeanor. On the one hand, they wanted workers to be friendly without being obsequious. Margaret said she preferred service that was "quick, unobtrusive, not fawning." Christina, a leisure traveler in her late twenties, liked service that was "friendly, not like 'you are the queen of the world.'" Yet workers should not become *too* friendly; as Andrew said, service "has to be respectful. You know, you're not looking for somebody who's going to be chatty necessarily. It's just the sense of recognition and caring." Finally, guests disliked workers who seemed to be looking down on them; Dorothy said, for example, "I have a very strong sensitivity to snobbism. I mean I really hate it."

Shirley's definition of luxury service focused on workers authentically legitimating guests' entitlement without drawing attention to it: "I guess it's a pretty subtle level of service that I'm trying to describe here, not making a huge fuss over you but just being glad that you're there, sort of signaling that to you, in a way, that nothing's too much trouble, but it's not obsequious and it doesn't make you feel awkward about asking for things." Implicit in all these requirements is that workers not highlight the disparity between themselves and guests either by locating themselves above guests (with snobbery) or below them (with fawning), preserving an image of egalitarianism within an asymmetrical relationship.

Evelyn, a leisure traveler in her fifties, described limits to both friendliness and formality, as they related to her husband, and coded appropriate worker behavior as a skill: "If he happens to like the person who he's dealing with and they establish a certain kind of camaraderie, then he's very happy. If it's somebody who's a little on the snobby side, it bothers him. . . . He likes people who have a sense of humor but not overly—you know, there's a fine line between hotel staff or waiters who are too friendly and too familiar, and that gets irritating. It's an art to know how to do it." When I asked if she thought much about the staff, she replied, "Only if they exceed the bounds that I would expect. If they're overly familiar I certainly notice it. If they're terribly snobby I notice it." Just as guests became routine for workers when they observed the contract, so workers became unnoticeable for guests. When they were overly familiar or too distant, workers broke the contract and became conspicuous.

Goffman writes that "by treating others deferentially, one gives them an opportunity to handle the indulgence with good demeanor."[30] Conversely, when workers withheld deference, guests enacted their own revenge, bringing their power over subordinate workers into the open. Guests in interviews mostly talked about enforcing their demands interactively (although they probably withheld tips as well). Adam said of speaking authoritatively to a snobby worker: "That's a case where—without expressing it in words—where [your] disdain for that kind of people can come across in your voice and in a very controlled way. You feel very good about being able to project that, and you're giving a message which is absolutely clear to the person on the other side of the desk."

Some guests coded workers as forcing them to change their tone. Virginia told me, in the context of claiming that she usually treated the workers very well, "I think you always have to make the effort to try. You know, you call up housekeeping and you're nice to them and ask them for that ironing board, and if it doesn't come then you might have to change your tone. . . . I mean it depends on how much patience you have." Kim, a young business traveler, told me, again in the context of saying she was nice to workers, "I would never talk down to them unless they pissed me off or whatever or were rude."

I saw this kind of behavior ethnographically as well. Some guests used what I came to think of as a tone of "authority in reserve." They were polite, but something about the way they communicated made it clear that they would cause a fuss if they did not get what they wanted. Beyond using this authoritative tone, sometimes guests raised their voices to workers or scolded them openly when they felt they were not getting what they deserved. Unlike workers, they did not have to take revenge invisibly. However, as I have said, this kind of behavior was rare. As a rule, the interaction operated smoothly, and the guest's demands were met without the need for open hostility. Of course, guests also had the option to complain to management if workers withheld service, but

as I have suggested, comment cards and letters rarely singled out particular workers for criticism. Most of the guests I interviewed said they
rarely bothered to complain if something in their stay went awry.

Even demanding guests tended to revert to a friendly demeanor when
their demands were met, as if they had simply had to exit the relationship
of mutuality temporarily in order to reassert their own authority. The
baroness de Bourgh became incensed when Royal Court staff could not
confirm that a fax of hers had been sent; she screamed at me for several
minutes on the telephone and generally treated me "like an idiot," as I
wrote in my notes. Yet I also noted that when we finally assured her it
had gone through, "she was really happy, not mean at all, she was actually kind of cute and grateful." Also at the Royal Court, I showed an
older couple to a room they felt was too close to the ongoing renovation.
The husband announced, sternly and definitively, "Staying even temporarily in that room is not an option." He threatened to leave the hotel
if he was not accommodated immediately. Jackie relocated the couple,
and they went out for a walk, asking us to order flowers for the new
room. When they returned, I told him the flowers had arrived and said "I
hope you like them"; he responded cheerfully, "Oh, I'm sure we will," as
if there had never been a problem. Having obtained their desire and
reestablished their authority, guests could return to the rules of the
business-as-usual interaction. (Workers, however, did not always see
them the same way afterward.)

Expectations of the Hotel

Beyond their individual relations with workers, guests also thought of
themselves as having an agreement with the hotel as an institution. In
comment cards and letters, guests often expressed gratitude to the hotel
itself. Mr. Rose, who had received a travel alarm clock to mark his twentieth stay, sent a thank-you note; he wrote, "The Luxury Garden is the
best hotel I ever stay in." Sometimes they used language such as "Thank
you for your hospitality," again coding the service as voluntary rather
than commodified. One guest wrote on a Luxury Garden comment card,
"Thank you so much for the wonderful stay. We were celebrating our

thirty-fifth anniversary and both our birthdays—the *gift* of champagne and strawberries at the start of our stay was a lovely *kind gesture"* (emphasis added). Here, the guest sees the amenities as voluntary gifts, as if they were not included in the price of the room.

By the same token, the hotel as an institution can violate the contract. Guests in both hotels griped about particular features of the rooms or the public areas of the hotel or about rooms that were not ready when they were supposed to be. Guests complained that renovations at the Royal Court prevented them from getting hot water. In fact, most of the complaints recorded on comment cards had to do with some kind of infrastructural problem, which guests saw as management's responsibility. While guests did occasionally get angry at individual workers for these failings, they were often able to separate the two, saying for example, "I know it's not your fault." Workers usually viewed demands related to such problems (which were beyond their own individual control) as reasonable. Indeed, they often sympathized with guests about these types of problem, as we have seen. They separated their own implicit contract with guests from the hotel's agreement, further decommodifying and individualizing the relationship.

When hotel policies made commodification too apparent, guests resisted. For example, several guests complained on comment cards about the price of small services or about being charged for items in the minibar. They seemed not to have a problem with the money itself but rather with the principle, writing, for example, "A minibar in a $500 room?!? Make it complimentary and charge $525." Another guest also wrote that management should charge more and eliminate the minibar fees, commenting, "Tipping and extras are a hassle, uncomfortable and inconvenient." Overall, guests implicitly described a contract in which their needs should be met in a friendly, caring way, without drawing attention to the commodification inherent in the service.

Guests often expected compensation *from the hotel* when something in their stay went awry. Margaret, for example, told me that when the hotel made a mistake, it would be all right "as long as they do something. A complimentary meal, champagne, cookies. I've never had a room comped, but that would be nice too. But yeah, they should do some-

thing." When the hotel failed to respond to guests' complaints, interviewees told me, they were unlikely ever to return.[31] (Of course, guests
sometimes took revenge on the hotel for the behavior of particular workers; as Adam and Rose told me about a worker in a French hotel who
was "extremely arrogant and snobby. . . . We would never go back there,
even if it was half price, because of the feeling we got there. It was just
not welcoming at all.")

As guests' demeanor changed toward particular workers once problems were resolved, so it changed toward managers, as representatives of
the hotel, when problems were rectified. One guest complained to Brad,
the Royal Court manager, because he had fallen in the bathtub. When he
subsequently went into the bar, Brad asked the bartender not to charge
him for anything. After a couple of glasses of wine, the guest emerged,
pleased and very appreciative of the gesture. Brad also told me that he
had sent a bottle of Evian to a guest who had been disturbed by the construction, and the guest had "loved it" and quickly gotten over his
annoyance. Brad said, "Even though our guests have a lot of money, they
still really like this," referring to the acknowledgement that these simple
gestures implied on behalf of the hotel's management, regardless of their
insignificant monetary value.

THE SPECIFICITY OF LUXURY

Robin Leidner has argued that customers "often treat interactions with
workers as a special category of encounter," in which the social command to treat others in ways that reinforce their dignity and individual
"sacredness," à la Goffman, does not apply.[32] Yet this social command
does seem to apply in luxury service, largely because of the moral norm
of reciprocity. This norm is widespread, which raises the question of why
such practices have not been found in other service work settings. Partly,
I believe, these findings are a matter of emphasis, because most
researchers have opted to be skeptical about the motivations and functions of reciprocity. The literature has failed to differentiate among structural asymmetry that provides the context for these relations, self-

subordination that is a feature of the job, and reciprocal interactions that may be experienced as both meaningful and positive by the participants.

But differences also exist between luxury hotel workers and those studied by scholars of other settings, especially domestic service. First, the race of workers varies. I worked with no African American interactive workers in either site, and clients may find it more difficult to treat white, Asian, and (the few) Latino workers as invisible, although this is a common dynamic in client interactions with black service workers.[33] On the other hand, the guests in my sites did have ongoing relationships with workers of color, as we have seen, including Haile, the Ethiopian doorman.

Organizational characteristics may play an especially important role in client-worker relations. Reciprocity is particularly easy in the luxury setting because of characteristics of the site, the consumer, and the product. First, the bureaucratized setting facilitates reciprocal behavior, especially in comparison with the personalistic situation of domestic servants. What Mary Romero calls "the struggle for control" over the labor process between domestics and their employers is not present between workers and hotel guests, because managers organize the labor process and regulate working conditions.[34] Guests do not have to establish their own authority and superiority vis-à-vis workers, because it has already been guaranteed for them in advance. Furthermore, deference and self-subordination are explicitly coded as part of the worker's job, so unlike employers of domestic servants (whose job description does not officially include deferential emotion work), hotel guests usually do not need to elicit emotional labor through subtle or overt means (though as I have shown, they will do this interactively when they have to). Thus, secure in the knowledge that their dominance is guaranteed by preexisting organizational arrangements, guests can develop relationships of reciprocity and equality with workers. The organizational context of the interaction changes the character of these relations by establishing the worker's obligation to the guest.

The hotel setting also encourages guests to cast relationships with workers as professional exchanges rather than as quasi-familial, as employers of domestic servants do. Uniformed, smiling workers project an air of competence and efficiency. Both perceptions of workers as professionals and the prestige of the hotel give workers a "status shield" that workers in lower-prestige occupations and settings lack.[35] Demographic similarity between workers and guests, as well as workers' superior knowledge in a variety of areas, makes it easier for guests to see them as professional. It is not coincidental that Max, the older, white, male concierge, had the most highly developed relationships with guests. Coding workers as knowledgeable and professional makes maternalism (or paternalism) an unlikely guest strategy. Likewise the gender dynamic between hotel workers and guests differs from that of domestic service; the hotel relationship often involves male customers and female workers or female guests and male workers, rather than a relationship between women, in which the employer must distance herself from the domestic servant thanks to her own subordinate gender status.[36]

In addition, the wealth of luxury guests may lead them to treat workers well. Wealthy customers may be informed by a sort of noblesse oblige toward workers, a sense of how servants should be treated that dovetails with the rules of the contract. This "status duty" complements the generalized norm of reciprocity.[37] Likewise, wealthy people may see no challenge to their own status in being friendly to workers. Ray Gold found that apartment building janitors (what we think of now as "supers") experienced less status competition with wealthier tenants than with middle-class tenants. Richer tenants treated workers respectfully and developed personal relations with them, rather than try, as the less wealthy tenants did, to depersonalize relations with them and constitute them as inferior.[38] We see a similar dynamic in the luxury hotel, in that wealthy guests do not feel competitive with workers for status. Guests' wealth allows them to tip generously, and they rarely complain about money, which minimizes conflict with workers. Thus, social distance provides both material and interactive benefits to workers.

The repeated visits of frequent guests to luxury hotels also play a role in their tendency to abide by the contract and to develop ongoing relationships with workers. Experience in the hotel trains them on the hotel's norms. Guests also feel accountable to workers in establishments to which they will be returning, for both instrumental reasons (they want good service next time) and norms of reciprocity (it is especially important to be nice to people you "know"). Fred Davis argues that the fleeting nature of relations between cab drivers and their "fares" nullifies the social constraints and "informal social control networks" operating in more predictable, repeated relationships. The opposite is true in luxury hotels, where personalized attention and a tendency for guests to return mean that workers may indeed remember clients. Rather than "relations between servers and served" becoming "reputationless, anonymous, and narrowly calculative," as Davis predicts of fleeting encounters, these relations in the hotel can become personal and reciprocal as they are extended through time.[39]

Finally, the character of the luxury product also influences guests' propensity to treat workers well. Unlimitedness breeds reciprocity: it is easier to be nice to workers who are responding to one's every need. When I asked Betty if she treated luxury and nonluxury hotel workers differently, she said, "Well, I try not to, but sometimes it's difficult . . . because I find that in many [nonluxury] hotels when you need something you have to make a case for it, instead of just a request, and then you're put on the defensive and it's difficult not to treat [the worker] differently." I asked, "So it's sort of easier for you to be nicer to the people in luxury hotels, because—" and she finished for me, "It is, because they're nicer to you." Because it is the worker's job to meet every guest request, no contradiction exists between the worker's and the guest's incentives. This harmony contrasts to nonluxury hotels, where time constraints and other managerial limits make acceding to guest requests more difficult for workers, sometimes trapping them between customer demands and managerial ones.[40]

Another dimension of luxury service that facilitates reciprocity is the recognition imperative itself. Guests identify their own labor as necessary to the interactive product they are trying to consume, because that product consists of a relationship. As Andrew put it: "I like to respect everybody as an individual. I mean, they are a person. They are more than just an employee. Where you have the opportunity to do that, I think you get a lot of gratification. . . . It changes the equation when it's more than just an employee relationship. . . . And if they care about you as a person, you care about them as a person." Mike, whom I quoted above as saying "you actually have to, in a way, merit that kind of treatment," also commented:

If you treat people well, they'll treat you well, and these folks can be
quite helpful to you if you treat them well consistently, and they can
just make your experience much nicer and much more personal. . . .
If you are courteous and respectful and appreciative of what they do,
that comes back to you many times over in terms of good, thoughtful
service and just in a more pleasurable environment. . . . I mean, I just
like people, right? . . . I mean, part of it's instrumental. Part of it's just
being a decent human being, and part of it's just interesting.

Hegel argued that the master must recognize the slave in order to constitute him as capable of recognizing the master; similarly, in hoping to cast
the recognition they consume as genuine, guests feel they need to reciprocate. Because the product is a relationship,[41] the guest must also work,
though his labor is not commodified.

These are the factors that encourage *guest* behavior of a particular kind.
Characteristics of luxury service also help *workers* to maintain a sense of
themselves as dignified, autonomous, and powerful. The imperative to
remember guests enhances predictability and hence self-protection
against negative legends, enabling reverse customization. Workers are
also able to develop relationships with guests they like, which many of
them enjoy. Furthermore, interactive workers' discretion allows them not
only to feel autonomous and skilled but also to resituate themselves as
equal by enacting these practices of reward and revenge when guests
refuse to respect the rules of the contract. Workers in more routine or constrained service jobs may not have the autonomous decision-making
capacity needed to do this. Indeed, even in luxury hotels, routine work
and limited discretion prevent workers in the back of the house from
enacting revenge and reward, even related to their minimal contact with
guests.[42]

CONSTITUTING EQUALITY

In the service work literature, reciprocity in the form of gifts, tips, or
"niceness" between customers and workers is typically considered
unusual or instrumental or both.[43] Some authors see practices of gift giv-

ing or tipping as establishing or reinforcing subordination because of their unilateral nature,[44] and many are skeptical about the possibility for "real" friendship to exist between workers and clients.[45] The imputed antagonism between workers and customers is reflected in the assumption that emotional labor in service work settings is inherently inauthentic, stressful, and potentially damaging to workers' sense of self.

These luxury hotel cases show that antagonism, instrumentality, and inauthenticity are not the only features of customer-worker interactions and that clients do not always serve a primarily oppressive role. In my sites, guests were usually respectful and courteous and often genuinely warm and generous toward workers. They developed ongoing relationships that helped workers become invested in their work.[46] Though these relationships involved ambivalence and contradiction,[47] both workers and guests experienced them as authentic and meaningful. They were not simply instrumental attempts by guests to get better service, and workers' responses to them were not instances of false consciousness or misunderstanding of the situation.

Indeed, this chapter has shown that relationships between workers and clients are also key to generating consent. William Whyte wrote of worker-manager relations in restaurants that "the exchange of favors or good turns is a vital element in good supervision. . . . No matter how much he is paid, [the restaurant worker] never feels that money alone entitles the employer to his all-out efforts. Such loyalty and devotion to the job cannot be purchased. They can only be won in human relations."[48] But in hotels, the *guests* are key players. Workers become personally invested in these relationships and in enforcing the rules that govern them; again, to accept these rules is also to accept the relations in which they are embedded, including unequal distribution of material resources and asymmetrical entitlement to physical and emotional labor.

These findings illustrate the "incomplete commodification" of emotion work, rather than a dichotomy between commodified and uncommodified relations.[49] Tips have long been considered to combine elements of both gifts and payment.[50] The presence of both emotional niceness and nonmonetary gifts in worker-guest exchanges further complicates this distinction. Personal ties and commercial exchange are intermingled, as they are in many kinds of relationships.[51] As we have seen, these forms of reciprocity indicate both personal relationships between workers and guests and workers' entitlement. Just as the tip hangs somewhere between "gift" and "payment," so the relationship between guests and workers combines elements of voluntary friendship and commodified employment relations.

Although reciprocity is often considered a crucial element of egalitarian society, some social theorists have shown how it plays into the legitimation and reproduction of inequality. Alvin Gouldner, for example, has argued that the social expectation of reciprocity preserves civility between higher- and lower-status people: "The norm of reciprocity . . . engenders motives for returning benefits even when power differences might invite exploitation. The norm thus safeguards powerful people against the temptations of their own status; it motivates and regulates reciprocity as an exchange pattern, serving to inhibit the emergence of exploitative relations which would undermine the social system and the very power arrangements which had made exploitation possible."[52] Pierre Bourdieu has made a similar point with his notion of "strategies of condescension," which are "those strategies by which agents who occupy a higher position in one of the hierarchies of objective space symbolically deny the social distance between themselves and others, a distance which does not thereby cease to exist."[53]

Judith Rollins argues that employers of domestic servants use maternalism to naturalize inequality by casting domestic servants' inferiority as innate.[54] She suggests that by constituting this natural inferiority, employers avoid acknowledging the injustice of the system and their own participation in it. My evidence suggests that the same objective— creating an implicit justification of unequal social relations—is achieved in the hotel, but through opposite means: guests, who wish not to feel exploitative, try to normalize inequality by denying it, constituting workers as inherently equal, primarily through reciprocity. Workers respond to and even demand this kind of treatment, participating in the intersubjective creation of an equal self.

This equality is established in several ways. First, the contract, the idea that each party has rights and responsibilities vis-à-vis the other, creates a sense of equivalence through mutual obligation and exchange. Because workers generally act first, guests are indebted to workers, rather than the other way around (this is one of the reasons workers in my sites disliked being tipped before they carried out the guest's request). Second, both workers and guests cast worker labor as voluntary, offered willingly by an independent agent. Workers negotiate their effort and enact revenge when they need to; guests treat workers well in an attempt to code the labor they consume as decommodified and not coerced. Third, developing meaningful relationships allows workers and guests to think of themselves as equal by virtue of sharing a common humanity. Though guests retain ultimate authority and entitlement to emotional and physical labor, as well as an extremely privileged structural position, observance of the "Golden Rule" establishes guests and workers as equal on a basic human level.

The contract can break down, as we have seen. When workers violate guest expectations, asymmetrical power relations and entitlements appear, as guests assert their greater authority explicitly. But workers neutralize these demonstrations and other violations with their own symbolic acts of revenge. These are moments of resistance, but in the long term, workers' defense of the contract serves to legitimate the rules of interaction. As long as guests constitute workers as entitled to good treatment, workers consent to observe guests' greater prerogatives.

In this process, workers and guests collaboratively reconstitute the social relation as an individual relationship. The ideas of common humanity and of independent agents participating in contracts cast both participants as individuals. Likewise, both financial and emotional interactive incentives exist between individual workers and particular guests, further distancing both types of actor from collective class identifications. The collective norm is observance of the contract, while transgression is coded as individual deviation. Finally, guests' propensity to separate their relation with the hotel as an institution from their relationships with workers as individuals reinforces the individualizing tendency.

Rather than obscure inequality, as others have suggested, these practices around reciprocity normalize guest entitlement to workers' labor.[55] Workers and guests do not cease to be aware of the asymmetries between them, but egalitarian interactions allow them to become taken for granted and not critiqued in any kind of structural way.

Somewhat ironically, normalization through individualization depends on both cultural norms and organizational characteristics. Everyday interactive work that is socially required outside the hotel comes into play within it; guests observe norms of reciprocal behavior, performing what Goffman calls the "joint ceremonial labor" people do to constitute themselves in particular ways.[56] This expectation most likely varies cross-nationally.[57] At the same time, both guests' inclination to treat workers well and workers' capacity to reconstitute themselves as powerful in the absence of good treatment depend on features of the luxury environment, as we have seen. Reciprocity as a mechanism of consent probably exists in interactive workplaces outside the United States and outside the luxury sector to a greater extent than other researchers have identified. But how the relations I have described play out is specific to the American luxury hotel.

In order for the contract to function, guests need to know the rules of the game. In chapter 6, I turn to guests' understandings of their own entitlement and how their experiences in the hotel itself shape these understandings.

SIX Producing Entitlement

In Garry Marshall's 1990 movie *Pretty Woman,* wealthy executive Edward (Richard Gere) hires a street prostitute named Vivian (Julia Roberts) to spend a week with him in a Los Angeles luxury hotel. In the course of her stay, Vivian is transformed from tacky hooker to upper-class lady. This transformation is mediated by the luxury hotel. Initially, the hotel's general manager, Barney Thompson (Hector Elizondo), threatens to throw her out, but he emerges later as the primary agent of her metamorphosis. While Edward is occupied with his business deals, the avuncular Barney acts as her tutor in the ways of the wealthy. After workers in a Rodeo Drive boutique scorn Vivian because of her "cheap" appearance, he delivers her into the hands of an accommodating saleswoman. Before she has to dine with Edward and his professional associates, he literally teaches her how to use a knife and fork, as well as the other accoutrements of the high-end restaurant table. When she emerges from the hotel, she has left her lower-class tastes and mores behind and is ready for a life of luxury consumption. After this transformation, commitment-phobe Edward decides he cannot live without her. Assisted by Barney and the hotel's limousine driver, he rescues her from her small walk-up apartment, where she no longer feels at home, and delivers her to the life she is now meant for.

Though different from Vivian in many ways, of course, the guests I interviewed described a similar transformation. Unlike the subjects of most studies of the upper class, many of my respondents had not come from wealthy backgrounds.[1] They were initially uncomfortable with their own consumption of luxury service. They also feared they did not belong or know how to behave in the luxury environment. Though the tutelage they received was more subtle than that in *Pretty Woman*, the hotel itself helped guests to become entitled consumers of luxury service.

I look first at how guests understood their own consumption. Many felt conflicted about spending money and about structural and interactive inequality with hotel workers. But they legitimated their own consumption of luxury service by mobilizing particular interpretations of themselves and workers to justify or neutralize disparity, just as workers did. We have seen that guests coded workers as equal; here again they invoke reciprocity as a leveling mechanism. Guests also used comparative strategies of self, taking not workers but their own social peers as objects of comparison, often using moral criteria. These strategies varied according to guests' reasons (business or leisure) for being in the hotel, their personal histories, and to a certain extent their gender. The organization of work in the hotel supported guests' capacity to make particular interpretations.

Second, I show how guests became comfortable in the luxury environment. The McDonald's clients Leidner studied were trained by the environment to fit themselves into the company's routine, to be ready with their orders when they reached the front of the line, to clean up after themselves, and so on.[2] Similarly, guests in the hotel setting learn their own obligations: the rules of tipping and reciprocity and the performance of class through appropriate dress and behavior. But they also become accustomed to their own entitlements, especially to workers' caring labor. Their insertion into this setting depends especially on workers' behavior, which indicates to insecure guests that they do belong in the luxury milieu, and also legitimates their superior entitlements vis-à-vis the workers themselves. Work routines, then, do not control customer demands, as they do at McDonald's; rather, they constitute demanding customers.[3]

Through the consumption of luxury service, the guest is constituted not just as a legitimate customer but also as a privileged subject. What appears as recognition of the individual's needs and desires is, in fact, a recognition of class prerogatives. Like schools, social clubs, and other upper-class institutions, the hotel helps guests to gain what Bourdieu, citing Goffman, called "a sense of one's place."[4] Like Vivian, guests emerge from the hotel with higher expectations and a new sense of entitlement.

CONFLICTED CONSUMPTION AND STRATEGIES OF LEGITIMATION

We have seen that for workers in my sites, getting paid was not enough to generate their consent to exert effort. Likewise, guests I interviewed did not feel that having money alone entitled them to consume service. Some guests felt "guilty" about spending money on luxury consumption. Linda, a leisure traveler in her fifties, told me she often asked herself, "What have I done to deserve this? Do I deserve it? Should I be doing this?" As a rule, this feeling was not related to the actual amounts of money guests had; for the most part they told me they would still feel the same way even if they had more money, or that they could already spend as much money as they liked.[5]

Many guests attributed their conflicted feelings about spending money and consuming labor to their upbringing. As Virginia told me, "It's not a matter of not affording it. It's a matter of, that's a lot of money to pay for this room that we're not even spending a lot of time in. . . . Because in our family, and I think in [my husband's] family, which is also Irish Catholic, you work really hard for the money that you make and you don't throw it away." She also believed that her reluctance to consume labor was due to her Catholic background. The staff at one luxury hotel had been very solicitous toward her after she had had surgery, offering to run her errands. Asked if she had taken the workers up on these offers, she said, "No, of course not. I'm Irish Catholic. You don't do that. Too much guilt involved." Andrew, a business traveler, described the influence of his "frugal" parents, especially his mother, saying, "I don't even tell her where I'm staying sometimes now, because she will make you feel a little guilty for spending money. . . . Sometimes I feel a little guilty, and I think it goes back to my roots." Notably, Andrew's mother had come from a wealthy family. He attributed her thrift to her sense of feeling different from other children when she arrived at school in a limousine.

Some guests, however, expressed no conflicts about spending money on luxury service, attributing their desire for it to their disadvantaged childhoods. Margaret, a leisure traveler in her late fifties, said of people who felt guilty, "Yeah, I don't know what that's about, because if you have it, I don't know why you don't enjoy it. What are you saving it for?" She contrasted herself to her ex-husband, who had been raised with money but had never found a way to enjoy it, whereas she had grown up in a poor family. Christina, a young leisure traveler, said her husband always stayed at the Ritz-Carlton, in a suite; she told me, "He just wants it because he grew up staying in Holiday Inns, and he likes the fact that he can do it."

Thorstein Veblen might have seen luxury hotels as sites of "conspicuous consumption" and "conspicuous leisure," in which individuals parade their consumption and their free time in order to obtain status.[6] But guests seemed to prefer not to see them that way.[7] Contradicting the idea that they were pursuing status rewards, several leisure travelers I interviewed claimed they did not always tell their friends or families which hotels they had chosen, for fear they would find spending on such hotels excessively extravagant. At the Luxury Garden, a guest asked me not to use hotel stationery for a fax she had asked me to send, telling me afterward, "I just didn't want it to be branded." Likewise, business travelers denied that the status of the hotel was important to them vis-à-vis their peers or business associates. Most said, in response to my question, that it was often a liability, because they were likely to be seen as overly extravagant by their own clients. Bob, a management consultant in his early thirties, told me, "We use what's called a 'blush test,' which is, if you imagine a situation where you're telling a client where you're staying, and you actually blush, then you shouldn't stay there." Although it is difficult to ascertain the truth of such claims, at the very least they indicate internal conflict among the consumers of luxury service.

Guests I interviewed were also torn about the inequality between themselves and workers. They rarely brought it up, which suggests that it was normalized for them just as it was for the workers. However, when I mentioned disparity, a majority acknowledged that they did notice it.[8] As Evelyn said, "I may not be consciously—when you're asking me, I realize I do feel that." Mike, a businessman in his late thirties, said he did think about disparity "from time to time. And I don't quite know what to do about that." Betty said, in response to my question, "Yeah, I do [think about the workers] because it's a hard life. . . . You think, well, gee, I wonder what their life is like when they're here dealing with people all the time who are spending three and four and five hundred dollars a day." Business and leisure travelers used a range of strategies to understand and justify these disparities.

Leisure Travelers: Distance and Denial

People I interviewed who traveled primarily for pleasure, especially women, distanced themselves from service in various ways. Some asserted that staying in luxury hotels was not important to them or that they were more interested in the amenities of the hotel than in the service. They spoke of being "embarrassed" by excessive attention. They also suspected that recognition was not authentic, mentioning that "they have it in the computer." Dorothy said, of being called by name:

> That doesn't mean a whole lot to me. I don't know—I'm just not—
> I'm not one of those people who—if I went every year to Paris and
> the same hotel it certainly would be nice to be remembered, not for
> any self-important reason, but just because when you love the city and
> you love the place you stay, it's nice to know that they remember you
> because you go there because you love it. . . . But I don't need a fuss to
> be made about me or anything like that.

Dorothy codes enjoyment of personalization as distastefully "self-important," contrasting it to a more genuine shared appreciation of a place. As I mentioned in chapter 1, many of the people who expressed this view were women, wives of wealthy businessmen; they preferred to think of themselves as unobtrusive, not demanding either personal recognition or services. They often characterized their husbands as being more interested than they in consuming recognition and in developing relationships with workers.

However, some of these women contradicted themselves, at times saying that personal attention or labor did not matter to them and later giving examples in which it clearly did. Evelyn, quoted above, was a woman in her fifties who traveled for leisure; she said, "Service doesn't mean as much to me as it does to other people." Her comments about a top-level Asian hotel, often ranked one of the best in the world, reflected this contradiction: "I walked in and I thought, what's so great about this hotel? [But] we went upstairs and came down and within half an hour everybody in the lobby knew our name. And I felt—*actually, I don't feel that's necessary, but I thought*—and the service was really outstanding, and the waiters and waitresses were just so pleasant" (emphasis added). Representing her desire for luxury as an offshoot of her husband's, Martha said, "When I travel by myself I usually stay in way lesser hotels. . . . But when I travel with Eric [her husband], I always stay in great hotels . . . because he loves it." When I interviewed Eric, I mentioned this comment; he responded skeptically, "I find *that* hard to believe." This ambivalence indicates internal tensions or conflicts over entitlement to luxury service.

Another strategy leisure travelers used in dealing with disparity was not to think about it, often commenting, "I'm not going to change the world." Linda said, "I block it out to get through the day," and made an analogy to oncologists or neurosurgeons whose patients frequently die and who have to desensitize themselves. She and others made comparisons to other parts of the world, such as India or Mexico, where inequality is more extreme than in the United States. Evelyn said, "I think it's like when you're traveling in India, which I did once. I mean if you look around, I mean, you can't stay there. You have to sort of, you might say, harden your heart a little bit. You can't be—if you're such a compassionate person that you feel for every person who is underprivileged and whatever, you have a terrible time. I mean you can't—I don't think I'm that kind of person. I just feel that I can't save the world." Right before making this comment, Evelyn told me, "I don't want to know these people. They don't mean a thing to me one way or the other. They're there to do a job." Her attempt to distance herself from workers indicates how she "hardens her heart" to them. When I asked if the disparity he noticed impeded his enjoyment of the hotel, Adam, a retired executive in his sixties who traveled extensively with his wife for pleasure, said:

> No, because people—you know, you can't play God, and I mean life is often not fair and you can only do what you can do, but you can't make a sociology case out of every person you meet. You have to—and certainly when you go to India, for God's sake—as one of our Indian friends said to us before we went, "when you travel in India you must know when to look and when not to look." So, I mean you can't tear yourself apart for all the ills of the world or you wouldn't be able to live your life. You can't do that.

Similarly, I asked interviewees if they tended to think about how much they were spending or whether their stay in the hotel was "worth it," and most said they did not think about it. Shirley said she wasn't interested in how they made the service happen, calling it "a fantasy": "I'm fascinated by it, but when I'm in the middle of it I just want to surrender to it. . . . I want to believe that they're glad to see me when I come through the door." Not thinking about how "they" make the service happen relieves the client of having to think about who the workers are or the situation they are in. This strategy may be part of the reason guests do not like to be reminded of the commodification of the service. And coding workers as *wanting* to serve them not only makes workers' labor feel more genuine but also allows guests to feel less exploitative.

Business Travelers: Engagement and Evaluation

Business travelers described a different orientation to luxury service. In counterpoint to the idea of hotel as fantasy, business travelers often evaluated the service as a business. These guests, especially men, were very interested in how it was produced and were often aware of the hotels' techniques for knowing their preferences or their names. As Tom, a business traveler, said, "I'm curious from a business management perspective. How do you run an organization that way to provide that level of service?" Andrew told me, "Being in business, I really think it all comes from the top. I think it's got to start with a general manager who cares about training his staff." Here guests cast themselves symbolically as quasi-managers rather than consumers.

In contrast to the women I described above, these male business guests said they did not mind that personalization was engineered; in fact, it indicated that the hotel was doing something right. At one luxury hotel, Mike told me, "Those guys [the staff] change over all the time, but they have a good preference file, and they call you by name, and that's nice. It makes it that much more personal and comfortable when you come in." Even if individual workers do not care about guests, Herbert commented, "institutionally they really do care." On more than one occasion in my field sites, male guests indicated that they understood the organizational standards of the luxury hotel; one man said to the front desk agents at the Luxury Garden, for instance, "You remember me; that's pretty good."

As they evaluated service from an imaginary managerial perspective, guests also shifted the burden of making workers happy onto the real management. Tom commented, "I think they've been *trained* [to know that] the only reason we're staying here is because of the wonderful service that they're giving us, so they're making this whole thing work. . . . I really like what I'm seeing in these hotels, and I think they've got the staff really committed." In our discussion of disparity, Betty said, "I would hope that at a luxury hotel, the compensation is better than it is at any other hotel," and she suggested that managers needed to be sure to treat the workers well. Rather than become quasi-managerial agents of control themselves, these guests wanted to believe that the legitimate agents of control—the actual managers—were benevolent toward workers.

Mitigating Disparity through Reciprocity

Both business and leisure guests described reciprocity as their main practical approach to closing the gap between themselves and workers. As we have seen, most clients espoused an explicit philosophy of reciprocity, rejecting the idea that because they were paying for the service they were not obliged to reciprocate. Reciprocity allowed guests to cast workers as equal in human terms, and at the same time guests described emotional reciprocity specifically as compensating for economic disparity. Adam, quoted above as saying "You can't change the world," added, "But you do what you can do. Certainly if you're blessed with any interest in other people, it goes a long, long way, and people sense that. They just sense that. I can't explain what I mean." Shirley, who admitted pangs of guilt about staying at hotels in developing countries, said, "I guess I sort of think, well I'll make the best of it. I'll be as pleasant as I can be, and I certainly won't be [an ugly American]." With housekeepers, she said, "I often try to engage in eye contact or a smile or something. I think that just makes me feel better," and laughed sheepishly.

Strategies of Self

In addition to practicing reciprocity, guests thought of themselves in ways that minimized social distance with workers, invoking reinterpretations of hierarchy such as those we saw in chapter 4. Some business travelers saw themselves as analogous to workers in terms of their dealings with their own customers. Bob, the management consultant introduced above, said, "I'm giving a professional service myself. So I understand what it is to have clients." Leisure travelers made analogies to guests in their own homes. Shirley told me, "I like to entertain, and I like to take care of people, in the sense that I like them to feel comfortable in my home, so I think there's part of that at work too. Sort of noticing how other people do that, whether it's a bed and breakfast or a luxury hotel." In both of these analogies, the guest occupies the place of the worker serving someone else.

Guests also considered luxury consumption as compensation for their own work. Bob saw the hotel stay as making up for his frequent travel and minimal free time:

You want to feel pampered. When you're on business trips, in some way your lifestyle is in duress, so you feel the need for an extra level of being

taken care of. . . . It actually does make a big difference psychologically. . . . And also, when your time becomes compressed, marginal
amounts of pleasure of any sort, people pay insane amounts of money
for that. When you have two hours in the day that are free, that's a vast
difference from having four or six hours free. . . . So you want a nice
dinner, and you want a nice place to stay, because marginally the enjoyment in your life is very small, so you want everything to be nice. That's
what it is. . . . Oh yeah, and you want [the company] to pay for it, because you're traveling and all that stuff. So you feel entitled.

Here Bob explicitly links entitlement to luxury consumption with his
own labor.[9] In a more succinct presentation of the same idea, a woman
checking into the Luxury Garden justified her need for a bigger room by
saying, "I work all day—I want a bathtub!" In some cases it was a
reward for work they had done earlier in their lives. Andrew told me,
"It's not that I deserve it, but it's that I've worked hard in my life, and I
have accomplished a lot in my career, and I kind of look at it as kind of a
reward for that work." Even leisure guests talked about the "work"
involved in planning their trips, which many, especially women, took
very seriously (many female guests in both my ethnographic sites certainly did). Some guests even said they needed pampering after they had
been "out all day" (sightseeing).

Some guests particularly valued expressions of empathy from workers, with the similar justification of having been traveling for a long time
or being tired. Mike said, "You tend to feel somewhat embattled by the
challenges of dealing with air travel and taxi cabs and all that sort of stuff,
and it's just nice to have a friendly face and a friendly voice." Martha told
me: "I think it's always nice to have somebody address you by your
name. . . . It makes you feel like you've come to a destination. I think it's
more a sense of 'you're finally here.' Especially when you've been traveling a long [way], in and out of cabs, you may not know where you're
going, or you're lost, to have somebody say, 'Oh, Mrs. Smith, we'll help
you with your bags,' you say, 'Oh good, thank God,' you know."

Guests in my sites, especially male business travelers, often tried to
elicit compassion from workers, citing the requirements of their own
jobs. While checking into the Luxury Garden, one man told the front desk

agents that he was taking the red eye flight to Detroit the next day, adding, "Don't everybody be jealous at once." Guests in both hotels, when requesting early wake-up calls, would often make comments along the lines of "Don't you feel sorry for me?" Guests thus cast workers as advantaged, playing into workers' own understanding of themselves as empathetic.

Betty, a businesswoman, told me hotel workers need to have "two things: respect for people and empathy. You [the client] have been traveling, you're coming in, you're in a strange environment. Just imagine if you [the worker] were in their place and [you] needed something or wanted something . . . wouldn't you want someone to do it for you?" This view assumes parity between the worker and the guest and codes the worker's efforts as voluntary and responsive to a "natural" desire. At the same time, she portrays workers as having power over her by virtue of their familiarity with the place and their capacity to make her happy.

Like workers, guests used strategies of comparison to others as well. Drawing especially on a moral repertoire, they contrasted themselves favorably to other wealthy people. Some characterized their own sense of entitlement as less than that of their friends or other guests they had seen in hotels.[10] As Sally, a fifty-five-year-old homemaker married to an attorney, said: "I think we are not in the income category that lots of our friends who travel to those places are. And I think when they do reach that income level, they just act—they just have a different mindset than I do. . . . They just expect that [treatment]. It's their due, in a way. And you know I just never did or probably ever will, even if I had a gazillion dollars and could stay in the Ritz in Paris any time I wanted."

Guests thought of themselves as less extravagant than these peers, describing limits on their spending. Though he had stayed in luxury hotels worldwide, Adam told me, "I would never stay at the [Hotel X] and pay, as a couple of our friends did, eight hundred or a thousand dollars a night. I mean I think that's—with all that's going on in the world, it would seem to me to be an excess of conspicuous consumption. And I just couldn't do that." The sense of putting some kind of a cap on what they spent allowed these guests to see their own demands as moderate in relation to real or imagined others who were not concerned with inequality or social issues. These guests used comparisons to negotiate symbolic limits to what was "reasonable." As we will see, however, what they consider reasonable for themselves is not the same as what they deem reasonable for workers.

They also saw themselves as nicer to workers than other guests in luxury hotels were, again invoking a norm of emotional reciprocity. As Herbert told me, "People basically don't treat people in the service environment very nicely, and I do." Andrew said, "I have certainly seen the situation of those who don't respect the staff, and that really bothers me. . . . [They have] a standoffish attitude or don't use expressions of appreciation. . . . It makes me uncomfortable." Virginia, who had lived for three months in a Four Seasons hotel after her apartment building flooded,[11] said:

> I did see people being rather impatient and rude to some of the staff people there. . . . There are some people that just put themselves on a level where they expect people to treat them on a higher level, I guess. They're there to be waited on. And I didn't feel that way when we were staying there. I felt it was very nice that these people did such a good job with what they did. Boy, were we lucky to be staying there. But I certainly didn't feel that we deserved it.

These legitimations through particular interpretations of self and other highlight guests' unwillingness to see themselves as entitled simply because they have the money to purchase the service. Instead, they use strategies similar to those of workers to minimize social distance. They cast themselves as disadvantaged or deserving, giving workers the power to make them feel better. And they relocate themselves according to a moral standard in comparison to people richer, less thrifty, or with a greater sense of entitlement than themselves.

Strategies of Other

Guests' views of interactive workers served to minimize the perception of inequality, often drawing on or dovetailing with the same images workers had of themselves. First, guests often thought of front of house

workers as professionals. Evelyn said she felt the disparity between herself and the housekeepers in hotels. But when I asked about interactive
workers, she responded: "Not so much with the front desk people . . .
because they have a different appearance. They just have a different
mannerism. You know, it's just obvious that they're not—even though
those people may not be making a lot of money, but they're dressed well.
They're either American, or they're trainees from France or something.
You just have a feeling they have a different level of education and that
they're more worldly." Shirley likewise acknowledged being aware of
inequality with housekeepers ("Oh yeah, I feel the disparity in our lives
very much") but not with front desk workers. When I asked her to
explain, she said, "I think probably there's a level of parity in the sophistication, you know—in the sense of the front desk people or the
concierge-level people, there's a level of professionalism. Do you know
what I mean? So it feels like a more direct service kind of a thing."
Demeanor, appearance, and sophistication are the signals of professionalism and, by extension, equality. Other interviewees invoked education
as a key to professionalism. And, as I suggest below, race seemed to play
a role.

Guests also thought of workers as holding their hotel jobs only temporarily, as Evelyn's invocation of "trainees" suggests. Mike spoke of
young desk clerks as doing their "first job" and said, "If it's a transitory
[job], then it's not a bad sort of stepping stone to doing something else."
Guests who had themselves come from disadvantaged backgrounds saw
workers as analogous to themselves at an earlier stage. Asked if he ever
felt glad not to have the kind of job housekeepers do, Eric said, "Well, I
kind of feel that way about most jobs. I kind of figure, boy, there's no way
I could work that hard again in my life." He then proceeded to talk about
the hard physical labor he used to do. By invoking their own experiences
of upward mobility, guests reassured themselves that workers were also
on their way up.

Some guests invoked the concepts of status by association and hotel
hierarchies, on which workers themselves also drew, suggesting that
workers were advantaged relative to others in their lives, both at and outside work. Mike spoke of the doorman at a Ritz-Carlton he frequented:

"In some respects, I think he feels, at least as far as when I've talked to him, he's got somewhat of a privileged position relative to some others." Virginia said,

> You get the feeling that there's a different pecking order, which of course there is. . . . There's probably a certain amount of status to be working behind the desk as opposed to doing the laundry-type thing. . . . They certainly come across like this is the best job they ever had. And I give them a lot of credit for that, because it can't be. But maybe for them it is, because there's probably a great deal of status for them to say that they work at the Four Seasons.

Similarly, some guests compared workers' lives with what they thought of as a reasonable standard of living, rather than with their own standard of living. Evelyn said, housekeepers "are probably very happy to have a job." Mike told me he thought about workers who might not move on to better jobs, such as the aforementioned doorman: "I think [he] provides exceptional service, and with the kind of tip income he gets for a high school degree, he probably actually does quite well for himself and feels pretty good about where he is in life." Several guests talked about how they noticed disparities between themselves and workers in less-developed countries, but they did not think about such disparities in the United States or Europe, the implication being that workers here are not especially badly off. As we have seen, guests also tended to invoke images of India or other developing countries when talking about inequality.

Guests thus set hotel workers up as suitable for comparison with both their fellow workers and their peers at home—but not with the guests themselves. They compare workers with those "below" them in terms of status or standard of living, while they contrast themselves, as we have seen, with other rich people who are "above" them in the sense of being willing to spend more money. In so doing, they avoid making direct comparisons between themselves and workers. Guests thereby establish workers as inhabiting a world distant from their own, just as workers often see guests as occupying a foreign social sphere in which money has different meanings. This use of a relativist measuring stick to evaluate workers' material conditions contrasts with the strategy of common humanity that underlies reciprocity. Workers are equal to guests in some fundamental human sense, but guests cast workers' material needs as less than their own by evaluating them in relation to an abstract standard.

Invisible Workers and Race

Strategies of self and other seemed to fail guests when they talked about back of house workers. Guests were more likely to express discomfort with the disparity between themselves and these workers. When I asked Evelyn if she thought about the lives of the people who worked in hotels, she responded: "Yes . . . I've noticed when they're foreign-speaking, Hispanic maids or whatever, it occurs to me what kind of lifestyle they have. . . . The disparity between haves and have-nots is very apparent to me. And I do feel a little uncomfortable with that." Other guests spoke of being sure to tip the housekeepers, because "they're the ones that really make the room so nice." As Sally said, "You're more inclined to be nicer to the maids than to the people at the front desk. . . . I think they're at the bottom of the totem pole, and they've got the worst jobs in the hotel practically. But they really are the ones making you the most comfortable." Again, women were much more likely to express this kind of sentiment.

Guests were especially upset by this work when they thought the worker was somehow inappropriate for it. Rose, for example, spoke compassionately of an Albanian housekeeper she had met in a French hotel. In Albania, this woman had been a professor, but she was now a political refugee. "So she was trying to make ends meet, and that really bothered us a lot, because she was a very highly educated woman who was doing domestic work." Dorothy described one hotel's butler service, in which the butler turned out to be a young Asian woman dressed in tails. This upset her: "It really bothered me to see this woman dressed up with this starched, pleated thing in front." When I asked why, Dorothy said, "That's a good question. I guess because she was young and beautiful, and did I think because she was Asian she must have been really smart? . . . I don't know. I know that we certainly never expected her when they said butler service."

Despite their claims of feeling bad for the housekeepers, however, guests sometimes used invisible labor for fun or allowed their children to do so. Andrew told me about a family trip to Asia, "We'd jokingly say, 'Let's push the call button and see how many seconds it takes for someone to arrive in the room.'" Dorothy recounted of a particular hotel, "My son was maybe twelve the first time we went. . . . He'd run out [of the room], and then he'd wait to see how long it would take them to refold the toilet paper. We couldn't figure out how they knew." The guests coded this as part of the mystique of the hotel, in a sense its power over them. But at the same time they were making use of their own power over a particular kind of human labor, which is especially easy to do when that labor is invisible.

These views of workers are implicitly racialized, which seems to lead to both a sense of guilt and the capacity to code work as invisible.[12] On the one hand, guests felt especially bad for workers of color—for example, the Hispanic maids to whom Evelyn referred above. The racial dimension also marked guests' expressions of concern about hotel workers in developing countries. On the other hand, despite their claims of discomfort, guests may be more likely to feel comfortable when workers doing back of house jobs are of particular racial or ethnic backgrounds. These workers may seem more appropriate for the job. As the quotes above suggest, white people or "model minority" Asians transgress the code of who a servant should be. And it seems unlikely that white guests would repeatedly push the call button if they thought a white worker would be coming to the door.[13]

Philosophies of Work and Class

Guests' views of workers were embedded in certain broader philosophies, suggesting in various ways that disparity was not, in fact, a problem. For example, a few guests I interviewed lamented that service is not respected as a profession in the United States, implying that if it were there would be no reason to worry about these workers being subordinate. Betty argued that lack of respect for service workers as professionals arose historically, thanks to an American resistance to making class distinctions: "[In Europe, service workers] were highly respected for what they did and appreciated. In other words, there was respect for them as people. . . . And in America we were so against class, with the idea that everyone is equal, that we never really developed the service industry as a profession. So the respect never was there. . . . And I think we need to do that." Betty invoked the same idea that we see in strategies of reciprocity: that respect for workers as people and as professionals mitigates structural inequalities. (She seemed to indicate that an attention to class would involve seeing professionalism rather than inequality.) Expressing a similar idea, Dorothy, who came from an immigrant family and had relatives in the restaurant business, said she felt that feeling sorry for workers implies that something is wrong with their jobs.

Guests also expressed a belief that people should not be defined by their jobs alone. Bob defined class as "social standing," unrelated to how much money one has, analogous to royalty or caste systems. He said, "There's no expectation on my side that [workers] should be in a different class. Once you walk outside of the hotel where they work, and you run into them on the street or whatever, they are another person. So there's nothing about their job that defines their social standing in my mind." In a sense, this view contradicts the idea that workers should be respected as professional, because it implicitly defines these jobs as low status.

In a similar vein, some guests proclaimed that "money isn't everything." Like workers, they reduced money to just one of many possible social advantages. Dorothy said, "I don't mean to sound heartless. I just think that other divisions in life about who's lucky and who isn't, at this point in my life, strike me as more serious." She cited "tragedies and illnesses" as fates worse than doing "what is considered a more menial job."

In general, these views of workers, which in many ways parallel those that workers themselves expressed, suggest that disparity is not such a big problem. Guests are deserving, disempowered, or equivalent to workers in their job of serving others. Workers are professionals, or they are upwardly mobile. The work they do is not degrading, and it doesn't define them anyway; money isn't everything; and they can make a reasonable living. Like workers, guests relocate themselves on these symbolic hierarchies; unlike workers, they attempt to avoid being at the top. Lamont found a similar process among American upper-middle-class men. As she argues, "By these shifts in hierarchies, equality can be maintained, at least at the symbolic level."[14]

Organizational Justifications

The organization of work in the hotel and the luxury product itself supported these understandings of work and class. First, the spatial division of labor removed from view the workers who were most different from guests and who therefore might evoke guilt in them. Dorothy, who usually traveled for pleasure, said, "I think for the most part, especially with the people who clean up, you hardly ever encounter them. I don't think [disparity] comes up, because you're rarely face to face. And there's rarely English spoken." Having admitted her discomfort with disparity with housekeepers, Evelyn told me, "I prefer not to see them." Other guests told me they could not comment on the condition of the housekeepers, because they ran into them so infrequently. This kind of response speaks to the expediency of hiding back of house workers from guests, who may be more aware of and more uncomfortable with social differences from them because of both the lower status of the job and the demographics of the workers.

Second, the imperatives of luxury service both obscure and normalize disparity. Friendly, "genuine" attention allows guests to feel that consuming luxury service is legitimate. Eric indicated that the absence of problems characteristic of luxury service meant he rarely thought about inequality: "No, I really don't think about it that much, to tell you the truth. . . . I haven't had situations where service has been bad or rude, certainly as it may happen from time to time in a restaurant, where you say to yourself, 'Who is this jerk working for five dollars an hour treating me like an idiot?'" I asked, "So it's almost because the service is good that you don't notice that?" Eric responded, "Right."

When I asked her about the social distance between herself and the workers, Virginia said: "I thought about that a lot when we were living [in the hotel]. . . . That's a situation that never makes me feel very comfortable. But again, with the staff there, they were just very, very upbeat and very nice. . . . The girl [who took care of our room], we just got to feel that she liked us and maybe she did some extra stuff for us that she wouldn't have done for somebody else." Workers' apparent eagerness to serve—to give the sense that "nothing is too much trouble"—masks the fact that it is work for them, which they provide but cannot consume. If guests look to workers for indications that consuming their labor is acceptable, chances are good they will receive these assurances. Virginia also highlights a special, individual relationship with the worker as a reason to feel comfortable with consuming service.

Finally, as we saw in chapter 5 and above, guests see themselves as having an agreement with the organization to provide services for money and to be responsible for its own workers. Thus, guests can be "free" to develop individual relationships with workers, whose working conditions and remuneration are not their province (unlike in the case of employers of domestic servants). This distinction, again, allows guests to see their relations with workers as decommodified and therefore voluntary on the part of the workers as well as themselves.

Overall, then, guests used various interpretive strategies, supported by organizational characteristics, both to deny and to legitimate their privilege vis-à-vis workers. At the same time, however, their experience in the hotel helped constitute their entitlement to luxury consumption.

PRODUCING THE PRIVILEGED SELF

In addition to *Pretty Woman,* many American films portray the luxury hotel as a site of class transformation. In Ernst Lubitsch's *Ninotchka* (1939), a dour Soviet bureaucrat, played by Greta Garbo, comes to appreciate the joys of romance, laughter, and capitalism (which are inextricably intertwined in the character of Leon, with whom she falls in love) during her stay in the "Royal Suite" in a Parisian luxury hotel. In *Blue Crush* (2002), young white surfer Anne Marie (Kate Bosworth) initially works as a housekeeper in an exclusive resort in Hawaii; after she is fired for yelling at a guest who has left his room a mess (an indicator of her inappropriateness for the job), she takes up with another guest, stays in the room she once cleaned, and learns to live in the lap of luxury. In *Maid in Manhattan* (2003), Jennifer Lopez plays Marisa, a hotel housekeeper who meets a rich politician while wearing a hotel guest's fancy clothes, falls in love with him, and overcomes her "maid" status by marrying him and becoming a hotel manager.[15] The hotels in these films serve as sites for the production and reproduction of the dominant class.[16]

This transformation really does take place in the luxury hotel. Although they enjoy the luxurious environment and service, many guests are insecure about their entitlement to luxury service and their capacity to "do class."[17] They talked about feeling intimidated, not knowing the rules of appearance and behavior, and not feeling that they belonged. Yet, the service itself, though it may be overwhelming at first, reassures anxious guests that they do belong there. Furthermore, guests not only express needs and desires but also learn what these are supposed to be through their experience in the hotel. The service guests receive creates and legitimates needs, and it helps guests to develop a sense of their own entitlement.

Fear of Not Belonging

A *New Yorker* cartoon of a few years ago, by Bruce Eric Kaplan, depicts a couple checking into a hotel. The desk clerk is saying, "Also included in the package is a vague sense of your not being good enough to stay here." Echoing this theme, several guests in my sites described feeling intimidated in the luxury setting in general and by the service in particular. Kim, a young business traveler, had stayed at the Luxury Garden before I interviewed her. She told me, "I found the Luxury Garden, when I first walked in, was definitely a little intimidating, more so than any place that I can recall staying at. . . . It's probably because of the look of the hotel, very serious, quiet." Shirley said, of an early experience at a Four Seasons hotel, "I felt a little bit like an impostor almost, in some ways. . . . It felt pretentious." She said the staff's anticipation of her needs initially "took me aback." I saw this intimidation ethnographically as well. Guests were sometimes visibly startled by having doors opened for them or being recognized. Occasionally they asked, "How did you know my name?" or, "How did you get my car here so quickly?"[18]

As we have seen, guests appreciated the idea that there were no limits in the luxury hotel. Yet at the same time, many guests indicated that they did have to observe rules of behavior, and they often felt insecure about knowing these rules. I have mentioned Mike's comment: "There are internal cultural norms of how you manage yourself in those places, and early on you don't know what those norms are." Guests did not always know, for example, whom and how much to tip or what they were allowed to request of workers.[19] Evelyn told me she was sometimes unsure if she was supposed to try to bribe workers to get a better room, and she said she never knew when to tip the concierge.

I also saw ethnographic evidence of this insecurity, which guests often resolved by asking workers what to do. The Royal Court guests from the rap magazine I mentioned in chapter 4 were clearly unfamiliar with many of the norms of the hotel; one asked me when I brought his car around, "Do I have to tip you?"[20] Another Royal Court guest asked me if he should tip workers all at once at the end of the stay or throughout.[21] Some guests in both hotels seemed unsure of how to give money to workers; they seemed to intuit that openly handing over the bills was somewhat gauche but had not mastered the idea of folding up the money or putting it in an envelope. A Luxury Garden guest was surprised to find out that the newspapers in the lobby were free; he also asked me if he should tip his massage therapist (he should—about 20 percent). The worker is the repository of knowledge here, which again gives her power in the local context of the hotel.

Guests, especially women, also described paying attention to rules about their appearance, and they described feeling very conscious of what others in the hotel were wearing. Virginia said of a luxury hotel, "I think I felt that I needed to look like I belonged there. I needed to get dressed up and not be in my sweatpants and T-shirt . . . [in] the higher end hotels, because you see people that come there either to stay or for meetings and stuff like that, they tend to dress nicely and look like they can afford to stay there, I guess, if that makes any sense." Rose suggested that her appearance was especially important for the treatment she received from workers, saying, "I feel only that sometimes we should look fairly nice when we walk into a hotel the first time, not be too slobby, because it might make a difference in the service or the way we're received."

Shirley invoked the idea of learning appropriate behavior in her discussion of becoming more secure in the hotel:

> For a long time I traveled with my Lands' End luggage. It was perfectly fine for me. Then it occurred to me that people had—that how you look when you go into a hotel like that has a different—people don't necessarily arrive in their jeans with their Lands' End duffel bag. That there's a look. I started to pay attention, just because I wanted not to be inappropriate, especially if it was a business situation with my husband, I certainly didn't want to call attention to myself in a way that might embarrass him, or—not that he's like that—but I think it's sort of coming to a role, that I should know how to handle those sort of situations. . . . I think I did, I started picking up a culture, I wanted to make sure I was playing by the right rules.

I asked, "And do you still feel sometimes like an impostor?" She answered, "Oh, sure. Yeah. Not as much as I used to, because I just decided, you know, I can play this role. Because there is a little bit of playing a role I think. Maybe it's less an impostor now and more that I'm just going to adopt that persona." She explained, laughing, "You know, the persona of somebody who knows how to walk into the lobby of the Four Seasons and handle herself."

This concern with looking the part indicates another way in which the hotel required work of its guests. They felt obliged not only to offer workers reciprocal emotional labor, as we have seen, but also to expend effort in trying to fit in. Here we see a particular performance of self as an element of guest behavior as well as that of workers.

Guests saw workers as powerful agents of this unfamiliar local culture. First, they feared workers' judgment. Sally felt extremely insecure in luxury hotels, even though she knew she was supposed to feel entitled by virtue of her payment:

> I think a lot of the [workers] are really intimidating, and I am just on edge the entire time. . . . I mean you get the idea that they're sizing up your

clothes the second you walk in. And I just don't care. I don't like that. I don't want to be a part of that. . . . I tend to be put off by all the welcoming people, you know. I just don't think they—I don't want them to—I hate being judged by all of them—that's just me. And I think that's the problem I have with the ultra, ultra, ultra hotels. . . . I mean it's the ones, the swallow-tail coat concierge that I think, oh, my God, I don't want to deal with this guy. And that's just me. I mean I'm just—I wish I were a little more secure in my—after all, I am paying, right?

Dorothy said, "I think if you don't get a suite they almost look down on you." Describing an occasion when she had requested a room change but had not wanted a suite, she recounted, "They made me feel that if I wasn't in a position to take the suite, why was I even complaining about the room?" Betty attributed to workers the power to decide if she belonged, regardless of whether she could afford the room: "There's a certain level of satisfaction in the fact that you can stay at a Ritz-Carlton if you want, but you don't want to be treated like a nobody walking in the door." When I mentioned this tendency to him, Alec at the Luxury Garden agreed, saying, "Some guests seem like they are afraid of me." By the same token, guests feared that workers would judge them for being extravagant; Tom said, "They are probably thinking this is pretty ridiculous that people are paying this kind of money to stay here."

Second, guests believed that the workers were in charge of guiding the interaction and establishing its limits. Shirley felt that the workers decided how much to connect with the guests, saying she tended to "take their cue." Andrew said that he and his wife "become as friendly as they let us become." These perceptions invert the luxury standard of letting guests initiate action and determine the tone of the contact.

Third, guests felt diminished when workers seemed to be giving more attention to other clients, indicating that they were more desirable. Christina told me about staying in a luxury hotel when a powerful corporate executive was also a guest; she was annoyed that workers in the restaurant called him by name and offered him extra orange juice but did not do the same for her and her husband. I saw this kind of comparison ethnographically as well. For example, one morning a walk-in customer at the Royal Court restaurant requested a window table. Although two were available, the walk-in guest later complained because the manager had seated Mr. Louis (a frequent hotel guest whom all the workers liked) first, at a table that the other man had thought of as "his." I wrote in my notes, "He basically accused [the manager] of caring more about the in-house guest. . . . It sounded like he had a huge inferiority complex."

Finally, and most surprising, several guests described feeling that the workers expected more demands from them than they were going to make, suggesting that their desires were inadequate. Sally told me, "I'm not going to be asking them to do a lot of things, and [there's] their expectation that I *should* ask them to do a lot of things." Eric described feeling uncomfortable, saying, "I'm much more relaxed in the way that I deal with people . . . [more than] I think a lot of people in hotels are or what the service staff expects you to behave like. . . . I think they expect you to behave in kind of a superior way, you know, that you should expect the solicitous behavior from them." These guests felt deficient because they suspected they were not demanding enough, that they did not inhabit or perform their status appropriately and somehow did not live up to workers' expectations. They also felt uncomfortable receiving the deference that they saw as a hallmark of luxury service.

Although ethnographic observation is less likely than interviews to yield such explicit statements, some guests in both hotels also demonstrated this class insecurity, seeming to project their own fears about entitlement onto the workers. For example, a guest at the Royal Court, already annoyed with the staff, became incensed when an assistant manager informed her that the Sunday *New York Times* she wanted would cost four dollars. She stated indignantly, "I can afford four dollars!" Later the manager said, "She accused me of thinking she couldn't afford it," though in fact he had just wanted to make sure she knew it was not free in order to minimize the possibility of displeasing her. In 2003, when the economy was weak, Luxury Garden managers told workers to let guests know how much extra services were going to cost (whereas before they had simply assumed the guest would not object to high prices). Alec told me that he had to frame this information delicately, to avoid offending guests by seeming to think them not rich enough, for instance, "I'll just put that ninety-five-dollar charge on your room account."

Guests often attributed their feelings of insecurity, like their conflicts about consumption, to their modest upbringings. Virginia, whom I quoted above as being ambivalent about spending money, said: "It's kind of like you weren't really born with a silver spoon in your mouth, and it doesn't always feel very comfortable when it's in there." The luxury hotel initially represented an unknown frontier of high-end splendor. As Mike put it, "I didn't know that beds came that big and that you had three-hundred-count linen. I didn't know what that was." Martha said of upscale hotels, "I didn't know they existed." The hotels are thus sites for the acquisition of a certain kind of cultural capital linked to consumption. Guests learn not only proper tastes and legitimate desires but also appropriate presentation of self and treatment of workers.

As we have seen, workers do in fact evaluate guests on these criteria—on their appearance, their behavior, and their "right" to stay in the hotel. The informants in my sample, at least before they learned the rules of the game, were the kind of guests whom workers might be especially inclined to look down on critically—or to condescend to sympathetically. At the same time, guests seemed to project an especially extreme version of class insecurity onto workers; for example, I do not believe workers judged guests for not demanding enough. However, the sense of disenfranchisement some guests feel in the hotel recasts workers as powerful and thus serves to minimize guests' perception of inequality with workers, just as it does for workers themselves. This sense of inadequacy itself obscures the guest's overall privilege and also helps to individualize the relation. These fears also demonstrate the importance to guests of their interactions with workers; whether accurate or imagined, workers' opinions about guests were meaningful to them. Money alone did not lead to a sense of entitlement or comfort.

Learning Luxury

In the 1946 Ernst Lubitsch film *Cluny Brown*, the title character, a young female plumber, recounts her experience having tea at the Ritz. She says, "It wasn't the tea [that I liked]; it was the 'Yes, miss?' and 'Crumpets, miss?' I didn't feel out of place at all." Like this character, guests who were uncomfortable in the hotel setting were made to feel comfortable by the workers and the luxury treatment. By observing the imperatives of luxury service, workers mitigated guests' sense of insecurity and alienation and legitimated both their presence in the hotel and their desires.[22]

Many guests said what they liked most about luxury hotels was that the workers treated them "like you belong" or "like a friend." Linda said she felt "more at home" when the staff knew her name. Guests invested workers with the power to decide whether they belonged or not. As Andrew put it, "When you're in an upscale hotel, you know you're in an upscale hotel, and let's just maybe analyze the other side of it. You certainly don't want to feel—you don't want the feeling that they know it's an upscale hotel and there's any doubt or any question that you should be there. I think the hotels that make you feel comfortable and almost like you're coming home, so to speak, I think that's a great feeling." Shirley said, "Part of being able to play the role was having them act like I belonged there. Just knowing my name and anticipating my needs in a certain way."

Eric, a self-made businessman and owner of a large company, described both his intimidation in the luxury environment and his process of acclimation to it:

> I don't think I stayed in a hotel until well after I got married. . . . I mean I remember when I was . . . college age and would drive down to Florida. We would always stay in these fleabag type hotels when we were kids,, with our buddies. Part of our goal was always—you drive by the good hotels and maybe go over there for a drink, and you hope that one day you could afford to stay there. . . . Some of these places can be a little bit stuffy, and it's not like staying at the Holiday Inn. . . . You've got kind of the beautiful people; it's very elegant and dignified. And you grew up on the southwest side of Chicago, and you end up going into a premier or first-class hotel the first time, and it can be very intimidating. . . . But the people are service personnel, and after you stay there you kind of feel like you end up belonging there.

Workers legitimated other kinds of consumption beyond simply staying in the hotel. I witnessed this process ethnographically in an encounter with Mrs. MacKenzie, who was planning to stay at the Luxury Garden on New

Year's Eve with her husband. She called the concierge desk in November to begin making their plans for the evening. At one point in our conversation, she was trying to decide between using a regular sedan or a limousine for the evening. Because she seemed to want the limo, I said, "Well, it's only once a year, you should have what you want." She answered, "You should be in sales," and decided to take the limo. After checking with the company, I called her back to let her know about the ten-hour minimum (meaning the cost would be seven hundred dollars plus tax and tip). I assumed she would change to a sedan, but she said, "I was thinking about what you said, and you're right; we don't do this very often, so I'm going to stay with the limo." I wrote in my notes, "It was as if I had just given her the justification she was looking for to spend more money."

Mrs. MacKenzie's response demonstrates, first, her own ambivalence about spending the money and, second, the power she projected onto me to give her permission to spend it. Not knowing her at all, I had simply happened upon a framing of the issue that resonated with her. It made no difference to me whether she used the limo or not; I was simply trying to customize my response to what she seemed to want to hear. My job was to empathize with her, and in doing so I unwittingly also legitimated a desire about which she felt conflicted. (Most concierges do have an economic motive to promote this kind of consumption because of their commissions; hence, their incentive structure makes it more likely that they will encourage high-level consumption and thus mediate transformation.)

Just as workers in the early twentieth century taught guests how to ride elevators,[23] the workers I observed trained guests on what their behavior should be in the hotel and elsewhere. I have described their subtle policing of the contract. More explicitly, workers answered the kinds of questions I have mentioned about tipping and appropriate dress. Max sometimes lauded guests for making an emotional connection. When a guest asked if she had to pay for the stamp he had given her, he responded, "Your smile is postage enough." On another occasion he told a guest who was thanking him, "Your smile made it all worthwhile."

Workers and managers clearly saw guests' expectations as created within the hotel. We have seen this implicitly in the ways they tried to control or limit guests' demands and behaviors, but workers also talked about it more explicitly. For example, they were wary of giving room upgrades. As Petra at the Royal Court told me, "You have to be careful about that, because there are a lot of people who will always want it if you do it for them once." At the Royal Court, workers and managers had to strategize about how to increase the low rates of frequent guests who had been staying at the hotel for a long time and had become accustomed to paying much less than others. At the Luxury Garden, Antonio talked explicitly about educating Dr. Kramer, who had requested a rental convertible. The guest had delayed in giving us his license information, so the car was not supposed to come until 12:30. It arrived at noon, but Antonio said, "Don't tell him, because he needs to wait. If we tell him, next time he'll expect it to be just as fast."

Workers' practices led guests to become comfortable with their own entitlement to stay in the hotel, to spend money, and to consume services that were initially unfamiliar. In this process, their perceptions of workers shifted. Shirley said that initially she had found workers in luxury hotels "kind of cool and sophisticated and a bit aloof." Later, demonstrating some ambivalence, she commented, "I think hotel people are much more friendly, much more accommodating than my first experience. And that could be more a reflection of my own insecurity at that level of hotel. But I have found them to be more—they extend themselves more than my first experiences. But I'm willing to guess that that could be as much my own awkwardness too."

In fact, over time, guests described taking a new approach to the workers, in which the guests defended their own entitlement and began to speak more authoritatively, interactively enforcing their rights. Adam talked about how he ensured that workers behaved as he wanted: "I think also it can be your air of confidence and the way it shows in your voice. I'm not talking about raising your voice but just the way you talk. If a front desk person is maybe a young person who's kind of snotty or arrogant and you just with your voice demand attention without raising it a decibel." I asked, "How do you think you are able to do that?" Adam answered, "Just experience and getting older and being secure." Eric, the guest quoted above as initially insecure, complained of a luxury hotel worker who told his assistant that they would not change the policy of a three-night minimum for him: "I was so flabbergasted by that, I ended up getting on the phone myself and talking to the reservationist, and I just said, 'Hey, if that's your policy, you just lost all of our company's business.'"

Andrew described refusing to accept a hotel room he did not like, even remembering the moment when he realized he could get what he wanted by behaving a certain way, though he did not want me to think he was too aggressive:

> This is something that I've gotten, I would say, a little more demanding [about], and I hope I don't come off as being a little more pushy when I make these statements. First of all, I ask at the front desk, Is this the best room available? And I remember in this particular German hotel—and I think this is kind of where I got to be a little more aggressive—they said, "This is a very good room." They took me up to the room and it looked like 1930s, you know, a prewar hotel room. I said to the bell boy, "This is unacceptable." So he called back down, got the keys to another room, took me there. It was a bigger room but still no charm, no nothing, again kind of a '30s, German modern kind of a thing. I said, "This is not acceptable." I said, you know, "I asked for one of your better rooms, and I don't consider this to be a better room." So he called back down. The next room they took us to was a two-room suite, very much in the Bavarian style, with wood canopy bed and just a lot of charm and everything. And I said, "This is an acceptable room. This is something that I will enjoy staying in." I just kind of realized that these rooms are there, and sometimes you have to ask for them and get a little pushy, I guess.

In these examples we see the birth of the "authority in reserve" tone that I described in chapter 5.

In my sites, some guests explicitly invoked their own experience in order to suggest that they could not be fooled. When a worker and then at a manager at the Royal Court told a caller, truthfully, that the hotel was full, she screamed at them, repeatedly saying, "I know you hold rooms. . . . I've stayed in hotels before!" A guest at the Luxury Garden complained to me that he had not been given a receipt after his rental car was returned; he said sternly, "I am a very experienced traveler, and I have never not gotten a receipt."

Bourdieu wrote that "having a million does not in itself make one able to live like a millionaire; and parvenus generally take their time to learn that what they see as culpable prodigality is, in their new condition, expenditure of basic necessity."[24] Over time luxury experience did become a need. Guests talked about how hard it was, having become accustomed to this level of consumption, to lower their expectations. Kim, who stayed in luxury hotels for business but was not wealthy, told me, "A luxury once tried becomes a necessity." She recounted:

> It's this terrible thing that happens. I mean when you travel for business like that, and then you really get used to it and you want to repeat it. I mean I can't believe I said this, but last Christmas I said to my sister, "I am *not* staying at the Holiday Inn," and she was like, "What the heck is wrong with the Holiday Inn?" Then I realized what has happened to me. I had to crack up weeks later when that statement was played back to me, like "What's the matter with me?" . . . You just get used to stuff, and it becomes—I think it's natural. I'm sure I'm not the only one like that.

Dorothy expressed a similar emotion, saying, "I think if I went to Venice and I went back to, you know, like I used to stay at [a midrange hotel], I think I'd feel bad. Because it's like when you get to be in first class sometimes, and when you have to go back in the back of the plane you know what goes on in front, so you feel bad."

Some guests expressed ambivalence about how wedded they were to this kind of consumption. When I asked Tom if it was hard for him to get used to staying in this type of hotel, he responded:

> The biggest shock is maybe how expensive some of these [hotels] were. And I guess the shock is maybe that once you've experienced it, you end up justifying that it's okay, that it's worth it. But if you think about it too hard it's hard to justify why you'd spend seven hundred dollars a night at a hotel. . . . It's like why is a hundred-dollar bottle of wine—is that ten times better than a ten-dollar bottle of wine? Probably not, but once you've tasted it—I guess if you're able to afford it, it's kind of a reward for your hard work. So I mean the same thing with any luxury item. . . . I don't think you can justify those kind of decisions on economic terms. . . . But if you try it and you like it, and you say "Gee, it's pretty nice."

Asked if he thought about how much the hotel cost, he said, "No. I think the first few times we might, but after you kind of have broken yourself into it, you realize it's a real special experience." Here he invokes compensation for his own work in the past as a legitimation of his consumption, but primarily he suggests that although luxury consumption does not make sense in "economic terms," it becomes something you want to continue to consume, as long as you don't "think about it too hard."

Other guests seemed invested in representing themselves as less desirous of this type of experience than perhaps they actually were. As I noted above, Martha portrayed herself as staying in luxury hotels to please her husband, but he disputed this account. Shirley told me in our telephone interview that she did not want to become too accustomed to consuming at this level. For example, she said about the upcoming trip she and her husband were taking to Europe, "We could easily be in a two-star place by the train station in a town in France, and that would be fine with me. It would." But her husband was laughing in the background; she chuckled and said, "My husband's saying, 'I don't think so.'" Still ambivalent, these guests were not willing to express luxury consumption as a basic need.

Hotel guests also talked about becoming entitled to consume the labor of others in realms besides their hotel stays. For instance, though her husband had been a successful businessman for many years, Martha had never hired workers when she hosted social functions. She expressed her newfound sense of entitlement when she told me, somewhat amazed, "This year I did have a Christmas party for people, and I didn't cook, for like the first time in my life. . . . The Ritz catered it. And it was, like, wonderful, because I just realized, wow, all these years you've worked like a dog, and now you can just have people come in and do that, you know, they'll do that. You can do that. You can have people come in." Intellectually she had known such a possibility existed, of course, but it had not felt like an option for her.

Guests also talked about how their sense of ambivalence was mitigated over time, indicating an acceptance of their privileged place in the world. I asked Shirley if she felt she was more accustomed to the disparity between herself and hotel workers than she used to be, and she said, "Yes. Yes, I think I'm more used to it. I try not to take it for granted, but yes." Linda told me of spending money on herself, "I just recently allowed myself to feel like, 'I *can* do it.'" She said that she was "learning not to think about it" and that "sometimes [self]-denial is a reflex, and it's liberating to realize that." Linda's comment indicates that the process of acceptance can involve closing down her awareness of disparity rather than constructing explicit justifications of it.

Not all the guests I interviewed expressed these doubts and insecurities about their belonging in the hotel. Those who came from wealthy backgrounds had long been accustomed to luxury consumption. Their dispositions already functioned to make them comfortable in this environment. However, the service functioned equally, albeit less dramatically, to maintain their sense of themselves as entitled luxury consumers. In this sense their feeling of entitlement was continually reproduced and reconstituted. Furthermore, these guests also talked about the importance of reciprocity and signaled tensions between seeing the worker as an equal human and benefiting from her willingness to serve.

Thus, the hotel is a site of the constitution of particular kinds of dispositions, where individuals are interpellated into their position as class subjects through their consumption of luxury service itself. Guests shift from performing to inhabiting the role. They become not only certain kinds of *customers* but also certain kinds of *people*—those who are especially entitled to care and labor. Practices that constitute what Althusser called "ideological recognition" are ongoing in the hotel, both in interactions between guests and workers and in the availability of certain other services involving human labor. Like religious ideology, luxury service hails consumers, telling them, "this is your place in the world," obtaining from them "the *recognition* that they really do occupy the place it designates for them as theirs in the world, a fixed residence: 'It really is me, I am here, a worker, a boss, or a soldier!'" In this context, the "practical rituals of the most elementary everyday life," including "the hand-shake, the fact of calling you by your name,"[25] and so on, are not only components of ideological recognition in some broad sense of interpellation generally but also elements of a more specifically classed recognition that tells guests and workers who they are, hailing them as subjects entitled to consume in a particular way.

This process can also be interpreted as a moment in the creation of habitus, à la Pierre Bourdieu. Habitus, a set of dispositions that structure action, develops in individuals, produced by "the conditionings associated with a particular class of conditions of existence."[26] The interpellative function performed by the hotel is a practical moment in the creation of habitus, the consumer's capacity to feel as though he belongs in the hotel and knows how to behave there. By extension, this brings about his sense of himself as enjoying, in a "natural" way, the prerogatives of the upper class. The hotel produces and reproduces these class dispositions.

THE CONSENTING CONSUMER

Scholars in both Marxist and Weberian traditions tend not to problematize wealthy people's consent to consume at the highest level possible or to participate in the social order that favors them. These scholars posit implicitly or explicitly that people have an innate, though not always conscious, interest in increasing their status or material advantages or both.[27] But my data on guests' conflicts about consumption show that it is not somehow psychologically automatic for high-end consumers, first, to take advantage of their social prerogatives and, second, to see these prerogatives as natural and unproblematic. The sense of entitlement to consume is an analytical problem, not an inherent feature of human nature or capitalist society.

This chapter has looked at how exactly members of the dominant class forge, in Paul Willis's terms, their "own legitimations."[28] Guests justify their conflicts about consuming luxury service just as workers resolve their discomfort with producing it: through interpretive, practical, and comparative strategies of self and other, which can be internally contradictory. They obscure their own privilege by trying not to think about it, making comparisons with people wealthier than they or mentally shuffling responsibility for workers' well-being onto managers. They mitigate their privilege by practicing reciprocity toward workers and casting them as equals. They justify entitlement by constructing themselves as deserving or dependent and as more moderate than their peers. They relativize it by thinking of workers as professionals, as temporarily in the job, as having status within the hotel, or as "not so badly off" in relation to a general idea of an acceptable standard of living.

These strategies depend on characteristics of individuals—especially their own background, their reasons for travel, and their gender (which is itself, of course, linked to broader social processes). Yet these strategies are also tied to features of the hotel itself, including service imperatives and the organization of work. Finally, these interpretations of self and other depend on the same culturally inflected repertoires of judgment we have seen in previous chapters. Racialized notions, imported from outside the hotel, of what kinds of people are appropriate for certain types of work also come into play.

Guest privilege is not only legitimated but also *constituted* in the hotel, principally in interactions between workers and guests. Guests' insecurities are mitigated by workers and services that tell guests they belong. They are shown what kinds of needs and wants are appropriate, and their sense of entitlement to consume workers' labor is expanded. At the same time, however, there are limits; workers cast entitlement as conditional by showing guests in subtle ways that expectations of them do exist, that they must play by the rules of the game. The hotel is a training ground for negotiating the relationship between obligation and entitlement that we have seen throughout this book. It is also a site of producing entitled subjects more generally, a place where people become accustomed to being served.

For my subjects who grew up in working- or middle-class circumstances, the need for the production of entitlement is especially clear, for it has not been shaped in the typical sites (families, exclusive schools, elite social clubs, and so on). In the hotel, entitlement depends on consuming the labor of others rather than on the explicit training and networking opportunities characteristic of sites in other studies. The service is accessible to anyone with the means to pay (rather than with a particular pedigree) and thus can be seen as an institution of social mobility. It not only reproduces the already-dominant class but also mediates the entitlement of the newly rich. Just like in the movies.

Conclusion

CLASS, CULTURE, AND THE SERVICE THEATER

In 1918, Herbert L. Stewart, a professor at Dalhousie University in Nova Scotia, published an article in the *American Journal of Sociology* critiquing luxury consumption, especially among the idle rich. Taking wealthy people to task for judging "the poor man who debases himself with liquor," he argued, "It may turn out that the life of idiotic ostentation makes humanity quite as despicable as the life of a drunkard, and that the image of God is less defaced in a saloon of the Bowery than in those jeweled birthday parties for dogs with which the New York Four Hundred disgust all civilized mankind." He wrote, "That much of this is, in the face of the world's needs, an enormity for which all defense is mere shamelessness no conscientious person will deny. . . . Take the advertisement of a present-day 'millionaire's hotel,' with the assurance it gives of 'the very last word in sumptuousness.' Is this not one of the features of our time upon which we all trust that a wiser age will look back, not only with condemnation, but with a sense of nausea?"[1]

More than half a century later, in the 1981 film *My Dinner with André*, which documents an extended philosophical conversation between Wallace Shawn and André Gregory, Gregory expresses a similar sentiment. But he links wealth to the entitlement to subordinated labor. He comments to Shawn:

> [I]f we allowed ourselves to see what we're doing every day, we might find it just too nauseating. I mean, the way we treat other people—I mean, you know, every day, several times a day, I walk into my apartment building. The doorman calls me Mr. Gregory, and I call him Jimmy. . . . Now already, what is the difference between that and the Southern plantation owner who's got slaves? You see, I think that an act of murder is committed at that moment, when I walk into my building. Because here is a dignified, intelligent man, a man of my own age, and when I call him Jimmy, then he becomes a child, and I'm an adult. Because I can buy my way into that building.[2]

Twenty-five years later still, as we have seen, Stewart's wiser age seems not to have dawned. Indeed, the nausea both Stewart and Gregory invoke seems to have been replaced by a hunger for upscale goods and services, fueling the growth of luxury consumption. This consumption depends on the high and growing incomes of those at the top, which have increasingly diverged from those at the bottom. Despite this inequality, ethical critiques like Stewart's and Gregory's are scarce in public discourse. Astronomical CEO salaries raise little public outcry, because cultural norms regarding appropriate compensation and inequality have shifted in the last twenty or thirty years.[3] More people than ever believe they can achieve a higher standard of living than their parents, and pundits and some scholars have declared "the end of class."[4]

How can the dynamics of production-consumption in the luxury hotel help us understand the legitimacy of class inequality in the service economy? How might we continue to investigate the link between service work and class? And what are the possibilities for social critique and change? These are the questions I explore in this conclusion.

SERVICE WORK AND CLASS ENTITLEMENTS

I have argued that interactive service complicates the traditional view of class in work. The traditional approach takes the point of (factory) production as the paradigmatic site of class exploitation and focuses on how labor processes generate alienation and resistance among workers. Even analyses of the service sector have drawn on this paradigm. But, in fact, the service sector—especially service that features class asymmetry between customers and workers—is different. New forms of inequality come into play, adding a further object of criticism to the traditional one of exploitation. At stake in the hotel is not only the production of inequality through the appropriation of labor effort but also workers' and clients' unequal entitlement to material and emotional resources. I have therefore focused not on relations of *exploitation in production* but on relations of *entitlement in production-consumption*.

These entitlements are class based, arising from the class positions of workers and clients, including their locations in global and local divisions of labor. Such entitlements have two aspects. First, unequal entitlements to material resources that exist outside the hotel determine workers' and guests' relative positions inside the hotel (guests pay to consume the hotel's product, while workers are paid to produce it). Second, by virtue of their greater material resources, guests receive more personal attention and labor than workers receive. Luxury service thus both *depends on* unequal entitlements to material resources and *guarantees* unequal entitlements to recognition.

Class not only structures these sites but is also "accomplished" interactively within them. As Amy Hanser writes, "Service interactions that involve acts of deference . . . become practical enactments of relative social locations, a 'doing' of social difference."[5] Workers and guests perform class in their appearance and demeanor as well as in their interactions. This "doing" of class is not unlike the doing of gender that many scholars have analyzed.[6] It is performative but not necessarily inauthentic; rather, this "acting" of class can feel genuine and natural for both workers and guests in the hotel.[7]

Furthermore, the effects of the luxury workplace—now the service theater—on workers differ from those usually described in the literature. Rather than foster resistance or alienate the worker from himself, relations of production-consumption here primarily *normalize* class entitlements, leading both workers and guests to take them for granted. This normalization is a paradoxical result of workers' and guests' strategies of self. Workers construct and defend nonsubordinate selves, drawing on local, organizationally and culturally inflected repertoires of selfhood to create and emphasize autonomy, authority, competence, prestige, benevolence, discernment, morality, and privilege. These self-constructions are not coping mechanisms that workers create to protect "authentic" selves that arise outside the labor process; rather, they depend on consenting participation in work. Guests, for their part, also work to create needy, deserving, and generous selves in order to overcome their fears of not belonging or of exploiting workers.

But these strategies for mitigating class entitlements also lead these actors to begin to take them for granted. Catering to guests' every need comes to seem reasonable to workers, just as having their needs catered to seems appropriate to guests. The material inequalities in which both are embedded recede into the background and are normalized.

FROM COMMODITY FETISHISM TO INTERACTIVE NORMALIZATION

Especially important here is that normalization depends on interaction. For Marx, the obscuring of exploitative production relations happened *outside* work, through commodity fetishism; when tangible goods were exchanged in the market, a "definite social relation between men" assumed "the fantastic form of a relation between things."[8] But in the service theater, where production and consumption are no longer separate, the interactive product is intangible, and inequality is obvious; no material object obscures awareness of social relations. Replacing the "ghostly objectivity" of the commodity, individual relationships among workers, managers, and clients normalize the patent inequalities of production-consumption.[9]

Individual relationships take primacy over class relations in several ways in the hotel. First, both guests and workers are created as independent individual actors.[10] Customized service indicates to guests that they are unique and deserving individuals. Workers are cast and cast themselves as autonomous individuals, making choices in games of money and skill, in which incentives and rewards are individual. Second, literal and symbolic interpersonal relationships underpin workers' sense of nonsubordinate, nonexploitative individual selfhood. Competitive and comparative relations with other workers help them establish autonomous, competent, and privileged selves. These lateral relations usually supersede any potential feeling of collectivity among workers, and they deflect attention from hierarchical relations with managers and guests. At the same time, worker comparisons with guests cast workers as personally superior and advantaged in a range of ways. In this process, guest wealth becomes an individual trait analogous to morality or intelligence.

Meaningful contact between individual workers and individual guests further recasts class relations as individual relationships, this time as relationships of equality. Despite the class gulf, both parties tend to focus on what they have in common rather than what separates them (an approach that managers also try to foster). Both workers and guests emphasize workers' entitlement to emotional and financial reciprocity. Often, long-term acquaintanceships or even friendships develop. Establishing and maintaining these connections helps both workers and guests to interpret their relations as egalitarian rather than subordinating. When guests transgress the implicit contract, workers punish them, symbolically reestablishing their own entitlements. But again, these punishments are couched in individual rather than class terms.

Scholars of work, therefore, must take positive interactions seriously rather than dismiss them as only performative, forced, or instrumental. The relationships that develop between guests and workers are not "false" or "imaginary" friendships. Indeed, their very meaningfulness is what makes them important for normalization. Rather than commodified interactions threatening authentic selfhood, as Hochschild and others would predict, authentic interaction threatens the possibility of social critique.[11]

SERVICE WORK AND SOCIAL REPRODUCTION

Worker-guest interactions in luxury hotels operate against the possibility of self-conscious class identifications, because they foster a sense of individual personality, individual interests, and individual relationships. But workers and guests nonetheless produce themselves and each other as classed subjects, in that they have particular understandings of their own entitlements and those of others. In consenting to produce and consume luxury service, they also consent to the broader idea that it is acceptable for some people (those with more material resources) to receive more attention and subordinating labor and for others to provide that attention and labor. These are not explicit legitimations; rather, they are implicit mechanisms that lead both workers and guests to feel comfortable on their own side of the front desk.

By shaping the entitlements and dispositions of workers and guests and constituting inequality as normal, the hotel is serving a function long associated with social institutions outside work: the function of social reproduction, or maintenance of the status quo. Institutions of social reproduction, such as families, schools, religious institutions, trade unions, and civic associations, shape people's dispositions, capacities, and common sense. Experiences in these social sites influence subjects' understandings of their own place in the world and reinforce the appearance of naturalness or inevitability of that world. For the most part, these theorists argue, subjects thus constituted will act in ways that reproduce rather than challenge the social order. They will choose their own subordination, in many cases. And they will actively consent to unequal social arrangements by participating in these institutions—voting, praying, attending school, and so on.[12] Although change is not impossible, it is unlikely.

These institutions have typically been located conceptually outside production, in the realm of ideology or culture. Work is usually considered to produce resisting rather than consenting consciousness. Scholars of gender have usefully transcended this distinction, showing how gender identities are constituted and normalized in a range of ways within as well as outside paid and unpaid labor.[13] To a lesser extent, researchers have connected the legitimation of racial inequalities to work, especially but not exclusively within paid household labor.[14] Bourdieu linked class dispositions and legitimations to market mechanisms by looking at the role of consumption in perpetuating social hierarchies.[15] But in general the production of class dispositions and consent to an unequal class order has not been associated with work; this separation has reinforced a conceptual separation between work and culture that dates back to the old Marxist distinction between base and superstructure.

In some ways, Burawoy's work is an exception to this trend. Drawing on Gramsci's claim that "hegemony [in the United States] is born in the factory," Burawoy brought reproduction into the workplace. He argued that consent is not located in nonwork institutions of civil society (as Gramsci had suggested was the case in Europe) or in the preexisting values and attitudes of workers. Rather, work arrangements and hierarchies of status and skill among workers explain their consent to exploitation in the labor process and, by extension, to capitalist relations.[16] But Burawoy was concerned only with the securing and obscuring of surplus value at the point of production. He did not connect worker subjectivities on the job to class identities or entitlements outside the factory.

Taking a different tack, Robin Leidner linked service work to culture outside work, arguing that because consumers are present at the "point of production" in service workplaces, interactions affect culture as a whole. In particular, Leidner feared that routinization in workplace interactions might spread to social intercourse generally, changing norms about how people should treat one another.[17] But she was less attentive to how cultural norms from outside work might affect relations within work. And, just as Burawoy left out the broader cultural issues of identities, meanings, and entitlements outside the workplace, Leidner left out structural issues of class and reproduction. She was concerned with the implications of interactions for incivility, not inequality. (Other "cultural" approaches to work in the symbolic interactionist tradition are even less concerned with class inequality; here, the term *cultural* usually indicates a delinking from structural relations.)[18]

What remains, then, is to bring these ideas together, to connect class to interactive work and culture. Identities and meanings are embedded in relations of production-consumption, which are themselves cultural. Workers and guests in the luxury hotel bring certain kinds of dispositions and entitlements with them, which shape their experiences and behavior in the hotel. But, at the same time, work organization, social relationships, and the distribution of labor in the hotel also shape these dispositions and entitlements. The production of dispositions in the hotel is presumably analogous to what happens in many other social institutions in which workers and clients also participate, including schools, families, clubs, and political organizations. Their experience in the hotel is unlikely to seem much different to them from their experiences in these other sites. I suggest that it should not seem so different to sociologists either and, thus, that dichotomies between inside and outside work, culture and production, are overstated.

In the luxury hotel, this combination facilitates social reproduction. Guests' sense of entitlement to the labor of others is solidified, as is their sense of reciprocal obligation to the individuals providing that labor. Workers' interests are constituted in such a way that providing their subordinated labor to others benefits them. Their sense of powerful selfhood is, for the most part, also reinforced. It seems likely that other sites of professionalized luxury service, including high-end restaurants, spas, exclusive recreational clubs, first-class airline cabins, fancy department stores, and bureaucratically organized personal services, also normalize existing social relations, legitimating and reproducing ideas about people and about class, race, gender, and so on. Professional and semiprofessional production-consumption may also be organized around class entitlements (much as gender inequalities operate in these relations).[19]

Not all service theaters, of course, will serve this function of reproduction. Some may encourage critique of these relations and engender worker alienation or resistance. In domestic service, for example, it appears that the organization of unequal entitlements produces resentment and resistance.[20] This difference may be due to consistent racial stratification between client-employers and domestic workers, the personalistic nature of the employment relation, and minimal symbolic and material benefits for domestic workers compared with the workers I have studied. In other service theaters, unequal entitlements between managers and workers may be more salient than those between customers and workers, and thus the function and character of production-consumption relations may be entirely different.

Many factors surely influence which inequalities characterize production-consumption relationships, how they are negotiated, and what that means for the production of workers' and clients' understandings of the world. We must consider variation in, among other factors, industry, sector (luxury or not), the tangibility of the product, worker and customer demographics, and labor market conditions (including the presence of unions). Organizational and cultural factors also matter, as we have seen. The comparison of the Luxury Garden and the Royal Court has highlighted organizational variation in resources that shape the interactions, strategies, and dispositions of workers and guests. Cultural repertoires and norms also influence ideas of status, morality, and reciprocity. Worker and client strategies of self, therefore, probably vary not only by organization but also regionally or cross-nationally.[21]

The general point is that we must devise more flexible concepts to describe and theorize sites of production-consumption, finding new ways both to map variation among service theaters and to incorporate a focus on interaction with a social critique. I have suggested emphasizing entitlement over exploitation, consent over control, and reproduction over resistance. Whatever the approach, we must open up the dichotomies that currently prevail in the critical sociology of work. To take for granted oppositions between production and culture, control and resistance, authentic and inauthentic selves, and workers and clients, constrains our analysis.

CRITIQUE, CONTESTATION, AND CHANGE

To think about the service theater as a site of social reproduction may seem depressing, because it suggests that change is unlikely. But social reproduction is never guaranteed; as Paul Willis has argued, "there is no inevitability of outcomes."[22] How can we think about challenging hegemonic ideas that cast class inequality as unimportant?

As this book goes to press, thousands of hotel workers are fighting for power in the industry. Beginning in 2004, members of UNITE HERE, a union known for its commitment to strategic and confrontational organizing, staged pickets, boycotts, walkouts, and strikes in their search for better contracts.[23] These workers have put themselves on the line not only for more favorable wages, benefits, and working conditions but also to achieve the goal of coordinating contract expiration dates in 2006, to give the union more national leverage. In June 2005, for example, workers in Los Angeles signed a contract in which they gave up a wage increase in order to ensure that their contract would also expire in 2006.[24] In the spring of 2006, the union drew on this strength to launch a campaign to pursue contracts and new organizing nationwide.

These workers do not appear to be consenting to unequal entitlements. Indeed, they are contesting employers' entitlement to benefit from the fruits of their labor without fairly· compensating them. They are defending their own entitlement to a living wage, to health and pension benefits, to decent working conditions and respect from managers. By seeking similar contract expiration dates, they have struggled to expand these entitlements to include collective power and leverage. These rights are of the utmost importance to all workers, especially to those in the low-paid jobs that characterize the contemporary service economy. These rights are also difficult to protect, because aggressive antiunion employers and conservative governments have abandoned the social contract that reigned in the United States in the postwar years.[25]

The actions of these workers and their unions, and others like them, are a vivid example of the revitalization of the labor movement, which, while tenuous, bodes well for the possibility of developing solidarity among workers and critiques of unequal entitlements within work. But what do they have to do with the workers at the Luxury Garden and the Royal Court, who made few moves toward unionization? It is, of course, because of union density and management's effort to avoid unionization that Royal Court and Luxury Garden workers earn a living wage—some of them significantly more than that—and receive solid health and pension benefits and protection from arbitrary dismissal. Ironically, though, these conditions probably act as a disincentive to unionize, since workers already enjoy many of the advantages of the union contract.

I suspect, however, that their lack of interest in unionization is also related to the stability of manager-worker and guest-worker relations, which reinforce each other. As union organizers know, it is often harder to organize front of house workers because of their relationships with clients.[26] At the Luxury Garden, managers tended not to transgress worker prerogatives related to autonomy and games, and they generated resources for powerful self-conceptions, such as discourses of prestige and a division of labor that allowed workers to make distinctions between themselves and their colleagues. At the same time, guest-worker relations lent workers status and helped to establish them as entitled. The managerial regime at the Royal Court was less stable, in that managers did not always uphold workers' self-conceptions. Here, relations with guests seemed to provide a reason for workers to stay on the job even when managers acted arbitrarily or unsupportively. (Looking at luxury hotels in an area of low union density, and perhaps comparing them with nonluxury hotels in the same place, would help to show whether guest-worker relations exert a stabilizing influence.)

Royal Court workers did withdraw consent when managers interfered with their autonomy and when their preexisting strategies of self could not mesh with the resources available to them on the job. But these withdrawals of consent happened on an individual basis; workers simply quit. The chances that these workers or workers in similar circumstances might take organized, collective action seem slim. Managers' violations of the established rules of the game might lead to organized action, but they would have to be major transgressions of workers' expectations.

But another crucial question emerges here: What are the possibilities for challenging unequal *worker-client* entitlements and dominant ideas about income and class inequality generally? The axis of contestation in the union dispute, as in most of the critical sociological literature on work, is between workers and employers. It is firmly located in the realm of production, in particular a concept of production that does not involve clients, who cannot be regulated by the employment contract.[27] What might contestation look like along the worker-client axis I have been talking about? Are there other ways to think about unsettling this relation besides as a by-product of worker-manager relations?

On the one hand, such contestation might involve withholding labor from guests. As we have seen, though, this was rare in my sites. Although workers sometimes punished individual guests for breaking the rules of the game, they very rarely withheld labor in any obvious way or for any length of time. When workers did withdraw consent by quitting, they almost never talked about inequality between themselves and guests as the reason; relations with managers were usually the source of their ire. In general, major problems between managers and workers would probably lead workers to further deny their effort to guests; this denial would occur most obviously in the form of a strike but could also play out in less dramatic ways, as indeed occurred when workers at the Royal Court became less invested in their jobs as a result of irritation with managers. But withholding labor from guests either as a result of conflict with managers or as a way to punish guests does not seem to challenge guests' entitlement overall.

What about developing a critical discourse about inequality? This also initially seems unlikely to occur. Elena, the Luxury Garden assistant manager I introduced in chapter 1, did draw on this kind of critique when she left the hotel (and the industry), deciding that she no longer wanted her job to be to ensure "that assholes enjoy their stay." She thought it was "silly to care about rich people getting everything they want." But Elena was unique among the workers I knew in her overt dissatisfaction with the subordinating imperatives of her job and the structural inequalities in which they were embedded.

Potential critiques, however, do appear in many of the workers' attitudes and discourses I have described. As we have seen, although workers gained literal and symbolic benefits from guest characteristics having to do with their wealth, they also sometimes denigrated individual guests' sense of entitlement. Workers marked guests as spoiled or excessively demanding, made occasional comments about lacking sympathy for rich guests, suggested that "these people have too much money," and noted the gulf between the guests and the homeless people outside the hotel's front door. Perhaps most important, workers' withdrawals of labor and strategies of self did reflect a sense of themselves as entitled and of equality as important. Throughout this book, I have avoided theorizing these behaviors as evidence of "resistance," because this concept seems so vague, implying a potential change without specifying what it would be. But I do see them as possible elements of a broader critical view of unequal entitlements. Gramsci believed that helping people develop a critique of their everyday understandings of the world, or "common sense," entailed using elements of common sense itself. Rather than introduce "from scratch" a new form of thinking, he argued for "renovating and making 'critical' an already existing activity."[28] The critical discourses workers apply to individual guests are the already existing activities that might be amplified.

Furthermore, we should not ignore the other side of this coin: the discomfort with consumption that hotel guests expressed. As we saw in chapter 6, they often felt guilty or unsettled about the acceptability of consuming luxury service, not only because of their fears about their own entitlement, but also because of their moral sense of fairness. Their reciprocal actions toward workers demonstrate this sense of obligation, and their interest, in many cases, in forming relationships with workers suggests that their uneasiness about their own entitlement might be amplified in these relationships.

But it is hard to see how consumption entitlements could be contested practically, especially in the service theater itself. In luxury hotels, workers cannot demand (through withdrawing their labor or any other means) that guests be less rich or less entitled to recognition, because the hotel's existence is predicated on these features. And, of course, the issue goes beyond the service theater itself, for class entitlements are embedded in cultures outside the hotel.

If the cultural consequences of service work take place largely in people's heads, contestation must also occur in discourses about common sense. Thus, perhaps incipient critiques and discomforts in the service theater can be attached to broader public discussions of class inequality. Although such discussions are rare, they may be on the rise. In 2005, for example, the *New York Times* published a popular book based on an in-depth series about class.[29] In the same year, debate raged at Harvard about whether students should be able to hire local maids to clean their dorm rooms.[30] In 2006, marchers for immigrant rights carried signs reading "Who cleaned your veggies today?" and "I cleaned your toilets today," highlighting their own subordinated physical labor and symbolically linking it to consumer privilege.

A range of organizations might provide ways of developing the partial and occasional critiques that emerge in workplaces into explicit critiques, as well as offering macrolevel discourses that tap into wealthy people's ambivalence about their own consumption. Unions in particular might broaden their scope beyond worker-employer relations to encourage these critiques. Progressive groups and political parties can do their part. And critical scholars of work could also spend more time thinking about alternatives. Like Herbert Stewart, we can begin to imagine a moral universe in which consuming this kind of service is seen as unnecessary or inappropriate. At the same time, we must connect theories of work to ideas about how to make people see, as André Gregory put it, "what we're doing every day."

APPENDIX A Methods

This study came about indirectly as a result of my volunteer work with the Hotel and Restaurant Workers Union (HERE, now UNITE HERE). I started working with one of the union's locals in 1995, participating in new organizing and contract campaigns in hotels and internal organizing among union members. I had begun working with the local as a result of my interest in immigrant workers, but I soon became fascinated with the hotel industry. At the same time, my academic focus shifted to the service sector, and I learned that very little sociological research on hotels existed.

Without a very specific idea of what I wanted to look at, I began preliminary research for this project in 1998, first reviewing sociological and industry literature in order to get a sense of the hotel sector. In late 1998, I conducted seven interviews with people in the hotel industry (two faculty members in different hotel management programs, the head of the local hotel association, one industry analyst, one former hotel general manager, one union representative, and the vice president of the Convention and Visitors' Bureau) and fifteen interviews with managers in ten local hotels. This sample included managers from four hotels in the high-end "competitive set" (meaning they competed primarily with one another), including the Luxury Garden and the Royal Court. Managers I met during this process allowed me to conduct half-day observations in the restaurants of the Luxury Garden and one other luxury hotel; in October 1999, I sat in on the Ritz-Carlton's two-day orientation for new employees. As I have mentioned in the introduction, these preliminary interviews and observations led me to narrow the focus of the project to luxury hotels.

Ethnography was clearly the best way to study the production and consumption of luxury service and the relations between guests and workers. I knew that much of what I was interested in was not necessarily conscious in the minds of the participants, and thus interviews would not have illuminated the process and relations I wanted to investigate. But I decided to use interviews with guests to explore their perspectives and experiences, which were harder to get at through participant observation.

This project combined inductive and deductive approaches. Once I had decided to look at the luxury sector, I started with a set of theoretically informed research questions (described in the introduction), rather than attempt to enter the sites without preconceptions and allow salient issues to emerge from the research, as grounded theorists advocate. When I was in the sites, however, I tried to be as open as possible to what I might find of relevance to my interests. In early writings about the project, I delineated my expectations explicitly, which allowed me later to notice phenomena I found surprising (for example, guest reciprocity toward workers and workers' positive feelings about guests). I took hundreds of pages of field notes and carefully coded and categorized both these notes and interview transcriptions. I was careful to make sure I had significant evidence of anything I planned to present as a finding.

In what follows, I first present specifics of both types of data collection, including their strengths and weaknesses, and then move on to discuss ethical and other methodological issues.

CONDUCTING PARTICIPANT OBSERVATION

Obtaining entrée to both hotels was, overall, easier than I had expected. I found that managers in both the Luxury Garden and the Royal Court were interested in the same topic I was—how to produce luxury service—so my desire to investigate this made sense to them. It is also common in the industry for hospitality management or culinary institute students to spend a few months in a hotel for training, so the idea was not completely foreign to managers. Though managers in both hotels justified certain decisions about my access to particular jobs in ways that did not ring true,[1] for the most part they were quite flexible and open to my participation.

After deciding to try to work in a luxury hotel, I initially focused on the Luxury Garden. It was one of two or three truly top hotels in the city at the time, and I had already conducted three managerial interviews there, as well as one observation. After I had several formal conversations in June 1999 with Sebastian, the acting general manager, and Alice, the human resources director, they agreed to take me on as an unpaid intern. They requested that I write a short report about the composition of the project, and Alice required me to submit a letter signed by my dissertation chair, stating that I had independent health insurance should I be injured on the job. I also promised to provide management with a report at the end of my fieldwork detailing my thoughts about how service could be improved in the hotel. Alice mentioned repeatedly that my expertise would help the hotel to perfect its "systems" (with which she appeared somewhat obsessed) and told me she was glad I had no background in hospitality, because I would be more "objective."

We scheduled my start date for August 1, 1999, and I attended the new employee orientation in July 1999. However, right before I was scheduled to begin, Alice called to postpone. She told me several workers and one or two managers had recently resigned, which left no one available to train me. We discussed the possibility of my coming on as a paid employee, but the hotel wanted a two-year commitment, and in any case I did not have the requisite experience. She asked me to wait a couple of months. I spoke with her again in September, when she told me it was still too soon because of continuing high turnover. In November, I met with François, the new rooms division manager. Both managers said they were still in favor of my participation, but they could not guarantee a start date.

As an alternative, Alice offered to help me contact human resources managers she knew in two other hotels, one of whom was Nicole at the Royal Court.[2] When I met with Nicole, I presented the project to her much as I had presented it to Alice and Sebastian, as a study of how luxury service is provided, and I offered to write a report on improving service. Nicole asked very few questions, indicating, I believe, that Alice had put in a good word for me as she had said she would, thereby legitimating my project (though the tight labor market probably didn't hurt either).

Nicole called the next day to offer me a position. Although I had said I would work free of charge, she wanted to pay me at the rate of $6.25 per hour (less than half of what other workers made).[3] She was under the impression that legal problems could ensue if I were not on the hotel's payroll (though Alice at the Luxury Garden, attentive as she was, had never mentioned this possibility). Nicole seemed interested in using me to find out what was going on among workers, although she denied that she wanted me to "spy" on them. She told me that other workers "wouldn't have to know" I was doing research, but I insisted that I not be undercover.

I started work at the Royal Court on January 3, 2000. I worked thirty-two hours per week, covering equal numbers of shifts among jobs in the front office (telephone operator, valet/bellperson, front desk, and room reservations) in my first six months there. Because of competition among employees for front desk work, it was a couple of months before I was scheduled to work at the desk, but Petra kept her promise to allow me to work there regularly in my last four months in the front office. I then moved on to room service and the restaurant for five weeks. After that, I spent one month in housekeeping, where I shadowed workers and was no longer paid. I worked on call for two months after that, working several shifts at the door and in room reservations.

I had interviewed the general manager and the hotel's founder (no longer with the hotel) in 1998; I interviewed the human resources director, the sales director, and the front office manager in the fall of 2000, right before I left the site. In December, Nicole called me and asked if I was planning to write a report. I told her that I would be happy to do so but that I had already told her everything relevant in the two or three meetings we had had while I worked there (I describe these comments below). She decided the report was not necessary. I also reviewed three months' worth of comment cards and letters from guests.

As my stint at the Royal Court came to a close, I needed to look for another site to use as a comparison. I considered trying to find a nonluxury property, but I was concerned that the Royal Court did not truly qualify as a luxury hotel and that the comparison was not justified. I later realized that luxury is often in the mind of the beholder, but at the time I worried that the hotel's chaotic management, its small size, and the absence of some of the practices I associated with luxury service meant it was not "luxurious enough." I was also interested in assessing the effects of organizational characteristics on the worker strategies and worker-guest relations that I had observed at the Royal Court; I felt this required me to look at a hotel with more consistent management strategies and corporate culture in particular.

In September 2000, I turned back to the Luxury Garden, which I was sure was as luxurious as they came, as well as corporately affiliated, and in which I already had contacts. After about a month of playing phone tag with Alice and François, I spoke to François, who did not sound enthusiastic (he told me the hotel was not very "pro-intern," which I had never heard in the initial phase of contact). But a few days later Antonio, the guest services manager, called me back and said I could start in a couple of weeks, and he was quite enthusiastic about my participation. I was never sure what had caused the shift; perhaps it was my training at the Royal Court or a labor shortage in the Luxury Garden.

I began work at the Luxury Garden on October 31, 2000, logging four shifts per week at the concierge desk. I was unpaid, but I could keep cash tips. (Eventually the concierge staff also decided to let me keep cash commissions for massages that I scheduled, which amounted to about twenty-five dollars per massage, though they kept all other commissions, which were included in their paychecks rather than distributed as cash. On two occasions before I started receiving massage commissions, Alec and Max, unsolicited, also gave me cash [$150 total] as a way of compensating me, since they garnered the noncash commissions from services I set up; thus, my presence increased their income while decreasing their effort.)

Because one of the concierges was on maternity leave and I had perhaps proved somewhat more competent than the managers might initially have imagined, Antonio wanted me to continue working at the concierge desk after the end of the month we had agreed that I would spend there. After two months, I reminded him of our agreement that I would work in a variety of jobs, and he scheduled me for several shifts at the door and for one full week in housekeeping. He also gave me one shift each in the business center, telephone operator station, and reservations. He asked me to extend the internship an extra month so that I would work through February, when Becky, the other concierge, was coming back to work, which I agreed to do.

When I left, in March 2001, I debriefed with Alice and gave her a four-page report reflecting on the internship. I mainly described that I had felt a little out of place as an intern (which I elaborate on below) and suggested some ways that interns might be more consistently integrated into the workplace. I also made a few suggestions for minor changes managers might make, such as posting the schedule at consistent times. Although Antonio had repeatedly expressed enthusiasm about talking to me about my observations at the concierge desk, he never followed up with me, and I did not pursue the issue (soon after, he left to become concierge manager at another upscale hotel).

I interviewed a Luxury Garden assistant human resources director, the food and beverage director, a restaurant manager, and the rooms division manager during my preliminary research in 1998–99. In the spring of 2001, I interviewed Alice, the human resources director, François, the resident manager, and the director of sales; I also reinterviewed Sebastian, the former rooms division manager and acting general manager, who had since been promoted to general manager. I also reviewed four months' worth of comment cards and letters.

The specifics of my access illustrated some of the differences between the hotels described in chapter 2. Luxury Garden managers required more documentation and also postponed my internship because of concerns about turnover and training. This stance contrasted sharply with the immediate acceptance of my proposal at the Royal Court. I felt that the tight labor market at the Royal Court explained managerial enthusiasm for the project, whereas at the Luxury Garden concern with service quality made management unwilling to take on someone with no training.

Differences in managerial characteristics also affected how I felt in each site. At the Royal Court, I felt like a "real worker." As far as I could tell, management treated me much like any other employee, except that I was allowed to move from job to job (and I was paid less). I had a paycheck, a mailbox, and several uniforms. I was included in department meetings and invited to the semiannual hotelwide party. Furthermore, I never had the sense that managers or other workers did not see me as a colleague (though my being a researcher was, of course, an added issue, as I discuss below). The relatively flat organizational hierarchy and the recency of many hires minimized the investment of most workers in being more skilled than I (with the exception of Hugh and Giovanna).

At the Luxury Garden, in contrast, I was very definitely an intern. I had no paycheck, no mailbox, and no uniform (managers said they had to special order concierge uniforms and it would take months for one to arrive, so I wore my own suit). I was not included in department meetings; in fact, Sydney and Antonio used me to cover the desk while they met with the others. I had to get special clearance from Alice to attend the off-site holiday party, where I was not given a ticket for the door prize raffle; at the rollout of the Celebrated Quality Standards I was also deemed ineligible for the door prize. I was not offered a Christmas ham or turkey as the other workers were. I was initially not invited to the department's holiday party. (Antonio was very apologetic about this oversight; he said he had left invitations in everyone's mailbox, but because I didn't have one, he had basically forgotten about me.) My colleagues at the concierge desk tended to monitor me more than they did one another. My coworkers in other departments, especially those I did not know well, also sometimes treated me as less competent, calling the desk and asking to speak to any of the other concierges, as if I were incapable of assisting them. Here there seemed to be an investment in placing me at the bottom of the more hierarchical structure.

On the other hand, I received significant positive feedback from Sydney and Antonio, far more than I had at the Royal Court. This may have been an attempt to recognize me emotionally, since I was not receiving monetary compensation, but I believe it also reflected the greater use of positive feedback generally at the Luxury Garden. On several occasions Antonio gave me a handwritten "five star" card praising me, sometimes accompanying a comment card or letter from a guest that included positive mention of my work. On one card he wrote, "Thank you for your excellent efforts! You have made a nice impact on all of us and we have decided not to let you leave. Keep it up! Thank you!" Sydney also told me how valuable I was and lamented that I would not be staying.

My relations with workers also reflected the sociability of the Royal Court and the professionalism of the Luxury Garden. I became very friendly with my coworkers at the Royal Court; at the end of my second month in the hotel I started going out socially with them fairly regularly, which continued until I left the hotel. Luxury Garden workers socialized less with one another, and as a consequence I spent less time outside work with them.

In the couple of years following my fieldwork, I continued to stop by each hotel and chat with workers at least a few times each year. I had drinks occasionally with Annie from the Royal Court, and I attended a couple of social events for Royal Court workers in 2001 and 2002. After leaving the Luxury Garden, I went out once for dinner with the concierge staff and saw Alec and Max socially every few months. Through these contacts I was able to keep abreast of developments within both hotels, particularly the effects of the economic downturn as well as changes in personnel and management.

GUEST INTERVIEWS

I conducted the nineteen interviews with guests in the fall of 1999, when I was waiting to find out about gaining access to the Luxury Garden. I would have preferred to conduct the interviews later, but I decided to start talking with hotel guests, unrelated to my two sites, because I had the time to do so in that period. Although there were problems with the sample, I was surprised to find later that my interview data matched my ethnographic experience quite well. Because of this correspondence and time constraints, I did not pursue further interviews at the end of the fieldwork.

The respondents were seven men and twelve women who had spent significant amounts of time in luxury hotels. Eight were primarily business travelers, while the rest mainly traveled for pleasure. Seventeen respondents were white, one was African American, and one was Asian American. Four were in their thirties, one was forty-six, eleven were in their fifties, and three were sixty or over. Although I did not ask them about their incomes and wealth specifically, about two-thirds said that they had enough money to spend it however they liked and that their spending habits would not change if they had more money. Several of these respondents or their spouses owned their own businesses. The remaining interviewees included three of the younger people, who traveled for business, and two of the older women. About half of my respondents said they did not come from privileged backgrounds.

Sixteen interviews were conducted over the telephone, and three in person. Each lasted between one and two hours. Seventeen were tape-recorded and transcribed; I took extensive notes on the other two. Thirteen of the interviews began with a family member of mine who had recommended four friends; these respondents in turn introduced me to others. Three other interviewees were recommended by friends or acquaintances of mine; one was a family member of mine; and two, a married couple, were family friends.

The sample was flawed in several ways in terms of representativity. First, of course, it was too small. Second, respondents were older than what appeared to me to be the average age of luxury travelers (they were more similar demographically to the guests at the Royal Court than to those at the Luxury Garden). Third, because the respondents were not far enough removed from me, they tended to be politically liberal and possibly more likely to be conflicted about their luxury consumption. Their discomfort with luxury consumption was also a function of their working- or middle-class backgrounds, in many cases; I do not know the extent to which this is true of the "average" luxury consumer. A more representative sample would probably have yielded more data about clients who are not ambivalent about their consumption. However, the characteristics of these respondents allowed me to look closely at the process of interpellation that I have described in chapter 6. It remains to be seen what proportion of luxury consumers go through a similar process and at what point in their lives.

DILEMMAS OF ETHNOGRAPHY

The greatest benefit of the ethnographic method, in my view, was the opportunity to observe relations, practices, and strategies that workers and guests might not have identified in interviews, because the idea of normalization by definition suggests that people do not notice what is normalized. The contradictory dimensions of workers' and guests' self-conceptions might not have emerged if they had been forced to articulate them explicitly, since what people say about themselves does not always reflect their practice. Likewise, the opportunity to observe and participate in interactions between workers and guests allowed me to see a positive dimension I might not otherwise have noticed. I suspect that in interviews workers would have highlighted the guests they remembered, who were often transgressors of the contract, and thus painted a more negative picture of these relations, rather than describe routine reciprocal interactions.

I believe this project especially sheds light on the limitations of conducting interviews with managers (or even participating in training) as a principal source of data. I suspect that had I interviewed only workers and managers I would have ended up with a disproportionate understanding of the importance of managerial activities. Managers tend to tout the official line in interviews; they may also believe that their efforts bear more fruit than is actually the case. It is tempting to use managers' views about what workers are supposed to do in order to discuss the standardization of personality in interactive work, but only observation over time can show what workers actually do, which is to integrate their outside-work selfhood with the selfhood that is expected of them on the job. However, participant observation entails a number of hazards, to which I tried to be attentive in the research.

Reliability and Validity

The first challenge of participant observation is common for ethnographers: I tended to become so involved in the work that it was hard to retain a researcher's perspective on what I was observing. As I wrote in my notes one day after a shift at the Royal Court, "I was thinking about the transition I make every day from ethnographer to worker—I come in and see all these things I want to write down, and then pretty soon they are all just normal and I don't notice them anymore." Features of the work or of guest relations that would have been noticeable to an outsider became normalized for me. To avoid forgetting, I tried to take as many notes as possible during my shift, scribbling in the bathroom or saving random scraps of paper that would remind me of what I had done all day.

Second, and related, is the possibility that the processes I identified were specific to me alone. Often, because I was the only one doing a job, I was aware of only my own reactions to it. Furthermore, of course, my perceptions may have been different from those of other workers doing jobs similar to mine. To the extent that selfhood external to work is in fact related to our selfhood at work, it is entirely possible that my upper-middle-class background and elite education (not to mention my own personal characteristics) affected my perceptions of relations with guests, managers, and other workers. For this reason, I have eliminated from the book most claims that were not corroborated by my observations of or discussions with other workers.

The third issue is the comprehensiveness of my understanding of different jobs in the hotel. I was extremely fortunate to gain access to hotels in which I was permitted to move around. Later, however, I realized that I should have been more observant in several areas. Most important, I never worked at the Luxury Garden front desk. Because concierges stood only a few feet away from the front desk agents, I assumed I would also be gathering data on them. In this presumption I was unwittingly drawing on my experience at the Royal Court, where the two jobs were combined. I later saw, however, that the specialized division of labor impeded my understanding of these workers' jobs, which were especially important because they were among the few positions in which workers had to do recognition work without tip compensation. Managerial authority may also have been more noticeable at the front desk than at the concierge desk, where we were largely unsupervised.

I wish I had acquired a better sense of what was going on in several other jobs as well. By only shadowing housekeeping workers, I missed the isolation and repetitiveness of the job and some of the strategies they used to make it more interesting, such as turning on the TV or the radio (though I did glean more information than I would have from cleaning or turning down rooms alone, since I was able to interview housekeepers informally as we worked). I also should have insisted on spending more time at the Luxury Garden front door; working only a few shifts there, I was not treated like an insider, and I undoubtedly missed some elements of the relations among the workers and perhaps their financial strategies. And I should also have worked mornings in room service at the Royal Court to see what games workers used when it was busy, rather than spend the entire five weeks on the slow night shift. Overall, however, I believe I was able to get a good sense of the range of jobs and the major differences among them.

Fourth, and finally, of course, is how workers treated me and the consequent accuracy of my impressions. A few workers initially seemed suspicious of my motives, though they usually expressed their wariness using humor. One or two coworkers at the Royal Court jokingly referred to me at first as a "mole." One cook there called me "double agent Rachel." Jackie told me after I had been at the Royal Court for a few months that Brad, the assistant manager, had initially thought I might be a spy sent by the owners. Sometimes workers made comments that made me feel awkward. Hugh once pointed out my note taking, which as a rule I tried to keep out of sight (though he also told me, "I hope management reads your report"). Carolyn at the Luxury Garden asked, jokingly, "Are we just guinea pigs to you?"

Workers sometimes asked what my research was about or how it was going. Several workers in both hotels told me they wanted to read the dissertation (usually referring to it as a paper) when it was finished. Clint frequently told me to "put *that* in your paper," and Frankie often asked when my book was coming out and whether I was going to be famous. Jackie told me after she quit the hotel (in my third month) that she had not wanted to ask me about the research because she had thought she might start acting differently around me. Jasmine said, "Don't make my character in your paper a weirdo." Some workers seemed slightly intimidated and shy about asking what my project was about. Overall, I had the sense that people were aware that I was doing research, but for the most part I did not feel as if they treated me differently.

However, I knew workers did not tell me certain things, especially those at the front door, with its air of intrigue and insider knowledge. Some front door workers at the Royal Court were wary of talking with me too much about the tension with managers and their illicit parking schemes. On one occasion Joel explicitly refused to let me in on a conflict he was having with another worker, saying, "I know you want it for your thesis." During the week that I was observing the front door at the Luxury Garden, Fred and Javier demonstrated in subtle ways that they did not want me to work with them. On the other hand, I am confident that the substantial amount I did learn about their strategies and schemes indicated that these workers did trust me. I probably never learned about some practices, but I suspect the strategies and relations I have described apply to these too.

The ways in which I differed from my coworkers probably also played a role in my capacity to fit in and thus may have influenced the information I gleaned. I was demographically similar to (though a few years older than) my white female coworkers at the Royal Court. And though the concierges at the Luxury Garden were older than I and either men or Asian women, we were·similar in terms of cultural capital. Among all these workers, I felt comfortable more or less from the beginning.

In housekeeping, however, I stood out because I was white. Guests once or twice assumed I was a manager, and it is possible that workers also thought I was supervising them (and these workers, with limited education and English skills, were especially unlikely to be familiar with what a dissertation is, although I explained it as clearly as I could when they expressed interest). I did have the advantage of being able to speak Spanish, which I used with some housekeepers. Although I may not have seen every shortcut workers used, my sense of their subordination to the pace of their work was overwhelmingly consistent. Furthermore, they told me about hiding from managers in order to avoid having their quota of rooms increased, and their general tone seemed to indicate their trust in me.

At the front door and in room service I was different because I am a woman (for work at the door, a women's uniform didn't even exist). During my first shift with Zeke and Frankie at the Royal Court, they seemed a little uncomfortable. When I went outside to begin the shift, Zeke joked, "What are we going to talk about? Usually it's cars, girls, and football." Arnold, a Royal Court valet, told me that the doormen were nicer to me than to the male valets because I am female (which I suspect was true), and often my male coworkers at the door would not accept tips from me that were due them. At the same time Joel doubted my capacity to lift heavy bags; likewise, room service workers did not believe I would be able to carry trays loaded with food.

Guests at both hotels also treated me differently from the male front door workers. They expressed surprise when they saw me at the front door or when I helped them with their luggage. Female guests frequently said, "Good for you!" or offered other supportive words or a thumbs-up. Male guests sometimes responded with positive but gendered comments such as, "I didn't expect such a pretty girl," or, to the doorman, "She's better looking than you are." On a few occasions male guests refused to let me carry their luggage. One man said to me, "I will never let a lady carry my bag. You can still come up with me, and I'll still tip you, but my mother wouldn't have it." On another occasion a guest asked, "Did I see you parking that [Mercedes] 600?" and then added, "You did a good job," which he probably would not have said to a male valet.

Some of these issues could and probably should have been addressed in formal interviews with workers. I could have filled in gaps in my data about particular jobs, as well as acquired a more explicit window on workers' self-understandings and tested out some of my conjectures. Furthermore, I also could have gathered more data on their lives and identities outside work, on how they understood the relation between work and not-work, and on their consumption patterns. I would also have liked to get a better understanding of their real and imaginary interlocutors in their lives outside work.

Ethical Questions

A number of ethical issues emerged in the course of this project. First, I wondered if I should disclose my political position—both my experience with the union and the reason for my interest in luxury service, which was that I found its availability unbelievable and basically unconscionable. I was fairly sure that if I had been forthright about either of these issues I would not have gained access.[4] However, given that I had no interest in muckraking or in union organizing in these hotels, I decided that I did not have an obligation to disclose my political views unless managers asked me directly, which they did not. Indeed, I was shocked by the extent to which they assumed I shared their interests.

I believe they made these assumptions for several reasons. It appeared to me that managers in both hotels, and many workers, thought I was studying hospitality management even when they had been told otherwise. I was perfectly forthright with everyone about being a graduate student in sociology, but managers and workers usually equated "student" with "hospitality school." Their lack of familiarity with sociology in general and dissertation writing in particular, of course, facilitated this equation. I also tried to appear professional in initial interviews, wearing a black suit and carrying business cards with the University of California seal (in the biggest size available) embossed on them. When workers asked me what my project was about, I was even more forthcoming, usually mentioning that I was interested in the disparity between workers and guests. Indeed, it was this admission that often elicited the most explicit statements about inequality.

Yet, my research may have been harmful to workers. The most immediate drawback was that my presence may have interfered with their income. The clearest example of this interference occurred when I was in room service at the Royal Court, and Patrick, the restaurant manager, took shifts from full-time workers Hao and Alejandro to give to me. I was not sure whether he was trying to help me out or if he was trying to lower his labor costs in the department by relying on my cheaper labor (or both). When I found out what he had done, I was horrified and asked him not to do it again. For the most part I tried to do the less lucrative outdoor job at the Royal Court door, and I often refused tips that other workers offered me, especially when they seemed totally unwarranted. In some cases, as I have shown, I became more invested in making tips than I should have been. In general, however, I don't think workers were negatively affected. My presence at the Luxury Garden created monetary gain for concierges, since they had to split their substantial commissions among only five people instead of six.

The other major ethical issue was one of worker confidentiality, both in the on-site gathering of data from and about workers and in writing about them. As a condition of access to both hotel sites, I had promised to make some kind of assessment for managers, which could obviously mean evaluating other workers. My strategy at the Royal Court, where I knew Nicole hoped I would be her informant, was to ignore her hints and to avoid talking with her, which was not hard, because she was rarely around (the executive offices were far removed from the areas in which I worked). When I did have to tell her what was going on (only a couple of times during my eight months there), I made sure to report only things I knew she already knew or very general information. For example, I brought up problems linked to training, turnover, and lack of positive feedback. I focused my information on managers; here my worker persona influenced me, because I was often irritated with managers and knew other workers were too. I figured that I was freer than other workers to speak and was in a sense representing them, though this approach may have violated an ethical responsibility to managers. On a couple of occasions Nicole asked me about specific workers, and I always spoke highly of them. In the report I wrote for the Luxury Garden, I made no references to specific workers except to mention that Alec and Max had been especially helpful to me.

Workers might also suffer negative consequences in their jobs from what is written here. I have given all workers pseudonyms (some of which they chose themselves), but they remain for the most part identifiable to their coworkers and superiors. Significant turnover among hotel staff in part mitigates this issue, especially among workers at the Royal Court, where almost all of the front of house workers with whom I worked had left as of 2004. I have also chosen not to include information I felt would be damaging to workers who remain at the hotels.

Workers may also feel I have violated their privacy, especially as they had no option *not* to participate in the research (per my human subjects approval of the ethnography, workers did not sign individual consent forms).[5] Lack of understanding of the nature of the project (and possibly feeling intimidated about asking me) might have made it hard for workers to censor themselves around me even if they wanted to. Despite knowing about the research, they were unconscious of my data collection much of the time, I am sure. Some workers may also feel I have used their friendship for instrumental reasons. I did not lie to workers, and I became friends only with those with whom I felt some real compatibility. And I have tried to be sparing in my use of personal information. But it is hard to separate a genuine personal interest in one's coworkers from the desire to obtain information from them. I can only say I felt both.

Like workers, guests in my sites had no choice about participating. Indeed, in contrast to workers, they were unaware that research was being conducted. Occasionally guests inquired into my life outside the hotel, and I usually tried not to give many details about what I was studying (they, too, often assumed it was hospitality management). They would not necessarily have consented to participate, given my access to intimate aspects of their lives. My presence, of course, violated the assumption guests implicitly make that workers will not be in a position to use their private information. However, I do not expect this research to have negative consequences for them, because I have removed identifying details. Those I formally interviewed signed consent forms and, I am fairly sure, understood what they were participating in.

A final ethical issue is, appropriately enough, one of reciprocity. As I have said, I have tried to keep my presence and research from negatively influencing workers, and I was honest with them about what I was doing. But I did not compensate any subjects (guests, managers, or workers) for their participation, either by paying them or by making a symbolic gesture of appreciation, such as taking them out for a meal. I tend to believe that ethnographic research is inherently asymmetrical, no matter what the subject's social position, because the researcher benefits from the research in a way that the subject almost always does not, and the subject runs risks that the researcher does not incur. When researchers are in socially privileged positions relative to their subjects, as I was in relation to the workers and some of the managers I studied (though not the guests), this asymmetry feels more acute.[6] But I generally see the gesture toward reciprocity as an attempt, not unlike that of hotel guests, to make the researcher feel less guilty by glossing over social differences and unequal entitlements.

I am also not sure the different degree of social asymmetry means that it is more ethically imperative to compensate, in my case, the workers in the research than it would have been to compensate the guests, given that the primary exploitative moment occurs in the act of study itself. Did I have an ethical obligation of reciprocity in response to guests and managers as well as to workers? One could argue that because the guests I interviewed had the opportunity to refuse to participate while workers did not, I had a greater obligation to workers. But then, are obligations to all coworkers equal, from primary informants with whom I worked every day to those I shadowed once or twice or never? In any case, I am not sure adequate means exist to compensate for the researcher's advantages.

But a more practical truth also exists: that once I started work in the hotels, questions of asymmetry and obligation receded in my thinking. I began to see my relationships with my coworkers through the lens of work itself, as colleagues and peers rather than as "subjects." I also found myself inserted into (and invested in) power relations on the job that did not necessarily favor me. In this context, a symbolic gesture of reciprocity would have felt inauthentic and paternalistic. But here I perhaps made the same mistake that hotel guests often do: I allowed collegial relationships that *felt* egalitarian to blind me to both my general social privilege relative to that of my coworkers and the exploitative aspect of the researcher-subject relation as a way of mitigating my discomfort with these advantages. Had I been more attentive, I might have found a third way, between a doomed attempt at compensatory reciprocity and the head-in-the-sand approach I ended up with, that could have recognized these workers for their contributions without falsely attempting to efface the asymmetry of the situation.

METHODOLOGY AND THE STUDY OF PRODUCTION-CONSUMPTION

I have advocated for the integration of production and consumption in the study of service work. This integrative approach is methodologically as well as theoretically challenging, especially given the focus on workplaces in the ethnographic study of work. This emphasis, first, reproduces the idea of a split between the at-work and the outside-work selves of workers, which can reify a perceived tension between authentic and commodified selfhood. It also reinforces the tendency to concentrate on workers and managers, excluding customers in two ways: in terms of their visible and invisible participation in the labor process, and in terms of their own experiences of consuming the service product.

One way to approach these challenges is to attempt to glean a more multifaceted understanding of a single worksite, primarily by integrating the client. This is what I have tried to do, first, by paying attention to client influences on a range of elements of workers' experiences—their responsibilities, the rhythms of work, their games, and their understandings of their jobs and of themselves—and, second, by attending to client experiences, primarily through interviews. It might be feasible to integrate client experience ethnographically, perhaps by findings sites of *collective* consumption in which the researcher could participate. This might be possible in hotels by participating in tour groups, for example. In trying to link the experience of work to life outside work, researchers in a single worksite could also do interviews with workers. Indeed, to look at the relation between what workers say about their work in interviews and what they actually do on the job would illuminate continuities and contradictions between explicit and implicit strategies (in my case, for negotiating inequality).

A second possibility is to use multisited ethnography, still linked to a single central site of production-consumption, to overcome the conceptual split between work and home, community, and leisure. This would mean shadowing workers and clients (and potentially managers) outside the central site as well as in it. Such an approach is more challenging, given that these actors tend to live in widely dispersed communities (and might not want to have people following them around all the time). But tracking even a few workers and clients through their daily routines can be useful. (This kind of design was very fruitful, for example, in Hochschild's book *The Time Bind* [1997].) Especially relevant to my cases is the possibility that when physically removed from their worksites, workers would express more open social criticism, as James Scott would suggest.[7] A third way might be to use immersion in a family or community to study the integration of multiple sites of production and consumption in daily life. Whatever the approach (and, of course, there are many other options), the importance of consumption, interaction, and self in the service society calls for a shift away from the methodological focus on workers and managers alone in the traditional workplace.

APPENDIX B Hotel Organization

Most hotels, including the Luxury Garden and the Royal Court, are organized into several departments, broadly differentiated between administration (sales, accounting, human resources) and operations. Operations is usually split into food and beverage and rooms divisions. Food and beverage (generally referred to as "F&B") comprises the hotel's restaurants and bars, banquets and catering departments, and room service. Rooms division usually includes the front desk, the front door (door attendants, bellpersons, valets), housekeeping, and sometimes engineering or security or both. Each department is typically guided by an upper-level manager; depending on the size of the hotel, these department heads may supervise a midlevel manager, who oversees assistant managers and supervisors, or the assistant managers/supervisors may report directly to the department head. In most hotels, including my sites, department heads (usually the sales and marketing director, the controller, the human resources director, the rooms division manager, and the food and beverage director) participate in an "executive committee," which also includes the hotel's general manager.

Figures 1 and 2 show the differences between the two hotels. The Luxury Garden followed a typical structure and was highly differentiated. The Royal Court was more laterally organized, in part because the hotel was smaller, but also because of its transitional state. For example, Petra, the front office manager, had not been given the post of rooms division manager because she was thought to be too young and inexperienced. Thus, the general manager himself supervised several of the functions associated with the division, including housekeeping. The Royal Court had no food and beverage director; the job was shared by three assistant managers and the executive chef.

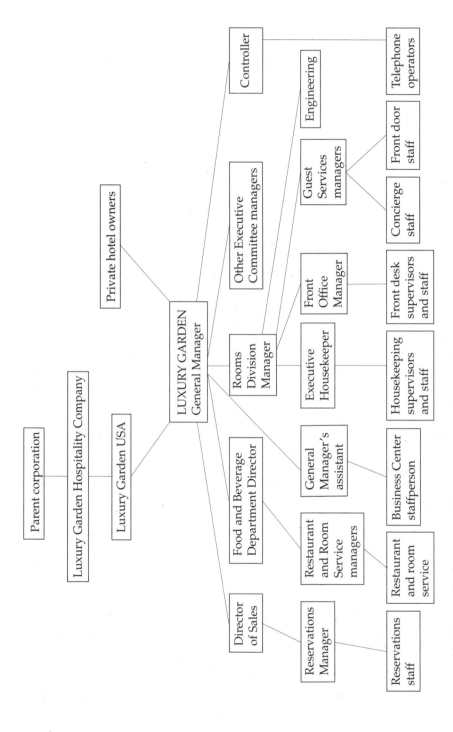

FIGURE 1. Luxury Garden organization

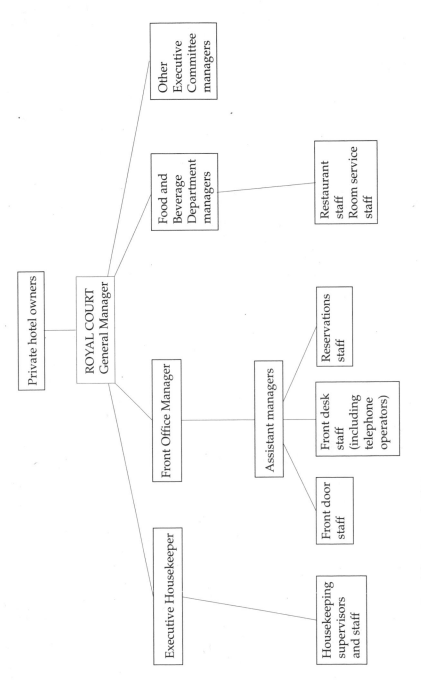

FIGURE 2. Royal Court organization

APPENDIX C Jobs, Wages, and Nonmanagerial Workers in Each Hotel

2000 – 2001

The following tables present the wages corresponding to different jobs, the demographics of workers in those jobs, and the differences in both between the Royal Court and the Luxury Garden.

TABLE 4 The Luxury Garden

Job	Hourly Wage ($)	Tips/Commissions	Worker Demographics
Front desk	15	No	Male and female White (U.S.-born), Latino, Chinese, Filipino
Concierge	15	Both, approx. $500 per week total	Male and female White (U.S.-born), Asian American
Telephone operator	14	No	Mostly female Latina
Reservationist	14	Sales incentives	Male and female White (U.S.-born), Asian American
Doorman	10	Tips: approx. $150 per shift No commissions	Male White (U.S.-born), Chinese
Bellman	9	Tips: approx. $100 per shift No commissions	Male White (U.S.-born), Filipino, Chinese, Latin American
Valet[a]	N/A	N/A	N/A
Room cleaner, turndown attendant	13–14	Tips very rarely	Female Primarily Chinese
Room service server	10	Tips: 15% of charge plus guest add-ons	Eastern European and other immigrants

[a] Valet parking is handled by the building's garage.

TABLE 5 The Royal Court

Job	Hourly Wage ($)	Tips/Commissions	Worker Demographics
Front desk, concierge	13	Both, approx. $50–$100 per week total	Male and female Mainly white (U.S.-born and European)
Telephone operator	13	No	Male and female Mainly white (U.S.-born and European)
Reservationist	13	No tips Minimal commissions for car services	Female White (U.S.-born and European)
Doorman	8	Tips: $60–$150 per shift No commissions	Male White (U.S.-born and European), Ethiopian
Bellman	7/10[a]	Tips: $80–$100 per shift No commissions	Male Latino, Filipino
Valet	10	Tips: $40 per shift No commissions	Male Latino, Filipino
Room cleaner, turndown attendant	12–13	Tips very rarely	Female Chinese, Filipino, Latin American
Room service server	9–10	Tips: 15% of charge plus guest add-ons and $2 per amenity	Male Chinese, Latino

[a] The two wages reflect what bellmen were ordinarily paid and what they were paid during the hotel's renovation. (See chapter 3, n. 21.)

Notes

INTRODUCTION

1. Four Seasons advertisement, *New York Times Magazine*, September 26, 2004.

2. The sociological literature on work in hotels is surprisingly limited. Hayner (1936) offers an early discussion of residential hotels and anomie. Contemporary researchers have tended to focus on manager-worker relations and control strategies (Jones, Taylor, and Nixon 1997; Madsen Camacho 1996; Mason 1989); characteristics of workers, jobs, and relations among workers (Prus and Irini 1980; Lennon and Wood 1989; Wood 1992, 1994; Stepick and Grenier 1994); and union representation and organizing (Zamudio 1996; Wells 2000; Bernhardt, Dresser, and Hatton 2003). These researchers do not explore the specificity of worker-guest relations or the particularities of luxury service. In their multiyear ethnographic study of Hawaiian resorts, Adler and Adler (2004) provide a comprehensive analysis of the types of workers and the organization of work in these sites and of workers' backgrounds and careers in the industry. However, much of their analysis is specific to the Hawaiian resort context, and they do not focus on worker-guest relations.

3. Veblen [1899] (1994). See Frank (1999) for a critique of luxury consumption, Twitchell (2002) for a celebration of the "democratization of luxury," and Brooks

(2000) for the claim that changes in the nature of high-end consumption indicate shifts in the nature of the upper class. None of these authors are sociologists.

4. Frank (1999: 18).

5. Frank (1999); Bleecker and Bleecker (2002).

6. Belluck (2002).

7. Bierck (2000).

8. Robinovitz (2002).

9. Harden (1999).

10. Goldin (2002); see also Kuczynski (2002). See Hospitality Net (2001) for a discussion of the recession-resistant nature of the hospitality industry.

11. Waggoner (2004).

12. Rozhon (2004).

13. Middle-class people are increasingly demanding luxury goods, in a trend some call the "democratization of luxury" or the "New Luxury" (Twitchell 2002; Turrell 2004; Silverstein and Fiske 2003; Danziger 2005). The New Luxury focuses on consumer goods and brands at the upper end but is not limited to the super-luxury level.

14. One particularly fascinating 2003 show, ABC's *The Family*, seemed to combine *Upstairs, Downstairs* with *Survivor*. Hosted by a dapper George Hamilton (often driving around in a golf cart), the program placed a middle-class extended family in a mansion in Palm Beach to compete for a million dollars while living in the lap of luxury. Contests involved "upper-class" activities with a twist, such as caviar-eating contests, playing donkey polo, and participating in an auction of participants' own portraits. Contestants were served by a staff of five professionals (chef, butler, housekeeper, stylist, and social secretary), who also formed the "secret board of trustees" that determined the final eliminations while convening in the basement wine cellar; these judges often based their decisions on the manners of the contestants.

15. *People* (2005).

16. Kuczynski (2004); Rozhon (2005); Tien (2002).

17. Williams (2005).

18. Both novels are based on the authors' personal experience. McLaughlin and Kraus (2002) worked as nannies in New York City; Weisberger (2003) worked for *Vogue*'s Anna Wintour.

19. Castells (1996).

20. Sassen (1991). Also see Sassen (1988) on the link between high-end professional workers and low-wage service jobs.

21. Macdonald and Sirianni (1996).

22. "Interactive service" may sound redundant; however, some service, such as that which hotel housekeepers provide, does not involve significant contact with clients.

23. Krugman (2002).

24. Since 1970, the share of total national after-tax income of the top 1 percent of families has doubled, to 14 percent, which is about equivalent to the share of the bottom 40 percent. In the last thirty years, average real annual compensation of the top one hundred CEOs rose from $1.3 million, thirty-nine times the pay of the average worker, to $37.5 million, more than a thousand times the average worker's earnings (Krugman 2002). In 2000, the four hundred wealthiest taxpayers in the United States reported over 1 percent of total national income, more than twice what they claimed in 1992 (Johnston 2003). See also Morris and Western (1999); Scott and Leonhardt (2005).

25. Bourdieu (1990).

26. For reviews, see Burawoy (1979); and Simpson (1989).

27. See, for example, Edwards (1979); Burawoy (1979, 1985); Zimbalist (1979); Littler and Salaman (1982); Reich, Edwards, and Gordon (1982); Knights and Willmott (1990); and Berberoglu (1993). See Smith (1994); and Wardell (1999) for reviews.

28. See, for example, Burawoy (1979); Edwards (1979); Stark (1980); and Knights (1990). For analyses of gender and the labor process, see Lee (1997); and Salzinger (2003).

29. More recent Marxist approaches (Wright 1997, e.g.) have emphasized unequal authority relations in production (not just unequal property relations) as a key element of class, which also fits into a model in which class is determined at work.

30. Everett Hughes (1952, [1971] 1984) and several of his students (Davis 1959; Gold 1952) looked at some service occupations. Their works, though insightful, did not analyze the specificity of service work vis-à-vis manufacturing (but see Whyte 1948). Analyses of clerical work in the labor process tradition tended not to look at client-worker interaction, rather likening the clerical workplace to the factory (e.g., Glenn and Feldberg 1979; de Kadt 1979). Despite his similar discussion of clerical work, Braverman himself did offer some discussion of characteristics particular to service work. Challenging Marx's interpretation, he pointed out that the relocation of personal services into profit-making enterprises turned "unproductive" into "productive" labor. "The very same labor may be either productive or unproductive, depending upon its *social* form. To hire the neighbor's boy to cut the lawn is to set in motion unproductive labor; to call a gardening firm which sends out a boy to do the job (perhaps even the same boy) is another thing entirely" (Braverman 1974: 412). He also prefigured contemporary discussions of service work by noting the simultaneity of production and consumption of an intangible object in retail. But rather than elaborate on this distinction, Braverman used it to suggest that fundamentally most service work was *not* different from manufacturing.

31. See, for example, Mars and Nicod (1984); Rollins (1985); Benson (1986); Sutton and Rafaeli (1988); Diamond (1990); Paules (1991); Sutton (1991); Romero (1992); Leidner (1993); Tolich (1993); Gottfried (1994); Pierce (1995); Gimlin (1996); Henson (1996); Lopez (1996); Macdonald and Sirianni (1996); Wharton (1993); Freeman (2000); Hondagneu-Sotelo (2001); Soares (2001); Tannock (2001); Rogers (2000); Smith (2001); Sallaz (2002); Lively (2002); Bolton and Boyd (2003); and Cohen (2004).

32. Hochschild (1983: 7).

33. Benson (1986); Leidner (1993).

34. Mills (1951).

35. See Wouters (1989); Tolich (1993); Wharton (1993, 1999); Steinberg and Figart (1999); Ashforth and Tomiuk (2000); McCammon and Griffin (2000); and Bolton and Boyd (2003).

36. Hochschild (1983); Leidner (1993). On routinization, see Ritzer (2000); and Alfino, Caputo, and Wynyard (1998).

37. Hochschild (1983) and Rollins (1985) argue this most explicitly, but it is implicit in many other discussions of worker identity, even in critiques of Hochschild (see, e.g., Wouters 1989; and Bolton and Boyd 2003). Others have questioned the inside-outside work dichotomy in services by highlighting worker identities as both producers and consumers (du Gay 1996; Benson 1986) but have not questioned this dichotomy in terms of relations between workers and customers.

38. On the first point, see Rogers (2000: 110); for the idea of preserving self-hood through resistance, see, for example, Paules (1991); Casey (1995); and Lively (2002).

39. See, for example, Hochschild (1983); Rollins (1985); Benson (1986); Paules (1991); Hall (1993); Leidner (1993); Pierce (1995); Erickson, Albanese, and Draulic (2000); Freeman (2000); Wood (2000); Kang (2003); Lan (2003); and Hanser (2005c).

40. For both a discussion of the challenges of producing service interactions in general and a study of McDonald's in particular, see Leidner (1993, 1996, 1999).

41. Distinct from "surface acting," which is *pretending* to feel, "deep acting" involves spontaneously expressing "a real feeling that has been self-induced," actually feeling what one is supposed to be displaying (Hochschild 1983: 35).

42. Fuller and Smith (1996).

43. Mars and Nicod (1984); Rollins (1985); Paules (1991); Romero (1992); Hall (1993); Fuller and Smith (1996); Gimlin (1996); Soares (2001); Rogers (2000); Rafaeli (1989); Rafaeli and Sutton (1990).

44. See, for example, Paules (1991); Gottfried (1994); Macdonald (1996); and McCammon and Griffin (2000).

45. For example, Gimlin (1996) argues that even when hair stylists can "imag-

ine" themselves to be friends with their customers, this relationship undermines their ability to think of themselves as professionals.

46. Leidner (1993) focuses on manager-worker and client-worker alliances rather than possible client-worker links. A few scholars indicate that working with customers is not all bad (see, e.g., Rafaeli 1989; Wouters 1989; Tolich 1993; and Cohen 2004), but they do so without theorizing these relations in much depth. For discussions of how organizational structure affects client-worker interactions among paralegals and hairdressers, see Lively (2002); and Cohen (2004). Hodson (2001) critiques the control-resistance dichotomy but does not attempt to theorize client-worker relations. Benson (1986) takes department store workers, managers, and customers seriously as separate but intertwined actors, but her historical method limits her discussion of interactions on the job.

47. Scholars have acknowledged the presence of interactive asymmetry between workers and customers, raising questions about how workers approach the deference, subordination, and low status associated with their occupations. Hochschild notes, for example, that "it is often part of an individual's job to accept uneven exchanges, to be treated with disrespect or anger by a client" (1983: 85; see also Paules 1991; Leidner 1993; and Soares 2001). But how class operates in service interactions themselves is rarely theorized in the literature. See Benson (1986) and Hanser (2005a, 2005b) for exceptions to this pattern. Both argue that class distinctions are reinforced in department stores offering personal service; Benson looks at department stores in the United States in the early twentieth century, while Hanser's focus is on retail in contemporary China.

48. Rollins (1985): 156–58.

49. Gold (1952).

50. Coser (1973); Shamir (1980); Bearman (2005).

51. Hughes ([1971] 1984); Hodson (2001).

52. See Benson (1986); and Leidner (1993: 24–31).

53. To take a gradational definition focused on socioeconomic status: guests in luxury hotels (and consumers of luxury services generally) have higher incomes, more education, more prestigious occupations, more wealth, and more social connections (which we could also call, following Bourdieu, economic, cultural, and social capital) than workers. From a relational standpoint, they are much more likely than workers to own capital and not to have to sell their labor for a wage. To use Weber's terminology, these workers and guests have unequal life chances in the market (as well as unequal status defined by consumption). Some guests would not be able to afford to stay in luxury hotels aside from their expense accounts, but even these guests are, on balance, better off than workers. And these less affluent guests are in the minority; most guests are either rich leisure travelers or well-compensated corporate executives, as I will describe in more detail later.

54. See Derber (1979) on the asymmetrical distribution of attention in society generally.

55. West and Fenstermaker (1995). See also Jackson (2002); and Bettie (2003). The questions of class that arise here are not about class location or exploitation of workers' labor effort for profit. Nor am I looking at class consciousness, manifested in individual attitudes, workers' self-identifications, or collective action (Halle 1984; Fantasia 1988; Freeman 2000).

56. The hotel names are pseudonyms, as are all names of people throughout. I have changed some minor details about the hotels in order to preserve confidentiality.

57. When discussing my sites specifically, as well as certain other specific sites, I use the words *doorman* and *bellman,* because these workers were all men. When describing the hotel industry in general, I have used the gender-neutral terms *door attendant* and *bellperson,* because some (though very few) women do work in these positions. I never heard anyone in the industry use the word *bellhop,* and union officials have confirmed that the term is no longer used. I use the term *front door workers* to denote door attendants, bellpersons, and valets.

58. I shadowed workers rather than doing the job myself because managers would not allow me to work as a housekeeper. During this period I was no longer paid. (See appendix A.)

59. Luxury hotels in this city were exclusively nonunion when I conducted this research.

60. Direct quotations from conversations with workers and guests in the hotels and from formal interviews with managers and guests are verbatim, though some are edited.

61. Burawoy (1979), chs. 4 and 5. See also Gramsci (1971); and Littler and Salaman (1982). For nuanced discussions of resistance and agency in contemporary workplaces, see Kondo (1990); and Freeman (2000).

62. See Hodson (1991), for example.

63. Hodson (1991) has offered the similar concept of "enthusiastic compliance," which is linked to pride, autonomy, and flexibility. I prefer to use *consent,* because it links work to unequal social relations at a broader level.

64. See Bearman (2005, ch. 5) for a discussion of doormen's strategies.

65. This argument pervades Bourdieu's work, but see especially Bourdieu ([1980] 1990).

66. On dispositions, see Bourdieu (1984).

67. See Lamont (1992). See also Freeman (2000).

68. Gouldner (1973).

69. See Lamont (1992: 241 n. 34) for a discussion of studies of egalitarianism in the United States. See Rafaeli and Sutton (1990) for a discussion of differences in cultural display rules in the United States and Israel.

70. My thanks to Karen Strassler for emphasizing the importance of this shift.

71. Goffman (1959); MacCannell (1973); Hannerz (1980).

72. Hannerz (1980: 210). See also Goffman (1959).

73. Roy (1953); Burawoy (1979).

ONE. "BETTER THAN YOUR MOTHER"

1. Jones, Taylor, and Nickson (1997: 546).

2. Quoted in Gillette (1998: 59).

3. Hochschild (1983: 7).

4. Benjamin (1988: 12, 21).

5. Berger (1997).

6. Williamson (1930).

7. Berger (1997: 22).

8. King (1957: 184, citing an 1841 article in the New Orleans *Picayune*).

9. King (1957); Berger (1997).

10. Groth (1994).

11. At the same time, ideals of rationalized service, associated with E. M. Statler, were also on the rise. See Wilk (2005) for a discussion of this period, including racialized notions of service in the late nineteenth century. See Benson (1986) for an analysis of lavish personal services in department stores in this period.

12. Nykiel (1989).

13. Industry analysts usually look at segmentation either by price (generating categories such as luxury, upscale, midprice, economy, and budget) or by service offered (full-service, limited-service, resort, convention, extended-stay) or by both. Size and regional variation are also important factors.

14. Dittman (1997); Walker (1993).

15. The Four Seasons chain claims credit for introducing or broadly implementing many of these services; see www.fourseasons.com.

16. Several changes supported this transition: the elimination of tax laws that gave incentives to own even unprofitable hotels; changes in contracts between management companies and owners, making management companies more accountable for profits; consolidation of large hotel companies through mergers and acquisitions, increasing corporate power; and the emergence of real estate investment trusts (REITs), which tend to focus on the bottom line because of concerns about shareholders and profit distributions. (See, for example, Sangree and Hathaway 1996; Urban Land Institute 1996; Dittman 1997; and PKF Consulting 1997.)

17. Binkley (1999).

18. Bernstein (1999).

19. Keates (1999). As of December 2002, 6.6 percent of total hotel properties (3,011 hotels) in the United States were defined as luxury (i.e., occupying the top 15 percent of average room rates); they comprised 767,294 rooms, or 17.6 percent of the total number of rooms. Twenty-one percent of total properties (9,941 hotels) were defined as upscale (occupying the next highest 15 percent of average room rates). These encompassed 1,153,814 rooms, or 26.5 percent of the total. (These figures were gathered by Smith Travel Research and provided to me by the American Hotel and Lodging Association's Information Center: www.ahla.com.)

20. In April 2003, the five-star luxury segment had the highest occupancy rate in the industry; although this rate was down from April 2002 and was due mainly to rate discounting, occupancy in luxury properties was at least 10 percentage points higher than in full-service midscale and economy properties (66.5 percent compared with 55 and 52.8 percent) (Sharkey 2003). In contrast to upscale, midscale, and economy hotels, those in the luxury segment experienced growth in room nights booked on the Internet and in revenue in the second quarter of 2002 compared with 2001 (Hotel Online 2002).

21. The Ritz-Carlton's revenue per available room grew 16.4 percent in North America in the second quarter of 2004 (Yee 2004a). Occupancy at the Four Seasons in the United States rose slightly, and room rates rose 6 percent in 2004 (Yee 2004b). See also Levere (2004).

22. See Mars and Nicod (1984).

23. As I will discuss in chapter 2, both hotels posted service standards guiding worker behavior.

24. Mann (1993); Dev and Ellis (1991). See also Bearman (2005) for a discussion of the tensions surrounding residential doormen's awareness of tenants' personal affairs.

25. In nonluxury hotels, personalization is usually limited to tracking repeat clients' preferences in terms of what type of room or newspaper they want.

26. Lipper (2000).

27. Maxa (2001); Rosenfeld (2001).

28. Keates (1998).

29. Bowen and Shoemaker (1998).

30. Dev and Ellis (1991).

31. Mann (1993: 56).

32. Although I did not explore the reasons for the gender dimension of this phenomenon in interviews, it may occur because women are more conscious of the labor involved in the service, having themselves performed domestic services similar to those offered in the hotel (or directed their own servants to perform them). For research on the gender and class contradictions among wealthy women, see Ostrander (1984); Rollins (1985); Daniels (1988); Odendahl (1990); and Kendall (2002).

33. Rosenfeld (2001).

34. Byrne (1998). See also Lipper (2000); and Jones, Taylor, and Nickson (1997).

35. In contrast, she appreciatively described a situation in which she had arrived hours late at a luxury hotel because the staff had given her bad directions; she told the front desk agent what had happened, and the woman came out from behind the desk, put her arm around Christina, and petted her dogs. Notably, Christina saw this incident as exemplifying *good* service, although it was the hotel's fault that she had gotten lost in the first place.

36. Veblen ([1899] 1994).

37. DeVault (1991).

38. Witchel (2000). "Bath butlers" at one Ritz-Carlton property will draw five different types of baths for guests (*Condé Nast Traveler* 2002).

39. Witchel (2000).

40. Shamir (1980).

41. Hochschild (1983: 6).

42. See Ellin (2004).

43. Gilbert (2001: 32).

44. Some might argue, following Waerness (1984), that luxury service is actually "personal service" rather than "caregiving," because it is unreciprocal and performed by a worker who is subordinate to the consumer. Yet researchers have found that these elements characterize many paid caregiving occupations as well as unpaid practices, suggesting that the distinction between "personal service" and "caregiving" is not a useful one (see Abel and Nelson 1990; Diamond 1990; and DeVault 1991). See also Himmelweit (1999).

45. Quoted in Picker Institute document, as cited in Stone (2000: 95); see also Wellin and Jaffe (2001: 9).

46. Diamond (1990); Abel and Nelson (1990); Lundgren and Browner (1990); Stone (2000).

47. DeVault (1991); Diamond (1990). I am grateful to Arlene Kaplan Daniels for pointing this out to me.

48. Himmelweit (1999: 35) argues that "caring ... specifically involves the development of a relationship, not the emotional servicing of people who remain strangers."

49. Rollins (1985); Hondagneu-Sotelo (2001).

50. Jennifer Bickham Mendez (1998) has looked at bureaucratized cleaning services in which primary relationships were between workers and managers, but these workers had very limited contact with their clients. Evelyn Nakano Glenn (1996) has argued that historically, workers in "public jobs," such as hotel maids, housemen, and janitors, preferred these to domestic servant jobs in private homes, because public jobs were impersonally bureaucratized and because workers were not isolated.

51. Julia Wrigley (personal communication) has suggested that employers in

private homes are able to make demands of household workers that they would not make of hotel workers because household work lacks formal codification of duties, so workers can be required to do almost anything. But, although they are more limited by virtue of their attachment to particular jobs, job descriptions and service standards for interactive workers in the luxury hotel rarely specify boundaries of exactly what types of tasks these workers are responsible for when it comes to ensuring guest satisfaction. I describe these standards more fully in chapter 2.

52. My experience at the Royal Court provides most of the data related to the work done in reservations, room service, and the restaurant and as telephone operator and valet, because I did not work for long in these positions at the Luxury Garden.

53. Housemen or runners are workers who do errands within the hotel for guests and other workers, delivering dry cleaning to guests or extra linens to housekeepers, for example. At the Royal Court these workers were all men, so they were called housemen, while at the Luxury Garden there were female runners. I use the term *runners* throughout.

54. Housekeepers also do emotional labor in that they have to suppress certain aspects of themselves to remain unobtrusive, as Dan Wilk points out (personal communication). However, given their extremely limited contact with guests, emotional labor is not as significant a part of the service they produce as it is for interactive workers.

55. See Adler and Adler (2004) for similar findings in Hawaiian resorts.

56. U.S.-born men in nonmanagerial positions that do not involve physical labor (i.e., front desk agents and concierges) are frequently openly gay. Their willingness to perform caring and deferential labor may be concomitant with less rigid definitions of masculinity than those associated with heterosexual men. There were no straight white men in nonmanagerial positions in either hotel in the areas in which I worked, except for restaurant servers.

57. Room cleaners' tasks also include changing the sheets and making the bed; emptying the trash in the room and the bathroom; tidying the room and arranging magazines and other amenities; dusting the room (including the TV, desk, minibar, bedside tables, drawers, framed pictures); cleaning all glass, mirrors, and the ice bucket; making sure the desk has the proper amount of stationery, pen and pencil, paper clips, and so on, and that the laundry bag, bathrobes, pillows, shoe mitt, sewing basket, and the designated number of several types of hanger are available and displayed correctly; removing dirty linens and towels and replacing them with clean ones; cleaning the bathroom floor, the shower, the toilet, and the bathtub; and vacuuming the carpet. Workers at the Luxury Garden have to fill the ice buckets in occupied rooms. Room cleaners are sometimes also responsible for placing a welcoming bowl of fruit in the rooms of arriving guests.

58. I saw firsthand the reason for this fear one evening when I was assisting Mei-Hwa with turndown service at the Luxury Garden. One couple who were in the room when we knocked did not want the service right then. They debated between themselves whether or when we should come back to do the service; they ended up deciding (it seemed to us) that they did not want it. The next day I found out they had complained that they had never received the service. I confirmed to the housekeeping supervisor that my interpretation was the same as Mei-Hwa's, but had I not been there it would have been her word against theirs, and because of her limited English it might have appeared that she had misunderstood them.

59. One Filipina housekeeper at the Royal Court had literally been enslaved by wealthy Filipino employers who had brought her to the United States; she had not seen her children since 1989 because, having escaped from her employers, she was afraid of reprisals should she return home. Another housekeeper's brother had been killed by the armed forces in her native El Salvador. Hence, their sense of alternatives was quite different from that of many other workers in the hotel.

60. At the Royal Court, reservationists and telephone operators were part of the front office administrative unit, and they were physically located right off the front desk area, so they participated in the same local culture. For this reason, I sometimes include them in the front of the house in the rest of the book.

61. Leidner (1993).

62. The assistant manager's job is not much better paid than line employees' work and involves longer hours and more customer abuse. Some workers refuse to become managers for this reason and in fact see themselves as privileged vis-à-vis managers; likewise, many young managers leave the industry (60 percent exit after the first year, according to the general manager at the Luxury Garden). Several of the young managers I worked with at both hotels, even those who had been professionally trained in hospitality management programs, felt burned out and were seriously considering other careers. However, while their consent to provide luxury service and carry out other managerial duties may not last, the incentive to which they are immediately responding is their prospect of advancement in the career, in which the assistant manager phase is considered a kind of hazing period. (Managers I interviewed pointed out that the hospitality industry is one of the few in which it is not necessary to have a college degree to get ahead, which may be a draw for some workers.)

63. Leidner (1993: 30–37). See also Benson (1986); and Sallaz (2002).

64. My thanks to Sean O'Riain for suggesting this formulation.

65. Shamir (1980); Hochschild (1983); Leidner (1993); Fuller and Smith (1996).

66. In popular film representations of hotel housekeepers, such as *Maid in Manhattan* (2002) and *Blue Crush* (2002), workers not only notice guests' possessions, especially their clothes, but also have the leisure to try them on. Quasi-

journalistic representations of housecleaning in private homes (Rafkin 1998; Ehrenreich 2001) also describe the authors' own voyeuristic practices, as does the work of French artist Sophie Calle, who worked as a chambermaid and took notes on and photographs of hotel guests' belongings and behaviors. But hotel housekeepers I worked with had neither time for nor interest in such antics. They rarely indicated any curiosity about the guests beyond whether they were messy or neat.

TWO. MANAGING AUTONOMY

1. These turnover rates were still far lower than those in nonluxury hotels; annual turnover frequently reaches 50 percent or higher in the industry as a whole.

2. I make this claim on the basis of reviewing several hundred guest histories as part of the telephone operator's job, which included going through piles of registration cards of recently departed guests and entering new information into the computer database.

3. The computer systems in both hotels did not track business and leisure, just the type of rate the guest paid; "rack," or official, rates were more likely to be paid by leisure travelers, while businesspeople used lower corporate rates.

4. See Hochschild (1983); McCammon and Griffin (2000); and Leidner (1999).

5. Mr. Weiss was the only manager in either hotel who was not called by his first name, though workers and managers did often refer to him by his initials. I do not know if he insisted on this treatment or if it had arisen out of respect for his age; he was in his sixties, unlike Sebastian, the general manager at the Luxury Garden, who was in his late thirties.

6. Fuller and Smith (1996); Hochschild (1983); Rafaeli (1989); Leidner (1993); Lopez (1996).

7. Kunda (1992); Leidner (1993); Casey (1995).

8. Kunda (1992); Bowen and Lawler (1995); Macdonald and Sirianni (1996); Jones, Taylor, and Nickson (1997).

9. See, for example, Kent (1990); Partlow (1993); and Hemp (2002). The company allows managers from other companies to attend its two-day employee orientation (for a five-hundred-dollar fee). I attended the orientation in October 1999, at a reduced fee, thanks to a manager in the training department whom I had interviewed the previous year.

10. The credo: "The Ritz-Carlton Hotel is a place where the genuine care and comfort of our guests is our highest mission. We pledge to provide the finest personal service and facilities for our guests who will always enjoy a warm, relaxed, yet refined ambience. The Ritz-Carlton experience enlivens the senses, instills well-being, and fulfills even the unexpressed wishes and needs of our guests."

The motto: "We are ladies and gentlemen serving ladies and gentlemen." The three steps of service: "1. A warm and sincere greeting. Use the guest's name, if and when possible. 2. Anticipation and compliance with guest needs. 3. Fond farewell. Give them a warm good-bye and use their names, if and when possible." The employee promise: "At the Ritz-Carlton, our Ladies and Gentlemen are the most important resource in our service commitment to our guests. By applying the principles of trust, honesty, respect, integrity and commitment, we nurture and maximize talent to the benefit of each individual and the company. The Ritz-Carlton fosters a work environment where diversity is valued, quality of life is enhanced, individual aspirations are fulfilled, and the Ritz-Carlton mystique is strengthened."

11. For example, the service basics include: "10. Each employee is empowered. For example, when a guest has a problem or needs something special you should break away from your regular duties, address and resolve the issue"; "13. Never lose a guest. Instant guest pacification is the responsibility of each employee. Whoever receives a complaint will own it, resolve it to the guest's satisfaction and record it"; "18. Take pride in and care of your personal appearance."

12. In some ways, though not all, these hotels conformed to Mars and Nicod's (1984) typology of hotels; the Luxury Garden was a "strong grid, weak group" site, while the Royal Court was "weak grid, strong group."

13. Despite the tight labor market, Luxury Garden managers were still somewhat selective about hiring, as my access shows. Major turnover in the summer of 1999 led managers to postpone my entry indefinitely because, they said, it would be too disruptive to other new workers. This decision was an early indicator that managers were more careful about hiring and training than their counterparts at the Royal Court, where Nicole, the human resources director, seized the opportunity to hire me despite my total lack of experience (see appendix A).

14. Managers also moved up within the hotel and in the company's hierarchy: the head of the U.S. division of the company had been the general manager of the Luxury Garden, and the current general manager had been the rooms division manager. (He and the resident manager were later promoted to oversee the opening of a Luxury Garden property in another city.) The human resources director had been the training manager, and the reservations manager for the U.S. division had been the reservations manager at the Luxury Garden.

15. The director of sales at the Luxury Garden told me that hotels oriented toward business travelers often categorize reservations with sales because of the importance of corporate rates, while hotels specializing in leisure travel tend to place reservations in the rooms division, as the Royal Court did.

16. The telephone operator did nothing besides manage the switchboard. Reservations agents were assigned specialized administrative tasks and specific areas of responsibility in addition to taking phone reservations. Back of house

workers besides housekeepers were divided into several categories: the runner did errands within the hotel for guests and workers, the linen person supplied linens, and the lobby person kept the public areas presentable.

17. Hochschild (1983); Leidner (1993); Kunda (1992); Casey (1995).

18. I attended the initial employee orientation in July 1999, although I did not begin working at the hotel until late October 2000 (see appendix A). It was very sophisticated and similar in tone to that of the Ritz-Carlton. It occupied two full days and focused on guest service in addition to basic issues such as benefits, safety standards, sexual harassment, and the Americans with Disabilities Act, and it featured appearances by members of the executive committee and the head of the U.S. division of the company.

19. These instances include those I have mentioned in chapter 1, of the concierges who gave up their shoes and convinced a department store to open early, the doorman who called the taxi company, the business center worker who ran to the Federal Express office with a guest's package, and the front desk worker who taped the basketball game on her VCR, as well as a bellman who loaned a guest his own car seat for the guest's child and a catering employee who calmed down the host of an important event by bringing her a favorite snack.

20. Workers at both hotels who had been employed at the Ritz-Carlton often painted a similar picture of corporate culture as increasing worker accountability. They saw the TQM program as coercive, suggesting that employee "empowerment" actually just made workers more vulnerable by increasing their responsibility. Workers could not turn to managers to solve problems, but they were punished for failing to satisfy guests.

21. Hochschild (1983).

22. Leidner (1996: 34).

23. This video told the story of an anthropomorphized complaint, which looked like an old cardboard box. He started out in "the Land of Business as Usual," where no one cared about him. He searched around in the Lands of "Big Promises," "Flashy Slogans," and so on, but still no one paid any attention. Finally, he arrived at "the Land of Complaints," where human-looking figures did listen to him—and he unburdened himself, after which they wrapped him up with colorful paper and a festive bow, and he turned into a gift.

24. Concierges frequently complained about Sydney and Antonio, in particular griping that they took long lunch breaks or otherwise disappeared without telling anyone where they were going and that they failed to take on extra responsibility when shifts needed to be covered on weekends or when workers were sick. Problems also arose because Sydney and Antonio shared managerial responsibilities, and it was not always clear which of them was in charge of the desk or of workers' requests and needs.

25. At the front door, a clearly established hierarchy and promotional order

existed. Often workers started in housekeeping as runners, were promoted to valet parker, then bellman, and then (theoretically) doorman. Some workers were hired as valets or bellmen and aspired to become doormen. Likewise in housekeeping, workers were occasionally promoted to supervisor. But these ladders ended at low-level managerial positions, which opened up only infrequently.

26. A single runner performed a wide variety of tasks, from delivering items to guests and workers to cleaning hallways, public areas, restrooms, and executive offices. Room cleaners and turndown attendants were sometimes scheduled to work full or partial shifts in the laundry. The room service office was located in a corner of the kitchen, and the restaurant cooks prepared room service orders.

27. There had been a rooms division manager who also supervised housekeeping and engineering, but Petra was thought to have too little experience for this kind of responsibility. She became the front office manager, and the housekeeping and engineering managers reported directly to the general manager.

28. These meetings took place approximately every three months; all the hotel's workers were invited, and about half attended.

29. The best example of fluctuating standards had to do with guest packages, especially those that arrived before the guest did. Managers kept changing the procedure for keeping track of these, which at various times included logging the package into a special binder, leaving a message for the guest, leaving a note in the computerized record for the manager, notifying the front desk via computer, and attaching a Post-it to the registration card. New ways to deal with packages proliferated, until finally in a department meeting Brad told us to "figure out a way that works and get someone to put up a memo," which, needless to say, did not occur. Several weeks later, new workers had clearly not been trained to use any of these approaches. Other procedures for which modifications were inconsistently executed included the system for printing out the letters thanking first-time guests for staying and inviting them back, the imperative to check all signatures on registration cards, the procedure for sending letters about late charges to guests, the way to charge minibar consumption, the use of special codes in the computerized guest records, the frequency with which bellmen would deliver messages to guest rooms, the color of pantyhose female workers were supposed to wear, and whether workers should deposit written messages inside guest rooms or slide them under the door. This continual flux in standards, combined with sporadic training, meant that no one, including managers, could be relied upon to know how things were supposed to be done at any given time.

30. At the time I began, the hotel was carrying out a program of job training funded by the state. Training topics included health and safety issues such as "blood-borne pathogens" and "back safety" as well as "interviewing skills," "upselling," and some computer training. Some training had been done in

customer service, but it was not mandatory for front office workers, nor was it ongoing.

31. See Hodson (1991) for a similar point.

32. Room service was very similar, because lack of supervision allowed workers to snack on various goodies and clown around. The restaurant servers played all kinds of games and practical jokes as well.

33. Susan Porter Benson makes a similar point when she shows that fragmented, inconsistent managerial authority in department stores and managers' dependence on workers facilitate the development of a work culture among saleswomen (1986: 230).

34. I realized a few weeks into my work at the Royal Court that I had not tried to converse with any of the Spanish-speaking workers even though I speak Spanish; I felt that I had ended up on the front office side of some invisible barrier until I made a conscious effort to communicate with those workers.

35. See, for example, Hochschild (1983); Casey (1995); and Bolton and Boyd (2003). But compare Littler and Salaman (1982).

36. See Jones, Taylor, and Nickson (1997).

THREE. GAMES, CONTROL, AND SKILL

Epigraph: *Ninotchka* screenplay by Charles Brackett, Billy Wilder, and Walter Reisch.

1. Burawoy (1979, 1985).

2. Using different language, Bourdieu makes the same point ([1997] 2000: 203–5). My thanks to Loïc Wacquant for pointing this out to me.

3. McCammon and Griffin (2000: 284); but see Sharone (2004) for a discussion of consent in high-tech work. For a discussion of piece rates in service work, in this case the incentives and negotiations around the sales quota, or "stint," in department stores, see Benson (1986: 248).

4. Burawoy (1985: 38). See also Whyte (1948, 1955); Roy (1953); and Burawoy (1979: 87).

5. Because housekeepers and turndown attendants in my sites (as in most hotels) had a fixed quota of rooms to service, their work was organized as a race against the clock. Guests' behavior affected their capacity to clean or turn down rooms quickly, and workers did think strategically about how to accomplish their tasks, but they had no control over final output.

6. Workers in different manufacturing jobs may also play multiple games, of course. Researchers such as Roy and Burawoy, who both worked in only one part of the factory, did not make these comparisons.

7. Whyte (1948); Roy (1953); Burawoy (1979).

8. See Sallaz (2002).

9. Burawoy (1979: 82).

10. See Davis (1959); Mennerick (1974); Shamir (1980); and Sallaz (2002) for discussions of worker typologies of customers.

11. Restaurant reservations constituted a similar game; the objective was to reserve as many tables as possible without compromising service quality by overbooking. Workers made fun of Patrick, the restaurant manager, for being inept at this game because of his fear of being too busy. He often closed down reservations at sixty-five "covers" (diners), whereas previous managers would go as high as one hundred.

12. Obtaining higher rates conflicted with the goal of selling out, of course, so reservationists had to balance selling more rooms with selling more expensive rooms. REVPAR (*revenue per available room*), an important industry measure, determines the average rate per room by adding up all the rates paid on a given night and dividing by the number of rooms in the hotel (even the unoccupied ones). Thus, fewer rooms occupied at a higher rate will yield the same REVPAR as more rooms occupied at a lower rate.

13. At the Luxury Garden, managers usually assigned rooms, and the hotel typically did not overbook, so workers did not play the blocking game unless they had to change room assignments at the last minute.

14. See Wilk (2005) for a similar claim about hotel workers in the first half of the twentieth century.

15. One international concierge association, Les Clefs d'Or (The Golden Keys), certifies concierges as members through a major take-home exam with a wide variety of questions pertaining to services, culture, and handling challenging requests from guests. The association's motto is "In Service through Friendship." Members of the association wear the group's emblem, crossed golden keys, pinned to their lapels. At the Luxury Garden, Charlotte and Sydney had earned their keys, and while I was there Max took the exam to gain entry. Although he made fun of himself for doing it, saying it was only for his "professional vanity," he took the test quite seriously. The local concierge association met monthly, partly to educate its members about local happenings, such as restaurant openings or special events. All the concierges at the Luxury Garden belonged to the local association, and Hugh and Giovanna at the Royal Court attended its meetings at least occasionally.

16. See also Mars and Nicod (1984).

17. Leidner (1993); Hochschild (1983).

18. Davis (1959: 164).

19. This was not always the case. See Wilk (2005) for a discussion of managers' efforts to abolish tipping in the early twentieth century.

20. Commissions for most services were paid by the vendor to the hotel and were included in workers' paychecks.

21. Prior to the remodeling, bellmen had made lower hourly wages (about seven dollars) because they received more tips, while valets were paid about ten dollars because they earned fewer and less generous tips (usually two dollars instead of five or ten). When the renovation began, management began to pay both types of job at the higher rate because of the bellmen's complaints that their tip income had dropped significantly with the lower occupancy of the hotel. Bellmen and valets on the same shift were reclassified as "bellman/valet" and were supposed to share the work, alternating between working inside as a bellman and working outside as a valet; working inside was more desirable because the tips were higher. The workers with less seniority, however (including me), usually ended up working outside. As we will see, this practice led to some conflict between bellmen and valets, as well as difficulty for me in knowing exactly how much each type of worker would earn in tips in a shift during which he worked only one job.

22. For other research on tip strategies, see Paules (1991); Butler and Skipper (1980); Butler and Snizek (1976); and Sallaz (2002). See Wilk (2005) for tip strategies in early twentieth-century hotels. See Lynn and McCall (2000) for data suggesting that tip size and service quality are correlated.

23. See Butler and Snizek (1976) for a discussion of similar "product promotional activity."

24. In regard to making out on the shop floor, see Burawoy (1979). I noticed more explicit money talk among tipped workers at the Luxury Garden, especially at the door. Workers at the Royal Court tended to be more discreet about money. However, Oscar, a doorman at the Luxury Garden who had also worked at the Royal Court, told me that front door workers there talked about money all the time, too, but that they would not do so in front of me, which I found plausible.

25. Roy (1953); Burawoy (1979).

26. See also Spradley and Mann (1975); Mars and Nicod (1984); Paules (1991); Wood (2000); and Sallaz (2002). See Hanser (2005a) for a discussion of workers using typologies of customers and negotiating effort in two department stores in China, where workers were paid on commission.

27. Paulo was dying of lung cancer but could not give up his job for financial and health insurance reasons. His willingness to play the game was decreased by the difficulty of physical exertion.

28. Whyte (1948).

29. Adler and Adler (2004: 104) found something similar in their study of Hawaiian resorts; one informant described an advance tip as "more like a bribe than a tip."

30. Mars and Nicod (1984); Lennon and Wood (1989).

31. I feel obliged to refrain from describing these practices in detail in order to protect worker confidentiality. The practices I do describe were known to management before I left the hotel.

32. Another possible practice was to use "gypsy limos" instead of taxis or car services to send guests to the airport, for which the doorman received a ten-dollar cash commission from the driver. I never saw any doormen at either hotel do this, although Zeke told me that it had been common at the Royal Court before management outlawed it (because these drivers did not carry insurance).

33. Burawoy (1979: 65−71).

34. This situation was somewhat unusual in that my position in relation to the other bellmen/valets was especially ambiguous; they treated me better in some ways and may have cheated me as well. My general feeling was that I should take the less lucrative spot outdoors, which I did, because this work constituted their livelihood. But this incident reveals that, at the same time, I was immersed in the logic of the tip and thus already somewhat resentful about it, enough to be angry when Carlos accused me of stealing his work, because I already felt that I had given up my "rightful" share to him.

35. Burawoy (1979).

36. Joel's need for assistance was complicated by his game of keeping cars at the curb. It was in his interest to wait to send the car to the garage until right before the meter reader was coming around, but if the car's owner did not appear he had to get the car to the garage as quickly as possible.

37. This situation arose when guests' bags were in storage because their rooms were not ready or when they were changing rooms. For a room move, front desk workers sometimes indicated whether there were guests in the room by writing "live move" or "dead move" on the bell slip with the room number. Workers dealt speedily with a live move, which had tip potential, whereas for a dead move they usually waited until they had extra time.

38. See Benson (1986: 247).

39. See, for example, Shamir (1980).

40. On professionalism among service workers, see Gimlin (1996); Freeman (2000); Cohen (2004); and Bearman (2005).

41. Because that decision was implemented before I arrived, I do not know whether it caused resistance among the doormen. I got the sense that front door games had never been as widespread at the Luxury Garden, at least partly because guests paid for parking at the front desk.

42. Pierce (1995); see also Henson (1996).

43. See Zelizer (1997).

44. And not all income-maximizing practices are games. Income maximization without game playing might be found in a workplace in which workers with minimal autonomy pursue economic incentives in isolation from others, such as some piecework situations. Such work organization would eliminate a collective culture of games and the constant comparison that goes on among workers.

45. See, for example, Leidner (1993); Soares (2001); and Tannock (2001).

46. See Paules (1991); and Sallaz (2002).

47. Gold (1952); Davis (1959); Hochschild (1983); Henson (1996); Salzinger (1991); Macdonald (1996).

48. Burawoy (1979: ch. 9).

FOUR. RECASTING HIERARCHY

Epigraph: *Maid in Manhattan* screenplay by Kevin Wade; story by John Hughes.

1. Michèle Lamont uses a similar idea of the comparative self (see, e.g., 2000: 102).

2. See Lamont (1992, 2000).

3. Mills (1951: 173).

4. See Rafaeli (1989: 259); also Kondo (1990) for an example of Japanese artisans who gained a similar sense of worth from their work in a prestigious enterprise. Freeman (2000) analyzes the construction of distinction and status among female office workers in Barbados, who often compared themselves with garment and electronics factory operatives.

5. See, for example, Coser (1973).

6. Jade, a business center worker who was also a dancer and a Pilates instructor, said hopefully of staying in luxury hotels, "I can't afford it now, but I might be able to some day." A room service order taker at the Royal Court told me he aspired to own luxury items; he liked working in the city because he could see "rich people, limos, and beautiful women."

7. Rollins (1985: 212–22); see also Gold (1952); Davis (1959); and McCammon and Griffin (2000).

8. See Bolton and Boyd (2003: 291) for a discussion of similar "philanthropic emotion management" among flight attendants.

9. Jackie's invocation of her "nature" paralleled other workers' use of a sense of authenticity. Workers often suggested that service work, especially in the luxury setting, requires a certain personality type or that they were especially well suited to it. Dirk told me, "To be a bellman you really need a particular kind of personality," which included being friendly and patient and having a good work ethic. Workers sometimes characterized their desire to work in the hotel as reflective of psychological deficiency. Alec, for instance, told me he was "codependent." Joel at the Royal Court joked that "everyone who does this kind of work was rejected as a child" and then said seriously that he did wonder if that was a factor. Hal, a waiter in the Royal Court restaurant, told me he did this work because he had "a need for approval."

10. See Gimlin (1996).

11. See Rollins (1985).

12. Pierce (1995); Hochschild (1983).

13. I could not find blue roses, despite spending half an hour going to the

stalls that were likely to have them. The blue orchid I finally procured sat on the counter for an hour or so waiting to be taken to the guest's room. Many workers admired it, but concierges disparaged it; the different responses signaled an implicit division between workers with high and low cultural capital.

14. See also Lamont (2000).

15. Lamont (2000: 111).

16. Willis (1977: 119).

17. See Salzinger (1991).

18. This strategy was also frequently used in the Ritz-Carlton orientation. For instance, the director of quality told the group, "Be proud of yourself because you are a Malcolm Baldrige winner." One trainer also asked employees what their friends and family had said when learning of their employment there; the answer he was seeking was "wow." The company's motto, "We are ladies and gentlemen serving ladies and gentlemen," reinforces both the exclusivity of the hotel and the parity between guests and workers.

19. Trainers at the Ritz-Carlton pursued a similar strategy, telling workers how much they would enjoy their new vocabulary in their daily lives. One told us, "You'll carry the culture with you" and "We'll make you a better person."

20. When I asked Alice about the inequality between workers and guests, she responded, "The feedback from guests is that their needs are basic, and regardless of financial disparity, workers can identify with that." She said that for people to identify with their jobs, "they need to focus on connections, not disconnections. If they thought about disparities they'd just feel disconnected. The 'connect' comes from knowing that basics are important," and again she mentioned Maslow's hierarchy of needs.

21. I realized when I began working at the Luxury Garden that concierges there did not have a sense of who the concierges at the Royal Court were, though they were acquainted with their counterparts at many other local hotels. When the Luxury Garden restaurant invited concierges from hotels all over the city to sample its fare, they did not issue invitations to the Royal Court, because they did not know which of the many people on the list to invite.

22. Goffman (1961: 320), emphasis in original.

23. Lamont (1992, 2000). For a similar critique, see Fantasia (2002).

24. Kondo (1990); du Gay (1996).

25. Lamont (2000: 147).

26. See Kondo (1990); and Salzinger (2003).

FIVE. RECIPROCITY, RELATIONSHIP, AND REVENGE

Epigraph: de Tocqueville (1862: 85).

1. Gouldner (1973: 247).

2. Gutek et al. (2000) characterize three levels of relationship between workers and customers in service environments: "service encounters" (interactions with no expectation of future contact), "pseudorelationships" (in which the customer may come back to the organization but not to the particular worker), and "service relationships" (in which the customer returns repeatedly to the same person providing the service). All three of these dimensions exist in hotels. Gutek et al. looked at services that can be provided by a single person, such as hairdressing and auto repair; because hotel services are organizationally embedded, the analogy is not precise, but the idea is similar.

3. In their study of Hawaiian resort hotels, Adler and Adler found that workers complained of mistreatment by guests more at elite than at nonelite resorts, but they also suggest that most workers had good relationships with guests (2004: 222).

4. Hochschild (1983: 108).

5. Mars and Nicod (1984: 61).

6. Fuller and Smith (1996).

7. Haile, the Ethiopian doorman at the Royal Court, laughed good-naturedly about a guest who always waved her tip around so everyone could see it. On another occasion he told me, "Hide your money," which was visible in my pants pocket; he showed me his special trick for folding it up very small without removing it from his pocket.

8. See Rollins (1985); and Romero (1992).

9. Hondagneu-Sotelo (2001).

10. Davis (1959); Rollins (1985).

11. See Ashforth and Tomiuk (2000); and Lamont (2000).

12. Paules (1991); Rollins (1985); Zelizer (1997).

13. See Lee (2002) on routine civility between workers and customers.

14. See Kondo (1990: 218).

15. As I have noted, workers sometimes disliked being tipped in advance; this practice not only interfered with games but also put workers in the position of owing the guest, when usually it was the other way around.

16. Hondagneu-Sotelo makes a similar point, arguing that many Latina domestics "prefer an employer who takes personal interest in them to an employer who pays more and treats them disrespectfully and coldly" (2001: 195).

17. Contract-violating behavior also paid off in a sense. That is, the demands of guests who complained aggressively were usually also met, because workers were eager to get rid of such people. However, the guest paid a price in terms of both revenge and his reputation among the workers, as I will discuss later in the chapter.

18. Whyte made a similar argument in his study of restaurant workers, arguing, "The waitresses had certain standards of behavior that they expected the cus-

tomer to live up to, and they took action to 'put him in his place' if he 'got out of line' " (1948: 93). See also Mars and Nicod (1984).

19. Goffman (1967: 88).

20. Hochschild (1983: 129); Leidner (1993: 192); Rollins (1985: 169); Ashforth and Tomiuk (2000). Hodson (1991) identifies detachment as a strategy for maintaining dignity.

21. Davis (1959); Paules (1991); Mars and Nicod (1984); Zelizer (1997).

22. Hochschild (1983); Paules (1991).

23. Paules (1991: 165).

24. However, for the most part managers implicitly or explicitly condoned revenge practices, provided they were not too blatant. In fact, assistant managers exhibited many of the same views as line workers, and even upper-level managers were sympathetic to workers' concerns.

25. Another punishment for guests, dispensed by managers rather than workers, was to be denied access to the hotel. Here managers used *their* discretion, sacrificing revenue to retain their own dignity and that of workers. One afternoon Patricia, the front office manager at the Luxury Garden, had a run-in with a guest who complained that he had been charged twenty-five dollars to have his car washed, and the inside had not been cleaned; he was very angry with her and treated her scornfully. She said afterward, "I was like, 'That's it. You are never coming back here. Over my dead body are you coming back.'" Haile told me proudly that Royal Court management had decided to "eighty-six" a guest who had been abusive to him.

26. Spradley and Mann (1975); Paules (1991); Hall (1993); Gottfried (1994); Macdonald (1996); McCammon and Griffin (2000).

27. Burawoy (1979: 83).

28. Other authors have noted that restaurant servers often perceive women as less friendly (see Hall 1993). Women acting with authority may be perceived as more transgressive than men exhibiting similar behavior; it may also be that women act more imperiously vis-à-vis workers because of their own lower social status, as Rollins (1985) argued in relation to employers of domestic servants.

29. Gouldner (1973: 250).

30. Goffman (1967: 83).

31. The tendency for guests to leave unsatisfied and never come back was a major preoccupation for managers in both hotels and in the industry as a whole. Particularly at the Luxury Garden, managers stressed the importance of finding out if problems had occurred and rectifying them immediately and appropriately.

32. Leidner (1993: 226).

33. Rollins (1985); see also Graham (1995); and Wrigley (1995).

34. Romero (1992: 147).

35. The quoted term is from Hochschild (1983: 163, 174–75).

36. Rollins (1985).

37. The quoted term is from Gouldner (1973: 249).

38. Gold (1952); see also Dill (1994); and Bearman (2005).

39. Davis (1959: 165).

40. Troyer, Mueller, and Osinsky (2000); Leidner (1993).

41. Stone, cited in Hondagneu-Sotelo (2001: 195); see also Himmelweit (1999).

42. Because the behaviors I have described depend on both the interactivity of the work and the discretion in it, back of house workers did not articulate the contract either implicitly or explicitly. Although room cleaners and turndown attendants usually described guests as "nice," they did not articulate expectations of guests as front of house workers did. Workers in semivisible back of house jobs, such as room service, sometimes complained about being treated as invisible, but their minimal discretion did not afford them much latitude in terms of negotiating effort. Because these workers gained professional pride from adhering to particular standards, as I have mentioned, they tended to observe routines even when surveillance was absent. Telephone operators' contact with callers was fleeting and routine and thus they did not use the strategies I have mentioned. Reservationists were more similar to front of house workers, as shown by the examples I have used, because they had more sustained interaction with callers.

43. See, for example, Hochschild (1983: 110); Romero (1992: 108); Pierce (1995: 163–69); Leidner (1993: 226); Rollins (1985: 187); and Rogers (2000).

44. Whyte (1948); Rollins (1985); Paules (1991); Romero (1992); Zelizer (1997).

45. For example, Gimlin (1996). Some researchers have shown that domestic workers benefit both materially and emotionally from personalistic relations with employers (Dill 1994; Parreñas 2001; Hondagneu-Sotelo 2001) or that workers sometimes enjoy their relations with customers (Rafaeli 1989; Leidner 1993; Smith 2001; Wharton 1993; Whyte 1948; Tolich 1993). But these positive relations have been little theorized, and the predominant sense is one of opposition between worker and customer.

46. See Himmelweit (1999); and Ashforth and Tomiuk (2000).

47. See Pratt and Doucet (2000).

48. Whyte (1948: 249–50).

49. Radin (1996). See also Himmelweit (1999).

50. See, for example, Mauss ([1950] 1990); Parry and Bloch (1989); Zelizer (1997: 240 fn. 13); and Bourdieu ([1980] 1990b, [1997] 2000).

51. See Zelizer (1997: 99).

52. Gouldner (1973: 247–48).

53. Bourdieu (1990: 126).

54. Rollins (1985: 198).

55. See, for example, Pierce (1995); and Hondagneu-Sotelo (2001) for practices that obscure inequality.

56. Goffman (1967: 85).

57. See Lamont (1992).

SIX. PRODUCING ENTITLEMENT

1. My sample is small and skewed toward newly wealthy people. See appendix A. For studies of the traditional upper class, see Domhoff (1974, 2002); Ostrander (1984); Cookson and Persell (1985); Odendahl (1990); Ostrower (1995); and Kendall (2002).

2. Leidner (1993). See also Benson (1986) on customer socialization in department stores and managers' (often fruitless) attempts to control customer behavior.

3. My thanks to Sean O'Riain for suggesting this formulation.

4. Bourdieu (1990: 128). See, for example, Cookson and Persell (1985); Domhoff (2002); Baltzell ([1958] 1971); Kendall (2002); and Bourdieu (1984).

5. Odendahl (1990) and Coles (1977) also signal this phenomenon.

6. Veblen ([1899] 1994: chs. 3 and 4).

7. See Holt (2000) for a claim similar to the guests'.

8. Hondagneu-Sotelo found that employers of domestic servants also felt guilty about disparity in resources and labor effort (2001: 180).

9. Thus, luxury hotel stays are the kind of "perk" that keeps workers in global services willing to work long hours (and travel) for a relatively small share of profits (Sassen 1991).

10. See Odendahl (1990) on wealthy philanthropists who compare themselves favorably to those who do not donate money.

11. This stay was paid for by insurance and demonstrated the opulence of their real home. As Virginia described it, "The insurance adjuster comes in and looks at where you're living and says, 'Okay, basically you can live anywhere, in any hotel you want to go to.'"

12. By the same token, I also believe it is likely that what Joan Scott calls the "legitimizing function of gender" (1988: 45) is operating among guests. Though recognition work is not necessarily performed by women in every instance, caring labor is archetypally feminized, and feminized labor is easier to consume without conflicts over subordination. I am grateful to Millie Thayer for pointing this out to me.

13. When I worked in room service I was surprised by the number of people who answered the door in their bathrobes, and it struck me that guests may be more comfortable opening the door to workers who do not look like them and will never be in the same social circle with them.

14. Lamont (1992: 42).

15. This film is especially interesting because Marisa is portrayed as both a Cinderella-like figure—already a princess, in maid's clothing—*and* a straight-talking, legitimate representative of the working class. In contrast to *Pretty Woman*'s Vivian, Marisa's essential self is not transformed; by the end, she can be both an authentic voice of the people, now with some workplace authority, and a rich man's wife.

16. They also serve as sites for the regulation of women's femininity and deviant sexuality. Julia Roberts's character shifts from exemplifying commodified sexuality to representing heterosexual monogamy. Even when her character thinks she and Gere are forever parted, she renounces prostitution; her experience of love and upper-class life has made it impossible for her to continue as a sex worker. Ninotchka is frumpy and asexual until she is transformed by love; the transformation is signaled by her purchase of a fashionable hat from the hotel's shop, a hat that she has initially derided as a symbol of capitalist decadence. The character in *Blue Crush* is at first deviant because she is single; in the end, she needs her boyfriend's encouragement to come back and win the big competition.

17. West and Fenstermaker (1995).

18. Another way workers preserved their own autonomy and authority was to avoid telling inquisitive guests how they acquired such knowledge, often saying something like, "That's our secret."

19. Unlike in restaurants, where the norm of tipping 15–20 percent is well known, guests have to learn specific norms of how much to tip workers according to their jobs and their effort. As I have noted, doormen and valets were usually tipped one or two dollars for getting cabs or cars, doormen and bellmen received two to five dollars per bag, and concierges might be given anything from five dollars for making a restaurant reservation to fifty dollars for making more complicated arrangements. See Bearman (2005) for tipping insecurities among tenants in doorman buildings.

20. I asked another guest in this group how he was doing, and he deadpanned, "Fittin' in," making a joke out of his sense of nonbelonging.

21. Tipping workers as you go ensures that the worker who actually did the work receives the tips; workers whom you want to tip may not be around when you are checking out, though of course it is possible to leave money for a specific worker. Also, as my discussion thus far suggests, not tipping when workers expect a tip—even if you are planning to tip them later—may indicate to them that you are not playing by the rules.

22. See Heiman (2004) for an argument about how upper-middle-class suburban residents play out class anxieties in relation to their babysitters; Hanser (2005b) for an analysis of "distinction work" in Chinese department stores; and Qayum and Ray (2003) on how relations with domestic servants serve class functions for their employers in India.

23. Wilk (2005: 317).

24. Bourdieu (1984: 374).

25. Althusser (1969: 163–66), emphasis in original.

26. Bourdieu ([1980] 1990: 52–53).

27. Veblen ([1899] 1994); Bourdieu (1984); Willis (1977). See Lamont (1992: 180, 185) for a critique similar to mine.

28. Willis (1977: 123).

CONCLUSION

1. Stewart (1918: 249, 251, 257).

2. Shawn and Gregory (1981: 81).

3. Krugman (2002).

4. See, for example, Scott and Leonhardt (2005).

5. Hanser (2005b).

6. See West and Zimmerman (1987); for specific analyses of work in this vein, see Leidner (1993); and Hanser (2005c).

7. For similar notions of class performance, see Jackson (2002); and Bettie (2003).

8. Marx ([1867] 1978: 321).

9. This process echoes Marx's description of feudal relations, in which "every serf knows that what he expends in the service of his lord, is a definite quantity of his own personal labor-power. . . . [In feudalism] the social relations between individuals in the performance of their labor, appear at all events as their own mutual personal relations, and are not disguised under the shape of social relations between the products of their labor" (Marx [1867] 1978: 325).

10. See Burawoy (1979).

11. DeMott makes a related argument about how critiques of the "decline of civility" serve simply to perpetuate the idea of a classless society; he suggests that the lack of civility is a form of resistance, "a flat-out, justified rejection of leader-class claims to respect" (1996: 14).

12. See, for example, Althusser (1969); Gramsci (1971); Willis (1977); Bourdieu ([1980] 1990); MacLeod (1995); and Lareau (2003).

13. See, for example, Milkman (1987); Hochschild (1983, 1989); Benson (1986); DeVault (1991); Leidner (1993); Pierce (1995); Salzinger (2003); and Hanser (2005c).

14. Rollins (1985); Hondagneu-Sotelo (2001); Parreñas (2001); Williams (2004).

15. Bourdieu (1984).

16. Burawoy (1979, quotation from xii).

17. Leidner (1993), especially the conclusion.

18. See, for example, Harper and Lawson (2003). Symbolic interactionists focusing on the microlevel might suggest that, in fact, interactive inequality does not exist in worker-client relationships, because unequal entitlements to recogni-

tion are actually made equal by the norm of reciprocity and other mechanisms. I hope I have made clear that while I think guests' reciprocal treatment of workers is meaningful and contributes to normalization, it is not the same as the recognition to which guests are entitled on the basis of their status within the hotel.

19. See, for example, Pierce (1995) on gender relations among attorneys and paralegals. Attorneys, financial advisers, and administrative and personal assistants of all stripes, for example, often work with people (including their own managers or client-employers) of much higher income and status, whom they must treat with kid gloves. These service theaters may serve social reproduction outcomes, normalizing differences in the ways the hotel does; we might expect a particular emphasis on professionalism or possibly aspirations here. Or we might find critique and resistance among less entitled workers.

20. Rollins (1985); Romero (1992). Some domestics do value these relations, however, at least some of the time (Hondagneu-Sotelo 2001). Furthermore, domestic service may serve to legitimate *employers'* privileged class position, much as consumption of luxury service reassures hotel guests of their entitlement. Judith Rollins (1985) has made this argument with regard to employers in the United States; Seemin Quayum and Raka Ray (2003) have shown that in India, the middle and upper classes constitute themselves as classed and modern subjects through their relations with domestic servants.

21. As Lamont (1992, 2000) has shown, work structures and workers' expectations of work vary cross-nationally, because they are in part shaped by state supports, union density, and political history, and judgments of self and other are mobilized differently in other countries. Likewise, the norm of reciprocity, the imperative to treat social "inferiors" as equals, and the ethic of "friendliness" that characterize the United States may be absent in other countries, especially in the service sector. For examples, see Rafaeli and Sutton (1990) on Israel; and Hanser (2005a) on China.

22. Willis (1977: 174); Gramsci (1971).

23. UNITE HERE, the union representing these workers, is the result of a 2004 merger between the hotel and garment workers' unions. This union is part of the Change to Win coalition, most of whose members disaffiliated from the AFL-CIO in 2005, in particular because of the CTW's desire to consolidate unions into industry-specific entities in order to gain more leverage vis-à-vis employers and their somewhat more radical stance on the need for worker organizing.

24. Their counterparts in Washington, DC, however, opted for significant wage increases and a contract expiration of 2007 (Veiga 2005).

25. See Fantasia and Voss (2004).

26. Stephanie Ruby (personal communication).

27. The emotional labor workers are required to perform can be a subject of union activity to a certain extent, but customer behavior cannot be.

28. Gramsci (1971: 330–31).

29. Correspondents of the *New York Times* (2005).

30. Belluck (2005).

APPENDIX A

1. When I moved to housekeeping at the Royal Court, I was told there were no openings for room cleaners, so the best way for me to see the job would be to shadow some of the room cleaners without receiving pay. But I realized when I started working there that housekeeping was experiencing a labor shortage. I do not know why management did not to want to hire me to work on my own, though I suspect the decision was at least partly related to the difficulty of conceiving of a white person in the job. The decision may also have had something to do with the limited amount of time I was going to be there, so it was not worth training me. Similarly, at the Luxury Garden, François told me before I started work that I could not work at the front desk because new workers had recently been hired for that station and were being trained. But in the four months I was there, only one new worker arrived at the front desk.

2. Alice also introduced me to Cynthia, a manager at another upscale hotel. Ironically, because this hotel was unionized, I would have had to start on the graveyard shift or not do actual work. Also, because this was a large, convention hotel, it met fewer luxury standards and thus was not ideal for my purposes.

3. Nicole justified this decision by referring to another woman who had wanted to work as an unpaid intern, using what I found to be shockingly racist language; she said, "She was colored—she was black, and I didn't want to seem like a slave driver." Desperate to find a research site and wary of antagonizing her, I let this comment pass.

4. This view was confirmed when I had lunch with the general manager of a new luxury hotel in the city during the time I was working at the Royal Court. Because he was, coincidentally, a friend of a friend of my family's and because he seemed like a fairly open person, I told him more about the project than I usually revealed to managers. He thought I was insane and jokingly called me a communist.

5. In order to obtain human subjects approval to conduct this study, I was required to get written consent from guests and managers whom I interviewed formally but not from workers or other guests in the hotels in which I worked, where all that was required was managerial permission.

6. An extensive literature exists on these ethical issues in qualitative fieldwork. For a useful review, see Wolf (1996a, 1996b).

7. Scott (1985: 321–22).

References

Abel, Emily, and Margaret Nelson. 1990. "Circles of Care: An Introductory Essay." In *Circles of Care: Work and Identity in Women's Lives*, ed. Emily Abel and Margaret Nelson. Albany: State University of New York Press.

Adler, Patricia, and Peter Adler. 2004. *Paradise Laborers: Hotel Work in the Global Economy*. Ithaca, NY: ILR Press.

Alfino, Mark, John S. Caputo, and Robin Wynyard, eds. 1998. *McDonaldization Revisited: Critical Essays on Consumer Culture*. Westport, CT: Praeger.

Althusser, Louis. 1969. "Ideology and Ideological State Apparatuses: Notes toward an Investigation." *Lenin and Philosophy and Other Essays*. London: New Left Review Editions.

Ashforth, Blake, and Marc A. Tomiuk. 2000. "Emotional Labour and Authenticity: Views from Service Agents." In *Emotion in Organizations*, ed. Stephen Fineman, 184–203. London: Sage.

Baltzell, E. Digby. [1958] 1971. *Philadelphia Gentlemen: The Making of a National Upper Class*. Chicago: Quadrangle Books.

Bearman, Peter. 2005. *Doormen*. Chicago: University of Chicago Press.

Belluck, Pam. 2002. "Doctors' New Practices Offer Deluxe Service for Deluxe Fee." *New York Times*, January 15.

————. 2005. "At Harvard, an Unseemly Display of Wealth or Merely a Clean Room?" *New York Times*, March 22.

Benjamin, Jessica. 1988. *The Bonds of Love*. New York: Pantheon.

Benson, Susan Porter. 1986. *Counter Cultures: Saleswomen, Managers, and Customers in American Department Stores 1890–1940*. Urbana: University of Illinois Press.

Berberoglu, Berch. 1993. *The Labor Process and Control of Labor*. Westport, CT: Praeger.

Berger, Molly. 1997. "The Modern Hotel in America, 1829–1929." Ph.D. dissertation, Department of History, Case Western Reserve University.

Bernhardt, Annette, Laura Dresser, and Erin Hatton. 2003. "The Coffee Pot Wars: Unions and Firm Restructuring in the Hotel Industry." In *Low-Wage America: How Employers Are Reshaping Opportunity in the Workplace*, ed. E. Appelbaum, A. Bernhardt, and R. Murnane. New York: Russell Sage Foundation.

Bernstein, L. 1999. "Luxury and the Hotel Brand." *Cornell Hotel and Restaurant Administration Quarterly* (February): 47–53.

Bettie, Julie. 2003. *Women without Class: Girls, Race, and Identity*. Berkeley: University of California Press.

Bierck, Richard. 2000. "First Class." *Seasons Guest Informant* (in-room magazine), Spring.

Binkley, Christina. 1999. "From Miami to Seattle, a Big Boom in Luxury-Hotel Construction." *Wall Street Journal*, September 30.

Bleecker, Arline, and Sam Bleecker. 2002. "Champagne Wishes, Dramamine Dreams." *San Francisco Chronicle*, January 13.

Bolton, Sharon C., and Carol Boyd. 2003. "Trolley Dolly or Skilled Emotion Manager? Moving on from Hochschild's Managed Heart." *Work, Employment and Society* 17 (2): 289–308.

Bourdieu, Pierre. [1980] 1990. *The Logic of Practice*. Stanford, CA: Stanford University Press.

————. 1984. *Distinction*. Cambridge, MA: Harvard University Press.

————. 1990. *In Other Words: Essays toward a Reflexive Sociology*. Stanford, CA: Stanford University Press.

————. [1997] 2000. *Pascalian Meditations*. Stanford, CA: Stanford University Press.

Bowen, D., and Lawler, E. 1995. "Empowering Service Employees." *Sloan Management Review* 36: 73–84.

Bowen, John, and Stowe Shoemaker. 1998. "Loyalty: A Strategic Commitment." *Cornell Hotel and Restaurant Administration Quarterly* 39 (February): 12–25.

Braverman, Harry. 1974. *Labor and Monopoly Capital: The Degradation of Work in the Twentieth Century*. New York: Monthly Review Press.

Brooks, David. 2000. *Bobos in Paradise*. New York: Simon and Schuster.

Burawoy, Michael. 1979. *Manufacturing Consent*. Chicago: University of Chicago Press.

———. 1985. *The Politics of Production*. London: Verso.

Butler, Suellen, and James K. Skipper. 1980. "Waitressing, Vulnerability, and Job Autonomy: The Case of the Risky Tip." *Sociology of Work and Occupations* 7 (4): 487–502.

Butler, Suellen, and William Snizek. 1976. "The Waitress-Diner Relationship." *Sociology of Work and Occupations* 3 (2): 209–22.

Byrne, Harlan. 1998. "The Secret: Service." Barron's Online, May 11.

Casey, Catherine. 1995. *Work, Self, and Society: After Industrialism*. London: Routledge.

Castells, Manuel. 1996. *The Rise of the Network Society*. Cambridge, MA: Blackwell.

Cohen, Rachel. 2004. "When It Pays to Be Friendly: Employment Relations and Worker-Client Interactions in Hairstyling." Paper presented at the American Sociological Association meetings, San Francisco, August.

Coles, Robert. 1977. *The Privileged Ones: The Well-off and the Rich in America*. Vol. 5 of *Children of Crisis*. Boston: Little, Brown.

Condé Nast Traveler. 2002. "50 New Hotels." May, 221.

Cookson, Peter W., and Caroline H. Persell. 1985. *Preparing for Power: America's Elite Boarding Schools*. New York: Basic Books.

Correspondents of the *New York Times*. 2005. *Class Matters*. New York: Times Books.

Coser, Lewis A. 1973. "Servants: The Obsolescence of an Occupational Role." *Social Forces* 52 (1): 31–40.

Daniels, Arlene Kaplan. 1988. *Invisible Careers: Women Civic Leaders from the Volunteer World*. Chicago: University of Chicago Press.

Danziger, Pamela. 2005. *Let Them Eat Cake: Marketing Luxury to the Masses — as well as the Classes*. Chicago: Dearborn Trade.

Davis, Fred. 1959. "The Cabdriver and His Fare: Facets of a Fleeting Relationship." *American Journal of Sociology* 62 (2): 158–65.

de Kadt, Maarten. 1979. "Insurance: A Clerical Work Factory." In *Case Studies on the Labor Process*, ed. Andrew Zimbalist. New York: Monthly Review Press.

DeMott, Benjamin. 1996. "Seduced by Civility: Political Manners and the Crisis of Democratic Values." *The Nation* (December 9): 11–18.

Derber, Charles. 1979. *The Pursuit of Attention: Power and Individualism in Everyday Life*. New York: Oxford University Press.

Dev, Chekitan, and Bernard Ellis. 1991. "Guest Histories: An Untapped Service Resource." *Cornell Hotel and Restaurant Administration Quarterly* 32 (August): 29–37.

DeVault, Marjorie. 1991. *Feeding the Family*. Chicago: University of Chicago Press.

Diamond, Timothy. 1990. *Making Gray Gold*. Chicago: University of Chicago Press.

Dill, Bonnie Thornton. 1994. *Across the Boundaries of Race and Class*. New York: Garland.

Dittman, David. 1997. "New Structures for an Old Industry." *Cornell Hotel and Restaurant Administration Quarterly* 38 (October): 3.

Domhoff, G. William. 1974. *The Bohemian Grove and Other Retreats: A Study in Ruling-Class Consciousness*. New York: Harper and Row.

———. 2002. *Who Rules America? Power and Politics*. 4th ed. Boston: McGraw-Hill.

du Gay, Paul. 1996. *Consumption and Identity at Work*. London: Sage.

Edwards, Richard. 1979. *Contested Terrain: The Transformation of the Workplace in the Twentieth Century*. New York: Basic Books.

Ehrenreich, Barbara. 2001. *Nickel and Dimed: On (Not) Getting by in America*. New York: Metropolitan Books.

Ellin, Abby. 2004. "True Hospitality: At Your Service and Then Invisible." *New York Times*, August 24.

Erickson, Bonnie, Patricia Albanese, and Slobodan Draulic. 2000. "Gender on a Jagged Edge: The Security Industry, Its Clients, and the Reproduction and Revision of Gender." *Work and Occupations* 27 (3): 294–318.

Erickson, Rebecca, and Amy Wharton. 1997. "Inauthenticity and Depression: Assessing the Consequences of Interactive Service Work." *Work and Occupations* 24 (2): 188–213.

Fantasia, Rick. 1988. *Cultures of Solidarity: Consciousness, Action, and Contemporary American Workers*. Berkeley: University of California Press.

———. 2002. Review of Michèle Lamont, *The Dignity of Working Men*. *Contemporary Sociology* 31 (2): 122–24.

Fantasia, Rick, and Kim Voss. 2004. *Hard Work*. Berkeley: University of California Press.

Fisher, William P. 1998. "Managing Your Boss." *Lodging Magazine* (December): 37.

Frank, Robert. 1999. *Luxury Fever: Money and Happiness in an Era of Excess*. Princeton, NJ: Princeton University Press.

Freeman, Carla. 2000. *High Tech and High Heels in the Global Economy: Women, Work, and Pink-Collar Identities in the Caribbean*. Durham: Duke University Press.

Fuller, Linda, and Vicki Smith. 1996. "Consumers' Reports: Management by Customers in a Changing Economy." In *Working in the Service Society*, ed. Cameron Lynne Macdonald and Carmen Sirianni. Philadelphia: Temple University Press.

Gilbert, Robert. 2001. "Marketing: High-Yield Strategies: Horst Schulze on How to Keep Guests—and Employees Happy." *Lodging Magazine* (July): 31–32.

Gillette, Bill. 1998. "Luxury Segment Players." *Lodging Magazine* (October): 54–59.

Gimlin, Debra. 1996. "Pamela's Place: Power and Negotiation in the Hair Salon." *Gender and Society* 10 (5): 505–26.

Glenn, Evelyn Nakano. 1996. "From Servitude to Service Work: Historical Continuities in the Racial Division of Paid Reproductive Labor." In *Working in the Service Society*, ed. Cameron Lynne Macdonald and Carmen Sirianni. Philadelphia: Temple University Press.

Glenn, Evelyn Nakano, and Roslyn Feldberg. 1979. "Proletarianizing Clerical Work: Technology and Organizational Control in the Office." In *Case Studies on the Labor Process*, ed. Andrew Zimbalist. New York: Monthly Review Press.

Goffman, Erving. 1959. *The Presentation of Self in Everyday Life.* New York: Anchor Books.

———. 1961. *Asylums.* Garden City, NY: Anchor Books.

———. 1967. *Interaction Ritual.* New York: Pantheon Books.

Gold, Ray. 1952. "Janitors versus Tenants: A Status-Income Dilemma." *American Journal of Sociology* 57 (5): 486–93.

Goldin, Davidson. 2002. "On the Rise: Private Charters." *New York Times*, January 13.

Gottfried, Heidi. 1994. "Learning the Score: The Duality of Control and Everyday Resistance in the Temporary-Help Service Industry." In *Resistance and Power in Organizations*, ed. John M. Jermier, David Knights, and Walter R. Nord. London: Routledge.

Gouldner, Alvin. 1973. "The Norm of Reciprocity." *For Sociology: Renewal and Critique in Sociology Today.* New York: Basic Books.

Graham, Lawrence Otis. 1995. *Member of the Club.* New York: HarperCollins.

Gramsci, Antonio. 1971. *Selections from the Prison Notebooks.* Edited by Quintin Hoare and Geoffrey Nowell Smith. New York: International Publishers.

Groth, Paul. 1994. *Living Downtown: The History of Residential Hotels in the United States.* Berkeley: University of California Press.

Gutek, Barbara, Bennett Cherry, Anita Bhappu, Sherry Schneider, and Loren Woolf. 2000. "Features of Service Relationships and Encounters." *Work and Occupations* 27 (3): 319–52.

Hall, Elaine. 1993. "Smiling, Deferring, and Flirting: Doing Gender by Giving 'Good Service.'" *Work and Occupations* 20 (4): 452–71.

Halle, David. 1984. *America's Working Man.* Chicago: University of Chicago Press.

Hannerz, Ulf. 1980. *Exploring the City.* New York: Columbia University Press.

Hanser, Amy. 2005a. "Counter Strategies: Service Work and the Production of

Distinction in Urban China." Ph.D. dissertation, Department of Sociology, University of California, Berkeley.

———. 2005b. "Is the Customer Always Right? Class, Service and the Production of Distinction in Chinese Department Stores." Unpublished paper.

———. 2005c. "The Gendered Rice Bowl." *Gender and Society* 19: 581–600.

Harden, Blair. 1999. "Molding Loyal Pamperers for the Newly Rich." *New York Times,* October 24.

Harper, Douglas, and Helene M. Lawson, eds. 2003. *The Cultural Study of Work.* Lanham, MD: Rowman and Littlefield.

Hayner, Norman. 1936. *Hotel Life.* Chapel Hill: University of North Carolina Press.

Heiman, Rachel. 2004. "Driving after Class." Ph.D. dissertation, Department of Anthropology, University of Michigan.

Hemp, Paul. 2002. "My Week as a Room-Service Waiter at the Ritz." *Harvard Business Review* (June): 50–62.

Henson, Kevin. 1996. *Just a Temp.* Philadelphia: Temple University Press.

Himmelweit, Susan. 1999. "Caring Labor." In *Emotional Labor in the Service Economy: Annals of the American Academy of Political and Social Science,* ed. Ronnie Steinberg and Deborah M. Figart, 27–38. Thousand Oaks, CA: Sage Periodicals Press.

Hochschild, Arlie. 1983. *The Managed Heart: Commercialization of Human Feeling.* Berkeley: University of California Press.

———. 1989. *The Second Shift.* With Anne Machung. New York: Viking.

———. 1997. *The Time Bind.* New York: Metropolitan Books.

Hodson, Randy. 1991. "The Active Worker: Compliance and Autonomy at the Workplace." *Journal of Contemporary Ethnography* 20 (1): 47–78.

———. 1995. "Worker Resistance: An Underdeveloped Concept in the Sociology of Work." *Economic and Industrial Democracy* 16: 79–110.

———. 2001. *Dignity at Work.* Cambridge: Cambridge University Press.

Holt, Douglas. 2000. "Does Cultural Capital Structure American Consumption?" In *The Consumer Society Reader,* ed. Juliet Schor and Douglas Holt. New York: New Press.

Hondagneu-Sotelo, Pierrette. 2001. *Doméstica.* Berkeley: University of California Press.

Hospitality Net. 2001. "Luxury Hotel Market Withstands Recession." www .hospitalitynet.org/organization/17005404.html, July 24.

Hotel Business. 2001. "Operators Are Redefining Luxury." www.hotelbusiness .com, March 21.

Hotel Online. 2002. "Report on Electronic Bookings for Worldwide Hotel Industry Shows Luxury Segment Leads the Way to Recovery in Q2." www.hotel online.com/News/PR2002_3rd/Aug02_eMonitor.html. Accessed May 1, 2006.

Hughes, Everett C. 1952. "The Sociological Study of Work: An Editorial Fore-word." *American Journal of Sociology* 57 (5): 423–26.

———. [1971] 1984. *The Sociological Eye.* New Brunswick, NJ: Transaction Publishers.

Jackson, John. 2002. *Harlemworld.* Chicago: University of Chicago Press.

Johnston, David Cay. 2003. "Very Richest's Share of Wealth Grew Even Bigger, Data Show." *New York Times,* June 26.

———. 2004. "Airlines Are Counting on Luxury Up Front." *New York Times,* November 21.

Jones, Carol, George Taylor, and Dennis Nickson. 1997. "Whatever It Takes? Managing 'Empowered' Employees and the Service Encounter in an Inter-national Hotel Chain." *Work, Employment and Society* 11 (September): 541–54.

Kang, Miliann. 2003. "The Managed Hand: The Commercialization of Bodies and Emotions in Korean Immigrant-Owned Nail Salons." *Gender and Society* 17 (6): 820–39.

Keates, Nancy. 1998. "Summer Travel: The New Perks." *Wall Street Journal,* May 29.

———. 1999. "The $500-a-Night Hotel Room: Not a Quick Ticket to Luxury." *Wall Street Journal,* April 30.

Kendall, Diana. 2002. *The Power of Good Deeds.* Lanham, MD: Rowman and Lit-tlefield.

Kent, William E. 1990. "Putting Up the Ritz: Using Culture to Open a Hotel." *Cornell Hotel and Restaurant Administration Quarterly* 31 (November): 16–24.

King, Doris Elizabeth. 1957. "The First-Class Hotel and the Age of the Common Man." *Journal of Southern History* 23 (2): 173–88.

Klueger, James, and Eliot Smith. 1986. *Beliefs about Inequality: Americans' Views of What Is and What Ought to Be.* New York: Aldine de Gruyter.

Knights, David. 1990. "Subjectivity, Power, and the Labor Process." In *Labour Process Theory,* ed. David Knights and Hugh Willmott. Basingstoke: Macmil-lan Press.

Knights, David, and Hugh Willmott, eds. 1990. *Labour Process Theory.* Basing-stoke: Macmillan Press.

Kondo, Dorinne. 1990. *Crafting Selves: Power, Gender, and Discourses of Identity in a Japanese Workplace.* Chicago: University of Chicago Press.

Krugman, Paul. 2002. "For Richer: How the Permissive Capitalism of the Boom Destroyed American Equality." *New York Times Magazine,* October 20, 62.

Kuczynski, Alex. 2002. "The Private Skies of the Very Rich." *New York Times,* October 7, Sunday Styles.

———. 2004. "In New York, Midas Fever Rises." *New York Times,* May 9.

Kunda, Gideon. 1992. *Engineering Culture.* Philadelphia: Temple University Press.

Lamont, Michèle. 1992. *Money, Morals, and Manners.* Chicago: University of Chicago Press.

———. 2000. *The Dignity of Working Men*. New York: Russell Sage.

Lan, Pei-Chia. 2003. "Working in a Neon Cage: Bodily Labor of Cosmetics Saleswomen in Taiwan." *Feminist Studies* 29: 21–45.

Lareau, Annette. 2003. *Unequal Childhoods*. Berkeley: University of California Press.

Lee, Ching Kwan. 1997. *Gender and the South China Miracle*. Berkeley: University of California Press.

Lee, Jennifer. 2002. *Civility in the City: Blacks, Jews and Koreans in Urban America*. Cambridge, MA: Harvard University Press.

Leidner, Robin. 1993. *Fast Food, Fast Talk: Service Work and the Routinization of Everyday Life*. Berkeley: University of California Press.

———. 1996. "Rethinking Questions of Control: Lessons from McDonald's." In *Working in the Service Society*, ed. Cameron Lynne Macdonald and Carmen Sirianni. Philadelphia: Temple University Press.

———. 1999. "Emotional Labor in the Service Sector." In *Emotional Labor in the Service Economy: Annals of the American Academy of Political and Social Sciences*, ed. Ronnie Steinberg and Deborah M. Figart. Thousand Oaks, CA: Sage Periodicals Press.

Lennon, J. John, and Roy C. Wood. 1989. "The Sociological Analysis of Hospitality Labour and the Neglect of Accommodation Workers." *International Journal of Hospitality Management* 8 (3): 227–35.

Levere, Jane. 2004. "Hotels Find New Demand for Concierge Luxury." *New York Times*, December 7.

Lipper, Hal. 2000. "Personalized Service at Top Hotels Gets Mixed Results, Survey Says." *Wall Street Journal*, January 21.

Littler, Craig, and Graeme Salaman. 1982. "Bravermania and Beyond: Recent Theories of the Labour Process." *Sociology* 16 (2): 251–69.

Lively, Kathryn. 2002. "Client Contact and Emotional Labor." *Work and Occupations* 29 (2): 198–225.

Lopez, Steve. 1996. "The Politics of Service Production: Route Sales Work in the Potato-Chip Industry." In *Working in the Service Society*, ed. Cameron Lynne Macdonald and Carmen Sirianni. Philadelphia: Temple University Press.

Lundgren, Rebecka, and Carole Browner. 1990. "Caring for the Institutionalized Mentally Retarded: Work Culture and Work-Based Social Support." In *Circles of Care: Work and Identity in Women's Lives*, ed. Emily Abel and Margaret Nelson. Albany: State University of New York Press.

Lynn, Michael, and Michael McCall. 2000. "Gratitude and Gratuity: A Meta-analysis of Research on the Service-Tipping Relationship." *Journal of Socioeconomics* 29: 203–14.

MacCannell, Dean. 1973. "Staged Authenticity: Arrangements of Social Space in Tourist Settings." *American Journal of Sociology* 79 (3): 589–603.

Macdonald, Cameron Lynne. 1996. "Shadow Mothers: Nannies, Au Pairs, and Invisible Work." In *Working in the Service Society*, ed. Cameron Lynne Macdonald and Carmen Sirianni. Philadelphia: Temple University Press.

Macdonald, Cameron Lynne, and Carmen Sirianni, eds. 1996. *Working in the Service Society*. Philadelphia: Temple University Press.

MacLeod, Jay. 1995. *Ain't No Makin' It*. Boulder, CO: Westview Press.

Madsen Camacho, Michelle. 1996. "Dissenting Workers and Social Control: A Case Study of the Hotel Industry in Huatulco, Oaxaca." *Human Organization* 55 (1): 33–40.

Mann, Irma S. 1993. "Marketing to the Affluent: A Look at Their Expectations and Service Standards." *Cornell Hotel and Restaurant Administration Quarterly* 34 (October): 54–58.

Mars, Gerald, and Michael Nicod. 1984. *The World of Waiters*. London: Allen and Unwin.

Marx, Karl. [1867] 1978. "Capital: Volume One." *The Marx-Engels Reader*, 2nd ed., ed. Robert Tucker. New York: W. W. Norton.

Mason, Simon. 1989. "Technology and Change in the Hotel Industry." Ph.D. thesis, Department of Sociology and Social Policy, University of Durham, England.

Mauss, Marcel. [1950] 1990. *The Gift: The Form and Reason for Exchange in Archaic Societies*. Trans. W. D. Hall. New York: W. W. Norton.

Maxa, Rudy. 2001. "The Savvy Traveler." Marketplace. National Public Radio, April 3–4.

McCammon, Holly, and Larry Griffin. 2000. "Workers and Their Customers and Clients: An Editorial Introduction." *Work and Occupations* 27 (3): 278–93.

McLaughlin, Emma, and Nicola Kraus. 2002. *The Nanny Diaries*. New York: St. Martin's Press.

Mendez, Jennifer Bickham. 1998. "Of Mops and Maids: Contradictions and Continuities in Bureaucratized Domestic Work." *Social Problems* 45: 114–35.

Mennerick, Lewis A. 1974. "Client Typologies: A Method of Coping with Conflict in the Service Worker-Client Relationship." *Sociology of Work and Occupations* 1 (4): 396–418.

Milkman, Ruth. 1987. *Gender at Work: The Dynamics of Job Segregation by Sex during World War II*. Urbana: University of Illinois Press.

Mills, C. Wright. 1951. *White Collar*. New York: Oxford University Press.

Morris, Martina, and Bruce Western. 1999. "Inequality in Earnings at the Close of the Twentieth Century." *Annual Review of Sociology* 25: 623–57.

Nykiel, Ronald A. 1989. *Marketing in the Hospitality Industry*. New York: Van Nostrand Reinhold.

Odendahl, Teresa. 1990. *Charity Begins at Home*. New York: Basic Books.

Ostrander, Susan. 1984. *Women of the Upper Class*. Philadelphia: Temple University Press.

Ostrower, Francie. 1995. *Why the Wealthy Give: The Culture of Elite Philanthropy.* Princeton, NJ: Princeton University Press.

Parreñas, Rhacel. 2001. *Servants of Globalization.* Stanford, CA: Stanford University Press.

Parry, Jonathan, and Maurice Bloch. 1989. *Money and the Morality of Exchange.* Cambridge: Cambridge University Press.

Partlow, Charles G. 1993. "How Ritz-Carlton Applies 'TQM.'" *Cornell Hotel and Restaurant Administration Quarterly* 34 (August): 16–24.

Paules, Greta Foff. 1991. *Dishing It Out: Power and Resistance among Waitresses in a New Jersey Restaurant.* Philadelphia: Temple University Press.

People. 2005. "Star Tracks." March 14, 20.

Pierce, Jennifer. 1995. *Gender Trials.* Berkeley: University of California Press.

PKF Consulting. 1997. *Trends in the Hotel Industry, USA Edition 1997.* San Francisco: PKF Consulting.

Pratt, Michael G., and Lorna Doucet. 2000. "Ambivalent Feelings in Organizational Relationships." In *Emotion in Organizations,* ed. Stephen Fineman, 204–26. London: Sage.

Prus, Robert, and Styllianoss Irini. 1980. *Hookers, Rounders, and Desk Clerks: The Social Organization of a Hotel Community.* Toronto: Gage Publishing.

Qayum, Seemin, and Raka Ray. 2003. "Grappling with Modernity: India's Respectable Classes and the Culture of Domestic Servitude." *Ethnography* 4 (4): 520–55.

Radin, Margaret Jane. 1996. *Contested Commodities.* Cambridge, MA: Harvard University Press.

Rafaeli, Anat. 1989. "When Cashiers Meet Customers: An Analysis of the Role of Supermarket Cashiers." *Academy of Management Journal* 32: 245–73.

Rafaeli, Anat, and Robert Sutton. 1990. "Busy Stores and Demanding Customers: How Do They Affect the Display of Positive Emotion?" *Academy of Management Journal* 33 (3): 623–37.

Rafkin, Louise. 1998. *Other People's Dirt.* New York: Plume.

Reich, Michael, Richard Edwards, and David Gordon. 1982. *Segmented Work, Divided Workers: The Historical Transformation of Labor in the United States.* New York: Cambridge University Press.

Ritzer, George. 2000. *The McDonaldization of Society.* New Century ed. Thousand Oaks, CA: Pine Forge Press.

Robinovitz, Karen. 2002. "Butlers behind Counters." *New York Times,* March 3, Sunday Styles.

Rogers, Jackie Krasas. 2000. *Temps: The Many Faces of the Changing Workplace.* Ithaca, NY: Cornell University Press.

Rollins, Judith. 1985. *Between Women.* Philadelphia: Temple University Press.

Romero, Mary. 1992. *Maid in the USA.* New York: Routledge.

Rosenfeld, Jill. 2001. "No Room for Mediocrity." *Fast Company* 50 (September): 160.

Roy, Donald. 1953. "Work Satisfaction and Social Reward in Quota Achievement." *American Sociological Review* 18: 507–14.

Rozhon, Tracie. 2004. "Even if Just a Bauble, Luxury Counts for Holidays." *New York Times*, December 12.

———. 2005. "Born with a Silver Spoon: No, That's So Ordinary." *New York Times*, April 17.

Sallaz, Jeffrey. 2002. "The House Rules: Autonomy and Interests among Service Workers in the Contemporary Casino Industry." *Work and Occupations* 29 (4): 394–427.

Salzinger, Leslie. 1991. "A Maid by Any Other Name: The Transformation of 'Dirty Work' by Central American Immigrants." In *Ethnography Unbound: Power and Resistance in the Modern Metropolis*, Michael Burawoy et al. Berkeley: University of California Press.

———. 2003. *Genders in Production: Making Workers in Mexico's Global Factories*. Berkeley: University of California Press.

Sangree, David, and Peter Hathaway. 1996. "Trends in Hotel Management Contracts: Shorter Lengths and Changing Fee Structures." *Cornell Hotel and Restaurant Administration Quarterly* 37: 26–37.

Sassen, Saskia. 1988. *The Mobility of Labor and Capital*. New York: Cambridge University Press.

———. 1991. *The Global City*. Princeton, NJ: Princeton University Press.

Scott, James. 1985. *Weapons of the Weak*. New Haven, CT: Yale University Press.

Scott, Janney, and David Leonhardt. 2005. "Class in America: The Shadowy Lines That Still Divide." *New York Times*, May 15.

Scott, Joan. 1988. *Gender and the Politics of History*. New York: Columbia University Press.

Sennett, Richard, and Jonathan Cobb. 1972. *The Hidden Injuries of Class*. New York: W. W. Norton.

Shamir, Boas. 1980. "Between Service and Servility: Role Conflict in Subordinate Service Roles." *Human Relations* 33 (10): 741–56.

Sharkey, Joe. 2003. "Occupancy Highest at Luxury Hotels." *New York Times*, June 10.

Sharone, Ofer. 2004. "Engineering Overwork: Bell Curve Management at a High-Tech Firm." In *Rethinking Time and Work*, ed. Cynthia Fuchs Epstein and Arne Kalleberg. New York: Russell Sage.

Shawn, Wallace, and André Gregory. 1981. *My Dinner with André: A Screenplay for the Film by Louis Malle*. New York: Grove Press.

Silverstein, Michael, and Neil Fiske. 2003. *Trading Up: The New American Luxury*. With John Butman. New York: Portfolio.

Simpson, Ida Harper. 1989. "Where Have All the Workers Gone?" *Social Forces* 67 (3): 563–81.

Smith, Vicki. 1994. "Braverman's Legacy: The Labor Process Tradition at 20." *Work and Occupations* 21 (4): 403–21.

———. 2001. *Crossing the Great Divide: Worker Risk and Opportunity in the New Economy.* Ithaca, NY: ILR Press.

Soares, Angelo. 2001. "Silent Rebellions in the Capitalist Paradise: A Brazil-Quebec Comparison." In *The Critical Study of Work: Labor, Technology, and Global Production,* ed. Rick Baldoz, Charles Koeber, and Philip Kraft. Philadelphia: Temple University Press.

Spradley, James, and Brenda Mann. 1975. *The Cocktail Waitress: Woman's Work in a Man's World.* New York: Alfred A. Knopf.

Stark, David. 1980. "Class Struggle and the Transformation of the Labor Process." *Theory and Society* 9: 89–130.

Steinberg, Ronnie, and Deborah M. Figart, eds. 1999. *Emotional Labor in the Service Economy: Annals of the American Academy of Political and Social Science.* Thousand Oaks, CA: Sage Periodicals Press.

Stenross, Barbara, and Sherryl Kleinman. 1989. "The Highs and Lows of Emotional Labor: Detectives' Encounters with Criminals and Victims." *Journal of Contemporary Ethnography* 17: 435–52.

Stepick, Alex, and Guillermo Grenier. 1994. "The View from the Back of the House: Restaurants and Hotels in Miami." With Hafidh A. Hafidh, Sue Chaffee, and Debbie Draznin. In *Newcomers in the Workplace: Immigrants and the Restructuring of the U.S. Economy,* ed. Louise Lamphere, Alex Stepick, and Guillermo Grenier. Philadelphia: Temple University Press.

Stewart, Herbert L. 1918. "The Ethics of Luxury and Leisure." *American Journal of Sociology* 24 (3): 241–59.

Stone, Deborah. 2000. "Caring by the Book." In *Care Work: Gender, Labor and Welfare States,* ed. Madonna Harrington Meyer. New York: Routledge.

Sutton, Robert. 1991. "Maintaining Norms about Expressed Emotions: The Case of Bill Collectors." *Administrative Science Quarterly* 36 (2): 245–68.

Sutton, Robert, and Anat Rafaeli. 1988. "Untangling the Relationship between Displayed Emotions and Organizational Sales: The Case of Convenience Stores." *Academy of Management Journal* 31 (3): 461–87.

Swartz, David. 1997. *Culture and Power: The Sociology of Pierre Bourdieu.* Chicago: University of Chicago Press.

Tannock, Stuart. 2001. *Youth at Work: The Unionized Fast-Food and Grocery Workplace.* Philadelphia: Temple University Press.

Thompson, Kay. 1955. *Eloise.* New York: Simon and Schuster.

Tien, Ellen. 2002. "Pulse: Mother's Day / A Portable Spa for Three Hours." *New York Times,* May 5.

Tocqueville, Alexis de. 1862. *Democracy in America.* Cambridge: Sever and Francis.

Tolich, Martin. 1993. "Alienating and Liberating Emotions at Work: Supermarket Clerks' Performance of Customer Service." *Journal of Contemporary Ethnography* 22 (3): 361–81.

Troyer, Lisa, Charles W. Mueller, and Pavel I. Osinsky. 2000. "Who's the Boss? A Role-Theoretic Analysis of Customer Work." *Work and Occupations* 27 (3): 406–27.

Turrell, Carter. 2004. "Luxury for the Masses." www.Forbes.com, July 13.

Twitchell, James B. 2002. *Living It Up: Our Love Affair with Luxury.* New York: Columbia University Press.

Urban Land Institute (PKF Consulting). 1996. *Hotel Development.* San Francisco: PKF Consulting.

Veblen, Thorstein. [1899] 1994. *The Theory of the Leisure Class.* New York: Penguin.

Veiga, Alex. 2005. "Hotel Union Says Lining Up Contract Dates Brings Leverage." *Miami Herald* online, www.herald.com, June 15.

Waerness, Kari. 1984. "The Rationality of Caring." *Economic and Industrial Democracy* 5: 185–211.

Waggoner, John. 2004. "Rich Are Spending, while Poor Tighten Their Belts." *USA Today,* July 23, B3.

Walker, Bruce. 1993. "What's Ahead: A Strategic Look at Lodging Trends." *Cornell Hotel and Restaurant Administration Quarterly* 34: 28–34.

Wardell, Mark. 1999. "Labor Processes: Moving beyond Braverman and the Deskilling Debate." In *Rethinking the Labor Process,* ed. Mark Wardell, Thomas Steiger, and Peter Meiksins. Albany: State University of New York Press.

Wardell, Mark, Thomas Steiger, and Peter Meiksins, eds. 1999. *Rethinking the Labor Process.* Albany: State University of New York Press.

Weisberger, Lauren. 2003. *The Devil Wears Prada.* New York: Broadway Books.

Wellin, Chris, and Dale Jaffe. 2001. "In Search of Personal Care." Working Paper no. 22. Center for Working Families, University of California, Berkeley.

Wells, Miriam. 2000. "Immigration and Unionization in the San Francisco Hotel Industry." In *Organizing Immigrants,* ed. Ruth Milkman. Ithaca, NY: ILR/Cornell University Press.

West, Candace, and Sarah Fenstermaker. 1995. "Doing Difference." *Gender and Society* 9 (1): 8–37.

West, Candace, and Don Zimmerman. 1987. "Doing Gender." *Gender and Society* 1: 125–51.

Wharton, Amy. 1993. "The Affective Consequences of Service Work: Managing Emotions on the Job." *Work and Occupations* 20 (2): 205–32.

——. 1999. "The Psychosocial Consequences of Emotional Labor." In *Emotional Labor in the Service Economy: Annals of the American Academy of Political and Social Science,* ed. Ronnie Steinberg and Deborah M. Figart, 158–76. Thousand Oaks, CA: Sage Periodicals Press.

Whitlock, Stephen. 1999. "It's the Little Things that Count." *Condé Nast Traveler,* April, 52.

Whyte, William F. 1948. *Human Relations in the Restaurant Industry.* New York: McGraw-Hill.

——. 1955. *Money and Motivation.* New York: Harper and Brothers.

Wilk, Daniel Levinson. 2005. "Cliff Dwellers: Modern Service in New York City, 1800–1945." Ph.D. dissertation, Department of History, Duke University.

Williams, Alex. 2005. "Wedding Singers? Not!" *New York Times,* November 20.

Williams, Christine. 2004. "Inequality in the Toy Store." *Qualitative Sociology* 27 (4): 461–86.

Williamson, Jefferson. 1930. *The American Hotel: An Anecdotal History.* New York: Alfred A. Knopf.

Willis, Paul. 1977. *Learning to Labor: How Working Class Kids Get Working Class Jobs.* New York: Columbia University Press.

Witchel, Alex. 2000. "At Hotels, the Butlers Are Doing It." *New York Times,* August 20.

Wolf, Diane. 1996a. "Situating Feminist Dilemmas in Fieldwork." In *Feminist Dilemmas in Fieldwork,* ed. Diane Wolf. Boulder, CO: Westview Press.

——, ed. 1996b. *Feminist Dilemmas in Fieldwork.* Boulder, CO: Westview Press.

Wood, Elizabeth Anne. 2000. "Working in the Fantasy Factory: The Attention Hypothesis and the Enacting of Masculine Power in Strip Clubs." *Journal of Contemporary Ethnography* 29 (1): 5–31.

Wood, Roy C. 1992. *Working in Hotels and Catering.* London: Routledge.

——. 1994. "Hotel Culture and Social Control." *Annals of Tourism Research* 21: 65–80.

Wouters, Cas. 1989. "The Sociology of Emotions and Flight Attendants: Hochschild's *Managed Heart.*" *Theory, Culture and Society* 6: 95–123.

Wright, Erik Olin. 1997. *Class Counts: Comparative Studies in Class Analysis.* Cambridge: Cambridge University Press.

Wright, Erik Olin, and Rachel Dwyer. 2000. "The American Jobs Machine." *Boston Review* 25, no. 6 (December).

Wrigley, Julia. 1995. *Other People's Children.* New York: Basic Books.

Yee, Amy. 2004a. "Demand for Luxury Helps to Lift Marriott." *Financial Times,* July 16, 25.

——. 2004b. "Demand for Luxury Increasing." *Financial Times,* November 5, 29.

Zamudio, Margaret. 1996. "Organizing the New Otani Hotel in Los Angeles: The Role of Ethnicity, Race, and Citizenship in Class Formation." Ph.D. dissertation, Department of Sociology, University of California, Los Angeles.

Zelizer, Viviana. 1997. *The Social Meaning of Money.* Princeton, NJ: Princeton University Press.

Zimbalist, Andrew, ed. 1979. *Case Studies on the Labor Process.* New York: Monthly Review Press.

Index

accountability to managers: corporate culture as a mechanism of, 22, 75, 76, 308n20; Luxury Garden workers, 71, 75, 76, 82–83, 85–86, 108; Royal Court workers and, 93, 109

aesthetics: displays of attentiveness to, 43–44, 50; of work, 74; worker judgments of guests, 155, 167–68, 174, 176. *See also* appearance; material luxury; taste

age: and guest-worker relations, 107, 191; Luxury Garden workers, 73, 107; luxury travelers, 278; Royal Court workers, 86–87, 107, 148

agency, 220; guests', 18, 112, 230; workers', 8–9, 16–17, 204, 244–45. *See also* authenticity; consent; resistance; revenge

airline workers, 123; flight attendants, 7, 45, 78, 166

alienation, service worker, from self, 8–9, 11, 15, 259–60

Althusser, Louis, 254

American Journal of Sociology, 257–58

antagonism: racial, 85; worker-client, 9, 136, 219; worker-coworker, 140, 141, 144, 150; worker-manager, 9–10, 136. *See also* conflicts

anticipation of guest needs, 25, 28, 32–38; domestic servant and hotel worker, 47–48; front of house workers, 49, 56; games reading guest expectations, 119; guest insecurity and, 242–43, 248; Luxury Garden, 33–37, 42, 67, 106, 127–28; Royal Court, 34, 37, 69, 91, 119; tipping game, 127–28

appearance: of guests, 167–68, 174, 199, 243–45, 247, 249; of workers, 70, 74, 88, 235, 245

asymmetry. *See* inequality

authenticity: constraints on, 102–3; in front of house work, 56; guest selfhood and, 46; performances and, 20, 259; reciprocity of guests and workers, 186, 210, 219, 261; Royal Court focus, 22, 69, 71, 72, 86, 89–95, 99, 104, 105, 108–9, 179–81; worker selfhood, 8–9, 11, 71, 285. *See also* sincerity authority: domestic servant lacking, 26; games and, 111; guests over workers, 151, 159, 186, 192, 211–12, 215, 221, 250–51, 317n28; local cultures of, 71; maternal, 47; and powerful selfhood of workers, 17–18, 157, 165; tone of "authority in reserve," 211–12, 251; workers constituting status with, 156–59, 180; workers over coworkers/ mutual regulation, 64, 72, 84–85, 86, 88, 96, 100–105, 109, 149–50, 156, 159; workers over guests, 165. *See also* control; empowerment; entitlement; managerial authority; organization of work

autonomy of workers, 21, 63, 141–50, 261; and games, 17, 109, 111, 124–25, 141–50, 151, 267; managers and, 11–12, 18, 22, 64, 86, 99–100, 143–50, 151, 267; powerful selfhood and, 11–12, 16–19, 109, 147–50, 267. *See also* consent by workers; control; discretion by workers; independence of workers

awards: concierge, 181, 311n15; Luxury Garden employees of the quarter/year, 77; Luxury Garden hotel, 65, 66, 177, 180–81; Malcolm Baldrige National Quality Award, 70, 315n18; Mobil, 66, 68, 160, 180–81; restaurants, 13, 65; Royal Court hotel, 68, 179; Royal Court "stars of reception" employees, 90, 102. *See also* ranking; rewards

back of house workers, 49–53, 51*table*, 57, 137, 141; awareness of structural inequality, 57–58, 61; demographics, 50, 53, 57, 58, 86, 104, 281, 305n58, 323n1; guests' awareness of structural inequality, 235, 237–38, 240; Luxury Garden, 50, 66*table*, 67, 74, 180, 292*table*, 305n58, 307–8n16; reciprocity constraints, 218, 318n42; Royal Court, 86, 88; tips and wages, 50, 61–62, 67. *See also* housekeepers; laundry services; noninteractive service work

back servers/busers, 40

bellmen/bellpersons, 40, 49, 56, 59, 159; conflicts with coworkers, 138–39; demographics, 50, 86, 281–82, 300n57; ethnographic observation, 13, 14, 273, 281–82; Luxury Garden, 67, 73, 74, 126, 129, 159, 193, 292*table*; name use by, 118; revenge for guest transgressions, 201; Royal Court,

86, 88, 118, 119, 126, 138–39, 293*table*, 312n21; tips, 125, 126, 127, 129, 138–39, 189, 292*table*, 293*table*, 312n21, 320n19; wages, 67, 292*table*, 293*table*, 312n21

benefits to workers: in authority and autonomy, 86; fringe benefits, 53, 65, 157, 266; of making guests feel better, 78; of structural inequality, 10

Benjamin, Jessica, 25

Blue Crush, 241–42, 305n66, 320n16

Bourdieu, Pierre, 17, 220, 225, 251–52, 254–55, 263, 299n53

Braverman, Harry, *Labor and Monopoly Capital*, 7, 297n30

Burawoy, Michael, 16, 111, 112, 129, 135–36, 138, 152, 263

busers/back servers, 40

business center, 27; Luxury Garden, 65, 74, 175; workers, 14, 139, 275

business travelers: conflicted entitlement to luxury service, 226, 229–30, 231–33; engagement and evaluation, 229–30, 231; expectations of workers, 209–10; interviewed, 277; Luxury Garden, 14, 67, 205; positive feedback from, 106–7; privileged compared with workers, 299n53; reciprocity with workers, 196, 206, 230–31; reservations categorized with sales, 307n15; room blocking games with, 117; room rates, 306n3; Royal Court, 13; tipping avoided by, 130; worker empathy for, 163–64

butlers: domestic, 47; luxury hotel, 40, 41

cab drivers: fleeting relationships, 124, 131, 217; tipping games, 124, 130, 131

capitalist labor relations, 7, 9–11, 263

care: reciprocity from guests in language of, 190, 191. *See also* caring labor/care work

career ladders: Luxury Garden, 73, 108; Royal Court and, 86–87, 308–9n25. *See also* promotion

caring labor/care work, 2–3, 26, 31, 47, 303n48; guest entitlement to, 19, 224; maternal/feminized, 21, 25–26, 38, 46–47, 48, 319n12; needs fulfillment, 36, 47; pampering, 38–44, 231–32; sincere, 45. *See also* anticipation of guest needs; emotional labor; empathy cars: "gypsy limos," 313n32; Luxury Garden chauffeur-driven house car, 65. *See also* cab drivers; valet parkers

Castells, Manuel, 5

Celebrated Quality Experience (CQE), at Luxury Garden, 80–81, 82

Celebrated Quality Standards (CQS), at Luxury Garden, 79–80, 92

Celebrated Standards Training (CST), at Luxury Garden, 79

chain hotels, 27

check-in and check-out times, Luxury Garden and, 37

civility, 220, 321n11. *See also* reciprocity in worker-guest relations

class, 12, 23, 300n55; backgrounds of wealthy guests, 15, 224, 226, 235, 254, 256, 277, 278; "democratization of luxury," 296n13; entitlements of, 5, 23, 258, 259–60, 264, 269; in hotel history, 26; interactions among individuals of different classes, 6, 11, 241, 260–62; interpellation into class positions, 23, 254–55, 278; mannerisms of, 177; performance of class/"doing class," 12, 20, 244, 246, 254, 259–60; work and, 3, 7, 12, 238–40, 297n29, 299n47. *See also* privilege; status; wealth; worker-guest inequality; working class

clerical work, 297n30

clients, 8; antagonistic relations with workers, 9, 136, 219; luxury service, 5; managerial control of, 9, 55; as managers, 9; monitoring of workers by, 57; selfhood in interactive services, 5–6. *See also* customer; guest; worker-employer relations

Cluny Brown (Ernst Lubitsch), 247–48

collective action, 300n55; consumption, 286; games, 111, 129, 313n44; individual interactions vs., 16–17, 19, 155, 182, 185–86, 204, 221, 267; lateral relations among workers and, 261; union, 266, 267. *See also* norms; organization of work

comment cards, 57, 107; complaints, 31, 42–43, 98, 106, 212, 213; managers posting, 84, 90, 98, 189; obscuring commodification of relationship with, 213; praising hotel, 37, 212–13; praising service, 33, 37–38, 41, 43, 84, 90, 98, 105–8, 189, 276; research review of, 14, 274, 275; rule-breaking approved of,

37–38; on speed of service, 41. *See also* letters from guests

commissions, 311n20; conflicts among workers over, 137; during ethnographic participation, 14, 274–75, 283; front and back of house workers, 50; games involving, 123, 125, 128–29, 133, 135, 137, 144; legitimating luxury consumption for, 249; Royal Court/Luxury Garden comparisons, 67, 68, 292*table*, 293*table*; wealth of guests compared with, 2; worker-coworker comparisons, 158. *See also* tips

commodification of relationship, 8, 192, 197, 218–21, 260–61, 285; obscuring, 178, 186, 189–91, 209, 212–13, 218, 221, 229, 241; sexual, 320n16. *See also* compensation

commodity fetishism, 260–61

community: doormen serving local "regulars," 133–34, 143–44, 146–47, 201; Luxury Garden workers, 75–79; multi-sited studies, 286; nonguests requesting services, 171; Royal Court, 91; worker comparison/superiority with outside, 22, 141, 155, 159–62, 183, 235–36. *See also* culture; demographics; organizational identity; sociability

comparison by guests, of selves with social peers/other guests, 224, 233–34, 245–46

comparison by workers, of selves, 176, 181–83; with communities outside the hotel, 22, 141, 155, 159–62, 183, 235–36; with co-workers, 17–18, 22, 140–41, 149, 151, 155–59, 178, 180, 181, 235–36, 261; with guests, 17–18, 22, 155, 162–81, 261; of guests acknowledging/not acknowledging effort, 196. *See also* judgment by workers; privilege; superiority of workers

compensation: corporate CEO, 5, 297n24; during ethnographic participation, 14, 129–30, 273, 274–75, 283; fringe benefits, 53, 65, 157, 266; for guest complaints, 213–14; to research subjects, 284–85; wealthiest taxpayers, 297n24. *See also* benefits to workers; commissions; income; perks; rewards; tips; wages

competence: workers evaluating guests', 167, 247; workers' strategies of, 140–42, 145. *See also* knowledge; skill competition: among workers, 126, 137, 273–74. *See also* comparison by workers; conflicts

complaints, guest, 316n17; anthropomorphized, 308n23; compensation from hotel for, 213–14; expectations and, 107–8, 122, 205, 211–13; about failures of labor, 31, 42–43, 98, 106; games to avoid, 113–14, 117, 118; about hotel structural and renovation problems, 31, 106, 164, 212–14; legitimation related to payment levels, 172, 173; Luxury Garden training in handling, 35–36, 78–79; wealth levels and, 122; workers fearing, 52–53, 57, 305n58; workers receiving, 136–37; workers' responses to, 35–37, 39. *See also* feedback

complaints, worker: about coworkers' English language competence, 85, 104, 141; about unequal entitlement of individuals, 17, 186, 204. *See also* conflicts; criticism; judgment by workers; limits; revenge

concierge floors, 28

concierges, 21, 27, 48–49, 56; conflicts between coworkers and, 139, 157–59, 308n24; cultural capital, 121, 157–59, 167, 169, 170, 281; displays of labor, 40; ethnographic observation, 13, 14, 274–75, 276, 279–80; games by, 118–20, 128, 130–31, 144; gender, 50; needs anticipation, 32, 33, 34; perks, 67, 68, 156–59, 179, 180; professional associations, 311n15; reciprocity with guests, 189, 191, 216; status by association, 161, 178; status over coworkers, 156–59, 170, 176–80; and structural inequality, 59; tips and commissions, 67, 125, 128, 129, 135, 137, 144, 158, 179, 189, 249, 283, 292*table*, 293*table*, 320n19; wages, 67, 68, 157, 158, 292*table*, 293*table*. *See also* Luxury Garden concierges; Royal Court concierge work at front desk

condescension: "strategies of," 220; by workers toward guests, 155, 162–71, 175–76, 178–82, 247. *See also* criticism; insecurity, guest; superiority of workers

confidentiality, research, 283–84, 300n56, 312n31

conflicts: worker-coworker, 18, 101, 103–4, 135–41, 144, 147–51, 157–62, 308n24, 312n21; worker-manager, 9–10, 18–19, 83, 113, 135–36, 145–50, 191, 268. *See also*

antagonism; competition; complaints; conflicts over guests' entitlement; contestation; criticism; resistance

conflicts over guests' entitlement, guests', 10, 225–41, 247, 255, 269, 278. *See also* critcism; entitlement of guests; limits

consent by consumers, 255–56, 262

consent by workers, 15–20, 57, 109, 262–64, 300n63; games and, 18, 111–13, 125, 144, 145–50, 151, 152; powerful selfhood and, 15–20, 72, 147–53, 260; reciprocity and, 186, 219, 221, 222; to research, 284, 285; unions and, 266. *See also* effort, worker; withdrawal of consent

consent to research by subjects, 284, 285

consistency: Luxury Garden managerial, 83–84, 143–44, 274. *See also* inconsistency; routinization; standardization

consumption: collective, 286; hierarchy perpetuated by, 263. *See also* customer; luxury consumption; production-consumption

contestation, 267–70; over games, 145–50; by unions, 266, 267–68. *See also* complaints; conflicts; criticism; resistance; revenge; withdrawal of consent

contract: of reciprocity between workers and guests, 23, 194–204, 206–16, 221, 278, 318n42; unionized hotels and, 65, 266. *See also* entitlement; expectations; rights; rules

control: games of, 110–53; of rewarding guests for niceness, 197–98; struggle for, 9, 215. *See also* authority; autonomy of workers; managerial control; powerful selfhood of workers

corporate culture, 17, 21–22, 70–71, 308n20; Luxury Garden, 21–22, 71, 75–79, 82, 108, 177, 274; Royal Court limited, 22, 71, 89–91, 93, 108–9. *See also* credo; organizational identity

costs: food, 58; managers skimping on scheduling to save labor costs, 139; newspapers, 243, 246; wages compared with costs of services provided, 6, 48, 60. *See also* room rates; suite rates

credo: Luxury Garden, 76, 77, 81; Ritz-Carlton, 32, 70, 76, 306n10; Royal Court and, 90

criticism: of guests by workers, 15, 17, 60–61, 154–55, 162–76, 180, 182, 185, 198–99, 247,

268–69; of inequality, 17, 60–61, 186, 204, 268–70; of luxury consumption, 61, 257–58; of managers by workers, 98–99, 102–3, 149; workers' mutual, 101, 103–4, 136–37, 140–43, 149–50; by workers outside the worksite, 286. *See also* complaints; condescension; conflicts; contestation; critique by workers; critique of inequality; feedback; judgment by workers; moral evaluations; superiority of workers

critique by workers: of guests, 169, 174, 183; of coworkers, 101, 141; of Royal Court management, 86. *See also* criticism

critique of inequality: absence of, among workers, 15, 17, 20, 21, 59, 183, 204, 222; possibility of, 169, 258, 261, 264, 265–70, 322n19. *See also* criticism; worker-guest inequality

cultural capital: concierges', 121, 157–59, 167, 169, 170, 281; worker education from guests in, 170–71; worker judgments of guests', 167–68, 169, 174, 178, 180; worker superiority in, 121, 157–59, 167–68, 169, 170, 174, 176, 178. *See also* knowledge; status

"cultural repertoires," 18, 176, 265. *See also* norms

culture: class and interaction connected to, 263–64; "shop floor," 16, 20, 22, 111; workplace, 71, 205–6. *See also* community; corporate culture; cultural capital; demographics; educational level; equality; language; organizational identity; reciprocity; service theater

customer: and class, 12; games by workers with, 22; interactions with service worker, 5–11; luxury consumption, 4, 28; managerial control of, 9, 55; manufacturing work, 8; research excluding, 285–86; unions and, 322n27; worker as "internal customer," 71. *See also* clients; consumption; customer feedback; customization; guest; interactive service work

customer feedback, 57, 66, 105–8, 189; complaints, 42–43, 98, 213; on "incredible service," 24–25, 33–34; managers posting, 76, 84, 90, 98, 189; monitoring workers with, 9, 57, 70. *See also* comment cards; complaints, guest; criticism; letters from guests

customization: reverse, 200, 218; worker-customer, 3, 29–30, 40, 54–56, 59, 107, 207, 261. *See also* personalization

Davis, Fred, 124, 127, 130, 217

deep acting, 9, 75, 78, 94–95, 298n41

deference, 12, 25, 28, 44–48, 215; deep acting, 78; domestic servant, 26, 47–48; front of house workers, 56; guest expectation of, 211; by guests to workers, 174; intangible, 49; "negative deference," 198–99; semivisible workers, 54, 58. *See also* subordination

demand. *See* customer

"democratization of luxury," 296n13

demographics, 108; ethnographic and other workers, 281, 321n1; front and back of house workers, 50, 57, 86; guests, 67, 69, 174–75, 278; interactive workers, 57, 73; Luxury Garden workers, 50, 73, 85, 107, 292*table*, 305n58; Royal Court workers, 50, 68, 86–87, 95–97, 104, 107, 148–49, 293*table*, 305n59, 323n1; worker-guest similarity, 191. *See also* age; educational level; family; gender; race/ethnicity

department stores, 4, 299nn46,47, 310n33

dependents, guests as, 45, 47, 177–78, 255

"deskilling," 7, 123, 146

The Devil Wears Prada, 5

dignity: workers', 11, 12, 20, 132, 214, 317nn20,25. *See also* personhood

discipline, of workers, 65, 80, 84, 94, 98, 99, 204

discretion, workers': games and, 130, 132, 144–45, 151–52; managerial inconsistency and, 99–104, 147; powerful selfhood and, 11–12, 17; revenge on guests, 200–204, 217, 317n25; rewarding guests, 197–98, 217; routinization and, 52, 54, 64, 79; semivisible, 54, 56. *See also* autonomy of workers

displays of labor, 38–44; escorting guests to hotel destinations, 38, 40, 126; guest entitlement to, 38–39, 160; guest reciprocity in, 192; invisible labor, 44, 50; pampering, 38–44, 231–32; speed of service, 38, 41, 113–23, 136, 151. *See also* caring labor/care work; effort, worker; emotional labor; physical labor; unlimited labor; visible labor dispositions: constituted in the hotel, 18–19, 107, 205, 249–50, 254–56, 262–65; preexisting, 18, 108, 152–53, 254, 263–64, 267. *See also* expectations; independence of workers; professionalism

division of labor: global and local, 259. *See also* hotel division of labor

dogs, guests', 31, 38, 303n35

"doing class"/performance of class, 12, 20, 244, 246, 254, 259–60

"doing gender," 259

domestic servants, 4, 237, 241, 318n45, 319n8; and gender, 47, 216, 302n32, 317n28; gifts from employers, 190; *Gosford Park*, 32; hotel work compared with, 21, 47–48, 303–4nn50,51; interactive subordination, 10, 21, 26, 47–48, 216; legitimating employers' privileged class position, 10, 322n20; maternalism by employers, 220; "psychological exploitation," 10; and reciprocity, 215–16; resentment and resistance, 264

doormen/door attendants, 49; conflicts, 146–48, 157, 191; demographics, 50, 86, 281–82, 300n57; display of labor and, 40; ethnographic observation, 14, 274, 275, 280; games, 125–34, 143–44, 146–48; invisibility, 194–95; local "regulars" served by, 133–34, 143–44, 146–47, 201; Luxury Garden, 65, 67, 74, 126, 127–28, 133–34, 143–44, 147, 160–61, 194–95, 280, 292*table*; name use by, 118; revenge on guests by, 201; Royal Court, 59–60, 69, 86, 88, 118, 126, 133–34, 146–48, 157, 180, 191, 293*table*; status by association, 160–61; status over coworkers, 156, 157, 180; and structural inequality, 59–60; tips, 67, 125–34, 146–48, 157, 189, 195, 281, 292*table*, 293*table*, 320n19; wages, 67, 156, 292*table*, 293*table*

dress. *See* appearance; uniforms

Dunhill store, Manhattan, 4

economics: boom (2000), 63–64; global, 5, 259; new economy, 1–23; "old" economy, 5–6; recessions, 4, 27. *See also* commodification of relationship; compensation; costs; labor; money; sales; wealth

educational level: workers', 53, 57, 61, 73, 235. *See also* learning; training

effort, worker, 25; games and, 16, 111–13, 127, 128, 129–33; guests not acknowledging, 195–96; guests recognizing, 189–92, 194; guests respecting, 187; limits set on, 19, 23, 48, 61–62, 113, 120–21, 128, 130–32, 137, 155, 164, 171–76, 183, 199–200, 204, 268–69; rewarding guests with, 197–98; voluntary appearance of, 44, 112, 118, 125, 132, 186, 198, 209, 212–13, 220, 221, 233, 241. *See also* consent by workers; displays of labor; performance; physical labor; unlimited labor

elder care work, 47

elevator operators, 40

Eloise (Thompson), 24

emotional labor, 8–9, 10, 303n48; defined, 25; "deskilling" of, 123; front of house workers, 56; housekeepers', 304n54; "incomplete commodification" of, 219–20; intangible, 49; reciprocity and, 193, 199–200, 215, 219–20, 244; unions and, 322n27; wealth of guest and, 122; withholding, 199–200. *See also* caring labor/care work; deference; emotional reciprocity/niceness/friendliness, worker-guest; empathy; needs; personalization; sincerity, worker

emotional reciprocity/niceness/friendliness, worker-guest, 134–35, 184–98, 205–12, 217–21, 261; egalitarian, 18, 19, 23, 185, 208, 231; guest-guest comparisons, 234, 245–46; and guest performance of self, 244; guests relying on workers to initiate, 245; workers praising guests for, 249, 318n42. *See also* civility; emotional labor; revenge; rewards

empathy: of workers with guests, 162–66, 174, 177, 179–81, 213, 232–33, 247, 249. *See also* sympathy

employee satisfaction survey, Luxury Garden, 76

employer-employee relations. *See* worker-employer relations; worker-manager relations

empowerment: managerial strategy of, 70, 71, 108–9, 308n20. *See also* powerful selfhood of workers

English language competence, 70; back of house workers, 53, 82, 85, 104, 141, 281, 305n58; coworker complaints about, 85, 104, 141; guest insecurities, 164; interactive workers, 57

entertainment: guest treatment of invisible

labor as, 238; worker discourses about guests, 15, 154–55, 162–63, 166–73, 180, 181, 195, 198–99. *See also* media; sociability

entitlement, class, 5, 23, 258, 259–60, 264, 269. *See also* entitlement of guests

entitlement of guests, 3, 12, 17, 31, 37–39, 206–14; conflicted, 10, 225–41, 247, 255, 269, 278; contestation of, 267–69; experienced by workers as individual situations, 17, 186, 204; games by workers and, 112–13, 125; interpellation into, 23, 254–55, 278; to labor abstention and luxury consumption, 23, 38–39, 42–43, 48, 160, 162, 169–76, 223–41, 259, 322n20; limits set by workers on, 23, 61–62, 155, 164, 171–81, 183, 268–69; morality evaluated by workers, 168–70, 247; normalization of, 15–20, 23, 61, 112–13, 125, 151, 155, 221, 260–61, 322n18; producing, 223–56, 259; reciprocity with workers and, 186, 198, 204, 206–14, 221, 269; reproducing, 242, 254–56, 262–65; revenge by workers, 198. *See also* consumption; expectations by guests; intersubjectivity; legitimation; privilege; rights; subordination, worker; unlimited labor; worker-guest inequality

entitlement of managers, 3; limited, 104, 108–9

entitlement of workers, 3, 18–19, 62, 109, 113; consent withdrawn for violation of, 109, 113, 146, 267–69; limited for new workers, 104; unions and, 266; worker-guest reciprocity, 185–86, 193–95, 220, 221, 267. *See also* equality; expectations by workers; intersubjectivity; privilege; rights

equality, 109; equal selfhood of workers, 109, 268–69; guests recasting hierarchy as, 220, 231, 239–40; professionalism signaling, 235, 255–56; reciprocity and, 18, 19, 23, 134–35, 185–94, 203–24, 230–31, 237–39, 255. *See also* inequality

escorting guests, to hotel destinations, 38, 40, 126

ethical questions: research, 282–85. *See also* moral evaluations; obligations

ethnicity. *See* immigrant workers; race/ethnicity

ethnography, 3, 14–15; dilemmas, 278–85; of domestic servants and employers, 10; of Hawaiian resorts, 295n2; inherently asymmetrical, 284–85; insecurity of guests, 242–43, 245, 246; interview data matching, 188, 277; on managerial strategies, 22, 108; managers allowing, 12, 272–76, 282–83; methodological advantages, 272, 278; multisited, 286; nonunion luxury hotels chosen for, 12–15, 300n59; reliability and validity, 279–82; surprises, 15, 60, 131, 185, 272, 277, 278, 319n13; of symbolic boundaries, 155, 182; workers legitimating luxury consumption, 248–49. *See also* participant observation; research

European hospitality students, 104, 149

exiting, 64; withdrawing consent by, 16–17, 113, 146, 150, 267, 268, 305n62. *See also* turnover

expectations by guests, 23, 206–7, 209–14, 252; business travelers, 106–7; constructed within the hotel, 23, 107, 225, 249–50; formed in other luxury hotels, 107–8; of hotel, 107–8, 207, 212–14; leisure travelers, 106–7; of Luxury Garden, 67; luxury service beyond, 57, 90; worker anticipation of/response to, 119; of workers, 122, 206–7, 209–14, 221, 239; workers violating, 221. *See also* contract; entitlement; needs; reciprocity in worker-guest relations

expectations by managers: of workers, 77, 113. *See also* luxury standards of service; organization of work

expectations by workers, 170, 267, 318n42, 322n21; of guests, 23, 192–97, 205, 246, 256, 318n42, 322n21; of reciprocity, 220, 222. *See also* contract; entitlement; reciprocity in worker-guest relations

exploitation, 10, 259, 260, 263; guest fear of exploiting workers, 19, 20, 186, 220, 229, 260. *See also* commodification of relationship

external labor markets: back of house work, 53; interactive workers, 57; tight, 13, 63–64, 70, 73, 87, 90, 95, 273, 275, 307n13

factory work. *See* manufacturing work

family: guests' dogs, 31, 38, 303n35; hotel recognition of guests', 28, 29, 30, 38; Royal Court small size like, 91; of workers, 73, 85. *See also* maternal care; race/ethnicity fear, guest, 269; of exploiting workers, 19, 20, 186, 220, 229, 260; of not belonging, 242–47, 260; of workers' judgment, 48, 244, 245, 246, 247. *See also* insecurity, guest; legitimation of luxury consumption

fear, worker, of guest complaints, 52–53, 57, 305n58

feedback: managerial, 96; workers' mutual, 100–102, 276. *See also* criticism; customer feedback; discipline; recognition of workers

films: luxury hotel as site of class transformation, 110, 154, 223–24, 241–42, 247–48, 320n15; name recognition by hotel workers, 24; needs anticipation by domestic servants, 32; women's femininity and deviant sexuality, 320n16; worker leisure, 305n66

fitness centers, 27, 65

"five-star service," 37, 66, 160, 276

flexible informality, Royal Court, 22, 71–72, 86–105, 149–50, 179–80, 205–6

flight attendants, 7, 45, 78, 166

food and beverage department, 63, 96, 161, 287. *See also* restaurant; room service

food service: fast food, 9, 54, 152; food runner, 13; speedy, 115. *See also* food and beverage department; restaurant; room service

formality/informality: Luxury Garden formality, 67, 143; "proper verbiage," 38–39, 91, 106, 177; of workers toward guests, 46, 69. *See also* friendliness; informality at Royal Court; professionalism

Four Seasons, 2, 25, 27, 28, 301n15; displays of labor, 38; guest-guest comparisons, 234; guest insecurity, 242, 245; international chain, 27; needs fulfillment, 34; occupancy rates, 302n21; personalized service, 31; sincerity of workers, 46

franchising, hotel, 27

frequent guests. *See* repeat/frequent guests

friendliness: Royal Court, 65, 69, 71, 99, 105–6, 205–6; U.S. ethic of, 322n21. *See also* emotional reciprocity/niceness/friendliness, worker-guest; informality; sociability

front desk agents, 48–49, 56, 59; conflicts with coworkers, 139; ethnographic observation, 13, 135, 273–74, 279–80; gender, 50; guest complaints made to, 137; Luxury Garden, 65, 67, 73, 74, 118–19, 158, 174,

279, 292*table*, 323n1; name use by, 118–19; sincerity of, 45; status compared with concierges, 156, 157; tips, 125, 158, 280, 293*table*; wages, 67, 158, 292*table*, 293*table*. *See also* front of house workers; Royal Court front desk agents

front door workers, 56, 262; ethnographic observation, 13, 14, 273–75, 280–83; gender, 50, 86, 281–82, 300n57; Luxury Garden (general), 74, 126–29, 292*table*; Royal Court (general), 138–39, 145–50, 179–80, 293*table*, 308–9n25; tips (general), 125–34, 138–39; worker-coworker conflicts, 138–39, 147; worker-manager conflicts, 145–50. *See also* bellmen/bellpersons; doormen/door attendants; valet parkers

front of house workers, 49–50, 51*table*, 55–57; awareness of structural inequality, 58–62; games, 118–20, 125–34, 143–44, 146–48, 152; and guest perspectives on inequality, 234–35; Luxury Garden, 50, 60–61, 74; reciprocity contract, 318n42; Royal Court, 50, 59–60, 68, 86–87, 88, 305n60; speed, 114; unionizing, 267; wages and working conditions, 50, 61–62. *See also* concierges; front desk agents; front door workers; interactive service work; restaurant

games, worker, 18, 22, 109, 110–53; autonomy and, 17, 109, 111, 124–25, 141–50, 151, 267; conflicts, 135–40, 147; contestation over, 145–50; defined, 111; income-maximizing, 124, 133–34, 151, 313n44; managerial regimes and, 111–14, 116, 117, 119, 123, 124–25, 134, 145–50, 267; manufacturing work, 16, 22, 111, 112, 123, 129, 130, 135–36, 138; restaurant reservations, 120, 130–31, 311n11; room assignment/blocking, 116–18, 311n13; room rate and sales maximization, 115–16, 122, 311n12; room service, 115, 130, 132–33, 280; rules, 125–27, 138–40, 143–50; saying no, 121; and selves, 17–18, 113, 121, 151–53; of speed, 113–23, 136, 151. *See also* "making out" games; money games

gender, 262, 264; "doing gender," 259; in films, 320n16; gay men in nonmanagerial positions, 304n56; and guest concerns with appearance, 243–44; and guest strategies of self, 224, 256; and guest-worker relations, 31–32, 107, 206, 216, 227–28, 230, 237, 281–82, 302n32, 317n28; Luxury Garden guests, 67; maternal care, 21, 25–26, 38, 46–47, 48; negative legends, 206; Royal Court guests, 69. *See also* stratification by gender

gifts: from concierges to front desk staff, 158; to domestic servants from employers, 190; to frequent guests from hotel, 30; from guests to workers, 184–85, 190, 191, 193–94, 218–20; from vendors to concierges, 157. *See also* tips

gift shop, Luxury Garden, 65, 74

Gilbert, Robert, 46

global economy, 5, 259. *See also* economics

Goffman, Erving, 20, 181, 198, 211, 214, 222, 225

Gold, Ray, 216

Golden Rule, 184, 221

Gosford Park, 32

Gouldner, Alvin, 208, 220

Gramsci, Antonio, 263, 269

greed, for tips, 129–30

Gregory, André, 270

guest: as agent, 18, 112, 230; in ethnography, 286; interviews, 14–15, 242, 272, 277–78, 284, 285, 286, 302n32, 323n5; no-show, 115–16; not employers, 48; packages, 309n29; privacy in research, 284; rules of behavior, 243–44, 249, 256; "walked" to another hotel, 116, 117, 136, 160, 172–73. *See also* clients; customer feedback; entitlement of guests; guest characteristics; guest desires; guest preferences; luxury consumption; needs, guest; personal information, guest; status of guests; strategies of guests; worker-guest inequality; worker-guest relations

guest characteristics, 27, 299n53; appearance, 167–68, 174, 199, 243–45, 247, 249; backgrounds, 15, 224, 226, 235, 254, 256, 277, 278; demographics, 67, 69, 174–75, 278; dependence, 45, 47, 177–78, 255; insecurity, 164–65, 242–47, 250, 253–54, 256, 320n19; of interviewed guests, 277, 278; at Luxury Garden, 14, 67, 205; privilege, 23, 162, 221, 225, 241, 247, 253, 255–56, 299n53;

at Royal Court, 13, 67, 69, 174–75, 205; "trailer trash," 154, 174; worker discourses about, 15, 154–55, 162–63, 166–73, 180, 181, 195, 198–99. *See also* business travelers; emotional reciprocity/niceness/friendliness, worker-guest; leisure travelers; repeat/frequent guests; transgressions, guest; wealth of guests

guest desires: recast as needs, 32, 34, 48, 178; Ritz-Carlton study on, 46; worker games to meet, 118. *See also* expectations by guests; guest preferences

guest preferences, 1–3, 28–32, 46–47, 69; front of house workers remembering, 56, 67; hotel computer history, 2, 30, 32, 54, 56, 67, 99–100, 106, 119, 163, 230, 306n2; housekeepers implementing, 52. *See also* needs, guest

habitus, 254–55

Hannerz, Ulf, 20

Hanser, Amy, 259

health care work, 47

Hegel, G. W. F., 218

hierarchy, 263; lateralism vs., 86–88, 101–2, 112, 136, 151, 155–59, 178, 180, 181, 235–36, 261; Luxury Garden hierarchical professionalism, 21–22, 71, 72–86; Luxury Garden internal, 21–22, 64, 71, 72–86, 143, 177, 276, 307n14; managerial regimes and, 21–22, 64, 71, 72–88, 143, 176–81, 276, 307n14; of needs (Maslow's), 178, 315n20; recasting, 22, 109, 140, 154–83, 204, 220, 224, 231, 239–40; Royal Court internal relations and, 86–88, 101–2, 139, 276, 308–9n25; shop-floor culture, 16, 111; symbolic ranking of workers vis-à-vis coworkers/guests/community, 22, 109, 153, 154–83. *See also* authority; class; comparison; condescension; entitlement of guests; hotel division of labor; inequality; privilege; ranking; status; subordination; superiority of workers

hiring: managerial strategies for, 69–70, 90, 145, 307n13. *See also* orientation, new employee; training

history: hotel's guest information, 2, 30, 32, 54, 56, 67, 99–100, 106, 163, 198, 230, 306n2; of luxury hotels, 26–28

Hochschild, Arlie: *The Managed Heart*, 7–9, 15, 25, 45, 78, 166, 187, 261; *The Time Bind*, 286

Hong Kong hotels, 29

hospitality industry: assumed to be research focus, 282–83, 284; college degree and career in, 305n62; literature, 2; students, 104, 149, 272, 305n62. *See also* airline workers; hotel industry; luxury hotels; restaurant

hotel: budget, 27; chain, 27; complex topography of, 48–49; convention, 27, 41; defined, 26; "heads in beds," 28; limited-service, 27; Mars and Nicod's typology, 307n12; midrange, 27, 37; "modern," 26; motor, 26–27; palace, 26. *See also* guest; luxury hotels; manager; physical aspects; production-consumption; service; worker

hotel division of labor, 26, 48–49, 108; and demographics of workers, 50, 68, 86–87, 95–97, 107, 293*table*; Luxury Garden, 18, 21–22, 71, 73–74, 83, 84–85, 107, 144, 176, 307–8n16; powerful selfhood of workers and, 17–18, 149–50, 176, 179–80, 267; Royal Court, 18, 22, 50, 68, 71, 86–89, 95–97, 101, 107, 126, 149–50, 179–80. *See also* back of house workers; front of house workers; interactive service work; invisible work; noninteractive service work; organization of work; semivisible workers; stratification; visible labor

hotel industry: changes in, 27; interviews with people in, 2, 14, 271–75, 278–79, 282, 305n62, 323n5; union density and activism in, 13. *See also* hospitality industry; hotel

hotel organization, 287, 288*fig*, 289*fig*. *See also* organizational characteristics

house car, Luxury Garden, 65

housekeepers, 21, 49, 50–53, 310n5; awareness of structural inequality, 58; emotional labor, 304n54; ethnographic shadowing of, 13, 14, 274, 275, 280, 300n58, 323n1; fear of guest complaints, 52–53; vs. fictional versions, 305–6n66; front of house workers' competence critiques of, 141; and games, 111; *Gosford Park*, 32; guest awareness of structural inequality with, 235, 240; legitimation of racial inequalities of, 263; Luxury Garden, 14, 65, 67, 74, 180, 292*table*,

305n58; race/ethnicity, 50, 104, 281, 305n58, 323n1; wages, 67, 292*table*, 293*table*. *See also* back of house workers; room cleaners; turndown attendants

housemen, 49, 304n53. *See also* runners

identity. *See* class; organizational identity; selfhood

immigrant workers, 5, 66*table*, 239, 271, 292*table*, 293*table*; back of house workers, 50, 53, 58, 86, 104; bellmen and valets, 86; busers, 40; English language competence, 53, 82, 85, 104, 141, 281, 305n58; European workers, 86, 87, 104, 149; Luxury Garden, 73; rights activism, 269–70; Royal Court, 86–87, 104; semivisible workers, 53

income: games to maximize, 124, 133–34, 151, 313n44; illicit games, 133–34, 143; inequality in, 6, 27, 48, 181, 258, 297n24. *See also* compensation; wages; wealth; worker-guest inequality

inconsistency: in Luxury Garden training, 79–80; of managerial authority in department stores, 310n33; Royal Court managerial, 22, 71, 86, 91, 92, 94, 95–100, 104–5, 108, 126, 145–50, 274, 309n29. *See also* consistency

independence of workers: from workplace, 18, 142–50, 179–81. *See also* autonomy of workers; selfhood of workers

independent ownership and management, of Royal Court, 13, 16, 22, 68, 86, 87

individual interactions: vs. collective action, 16–17, 19, 155, 182, 185–86, 204, 221, 267; complaints about inequality, 17, 186, 204; game rewards, 112; among people from different classes, 6, 11, 241, 260–62; reciprocity, 186, 189, 204, 221–22. *See also* interaction; personalization; personhood; relationship; selfhood

inequality: criticism of, 17, 60–61, 186, 204, 268–70; income, 6, 27, 48, 181, 258, 297n24; research process and, 284–85; unions contesting, 266, 267–68. *See also* class; entitlement; normalization of inequality; obscuring inequality; privilege; subordination; wealth; worker-guest inequality

informality at Royal Court, 16, 179; flexible, 22, 71–72, 86–105, 149–50, 179–80, 205–6;

mutual regulation, 86, 88, 96, 100–105, 109, 149–50. *See also* friendliness

information, guest. *See* personal information, guest

insecurity, guest, 164–65, 242–47, 250, 253–54, 256, 320n19. *See also* condescension, by workers toward guests; fear, guest

instrumentality: worker-guest relations, 197, 207–8, 216–17, 218–19, 261. *See also* service

intangible product: in service work, 7–8, 11, 47, 49, 53, 55–56, 111–12, 123, 260. *See also* invisible work

interaction: rules of, 204, 219, 221; scripted, 9, 55. *See also* individual interactions; interactive service work; positive interactions

interactive inequality. *See* worker-guest inequality

interactive service work, 5–6, 25, 49, 296n22; domestic servants, 10, 21, 26, 47–48, 216; ethnographic observation of, 12–15, 135, 271–83, 300n58, 323n1; fear of guest complaints rare in, 57; intangible product, 7–8, 11, 47, 49, 55–56, 111–12, 123; internship, 14, 273, 274, 275, 276, 323n3; noninteractive workers' limited, 21, 49; "producer services," 5; scripting, 9, 55; of semivisible workers, 54, 58; voluntary appearance of, 44, 112, 118, 125, 132, 186, 198, 209, 212–13, 220, 221, 233, 241. *See also* consent by workers; demographics; emotional labor; front of house workers; games, worker; positive interactions; relationship; reservationists; selfhood; skill; sociology of work; speed of service; subordination; telephone operators

intern: at Luxury Garden, 14, 273, 274, 275, 276; Royal Court and, 323n3

internal labor markets, 108, 177; Luxury Garden, 64, 73–74, 83, 108; Royal Court, 64, 86–87, 180, 308–9n25. *See also* career ladders; hotel division of labor; promotion; turnover, hotel workers; worker-coworker relations

interpellation, into class positions, 23, 254–55, 278

intersubjectivity: worker-guest, 25, 185–97, 220. *See also* reciprocity in worker-guest relations; recognition

interviews: guest, 14–15, 242, 272, 277–78, 284, 285, 286, 302n32, 323n5; hotel industry

people, 2, 14, 271–75, 278–79, 282, 305n62, 323n5; participant observation compared with, 188, 242, 272, 277, 278, 282

invisible work, 49, 50–53; caring labor, 40–41, 44; critiques of competence, 141; front of house workers, 55–56; guest awareness of structural inequality, 237–38; guest discomfort if made apparent, 44; guest entertainment with, 238; guest treatment of labor as, 194–95, 215, 318n42; need anticipation, 34; race and, 237–38, 310n34; revenge and, 199, 204, 211; specialization, 74; worker awareness of structural inequality, 57–58, 61. *See also* back of house workers; displays of labor; noninteractive service work

job characteristics, 48–53, 51*table*, 292*table*, 293*table*. *See also* back of house work; compensation; demographics; front of house work; hotel division of labor; interactive service work; invisible work; noninteractive service work; relationship; semivisible workers; visible labor

judgment by workers, 17, 22; of guests, 17, 22, 155, 162–76, 178, 180, 182–83, 185, 194, 198–99, 247; guests' fear of, 48, 244, 245, 246, 247. *See also* comparison by workers; criticism; superiority of workers; transgressions, guest

Kaplan, Bruce Eric, 242

Kasikci, Ali, 32

knowledge, workers', 157; in comparison with guests, 163, 165, 178–79, 181; in comparison with managers and coworkers, 149, 155; concierge associations and, 121; condescension based on, 166, 178–79; of coworkers' competence, 141; guests failing to respect, 195; guests recognizing, 187, 194; insecure guests drawing on, 164–65, 243, 256; managers failing to respect, 142; and professionalism, 216. *See also* competence; cultural capital; personal information, guest

Kozlowski, Dennis, 5

labor: capitalist labor relations, 7, 9–11, 263; guest abstention from and consumption of,

labor *(continued)*
38–39, 42–43, 48, 160; labor movement, 266. *See also* displays of labor; division of labor; effort, worker; external labor markets; internal labor markets; labor process; unions; unlimited labor; work
labor process: gender and, 297n30; guest's role in, 22, 286; in hotels, 21, 49, 53, 215; theory, 7–11, 21, 259, 260, 263; worker selfhood and, 260. *See also* games, worker; organization of work
Lamont, Michèle, 169, 182, 240, 314n1, 322n21
language: "proper verbiage," 38–39, 91, 106, 177. *See also* English language competence
lateral relations, workers': and collective action, 261; comparison, 17–18, 22, 140–41, 151, 155–59, 178, 180, 181, 235–36, 261; competition, 126, 137, 273–74; vs. hierarchy, 86–88, 101–2, 112, 136, 151, 155–59, 178, 180, 181, 235–36, 261. *See also* mutual relations, workers'
laundry services, 27, 49; Luxury Garden, 65, 74; Royal Court on-site, 68, 309n26
learning: to consume luxury, 223–24, 244, 247–55. *See also* educational level; training
legitimation of guest needs, 25, 28, 32–38, 42, 56
legitimation of inequalities: racial, 262–63. *See also* entitlement; legitimation of luxury consumption
legitimation of luxury consumption: by guests, 224, 225–41, 255–56, 260, 262; by workers, 23, 25, 28, 32–38, 42, 45, 56, 175–76, 181, 210, 248–56, 260, 262, 322n20. *See also* entitlement of guests; normalization; obscuring inequality
Leidner, Robin, 9, 54, 55, 56, 214, 224, 263, 299n46
leisure travelers: conflicted entitlement to luxury service, 226, 227–29, 231; distance and denial, 227–29; expectations of workers, 209–10; inequality with workers, 299n53; interviewed, 277; positive feedback from, 106–7; reciprocity with workers, 196, 205, 230–31; room rates, 306n3; Royal Court, 13, 69, 205
letters from guests, 57; ethnographic review of, 14, 274; managers posting, 76, 84, 90,

189; praising hotel, 212; praising service, 36, 84, 90, 105–8, 121, 189, 197, 276. *See also* comment cards
limits: to guest entitlement, 23, 61–62, 155, 164, 171–81, 183, 268–69; to worker's effort, 19, 23, 48, 61–62, 113, 120–21, 128, 130–32, 137, 155, 164, 171–76, 183, 199–200, 204, 268–69. *See also* unlimited labor
literature: hospitality industry, 2; industrial relations, 111; on luxury consumption, 3, 257–58, 270, 295–96n3. *See also* research
locker rooms, workers', 60, 61, 74
luxury: "democratization of"/"New Luxury," 296n13; features, 17, 25; "mass luxury," 4; in media, 4–5; specificity of, 214–18. *See also* luxury consumption; luxury product; material luxury; wealth
luxury consumption, 257–58; conflicted, 225–41, 247, 255, 278; consenting, 255–56, 262; "conspicuous consumption," 226; criticism of, 61, 257–58; guest comparison with others in, 233–34; guest entitlement to, 23, 38–39, 42–43, 48, 160, 162, 169–76, 223–41, 259, 322n20; guest perspectives on, 23, 223–56, 269; increasing demand for, 3–5, 6, 258; learning, 223–24, 244, 247–55; literature on, 3, 257–58, 270, 295–96n3. *See also* legitimation of luxury consumption; production-consumption
Luxury Garden, 2, 64–67; mystery shoppers, 14, 81, 84, 98; organizational characteristics, 65, 66*table*, 73–74, 287, 288*fig*, 307n15; organizational structure, 287, 288*fig*; ownership, 66, 73; ranking and awards, 65, 66, 106, 176–77, 180–81; room and suite rates, 2, 14, 66, 67; status by association with, 18, 159–61, 172, 177, 178; taste of workers influenced by, 171; in typology of hotels, 307n12; worker-to-room ratio, 65
Luxury Garden concierges, 73–75, 83, 94, 107, 145, 181, 292*table*; conflicts among, 308n24; cultural capital, 157, 281; ethnographic observation, 279–80; games, 118–19, 120, 131, 144; reciprocity with guests, 191; and Royal Court concierges, 149, 315n21; status by association, 178; tips and commissions, 67, 125, 129, 137, 144, 283, 292*table*; wages, 67, 292*table*
Luxury Garden guests: characteristics, 14, 67,

205; feedback, 42–43, 70, 84, 105–7, 189; insecurity, 242, 245; needs anticipation/fulfillment/legitimation, 33–37, 42, 67, 78–79, 106, 127–28; personalized service, 28–31, 42, 106; repeat, 67, 206. *See also* worker-guest relations

Luxury Garden Hospitality Company (LGHC), 66, 288*fig*

Luxury Garden managerial regime, 63, 70, 72–86, 72*table*, 97; authority, 83–84, 143–44, 274, 280; and autonomy of workers, 72–86, 141–45, 267; consistency, 83–84, 143–44, 274; corporate culture, 21–22, 71, 75–79, 82, 108, 177, 274; ethnographic report to, 273, 275; ethnography allowed by, 12, 272–73, 274, 275–76; hierarchy, 21–22, 64, 71, 72–86, 143, 177, 276, 307n14; interviews, 14, 271, 272–73, 275; organizational identity, 75–79, 81, 82, 91, 99, 108, 144–45; race/ethnicity, 73; and superiority of workers, 176–79; surveillance/monitoring of workers, 70, 71, 77, 83–85, 108; unionizing and, 267; worker-manager relations, 76, 83–84, 89, 108, 143–44, 189. *See also* Luxury Garden professionalism

Luxury Garden professionalism, 18, 67, 72–86, 141–45, 149, 277; guest descriptions of, 65, 105–7; hierarchical, 21–22, 71, 72–86; luxury standards of service, 38, 45, 75–83, 85–86, 92, 106, 145; managerial authority, 83–84, 143–44, 274, 280; organization of work, 72–74, 144–45, 265; worker-guest relations, 205, 206

Luxury Garden workers, 18, 65, 67, 72–86, 141–45, 267, 292*table*; awards, 77, 181, 311n15; bellmen, 67, 73, 74, 126, 129, 159, 193, 292*table*; community, 75–79; demographics, 50, 73, 85, 107, 292*table*, 305n58; doormen, 65, 67, 74, 126, 127–28, 133–34, 143–44, 147, 160–61, 194–95, 280, 292*table*; employee satisfaction survey, 76; ethnographic observation, 12, 14, 16, 271–83, 323n1; front desk, 65, 67, 73, 74, 118–19, 158, 174, 279, 292*table*, 323n1; housekeepers, 14, 65, 67, 74, 180, 292*table*, 305n58; intern, 14, 273, 274, 275, 276; internal labor market, 64, 73–74, 83, 108; labor division, 18, 21–22, 71, 73–74, 83, 84–85, 107, 144, 176, 307–8n16; needs anticipation/

fulfillment/legitimation by, 33–37, 42, 67, 78–79, 106, 127–28; number of, 66; orientation, 14, 75–79, 93, 145, 177–78, 273, 308n18; perks, 67, 73, 157; reservationists, 67, 73, 74, 292*table*, 307n16; room service, 65, 74, 292*table*; runners, 304n53, 308n16; telephone operators, 14, 67, 73, 74, 292*table*, 307n16; tips (general), 67, 125–29, 292*table*; training, 33, 35–36, 75–82, 91, 93, 145, 177–78; turndown attendants, 14, 292*table*, 305n58; turnover, 64, 206, 273, 307n13; valet parkers, 65, 74, 126, 292*table*; wages (general), 67, 68–69, 108, 158, 266, 292*table*; withdrawing consent, 17–18, 61–62; worker-coworker relations, 84–86, 104; worker-manager relations, 76, 83–84, 89, 108, 143–44, 189. *See also* Luxury Garden concierges; Luxury Garden professionalism; worker-guest relations

luxury hotels, 1–2, 11–15, 302n19; history, 26–28; international chains, 27; nonluxury hotels compared with, 25, 29, 41, 217, 267, 274, 302n25, 306n1; nonunion, 12–15, 65, 266–67, 300n59; occupancy rates, 28, 302nn20,21; trophy, 27. *See also* hospitality industry; Luxury Garden; luxury product; Royal Court

luxury product, 24–62, 217, 240–41. *See also* luxury service; material luxury; physical aspects; production-consumption

luxury service, 5–6, 11–15, 24–62; elements, 25, 28–48, 303n44; extreme, 4, 40; "five-star," 37, 66, 160, 276; like maternal care, 21, 25–26, 38, 46–47, 48; and new economy, 1–23; reciprocity facilitated by, 217–18; and social reproduction, 264; transnational companies, 5. *See also* guest; luxury consumption; luxury product; luxury standards of service; manager; worker

luxury standards of service, 17, 47; games and, 118–21, 124, 128, 140–41, 145, 151; Luxury Garden, 38, 45, 75–83, 85–86, 92, 106, 145; obscuring and normalizing disparity, 240–41, 248; Ritz-Carlton, 70–71, 91–92, 102, 307nn10,11; Royal Court and, 38, 45, 54, 89–95, 102–3, 108–9; status by association with, 159–61; worker subordination, 21, 23, 45, 59, 60, 118–21, 182–83, 204, 268, 303n44. *See also* customization;

luxury standards of service (*continued*)
deference; discretion by workers; displays
of labor; emotional labor; recognition of
guests; sincerity, worker; speed of service;
standardization

Maid in Manhattan, 154, 242, 305n66, 320n15
"making out" games, 146, 152; manufacturing work, 16, 111, 112, 123, 129, 130, 135–
36, 138
Malcolm Baldrige National Quality Award,
70, 315n18
manager, 8, 18–19, 287, 305n62; in capitalist
labor relations, 7, 9–11; client as a kind of,
9; entitlement of, 3, 104, 108–9; front of
house, 56; interviews, 2, 14, 271–75, 278–
79, 282, 305n62, 323n5; name, 306n5; "quality," 71. *See also* hotel division of labor;
managerial authority; managerial control;
managerial regimes; strategies of managers; worker-manager relations
managerial authority, 63–109; consistent, 83–
84, 143–44, 274; ethnography allowed by,
12, 272–76, 282–83; expectations of workers, 77, 113; and game rules, 125, 126–27,
138–40, 143–44, 145–50; inconsistent, 22,
71, 86, 91, 92, 94, 95–100, 104–5, 108, 126,
145–50, 274, 309n29, 310n33; Luxury Garden, 83–84, 143–44, 274, 280; "pissing on
trees," 97; Royal Court, 22, 71, 86, 91, 92,
94, 95–100, 104–5, 108, 126, 145–50, 274,
309n29; and worker autonomy, 11–12, 18,
22, 64, 86, 99–100, 143–50, 151, 267. *See also*
consent by workers; hiring; managerial
regimes; orientation; training
managerial control, 21, 52, 53, 108–9; of
client/customer, 9, 55; discipline of workers, 65, 80, 84, 94, 98, 99, 204; of production,
9, 89, 113; and revenge, 19, 317nn24,25; by
rewards to workers, 47, 75, 76, 105, 108. *See
also* consent by workers; luxury standards
of service; managerial authority; managerial regimes; monitoring of workers; strategies of managers
managerial regimes, 72*table*, 109, 176–81,
230, 287; and worker games, 111–14, 116,
117, 119, 123, 124–25, 134, 145–50, 267. *See
also* Luxury Garden managerial regime;
managerial authority; managerial control;

organizational identity; organization of
work; Royal Court managerial regime;
worker-manager relations
Mandarin Oriental hotel, Hong Kong, 29
manufacturing work, 6–11, 297n30; capitalist
labor relations, 7, 9–11; conflicts among
workers, 138; games, 16, 22, 111, 112, 123,
129, 130, 135–36, 138; "old economy," 5–6;
"shop floor" culture, 16, 20, 22, 111
marital status, hotel worker, 73, 87
marketing research, 30
markets, 4. *See also* economics; external labor
markets; hospitality industry; internal
labor markets; service
Marriott, 27
Marxism: alienation, 8; base-superstructure
distinction, 263; Braverman and, 7, 297n30;
capitalist labor relations, 7, 9–11; commodity fetishism, 260; consenting consumption, 255; feudal relations, 321n9; service
work as "unproductive labor," 7; unequal
authority relations in production, 297n29
Maslow, Abraham, "hierarchy of needs,"
178, 315n20
material luxury, 25, 26, 50–52; Luxury Garden, 65; personalized, 30, 43; Royal Court,
30, 68; tangible, 49, 52, 53, 55. *See also*
compensation; gifts; physical aspects;
wealth
maternal care, luxury service like, 21, 25–26,
38, 46–47, 48
maternalism, by employers of domestic servants, 220
McDonald's, 9, 54, 55, 122, 224, 225
media: luxury omnipresent in, 4–5, 296n14;
novels, 5, 15; television shows, 4, 296n14.
See also films
methodology, research, 12–15, 271–86
Mills, C. Wright, 8
mission statement: Luxury Garden, 75–76;
Royal Court, 90
Mobil rankings, 66, 68, 160, 180–81
money: guest views of, 239, 247; recasting
the meaning of, 122–23, 125, 135, 151, 169,
182, 239, 247; worker judgments about
guests', 175. *See also* economics; income;
money games; wealth
money games, 112, 122–35, 312n24. *See also*
tipping games

monitoring of workers: by clients/customer, 9, 57, 70; by coworkers, 100–101, 276; by managers, 52, 55–57, 70–71, 83–84, 97–98, 108; with mystery shoppers, 14, 57, 81, 84, 98. *See also* criticism; feedback; surveillance

moral evaluations: of guests by workers, 155, 166, 168–70, 176, 247. *See also* ethical questions; judgment by workers; norms

motto: Les Clefs d'Or, 311n15; Luxury Garden, 76; Ritz-Carlton, 70, 307n10, 315n18

movies. *See* films

mutual relations, workers': assistance, 101; criticism, 101, 103–4, 136–37, 140–43, 149–50; feedback/recognition, 100–102, 276; regulation, 64, 72, 84–85, 86, 88, 96, 100–105, 109, 149–50, 156, 159; surveillance, 101–2, 149; training, 52, 100–101, 150, 156. *See also* lateral relations, workers'

My Dinner with André, 258

mystery shoppers, 14, 57, 81, 84, 98

names: guests going by first names, 187–88; guests reciprocally using workers', 187; guests unequally not remembering workers', 209; guests using workers' first names, 44; for managers, 306n5; worker deference in using guest titles of address, 44, 54; workers recognizing guests', 18, 28, 30–32, 54, 56, 67, 91, 92, 118–19, 209, 227–28, 232, 242–43, 248

The Nanny Diaries, 5, 15

needs, guest, 34–35; desires recast as, 32, 34, 48, 178; fulfilling, 25, 28, 34–36, 47, 49; legitimating, 25, 28, 32–38, 42, 56; Luxury Garden workers' responses to, 33–37, 42, 67, 78–79, 106; Maslow's "hierarchy of needs" and, 178, 315n20; rule-breaking to meet, 37–38, 45; worker empathy and condescension toward, 163–66. *See also* anticipation of guest needs; recognition of guests

new economy, 1–23

New Luxury, 296n13

newspapers: costs of, 243, 246; detail of presentation, 43; displays of labor delivering, 40; guest preferences in, 302n25

New York Times, 4, 269–70

niceness. *See* civility; emotional reciprocity/niceness/friendliness, worker-guest

Ninotchka (Ernst Lubitsch), 110, 241, 320n16

noninteractive service work, 13–14, 21, 44, 49. *See also* back of house workers; housekeepers; invisible work; laundry service; room service

normalization of inequality, 17, 21–22, 57–62, 72; breakdown of, 61; division of labor and, 26; ethnographic method and, 278, 279; with games, 22, 112, 122, 125, 134–35, 151; guest conflict over, 227; guest entitlement, 15–20, 23, 61, 112–13, 125, 151, 155, 221, 260–61, 322n18; through individual interactions, 221–22, 260–62; with luxury service imperatives, 240–41, 248; reciprocity and, 186, 204, 220, 221–22; subordination of workers and, 17, 22, 62, 122–23, 125, 134–35, 155, 181–82, 185–86, 204, 260, 262; wealth of guests, 59, 134–35. *See also* legitimation

norms, 265; of personhood, 77–78; of reciprocity, 18, 19, 23, 186, 204, 207–9, 214–17, 221–22, 234, 322n21; tipping, 320n19. *See also* contract; moral evaluations; obligations; rules

obligations: of guests to workers, 23, 207–9, 221, 224, 269; of researcher to research subjects, 284–85; of workers to guests, 23, 215, 221. *See also* reciprocity in worker-guest relations; responsibilities; work

obscuring inequality: commodification/decommodification, 178, 186, 189–91, 209, 212–13, 218, 221, 229, 241; with games, 111, 113, 152–53; guest-worker reciprocity and, 185, 186, 189–91, 208, 209, 212–13, 218, 221, 255; with luxury service imperatives, 240–41, 248; by worker self-subordination, 57–62. *See also* normalization of inequality

"old economy," manufacturing jobs, 5–6

organizational characteristics: in client-worker relations, 215, 274; guest legitimation of privilege supported by, 241; Luxury Garden, 65, 66*table*, 73–74, 287, 288*fig*, 307n15; normalization through individualization depending on, 222; powerful selfhood of workers and, 17–20; Royal Court, 65, 66*table*, 274, 287, 289*fig*. *See also* managerial regimes; organization of work

organizational identity: Luxury Garden, 75–
79, 81, 82, 91, 99, 108, 144–45. *See also*
authenticity; community; corporate
culture; credo; mission statement; motto;
status by association

organizational structure, 287; Luxury Garden,
287, 288*fig*; Royal Court, 287, 289*fig*

organization of work, 22, 26, 49, 71, 215; and
guest awareness of inequality, 224, 240–41,
256; Luxury Garden, 72–74, 144–45, 265;
powerful selfhood of workers and, 16–19,
149–50, 152–53; Royal Court, 88, 97, 149–
50, 179, 265; spatial, 74, 88, 126, 240. *See
also* hotel division of labor; managerial
control

orientation, new employee, 93; ethnographic
observation, 14, 273; Luxury Garden, 14,
75–79, 93, 145, 177–78, 273, 308n18; Ritz-
Carlton, 271, 306n9, 308n18, 315n18; Royal
Court, 14, 90–93, 179. *See also* hiring;
training

overbooking, 115–16, 117, 136, 160, 172–73

ownership: Luxury Garden, 66, 73; Ritz-
Carlton, 27; Royal Court independent
management and, 13, 16, 22, 68, 86, 87

packages, guest, 309n29

packing and unpacking services, 38, 65

pampering, 38–44, 231–32

participant observation, 12–16, 25, 271–85;
and compensation, 14, 129–30, 273, 274–
75, 283; of guest insecurity, 164–65, 246; of
guest unpredictability, 115; interview data
compared with, 188, 242, 272, 277, 278, 282;
at Luxury Garden, 12, 14, 16, 271–83,
323n1; protection of subjects, 323n5; reliability and validity, 279–82; at Royal Court,
12–15, 135, 271–83, 300n58, 323n1. *See also*
ethnography

Peninsula Beverly Hills, 30, 32

performance, 20, 244; of class/"doing class,"
12, 20, 244, 246, 254, 259–60; deep acting,
9, 75, 78, 94–95, 298n41; mystery shoppers
rating, 84; tip strategy, 128; withholding
emotional labor, 199–200. *See also* criticism;
feedback; games, worker; monitoring of
workers; self-subordination of workers to
guests; service theater

perks: Luxury Garden, 67, 73, 157; luxury
hotel stays as, 231–32, 319n9; and powerful selfhood of workers, 155, 156–59; Royal
Court, 68, 157, 179, 180

personal information, guest, 29–30, 56, 166,
178, 180, 193, 320n18; hotel computer database of, 2, 30, 32, 54, 56, 67, 99–100, 106,
119, 163, 198, 227, 230, 306n2; privacy in
research, 284; workers' "consciousness of
the Other," 163. *See also* guest preferences;
names

"personality market," 8

personalization, 1–3, 25–32; displays of
labor, 38–44; failures of, 31, 42; front of
house work, 56; guest perspectives on, 31–
32, 227–28, 230, 302n32; intangible, 49;
Luxury Garden, 28–31, 42, 106; nonluxury
hotels, 29, 302n25; stationery, 30, 31, 40; of
workers by guests, 187. *See also* customization; guest preferences; individual interactions; personal information, guest; recognition of guests

personhood: corporate norms of, 77–78;
guests recognizing/violating workers',
18, 186, 187–88, 191, 194–95, 204; workers
recognizing guests', 31, 39, 46, 92. *See also*
dignity; selfhood

physical aspects: of hotels, 25, 26, 27, 30,
65, 68; hotel work space, 74, 88. *See also*
aesthetics; appearance; material luxury;
physical labor; room rates; technology

physical labor, 16; back of house workers, 50;
domestic servant, 26; front of house workers, 40, 49, 50, 56; gay men in nonmanagerial positions and, 304n56; guest background of, 235; guest's entitlement to, 38–
44, 221; of immigrant rights activists, 269–
70; invisible, 49, 50; semivisible workers',
54; speedy, 54; unlimited, 21, 25, 28; visible,
40, 49; withholding, 19, 200. *See also* effort,
worker

Pierce, Jennifer, 148, 166

positive interactions, 9, 10, 184–85, 214–15,
261, 318n45; as crucial feature of luxury, 25,
186; ethnographic surprise, 15, 185, 272,
278; repeat guests as positive legends, 193,
198, 205. *See also* customer feedback; reciprocity; recognition

power. *See* authority; control; empowerment;
entitlement; powerful selfhood of workers

powerful selfhood of workers, 13, 15–20, 109, 147–53, 264; autonomy and, 11–12, 16–19, 109, 147–50, 267; condescension/criticism/empathy toward guests, 155, 162–82, 232–33, 249; dignity, 11, 12, 20, 132, 214, 317nn20,25; distanced from working class, 162; games and, 113–14, 121, 152–53; hotel division of labor and, 17–18, 149–50, 176, 179–80, 267; individual interactions and, 261; limiting entitlement of guests, 23, 61–62, 155, 164, 171–78–81, 183; managerial strategy of empowerment, 70, 71, 108–9, 308n20; multiple symbolic hierarchies and, 22, 109, 153, 154–83; and prestige, 17–18, 111, 153, 155, 156–62, 180–81, 267; reciprocity and, 18, 232–33, 234; revenge expressing, 198, 204; strategies by workers for, 17–18, 22, 23, 48, 72, 113, 141–50, 152, 171–76, 183, 204, 260–65, 267. *See also* consent by workers; resources for workers' self-construction; strategies of self; superiority of workers

predictability: of frequent guests, 202; worker game strategy, 114, 115, 123, 129–33, 312n29. *See also* anticipation of guest needs; unpredictability

preferences. *See* guest preferences

prestige: powerful selfhood of workers and, 17–18, 111, 153, 155, 156–62, 180–81, 267. *See also* status

Pretty Woman (Garry Marshall), 223–24, 241, 320nn15,16

privilege, 181; consumer of immigrant services, 269–70; domestic service employers, 322n20; guest, 23, 162, 221, 225, 241, 247, 253, 255–56, 299n53; guest background, 277; hotel worker community, 90, 178, 235–36; of researcher, 284–85; workers over coworkers, 18, 156–59, 170, 176–80, 261; workers over managers, 305n62. *See also* entitlement of guests; status; superiority of workers; wealth

"producer services," in new economy, 5

production: axis of contestation in, 267; capitalist, 7, 112; of consent, 151, 152, 263; of dispositions, 18, 107, 205, 249–50, 254–56, 262–65; of entitlement/inequality, 223–56, 259; exploitative, 259, 260, 263; managerial control, 9, 89, 113; point of, 152, 183, 263; of

privileged self, 241–55; of services, 48–57; social reproduction institutions outside of, 260; unequal authority relations in, 297n29. *See also* division of labor; production-consumption; service product; work

production-consumption, 8, 11, 20–21, 263–65; entitlement in, 223–56, 259, 260–61, 264; guest reciprocity and, 192; guest selfhood and, 19, 241–55; studies, 14, 272, 285–86, 297n30; worker strategies, 18–19, 112, 183. *See also* consumption; production; service theater

professionalism, 142–50; and class, 238–39; as equality with guests, 235, 255–56; guests failing to recognize, 195; powerful selfhood of workers, 17–18, 148–50, 153, 179–81, 195; Royal Court managers and, 96, 103, 143; and worker-guest reciprocity, 195, 205, 206, 215. *See also* Luxury Garden professionalism

promotion: worker, 73, 87, 308–9n25. *See also* career ladders

"proper verbiage," workers to guests, 38–39, 91, 106, 177

"psychological exploitation," employer-employee relations, 10

punishment. *See* discipline; revenge

"quality managers," 71

quitting. *See* exiting

race/ethnicity: in earlier grand hotels, 26; ethnographic observation and, 281; guest awareness of structural inequality, 237–38, 256; and guest-worker relations, 107, 191, 215; intern, 323n3; invisible work and, 237–38, 310n34; legitimation of inequalities, 262–63; Luxury Garden guests, 67; Luxury Garden managers, 73; Luxury Garden workers, 50, 73, 85, 292*table*, 305n58; Royal Court guests, 67, 69, 174–75; Royal Court manager-worker socializing, 96–97; Royal Court workers, 50, 68, 86–87, 95–97, 104, 107, 293*table*, 305n59, 323n1; semivisible workers, 53, 73, 86. *See also* immigrant workers; stratification by race/ethnicity

ranking: Luxury Garden, 66, 106, 176–77, 180–81; Mobil, 66, 68, 160, 180–81; Royal Court, 68. *See also* awards; hierarchy

reciprocity in researcher-research subject relations, 284–85
reciprocity in worker-guest relations, 17–19, 23, 184–222, 237, 261, 264; contract, 23, 194–204, 206–16, 221, 278, 318n42; equality/inequality and, 18, 19, 23, 134–35, 185–94, 203–24, 230–31, 237–39, 255, 269, 321–22n18; ethnographic surprise, 185, 272, 278; financial/material, 18, 19, 23, 189–90, 193–97, 221, 261; norm, 18, 19, 23, 186, 204, 207–9, 214–17, 221–22, 234, 322n21; recognition, 25, 185–97, 220; unionizing and, 267. *See also* emotional reciprocity/niceness/friendliness, worker-guest
recognition of guests, 48; front of house workers, 55–56; "ideological," 254; by name, 18, 28, 30–33, 54, 56, 67, 91, 92, 118–19, 209, 227–28, 232, 242–43, 248; needs, 34–38; by noninteractive workers, 49; personhood, 31, 39, 46; reciprocal, 25, 185–97, 220; rewards from workers, 197–98, 205; technological aid with, 2, 32, 56, 67, 106, 119, 227, 230; tipping strategy, 127. *See also* anticipation; guest preferences
recognition of workers: awards, 77, 90, 102, 181, 311n15; guest failures in, 18, 142, 165, 173, 194–96; by guests, 18, 25, 48, 185–97, 204, 220; "ideological," 254; by Luxury Garden managers, 75, 76, 83, 84, 108, 189; mutual, 101–2, 276; reciprocal, 25, 185–97, 220; of researcher, 276; rewards from managers, 47, 75, 76, 108; by Royal Court managers, 83, 90–91, 98, 101–2, 189. *See also* compensation; feedback; promotion; tips
regulation: mutual, 64, 72, 84–85, 86, 88, 96, 100–105, 109, 149–50, 156, 159. *See also* authority; autonomy of workers; control
relationship, 184–222; capitalist labor relations, 7, 9–11, 263; fleeting encounters, 53, 124, 131, 186, 217, 318n42. *See also* commodification of relationship; individual interactions; worker-coworker relations; worker-employer relations; worker-guest relations; worker-manager relations
repeat/frequent guests: accumulation of knowledge about, 163; hotel history of preferences, 30, 56, 99–100, 163, 230; Luxury Garden, 67, 206; negative legends, 198, 205, 206, 218; personalization for, 29, 30, 31, 40, 43, 56; positive legends, 193, 198, 205;

qualification as, 172; rate increases for, 250; reciprocity with workers, 185, 186, 187–88, 191–93, 198–200, 202–3, 205, 206, 216–17; Royal Court, 69, 206; tipping games with, 131–32, 151; worker revenge on, 199, 200, 202–3; worker rewards to, 198; workers' longstanding relationships with, 47, 185, 186, 215, 217, 261
reproduction, social. *See* social reproduction
research: confidentiality, 283–84, 300n56, 312n31; ethical questions, 282–85; marketing, 30; methods, 12–15, 271–86. *See also* ethnography; interviews; literature; sociology of work
reservationists, 49, 53, 58, 318n42; awareness of structural inequality, 60, 122–23; ethnographic observation, 13, 14, 273, 274, 275; games, 115–17, 135, 311n12; Luxury Garden, 67, 73, 74, 292*table*, 307n16; restaurant, 120, 130–31, 311n11; Royal Court, 54, 55, 88, 116–17, 163, 293*table*, 305n60; wages, 67, 292*table*, 293*table*
reservations, 30, 40, 49; categorized with sales or rooms division, 74, 307n15; games involved with, 115–16, 117, 120, 122, 311nn11,12; maximizing room sales, 115–16, 122, 311n12; overbooking, 115–16, 117, 136, 160, 172–73; restaurant, 120–21, 125, 130–31, 311n11; "walking"/relocating to another hotel, 116, 117, 136, 160, 172–73. *See also* room rates; suite rates
resistance, worker, 9, 262–63, 268–69, 321n11; domestic servants, 264; and games, 151, 152; revenge as, 186, 204; selfhood and, 16, 19, 152, 182–83, 268–69. *See also* contestation; exiting; limits; revenge; withdrawal of consent
resources for workers' self-construction, 17–19, 152–53, 260; games, 113; managerial provision of, 9, 21–22, 64, 70–79, 94–95, 108, 109, 144–45, 177–78, 267; organizational context, 155, 177–83. *See also* dispositions; powerful selfhood of workers; strategies of self; transformation
respect. *See* personhood; recognition
responsibilities: guest, 206–14, 220–21; worker, 220–21. *See also* contract; expectations; luxury service; norms; obligations
restaurant: busers, 40; cooks and kitchen staff, 49; empathy of staff, 163; ethno-

graphic observation, 274; fast food, 9, 54, 152; food runners, 13; games connected with, 119, 120–21, 311n11; Luxury Garden award-winning, 65; reservations, 120–21, 125, 130–31, 311n11; Royal Court, 13, 37, 60, 119, 129, 162, 167, 309n26, 310n32; rule-breaking to meet needs, 37; servers, 49, 119, 129, 174, 304n56, 310n32; tipping norms, 320n19

restroom attendants, 40

retail sector, 4, 297n30, 299nn46,47, 310n33

revenge: guests on hotel, 214; guests on workers, 211; workers on guests, 19, 184, 186, 197–206, 211, 217, 221, 316n17, 317nn24,25. *See also* limits; resistance

rewards: guest luxury labor for workers, 192; to guests by workers, 197–98, 205, 217; to workers of games, 112, 153; to workers by managers, 47, 75, 76, 108. *See also* autonomy of workers; awards; compensation; promotion; recognition of workers; tips

rights: guest, 19, 23, 206–14, 220–21, 250; immigrant, 269–70; worker, 18–19, 194, 220–21, 266, 269–70. *See also* contract; entitlement; expectations

Ritz-Carlton, 27, 28, 99; credo, 32, 70, 76, 306n10; employee promise, 70, 307n10; ethnographic observation, 271; and guest desires, 46; managerial strategies, 70–71, 75, 76, 91; motto, 70, 307n10; 315n18; orientation, 271, 306n9, 308n18, 315n18; personalization, 30; revenue per available room, 302n21; rule-breaking to meet guest needs, 37–38; service basics, 70, 307nn10,11; standards, 70–71, 91–92, 102; Total Quality Management (TQM), 70–71, 308n20; training, 71, 91, 315nn18,19

"role distance," 142–50

"role embracement," 141–42

Rollins, Judith, 10, 163, 220, 322n20

Romero, Mary, 215

room assignment/blocking: games with, 116–18, 311n13; revenge of workers and, 200, 201; upgrades, 173, 178–79, 201, 250

room cleaners, 49, 50, 52, 304n57, 309n26; ethnographic shadowing of, 13, 14, 323n1; Luxury Garden, 14, 292*table*; mutual assistance, 101; and reciprocity contract, 318n42; Royal Court, 13, 52–53, 293*table*, 321n1. See *also* housekeepers; turndown attendants

room rates: care work differentiating, 47; entitlement to services related to, 37, 172, 173; and expectations, 107, 122; game of maximizing, 115–16, 122, 311n12; guest insecurity and, 245; limits of entitlement and, 173, 178–79; Luxury Garden, 2, 14, 66, 67; market demand and, 27; occupancy rates and, 28, 302nn20,21; "rack," 11, 306n3; revenge of workers and, 200, 201; REVPAR, 311n12; Royal Court, 13, 68; status by association, 160; upgrades, 173, 178–79, 201, 250; "upselling," 116; and worker awareness of structural inequality, 58, 122–23. See *also* reservations; suite rates

rooms division, 287, 307n15. See *also* front desk agents; front door workers; housekeepers; reservations

room service, 49, 53, 54, 55; awareness of inequality, 58; caring labor, 36; for dogs, 38; in *Eloise*, 24; ethnographic observation, 13, 115, 274, 280, 281, 283; front of house workers criticizing, 137, 140–41; games, 115, 130, 132–33, 280; gender of workers, 281, 292*table*, 293*table*; Luxury Garden, 65, 74, 292*table*; as marker of luxury to workers, 160, 175; Royal Court, 13, 54, 161, 274, 280, 293*table*, 309n26, 310n32; speed, 41, 115; technology, 54; tips, 50, 130, 132–33, 292*table*, 294*table*. See *also* semivisible workers

routinization, 9; discretion and, 52, 54, 64, 79; of emotional labor, 8; and games, 111, 151–52; interactive vs. noninteractive work, 21, 54, 57; McDonald's, 9, 54, 55, 224, 225; semivisible work, 54–56, 58; sincerity vs., 45–46; for speed, 114. See *also* scripting; standardization

Roy, Donald, 129

Royal Court, 30, 64–65, 68–69; friendliness, 65, 69, 71, 99, 105–6, 205–6; organizational characteristics, 65, 66*table*, 274, 287, 289*fig*; organizational structure, 287, 289*fig*; owned independently, 13, 16, 22, 68, 86, 87; ranking and awards, 68, 179; restaurant, 13, 37, 60, 119, 129, 162, 167, 309n26, 310n32; room and suite rates, 13, 68; status by association with, 90, 95, 159–61; in typology of hotels, 307n12; worker-to-room ratio, 65, 68. See *also* Royal Court renovation

Royal Court concierge work at front desk, 88, 148, 149–50, 179–80, 315n21; cultural capital, 157; demographics, 107, 149, 293*table*; ethnographic observation, 135, 279; guest expectations, 107–8; money games, 125, 129, 135; perks, 68, 157, 179, 180; training and evaluations, 94; wages, 68, 293*table*

Royal Court front desk agents, 89, 101, 293*table*, 305n60; authenticity, 69; demographics, 86–87; ethnographic observation, 101, 135, 279–80; games, 116–17, 125, 129; turnover, 64, 283–84. *See also* Royal Court concierge work at front desk

Royal Court guests: characteristics, 13, 67, 69, 174–75, 205; complaints about renovation, 31, 106, 164, 212–14; feedback, 70, 90, 98, 105, 107, 189; needs anticipation/ fulfillment/legitimation, 34, 37, 69, 91, 119; repeat, 69, 206. *See also* worker-guest relations

Royal Court managerial regime, 63, 70, 72*table*, 86–105, 143; authenticity focus, 22, 45, 54, 69, 71, 72, 86, 89–95, 99, 104, 105, 108–9, 179–81; and autonomy of workers, 86, 99–100, 146–50, 267; ethnography allowed by, 12, 272, 273–74, 275–76; flexible informality, 22, 71–72, 86–105, 149–50, 179–80, 205–6; inconsistent authority, 22, 71, 86, 91, 92, 94, 95–100, 104–5, 108, 126, 145–50, 274, 309n29; interviews, 14, 271, 274; laissez-faire, 83, 96; limited corporate culture, 22, 71, 89–91, 93, 108–9; luxury standards of service, 38, 45, 54, 89–95, 102–3, 108–9; organization of work, 88, 97, 149–50, 179, 265; "stars of reception" program, 90, 102; stratification by race/ ethnicity, 95–97; turnover in, 64, 95; unionizing and, 267, 268; worker conflicts with, 145–50, 268; worker-manager relations, 83, 89–91, 96–99, 101–2, 189

Royal Court renovation, 98; guest complaints about, 31, 106, 164, 212–14; and turnover, 64, 89–90, 104–5; wages and tips affected by, 126, 148, 312n21

Royal Court workers, 293*table*; bellmen, 86, 88, 118, 119, 126, 138–39, 293*table*, 312n21; competition among, 137, 273–74; conflicts with managers, 145–50, 268; demographics, 50, 68, 86–87, 95–97, 104, 107, 148–49,

293*table*, 305n59, 323n1; doormen, 59–60, 69, 86, 88, 118, 126, 133–34, 146–48, 157, 180, 191, 293*table*; ethnographic observation, 12–15, 135, 271–83, 300n58, 323n1; handbook, 45, 91; housemen/runners, 13, 304n53, 309n26; internal labor market, 64, 86–87, 180, 308–9n25; labor division, 18, 22, 50, 68, 71, 86–89, 95–97, 101, 107, 126, 149– 50, 179–80; mutual regulation, 86, 88, 96, 100–105, 109, 149–50; needs anticipation/ fulfillment/legitimation by, 34, 37, 69, 91, 119; number of, 68; orientation, 14, 90–93, 179; perks, 68, 157, 179, 180; reservationists, 54, 55, 88, 116–17, 163, 293*table*, 305n60; room cleaners, 13, 52–53, 293*table*, 321n1; room service, 13, 54, 161, 274, 280, 293*table*, 309n26, 310n32; surveillance/ monitoring of, 70, 97–98, 99, 100–101; telephone operators, 13, 54, 55, 88, 98, 101, 180, 184, 293*table*, 305n60; tips (general), 68, 125, 146–48, 157, 293*table*; training, 71, 87, 88, 91, 92–95, 100–105, 148, 149–50, 156, 309–10n30; turnover, 64, 89– 90, 95, 104–5, 206, 283–84; valet parkers, 86, 126, 138–39, 147, 157, 293*table*, 312n21; wages (general), 65, 68–69, 266, 293*table*; withdrawal of consent, 17–18, 109, 143, 145–50, 267; worker-coworker relations, 64, 72, 84, 86, 88, 96, 100–105, 147, 149– 50, 180, 310n34; worker-manager relations, 83, 89–91, 96–99, 101–2, 189. *See also* Royal Court front desk agents; worker-guest relations

rudeness: guest, 78, 132, 166, 193, 195, 198– 200, 203, 204, 234; worker, 128, 204, 240

rules: games, 125–27, 138–40, 143–50; guest behavior, 243–44, 249, 256; of interaction, 204, 219, 221; rule-breaking to meet guest needs, 37–38, 45; tipping, 125–27, 138–39, 146–50, 320n21. *See also* contract; norms; transgressions

runners, 49, 53, 54, 55, 58, 304n53; Luxury Garden, 304n53, 308n16; Royal Court, 13, 304n53, 309n26. *See also* semivisible workers

St. Regis, New York, 40, 41

sales: reservations categorized with, 74, 307n15; worker game of maximizing, 115–

16, 122, 311n12. *See also* room rates; suite rates

Schulze, Horst, 46

Scott, James, 286

scripting: of interactions, 9, 55. *See also* standardization

security, 287; surveillance cameras, 56, 83–84, 97. *See also* insecurity, guest

selfhood, 11; of guests, 5–6, 19, 46, 224, 231–34, 241–56, 260, 265, 278. *See also* dispositions; individual interactions; intersubjectivity; personhood; selfhood of workers; strategies of self

selfhood of workers, 5–6, 8–12, 15–20, 109, 261, 320n15; alienated, 8–9, 11, 15, 259–60; at-work/outside-work, 8–9, 11, 15, 18, 142–50, 179–83, 259–60, 264, 279, 285–86, 298n37; authentic, 8–9, 11, 71, 285; equal, 109, 268–69; ethnographic method and, 278, 279; games and, 17–18, 113, 121, 151–53; independent from workplace, 18, 142–50, 179–81; managerial inconsistency and, 145–50, 267; managerial transformation of, 9, 21–22, 70–71, 75–79, 94–95, 108–9, 177–78, 308n20; professional, 17–18, 148–50, 153, 179–81, 195. *See also* autonomy of workers; comparison by workers; entitlement of workers; intersubjectivity; powerful selfhood of workers; resources for workers' self-construction; self-subordination of workers to guests; strategies of self

self-regulation, 22, 104, 109. *See also* authority; autonomy of workers; self-subordination of workers to guests

self-subordination of workers to guests, 11, 12, 19, 21, 48, 214–15, 262, 264; games and, 112–13, 122–23, 125, 132, 152; interactive vs. invisible workers, 50, 57–58, 59; limits to, 23, 48, 171–76, 183; worker awareness of structural inequality and, 15–16, 21, 57–62, 122–23, 134–35, 155, 204. *See also* deference; effort, worker; entitlement of guests; powerful selfhood of workers

semivisible workers, 49, 53–55, 58, 112, 318n42; race/ethnicity, 53, 73, 86; speed, 114, 115, 151–52. *See also* housemen; reservationists; room service; runners; telephone operators

servants. *See* domestic servants

service: hotel, 2, 28, 48–57. *See also* consumption; luxury service; production

service economy: new economy as, 5–6. *See also* service

service product, 48–57; intangible, 7–8, 11, 47, 49, 53, 55–56, 111–12, 123, 260; tangible, 49, 52, 53, 55. *See also* luxury product; luxury service; service work

service standards. *See* luxury standards of service; standardization

service theater, 20–21, 48–57, 205; contestation of entitlements, 269–70; games, 22, 111–12; normalization of entitlements, 260–61, 322n19; social reproduction site, 262–65, 322n19. *See also* organization of work; performance; production-consumption

service work. *See* interactive service work

service worker, 3; alienation from self, 8–9, 11, 15, 259–60; appearance, 70, 74, 88, 235, 245; ethnographic observation of, 12–16, 135, 271–83, 300n58, 323n1; "going into robot," 15; interviewing, 280, 282, 286, 323n5; "unproductive labor," 7. *See also* demographics; domestic servants; entitlement of workers; exiting; hiring; hotel division of labor; interactive service work; internal labor markets; job characteristics; Luxury Garden workers; noninteractive service work; organization of work; relationship; Royal Court workers; selfhood of workers; service theater; sociology of work; strategies of workers; stratification by gender

sexuality, 320n16

Sharp, Isadore, 25

"shop floor" culture, 16, 20, 22, 111. *See also* manufacturing work

sincerity, worker, 20, 25, 28, 44–46; guest sincerity aiding, 187; Royal Court, 45, 54, 91–92; semivisible workers, 54. *See also* authenticity

skill, worker: "deskilling," 7, 123, 146; games of, 110–53; minimal division of labor and, 148; powerful selfhood of workers and, 17–18, 147–50; and prestige, 161. *See also* comparison by workers; competence; criticism

sociability: hotel events for workers, 77, 85, 91, 105, 181, 276, 277; manager-manager

sociability (*continued*)
socializing, 97; manager-worker socializing, 96–97, 99; Royal Court workers on the job, 85, 100, 103–5, 276–77, 310n34; worker-coworker socializing outside hotel, 14, 85, 276–77; worker-guest inside hotel, 106, 107; worker-guest socializing outside hotel, 188, 191. *See also* entertainment; friendliness

social life and position. *See* class; community; culture; demographics; disposition; sociability; status

social reproduction: of inequality, 11, 220, 242, 254–56, 262–65, 322n19. *See also* normalization of inequality

sociology of work, 6–11, 282–83; airline, 7, 45, 78, 123, 166; axis of contestation, 267; cab drivers, 124, 130, 131, 217; caregiving occupations, 303n44; class in service interactions, 299n47; client-worker relations, 9, 186, 214, 222, 295n2, 299n46, 318n45; dichotomies, 11, 219, 264–65, 285–86, 298n37; games, 111, 151–52; hotel work, 3, 133, 271, 295n2; interactive service work, 7–11, 15, 21, 57, 222, 297n30, 299n47; legitimation of racial inequalities, 262–63; luxury service, 3; managerial strategies, 108; McDonald's, 9, 54, 55, 122, 224, 225; revenge, 203; Whyte, 219, 316–17n18; Willis, 169, 255, 265. *See also* Burawoy, Michael; ethnography; Hochschild, Arlie; Lamont, Michèle; Leidner, Robin; manufacturing work; research; Rollins, Judith

spa, 27, 36, 189

speed of service, 38, 41; games of, 113–23, 136, 151

spending. *See* consumption

standardization: of procedures, 9; Ritz-Carlton, 91–92, 102; room cleaning, 52; Royal Court, 102–3; scripting of interactions, 9, 55; worker appearance and behavior, 70. *See also* consistency; luxury standards of service; routinization; training; uniforms

"stars of reception" program, Royal Court, 90, 102

stationery: luxury hotel, 226; personalized, 30, 31, 40

status, 226, 299n47; hotel, 18, 90, 95, 155,
159–61, 171–81, 216, 235–36; workers vs. coworkers, 156–59, 170, 176–80. *See also* class; hierarchy; income; prestige; privilege; status by association, workers'; status of guests; subordination; superiority of workers

status by association, workers', 159–62; with guests, 155, 161–62, 175–76, 182, 267; with hotel, 18, 90, 95, 155, 159–61, 171–81, 216, 235–36, 315n18. *See also* cultural capital; prestige

status of guests, 76; powerful selfhood of workers and, 155, 169, 171–76; VIP, 172–73, 178–79; worker status by association with, 155, 161–62, 175–76, 182, 267. *See also* class; entitlement of guests; repeat/frequent guests; wealth

Stewart, Herbert L., 257–58, 270

strategies of guests, 23; legitimation, 224, 225–41, 255–56, 260, 262; selfhood, 5–6, 19, 46, 224, 231–34, 241–56, 260, 265, 278. *See also* comparison by guests

strategies of managers, 64, 69–72, 108; empowerment, 70, 71, 108–9, 308n20; hiring, 69–70, 90, 145, 307n13; recognition of workers, 75, 76, 83, 84, 90–91, 98, 101–2, 108, 189; Ritz-Carlton, 70–71, 75, 76; status by association, 90, 95, 177, 178, 179; transformation of workers, 9, 21–22, 70–71, 75–79, 94–95, 108–9, 177–78, 308n20. *See also* corporate culture; managerial control; organization of work; professionalism; routinization; standardization; training

strategies of other, guest perceptions of workers, 234–37, 255–56

strategies of self: guests', 5–6, 19, 46, 224, 231–34, 241–56, 260, 265, 278; workers', 17, 22, 113, 141–53, 260, 265, 267. *See also* legitimation of inequalities; normalization of inequality; resources for workers' self-construction; selfhood; status

strategies of workers, 22, 23; competence, 140–42, 145; condescension, 155, 162–71, 175–76, 178–81; deep acting, 9, 75, 78, 94–95, 298n41; independence from workplace, 18, 142–50, 179–81; prediction, 114, 115, 123, 129–33, 312n29; strategies of self, 17, 22, 113, 141–53, 260, 265, 267; typology, 114–17, 119, 123, 124, 130, 132, 151. *See also* comparison by workers; consent by workers; entitlement of workers; games, worker; judgment by workers; powerful selfhood of workers; professionalism; self-subordination

stratification by gender, 9, 216, 292*table*, 293*table*, 319n12; back of house workers, 50, 86, 281, 292*table*, 293*table*; domestic servants, 47, 216; front of house workers, 50, 68, 107, 149, 281–82, 292*table*, 293*table*, 300n57; housemen, 304n53; telephone operators, 156, 292*table*, 293*table*

stratification by race/ethnicity, 21, 292*table*, 293*table*; back of house workers, 50, 53, 58, 73, 86, 104, 281, 292*table*, 293*table*, 305n58, 323n1; domestic servants, 47; and English language competence, 53, 57, 82, 85, 104, 141, 281, 305n58; front of house workers, 57, 68, 73, 107, 292*table*, 293*table*; Royal Court managers, 95–97

structural inequality. *See* worker-guest inequality

subjectivity. *See* selfhood

subordination, worker, 6, 9–10, 15–16, 26, 44–45, 57–62, 165; domestic servants, 10, 21, 26, 47–48, 216; immigrant rights activists, 269–70; judgments of guests and, 169–70; in luxury standards of service, 21, 23, 45, 59, 60, 118–21, 182–83, 204, 268, 303n44; noninteractive work and, 21; performances of, 20; philosophies of class and, 238–39; reciprocity with guests and, 23, 185–86, 192–93, 218–19; reframed and normalized, 17, 22, 62, 122–23, 125, 134–35, 155, 181–82, 185–86, 204, 260, 262; revenge and, 204, 211; semivisible workers and, 58; skill and, 114, 115, 152; wealth as entitlement to, 258; workers' strategies of powerful selfhood vs., 17–18, 22, 23, 48, 72, 152, 171–76, 183, 204, 261, 264. *See also* effort, worker; self-subordination of workers to guests

suite rates: guest insecurity and, 245; Luxury Garden, 2, 14, 66; Royal Court, 13, 68. *See also* room rates

superiority of workers, 181–83; to communities outside the hotel, 22, 141, 155, 159–62, 183, 235–36; to coworkers, 17–18, 22, 109, 140–41, 151, 153, 155–59, 176–81; to

guests, 17, 22, 109, 121, 153, 154–55, 162–76, 181, 261; Luxury Garden managerial regime and, 176–79; to managers, 149. *See also* comparison by workers; condescension; judgment by workers; powerful selfhood of workers; status

supervision. *See* managerial control; monitoring of workers

surplus value, 16, 263

surveillance: cameras, 56, 83–84, 97. *See also* surveillance of workers

surveillance of workers, 56–57, 70–71; Luxury Garden, 70, 77, 83–85, 108; mutual, 101–2, 149; Royal Court, 70, 97–98, 99, 101. *See also* monitoring of workers

sympathy: of workers with guests, 35–37, 45, 162–66, 213, 247. *See also* empathy

tangibility of product: intangible service products, 7–8, 11, 47, 49, 53, 55–56, 111–12, 123, 260; tangible service products, 49, 52, 53, 55. *See also* invisible work; physical aspects; visible labor

taste, guest: workers emulating, 170–71, 177; workers evaluating, 167, 247. *See also* aesthetics

technology, 309n29; computerized guest information, 2, 32, 54, 56, 67, 99–100, 106, 119, 198, 227, 230, 306n3; fast food workers', 54; human labor instead of, 40; as indicator of lack of authenticity, 32, 45; managerial provision of, 83; in "modern" hotels, 26; Royal Court compared with Luxury Garden, 94; semivisible work, 54, 110, 306n2; in service theater, 49; surveillance, 56–57, 83–84, 97–98; training in, 309n30; worker conflict over, 136

telephone operators, 49, 53, 58, 318n42; ethnographic observation, 13, 14, 273, 275, 306n2; Luxury Garden, 14, 67, 73, 74, 292*table*, 307n16; Ritz-Carlton, 93; Royal Court, 13, 54, 55, 88, 98, 101, 180, 184, 293*table*, 305n60; status, 156, 180; wages, 67, 292*table*, 293*table*

television shows, 4, 296n14

Thompson, Kay, *Eloise*, 24

time: check-in and check-out times, 37; eight-hour work shifts, 65; fixed quota of rooms to service, 310n5; hourly wages, 65, 67;

time *(continued)*
    twenty-four-hour room service, 65. *See also*
    effort, worker; speed of service
tipping games, 112, 123–35, 151–52, 175, 194,
    312–13; greed, 129–30; rules of, 125–27,
    138–39, 146–50, 320n21; strategies of, 127–
    29; talking about, 129, 312n24
tips: advance, 132, 312n29, 316n15;
    bellmen/bellpersons, 125, 126, 127, 129,
    138–39, 189, 292*table*, 293*table*, 312n21,
    320n19; concierges, 67, 125, 128, 129, 137,
    144, 158, 179, 189, 292*table*, 293*table*,
    320n19; conflicts between workers over,
    104, 136–40, 147–48, 157; doormen/door
    attendants, 67, 125–34, 146–48, 157, 189,
    195, 281, 292*table*, 293*table*, 320n19; front
    and back of house workers, 50; front desk
    agents, 125, 158, 280, 293*table*; guests
    neglecting, 130, 195–96; guest uncertain-
    ties about, 243, 320n19; Luxury Garden
    (general), 67, 125–29, 292*table*; niceness
    and, 193, 196–97, 207–8; obligatory, 207–9;
    during participant observation, 129–30,
    274–75, 283; performing gratitude for, 193;
    as reciprocity, 184, 189, 191–97, 201–2, 204,
    206, 207, 216, 218–21; refusing, 201–2;
    room service, 50, 130, 132–33, 292*table*,
    294*table*; Royal Court (general), 68, 125,
    146–48, 157, 293*table*; Royal Court renova-
    tion and, 126, 148, 312n21; turndown atten-
    dants, 44; valet parkers, 125, 126, 138–39,
    147, 157, 293*table*, 312n21, 320n19. *See also*
    tipping games
Tocqueville, Alexis de, 184
Total Quality Management (TQM), Ritz-
    Carlton, 70–71, 308n20
training: discipline instead of, 80; for domes-
    tic servants, 4; etiquette, 177; of guests by
    workers, 249–50; hospitality management
    or culinary institute students, 104, 149, 272,
    305n62; on the job, 71, 80, 93; Luxury Gar-
    den, 33, 35–36, 75–82, 91, 93, 145, 177–78;
    Luxury Garden inconsistent, 79–80; man-
    agers transforming workers through, 9, 21–
    22, 70–71, 75–76, 94–95, 177–78; mutual
    by workers, 52, 100–101, 150, 156; Ritz-
    Carlton, 71, 91, 315nn18,19; Royal Court
    and, 71, 87, 88, 91, 92–95, 100–105, 148,
    149–50, 156, 309–10n30. *See also* hiring; ori-
    entation, new employee; standardization

transformation: of guests into luxury con-
    sumers, 223–24, 244, 247–55; of workers
    by managers, 9, 21–22, 70–71, 75–79, 94–
    95, 108–9, 177–78, 308n20. *See also* empow-
    erment; legitimation; normalization
transgressions, guest, 166–71, 174–75; break-
    ing contract of reciprocity, 198–204; ethno-
    graphic method and, 278; failures in recog-
    nition of workers, 18, 142, 165, 173, 194–
    96; negative legends, 198, 205, 206, 218;
    revenge by workers for, 19, 184, 186, 197–
    206, 211, 217, 221, 316n17, 317nn24,25;
    rudeness, 78, 132, 166, 193, 195, 198–200,
    203, 204, 234. *See also* exploitation; moral
    evaluations; rules
transport. *See* airline workers; cars; escorting
Tremont Hotel, Boston, 26
turndown attendants, 49, 309n26, 310n5;
    demographics, 50, 292*table*, 293*table*; dis-
    plays of labor, 40–41, 50; ethnographic
    shadowing of, 13, 14; "invisible" labor
    made apparent, 44; Luxury Garden, 14,
    292*table*, 305n58; and reciprocity contract,
    318n42; routinization, 52; Royal Court,
    13, 293*table*. *See also* housekeepers; room
    cleaners
turnover, hotel workers, 283–84, 306n1; Lux-
    ury Garden, 64, 206, 273, 307n13; Royal
    Court, 64, 89–90, 95, 104–5, 206, 283–84.
    See also exiting
typology: of hotels, 307n12; worker strategies
    of, 114–17, 119, 123, 124, 130, 132, 151

uniforms: Luxury Garden, 74; Royal Court,
    88
unions, 13, 170, 266–67, 322n27; disciplinary
    proceedings, 65, 94; nonunion luxury
    hotels, 12–15, 65, 266–67, 300n59; research
    ethics and, 282; strike, 268; UNITE HERE,
    266, 271, 322n23; and workers distancing
    from working class, 162
UNITE HERE, 266, 271, 322n23
unlimited labor, 6, 41–43, 47, 48; deference
    in, 45; games and, 118, 120–21, 123, 128,
    130–32; and guest insecurity with rules of
    behavior, 243; and legitimation of guest
    entitlement, 42, 175–76, 260; physical, 21,
    25, 28; and reciprocity, 217; rule-breaking
    to meet needs, 37–38. *See also* effort,
    worker; limits

unpredictability: of guest requests, 54, 56, 64, 113–15, 117–18, 123–24, 132–33; of tipping, 127. *See also* predictability

valet parkers, 49; conflicts among workers, 138–39, 147, 157; ethnographic observation, 13, 273, 281–82; gender, 50, 86, 281–82, 292*table*, 293*table*; Luxury Garden, 65, 74, 126, 292*table*; and nonguests, 201; Royal Court, 86, 126, 138–39, 147, 157, 293*table*, 312n21; tips, 125, 126, 138–39, 147, 157, 293*table*, 312n21, 320n19; wages, 293*table*, 312n21
Veblen, Thorstein, 3, 38, 226
VIP status of guests, 172–73, 178–79. *See also* repeat/frequent guests
visible labor, 38, 40, 41, 55–56, 112. *See also* displays of labor; front of house workers; interactive service work; invisible work; semivisible workers
voluntary behavior, 197; guest reciprocity, 190, 213, 220, 241; worker effort appearing to be, 44, 112, 118, 125, 132, 186, 198, 209, 212–13, 220, 221, 233, 241. *See also* authenticity; self-subordination of workers to guests

wages, 2, 50, 65, 292*table*, 293*table*; bellmen/bellpersons, 67, 292*table*, 293*table*, 312n21; concierges, 67, 68, 157, 158, 292*table*, 293*table*; vs. cost of services provided, 6, 48, 60; doormen/door attendants, 67, 156, 292*table*, 293*table*; during ethnographic observation, 273, 274, 283; front and back of house workers, 50, 61–62; front desk agents, 67, 158, 292*table*, 293*table*; hourly, 65, 67; for "labor of love," 191–92; Luxury Garden (general), 67, 68–69, 108, 158, 266, 292*table*; manufacturing piece rates, 111, 112; "producer services," 5; Royal Court (general), 65, 68–69, 266, 293*table*; Royal Court renovation and, 126, 148, 312n21; unionized hotels, 65, 67; unions and, 266; valet parkers, 293*table*, 312n21. *See also* compensation; income
wake-up calls, 41
Waldorf-Astoria, 26
wealth: as entitlement to subordinated labor, 258; media details of, 4–5; "new Gilded Age," 6; "recession proof," 4; and servants,

4, 10; share of total national after-tax income, 297n24. *See also* compensation; luxury; money; wealth of guests
wealth of guests, 2, 299n53; backgrounds not wealthy, 15, 224, 235, 256, 277, 278; backgrounds wealthy, 226, 254; business travelers not wealthy, 252; comparisons to other wealthy people, 233; interviewed, 277; normalizing, 59, 134–35; reciprocity, 216; as resource for workers' self-construction, 17; workers' awareness of, 58–61; workers' condescension to, 165–66; workers' games and, 122, 134–35, 151, 161; workers' moral evaluation about, 168–70, 247; workers' status by association with, 161–62. *See also* money; worker-guest inequality
Weber, Max, 255, 299n53
Whyte, William, 219, 316–17n18
Williams, Serena, 4
Willis, Paul, 169, 255, 265
withdrawal of consent, 16–18, 62, 109, 113, 267–69, 321n11; by exiting, 16–17, 113, 146, 150, 267, 268, 305n62; Luxury Garden workers, 17–18, 61–62; Royal Court workers, 17–18, 109, 143, 145–50, 267. *See also* resistance, worker
work: aesthetics of, 74; and class, 3, 7, 12, 238–40, 297n29, 299n47. *See also* effort, worker; invisible work; job characteristics; labor; manufacturing work; organization of work; skill; sociology of work; visible labor; worker
worker: "internal customer," 71. *See also* labor; manager; relationship; service worker; strategies of workers
worker-coworker relations: competition, 126, 137, 273–74; conflicts, 18, 101, 103–4, 135–41, 144, 147–51, 157–62, 308n24, 312n21; discourses about guests, 15, 154–55, 162–63, 166–73, 180, 181, 195, 196, 198–99; ethnographic observation and, 276–77, 280–81, 282–83; games and, 111, 112, 126, 135–41; Luxury Garden, 84–86, 104; of privilege, 18, 156–59, 170, 176–80, 261; Royal Court, 64, 72, 84, 86, 88, 96, 100–105, 147, 149–50, 180, 310n34; sociability on the job, 85, 100, 103–5, 276–77, 310n34; socializing outside hotel, 14, 85, 276–77; superiority/comparison, 17–18, 22, 109, 140–41, 149, 151, 153, 155–59, 176–81, 235–36, 261.

worker-coworker relations *(continued)*
See also lateral relations, workers'; mutual
relations, workers'

worker-employer relations: exploitative, 10,
259; guest-hotel worker relations differing
from, 48; unions and, 266–67, 270. *See also*
domestic servants; hiring; orientation,
new employee; training; worker-manager
relations

worker-guest inequality, 6, 10–12, 259, 282–
83, 299n53; contestation of, 267–69; criticism of, 17, 60–61, 186, 204, 268–70;
exploitation concern of guests, 19, 20,
186, 220, 229; guest awareness of, 210,
221–22, 224, 235, 237–38, 240–41, 256;
guest perspectives on, 188, 227–56;
reciprocity and, 18, 19, 23, 134–35, 185–94,
203–24, 230–31, 237–39, 255, 269, 321–
22n18; social reproduction of, 11, 220, 242,
254–56, 262–65, 322n19; worker awareness
of, 15–16, 21, 57–62, 122–23, 134–35, 155,
204, 221–22; worker games and, 112–13,
122–23, 125, 134–35; worker status by
association, 155, 161–62, 175–76, 182,
267. *See also* class; consent by workers; deference; economics; entitlement; equality;
hierarchy; normalization of inequality;
obscuring inequality; self-subordination
of workers to guests; subordination,
worker; superiority of workers; worker-
guest relations

worker-guest relations, 9, 18–19, 25, 111–53,
162–82, 184–222, 316n2; "boundary-open,"
188; comparison/superiority of workers,
17–18, 22, 109, 121, 153, 154–55, 162–81,
261; condescension by workers, 155, 162–
71, 175–76, 178–82, 247; criticism by workers, 15, 17, 60–61, 154–55, 162–76, 180, 182,
185, 198–99, 247, 268–69; demographic
similarity, 191; dependence of guests, 45,
47, 177–78, 255; empathy/sympathy by
workers, 35–37, 45, 162–66, 174, 177, 179–
81, 213, 232–33, 247, 249; fear of guest com-

plaints, 52–53, 57, 305n58; fear of worker
judgments, 48, 244, 245, 246, 247; gender
and, 31–32, 107, 206, 216, 227–28, 230, 237,
281–82, 302n32, 317n28; instrumental, 197,
207–8, 216–17, 218–19, 261; obligations, 23,
207–9, 215, 221, 224, 269; ongoing, 47, 185,
186, 215, 217; race/ethnicity and, 107, 191,
215; rule-breaking appreciated by guests,
37–38, 45; sociable, 106, 107, 188, 191;
thanks from guests to individual workers,
189, 196, 197; unionizing and, 267;
unpredictability/predictability of guest
requests, 54, 56, 64, 113–15, 117–18, 123–
24, 129–33. *See also* authenticity; authority;
commodification of relationship; customer
feedback; discretion by workers; effort,
worker; entitlement; expectations; games,
worker; individual interactions; interactive
service work; intersubjectivity; judgment
by workers; limits; needs, guest; personalization; personhood; positive interactions;
reciprocity in worker-guest relations;
revenge; service; sociology of work;
tips; transgressions, guest; worker-guest
inequality

worker-manager relations, 18; conflicts, 9–
10, 18–19, 83, 113, 135–36, 145–50, 191,
268; criticism by workers, 98–99, 102–3,
149; discipline of worker, 65, 80, 84, 94, 98,
99, 204; ethnographic observation and, 283;
games and, 125, 126–27, 138–40, 143–50,
151; Luxury Garden, 76, 83–84, 89, 108,
143–44, 189; monitoring by managers, 52,
55–57, 70–71, 83–84, 97–98, 108; privilege
of workers, 305n62; restaurant, 219; Royal
Court blurred boundaries, 89, 96–97, 99;
socializing, 96–97, 99; unionizing and,
267. *See also* accountability to managers;
managerial authority; training; worker-
employer relations

working class, 6, 162, 320n15. *See also* labor;
worker

work shifts, eight-hour, 65

Text: 10/14 Palatino
Display: Bauer Bodoni and Univers Condensed Light
Compositor: BookMatters, Berkeley
Printer and binder: Maple-Vail Manufacturing Group
Indexer: Barbara Roos